Lynching and Spectacle

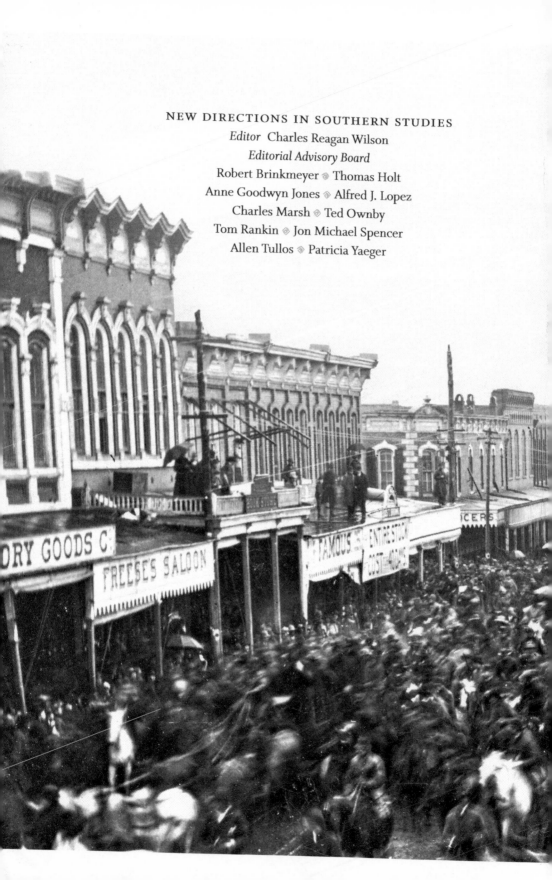

Lynching and Spectacle

Witnessing Racial Violence in America, 1890–1940

AMY LOUISE WOOD

THE UNIVERSITY OF
NORTH CAROLINA PRESS
Chapel Hill

Portions of chapter 3 appeared in "Lynching Photography and the Visual Reproduction of White Supremacy," AMERICAN NINETEENTH CENTURY HISTORY 6 (September 2005): 373–99, and are reprinted by permission from the Taylor and Francis Group.

Designed by Rebecca Evans
Set in Whitman with MiniPics Zafrica
by Tseng Information Systems, Inc.
Manufactured in the United States of America

The paper in this book meets the guidelines for permanence and durability of the Committee on Production Guidelines for Book Longevity of the Council on Library Resources.

The University of North Carolina Press has been a member of the Green Press Initiative since 2003.

Library of Congress Cataloging-in-Publication Data
Wood, Amy Louise.
Lynching and spectacle : witnessing racial violence in America, 1890–1940 / Amy Louise Wood.
p. cm. — (New directions in southern studies)
Includes bibliographical references and index.
ISBN 978-0-8078-3254-7 (cloth : alk. paper)
1. Lynching—United States—History. 2. Violence—United States—History. 3. Hate crimes—United States—History. 4. United States—Race relations—History. I. Title.
HV6457.W66 2009
364.1'34—dc22   2008045194

13 12 11 10 09 5 4 3 2 1

THIS BOOK WAS DIGITALLY PRINTED.

To my parents

CONTENTS

FIGURES

ACKNOWLEDGMENTS

I AM INDEBTED to many people who have contributed to this project in immeasurable ways. I first want to thank the many librarians and archivists across the country who helped me patiently and graciously, even if, at times, I was digging up the grimmest memories of their communities. I also want to acknowledge the Institute of the Liberal Arts at Emory University and the College of Arts and Sciences at Illinois State University for providing generous research funding to support this project. Greg Maier at Illinois State's Center for Teaching, Learning, and Technology kindly assisted in preparing images for the book.

I wish to thank the National Association for the Advancement of Colored People for authorizing the use of the images reproduced in figures 3.13, 6.6, 6.11, and 7.8, and Crisis Publishing Co. Inc., the publisher of the magazine of the National Association for the Advancement of Colored People, for authorizing the use of the advertisement reproduced in figure 6.8. I also thank the Taylor and Francis Group and *American Nineteenth Century History* for allowing me to reprint portions of "Lynching Photography and the Visual Reproduction of White Supremacy," which appeared in the journal in September 2005.

I am especially grateful to Harry Watson and the Center for the Study of the American South at the University of North Carolina at Chapel Hill for a fantastic fellowship year that allowed for the completion of this book. I am indebted to the staff at UNC Press, in particular Paul Betz and the freelance copyeditor Anna Laura Bennett, who shepherded this book to publication with care and professionalism. David Perry deserves special thanks for his enthusiasm for this project, as well as for his advice and patience. His calm and good humor have provided a much needed counterweight to my nerves and doubts.

I have had the good fortune to have many teachers and mentors who shaped this project in ways they might not even be aware of, including Dan Carter, Kate Nickerson, Gary Laderman, Amy Lang, Cris Levenduski, Jonathon Prude, Jay Watson, James Roark, Ted Ownby, and especially Allen Tullos. Matthew Bernstein warrants particular mention for his interest in my work. He read my film chapters carefully and thoroughly and provided much needed advice and encouragement throughout this process. My debt to Charles Wilson is incalculable. I will always be grateful for the way he welcomed this New Englander, wildly out of place in Oxford, Mississippi, into the field of southern studies. It was under his tutelage that I became interested in the issues that gave seed to this book, and I appreciate that his faith in this project was enough that he sought it out for UNC Press.

This project has benefited enormously from the advice and feedback of a number of other scholars, including Bruce Baker, Deborah Barnes, William Carrigan, Mary Frederickson, Anne Goodwyn-Jones, Trudier Harris, Don Mathews, and Charles Musser. Fitzhugh Brundage read the entire manuscript twice and offered invaluable suggestions for improvement. I cannot begin to express my appreciation for his encouragement and support.

Over the years, many friends and colleagues have read parts of this book in one form or another. I thank Shelby Balik, Katherine Charron, Jay Garcia, Adrienne Lentz-Smith, Brian Luskey, Gregory Renoff, Emily Satterwhite, and John Sweet for questioning my arguments, organizing my thoughts, and editing my prose. Bland Whitley, in particular, was a careful reader and editor of several chapters, going beyond the call to track down sources and read revisions at the last minute. I owe a special debt to Jennifer Meares, who has read this manuscript in draft form more thoroughly than anyone else. Not only is she an exceptional editor, but she has an incredible gift for drawing out the core of any argument and leading me to what I want to say.

There are a number of other people in my life who have listened with patience as I dwelled on this grim topic, who have provided suggestions and posed questions that have shaped my thinking, or who have simply offered moral support, including Marni Davis, Steve Farrelly, Karen Glynn, Alan Lessoff, Bill Philpott, and Kerry Taylor. Sarah Torian and Bland Whitley not only afforded me with an excuse to "do research" in Richmond, Virginia, but have remained incredibly loyal and generous friends. Jennifer Meares and Amy Viar offered me the warmth and joy of a second home in Atlanta and much needed diversion over the years. Saul Tobias, who always surprises me with his estimation of my talent, provided his unwavering encouragement and good cheer. And Jennifer Shaw has been a tremendous friend and, without doubt, my biggest advocate. I am thankful for all these friends.

This book is dedicated to my parents, Gordon and Louise Wood, to whom I owe everything.

Lynching and Spectacle

The mob yelled. Its yell echoed against the skeleton stone walls and sounded like a hundred yells. Like a hundred mobs yelling. Its yell thudded against the thick front wall and fell back. Ghost of a yell slipped through the flames and out the great door of the factory. It fluttered like a dying thing down the single street of a factory town. Louisa, upon the step before her home, did not hear it, but her eyes opened slowly. They saw the full moon glowing in the great door. The full moon, an evil thing, an omen, soft showering the homes of folks she knew.

JEAN TOOMER ◈ "Blood-Burning Moon" (1923)

The hostility of the whites had become so deeply implanted in my mind and feelings that it had lost direct connection with the daily environment in which I lived; and my reactions to this hostility fed upon itself. . . . Tension would set in at the mere mention of whites and a vast complex of emotions, involving the whole of my personality, would be aroused. It was as though I was continuously reacting to the threat of some natural force whose hostile behavior could not be predicted. I had never in my life been abused by whites, but I had already become conditioned to their existence as though I had been the victim of a thousand lynchings.

The penalty of death awaited me if I made a false move and I wondered if it was worth-while to make any move at all. The things that influenced my conduct as a Negro did not have to happen to me directly; I needed but to hear of them to feel their full effects in the deepest layers of my consciousness. Indeed, the white brutality that I had not seen was a more effective control of my behavior than that which I knew. The actual experience would have let me see the realistic outlines of what was really happening, but as long it remained something terrible and yet remote, something whose horror and blood might descend upon me at any moment, I was compelled to give my entire imagination over to it, an act which blocked the springs of thought and feeling in me, creating a sense of distance between me and the world in which I lived.

RICHARD WRIGHT ◈ *Black Boy* (1937)

INTRODUCTION

COMPARED TO OTHER FORMS of terror and intimidation that African Americans were subject to under Jim Crow, lynching was an infrequent and extraordinary occurrence. Black men and women were much more likely to become victims of personal assault, murder, or rape than lynching, and, as Richard Wright explained, they withstood all sorts of injuries and insults on a daily basis. But the news of a lynching shook Wright to his core. Despite, or even because of, its relative rarity, lynching held a singular psychological force, generating a level of fear and horror that overwhelmed all other forms of violence. Even one lynching reverberated, traveling with sinister force, down city streets and through rural farms, across roads and rivers. As Jean Toomer described it, one mob's yell could sound "like a hundred mobs yelling," and the specter of the violence continued to smolder long after it was over, "soft showering the homes of folks" like the ominous full moon in his story. All the everyday humiliations and hostilities that black southerners endured under Jim Crow could, in fact, be distilled into the experience of lynching, so that it came to stand as the primary representation of racial injustice and oppression as a whole. To be black in this time, according to Wright, was to be "the victim to a thousand lynchings."[1]

Lynching assumed this tremendous symbolic power precisely because it was extraordinary and, by its very nature, public and visually sensational. Those lynchings that hundreds, sometimes thousands, of white spectators gathered and watched as their fellow citizens tortured, mutilated, and hanged or burned their victims in full view were, for obvious reasons, the most potently haunting. The sheer brutality of these mobs, as well as their flagrant disregard for legal order and authority, shocked and terrified because they struck against common notions of what civilized people could or should be capable of. But even less obtrusive lynchings, in which mobs or posses of a few men hanged their victims away from public view, re-sounded. Although relatively private, they were still sensational. They were often deliberately performative and ritualized, as if mobs expected their violence to be noticed. They were then frequently made public—even spectacular—through displays of lynched bodies and souvenirs, as well as through representations of the violence that circulated long after the lynch-ings themselves were over: photographs and other visual imagery, ballads and songs, news accounts and lurid narratives.[2] Lynching, indeed, carried cultural force as a form of racial terror through its most sensational manifes-tations. Terrifying images of white power and black helplessness refracted not only into black homes and communities but across the American racial landscape. This is not to minimize the actual violence that mobs exacted on the bodies of their victims or the terrible consequences of so many lost lives. But even that violence and those deaths were themselves representa-tional, conveying messages about racial hierarchy and the frightening con-sequences of transgressing that hierarchy.

African Americans, however, did not need to see a lynching to be terror-ized by it, to feel, according to Wright, that "penalty of death" hanging over them at every waking moment. As Wright explained, "The white brutality that I had not seen was a more effective control of my behavior than that which I knew. The actual experience would have let me see the realistic outlines of what was really happening, but as long as it remained something terrible and yet remote, something whose horror and blood might descend upon me at any moment, I was compelled to give my entire imagination over to it." Lynching terrorized Wright because it existed purely in the realm of representation, as horrific images that haunted his consciousness, images that, he wrote, "blocked the springs of thought and feeling in me, creating a sense of distance between me and the world in which I lived."[3] It was the spectacle of lynching, rather than the violence itself, that wrought psycho-logical damage, that enforced black acquiescence to white domination.

Even more, mobs performed lynchings as spectacles for other whites. The rituals, the tortures, and their subsequent representations imparted powerful messages to whites about their own supposed racial dominance and superiority. These spectacles produced and disseminated images of white power and black degradation, of white unity and black criminality, that served to instill and perpetuate a sense of racial supremacy in their white spectators. Lynching thus succeeded in enacting and maintaining white domination not only because African Americans were its targets but also because white southerners were its spectators.

The cultural power of lynching—indeed, the cultural power of white supremacy itself—rested on spectacle: the crowds, the rituals and performances, and their sensational representations in narratives, photographs, and films. This book is about how and why those spectacles came to be and the cultural work they performed. It is about why so many otherwise ordinary and law-abiding white southerners wanted to participate in and watch extraordinary acts of violence and what it meant for them to do so. The spectacle of lynching emerged from and coincided with other practices and forms of spectacle and spectatorship at the turn of the century, and it drew cultural force from them. These other forms included both the traditions of public executions and religious ceremonies and modern visual media, like photography and cinema. To understand lynching in relationship to these other forms of spectacle is not only to comprehend the excessive and horrifying cruelty of lynching but also to make sense of the impulse that compelled so many people to look at scenes of torture and suffering with eagerness and approval, an impulse that extended beyond racism or psychological sadism.

Although lynching stood at the center of a long tradition of American vigilantism, the practice increased dramatically in both frequency and intensity after the Civil War and Reconstruction, peaking from the 1890s through the first decade of the twentieth century. At this time, lynching became a predominantly southern, racialized phenomenon, as white southerners sought to restore their dominance in the face of emancipation and the threat of black enfranchisement and social autonomy. Determining the exact number of lynchings that were committed in the late nineteenth and early twentieth centuries is a formidable task, since the definition of a lynching was itself open to contestation and change, and organizations such as the National Association for the Advancement of Colored People (NAACP), the Tuskegee Institute, and the *Chicago Tribune* kept varying kinds of records. In addition, many lynchings were not recorded. Despite these qualifications, we can ascertain that, between 1880 and 1940, white mobs in the South killed at least 3,200 black men.[4]

Southern mobs in this period also were more likely to lynch their black victims openly and with excessive force, exacting unprecedented tortures and mutilations. To be sure, not all lynchings happened in the South, nor were African American men the only victims. Lynchings were perpetrated and defended in surprisingly similar ways across state and sectional borders. Mobs also attacked white men; Native Americans; Chinese, Mexican, and other immigrants; and African American women in significant numbers.[5]

Nevertheless, the vast majority of lynchings at the turn of the century took place in former slave states, and the overwhelming majority of those were perpetrated against black men. Even more important here, most Americans at the turn of the century understood lynching as a southern practice and as a form of racial violence that white mobs committed against African American men. The South was widely considered to be, as H. L. Mencken deemed it, "the lynching belt," a reputation that many white southerners eventually struggled to disavow.[6] Just as lynching served as the defining metaphor for racial oppression in the early twentieth century, it also became an identifying marker of the South, especially the Deep South.

For this reason, this study begins in the South. The power of the lynching spectacle derived from the social and cultural particularities of the Jim Crow South and cannot be understood outside them. Indeed, once that spectacle was disseminated nationwide, particularly through photographs and motion pictures, its ideological significance and force changed altogether. The same images that had constructed and reinforced white supremacy came to have an alternative symbolic power, one that gave vitality and strength to the antilynching movement. The most public and sensational manifestations of lynching that had made the violence so terrorizing also became the tools through which lynching opponents could deflate that terror. In short, if lynching rested on spectacle, it also fell on spectacle. This book traces that cultural shift, which brought the eventual curtailment of lynching after World War I.

The term "witnessing" underlies the notion of spectatorship considered here. "Witnessing" refers not only to public testimonials of faith or truth but also to the act of being a spectator of significant and extraordinary events. A spectator or a bystander becomes a witness when his or her spectatorship bears a legal, spiritual, or social consequence; when it can establish the true course or meaning of an event or action; or when it can confer significance or value on an event. To act as a witness is thus to play a public role, one that bestows a particular kind of social authority on the individual, at the same time that it connects that individual to a larger community of fellow witnesses.[7]

The act of witnessing, in this respect, unites the disparate, if not competing, cultural spectacles of executions, religious rituals, photography, and motion pictures. These phenomena were anchored in similar conceptions of truth and evidence, and they established comparable modes of spectatorship. Southerners transferred the notions of witnessing generated in these social practices to the lynching spectacle. The act of witnessing a lynching, even in photography and film, lent the authority of both divine truth and irrefutable proof to white supremacist ideology and helped produce a sense of superiority and solidarity among otherwise different white southerners. Antilynching activists, in turn, relied on witnessing to convey an alternative truth about lynching. In using photographs and films to offer visual testimony to the cruelty that lynch mobs so unashamedly committed, lynching opponents trusted the same assumptions about spectatorship that bolstered prolynching thought—that to see an event was to understand its truth. They accordingly hoped that visual images of lynching would impel Americans to bear witness, to take moral and social responsibility for the brutal injustice of lynching.

As a study of spectacle and sensationalism, as well as the relationship between the local and the national, this book is also about lynching's fraught connection to modernity. When activists, cultural critics, and scholars in the early twentieth century investigated lynching as a social phenomenon, most considered it a backwoods remnant of an archaic and barbaric impulse toward vengeance—a sign that the South and other regions that still lynched were disconnected not only from American ideals but from modern civilization. Some also reasoned that the spectacle surrounding lynching derived from the South's cultural isolation—that it, in Mencken's words, took "the place of the merry-go-round, the theatre, the symphony orchestra, and other diversions common to large communities." Lynching would wane, it was assumed, only when southerners became less rural and isolated and developed not only a more enlightened respect for legal institutions and state power but more modern forms of amusement. This view reflected a broader liberal faith in this period that modernization, as it brought social and economic improvement, acted as a progressive force, one that would sway rural Americans to abandon their local prejudices and conflicts, especially racial ones, in favor of democratic and egalitarian ideals.[8]

Racial violence surged at the turn of the century, however, not because southern communities were cut off from modern institutions and customs but because they were undergoing an uncertain and troubled transformation into modern, urban societies. The devastation and uncertainties of the rural economy after the Civil War pushed increasing numbers of southerners, white and black, off the farm, and as northern investment poured into the South, cities and towns grew in area and population. The most spectacular lynchings took place not in the countryside but in these newly urbanizing places, where mobs hanged their victims from telegraph and telephone poles and where streetcars and railroads brought crowds to witness the violence. Even the smallest towns were undergoing an urbanization process of sorts. They were experiencing changes that white citizens regularly celebrated as progressive while lamenting what they saw as the corrosive effects of these changes on the social order.

The particular urgency and intensity with which white southerners lashed out at alleged black criminals stemmed from fears and anxieties that modernization generated. The expansion of commercial markets for rural crops, as well as the rise of new industries, such as logging and turpentine, brought new kinds of traffic and occupations to towns and cities. In this new environment, traditional forms of authority—the patriarchal household, the church, the planter elite—were called into question, and traditional notions of community, in which people could claim familiarity and kinship with their neighbors, were no longer as relevant. This new social order most threatened white dominance, as urban spaces and establishments brought whites and blacks together in new kinds of interactions and exchanges, and as many African Americans came to expect the same legal and civil rights accorded to whites. It was in response to these changes that white southerners, beginning in the 1890s, sought to reassert their racial privileges and authority through Jim Crow laws and ordinances and through the systematic disenfranchisement of former slaves and their offspring.[9]

Many white southerners expressed their apprehension about economic and political dislocations and disruptions as anxieties about moral dissolution and personal safety. That is, amid the upheavals of the New South, white southerners insisted that, above all, their moral and physical integrity was at stake. Industry drew laborers—mostly young, unattached men, black and white—into towns and cities, and these men were more likely to commit crimes, engage in violence, and indulge in behaviors like drinking, gambling, dancing, and sexual activities, that the middle classes of both races deemed immoral and socially dangerous. Establishments like saloons, pool halls, and brothels proliferated to accommodate these newcomers and made crime and moral vice seem even more conspicuous and threatening. White southerners' larger prejudices against and suspicions of African Americans unavoidably permeated their concerns about crime and immorality. Many white southerners fervently believed that this new environment had unleashed an innate propensity for violence and sexual transgression in African American men. Stories of black crime and moral dereliction dominated southern newspapers, which further fueled racial fears.

It was in this context of heightened alarm that white southerners felt inclined and justified to lynch African Americans with such unbridled fury. Lynchings tended to occur in places that were already wrestling with problems of crime and anxieties about moral decay, where lynchings were understood to be just and necessary retributions against abominable crimes, a means to ensure not only white dominance but the larger social and moral order. It was also in this context that the figure of the black brute rapist, who lustfully yearned to attack and violate white women, seized the white southern imagination. Although most lynchings did not stem from allegations of black rape, the specter of violated white women lay at the center of prolynching rhetoric and instigated the most horrific lynching tortures and spectacles. The figure of the black rapist struck at the heart of the matter — that black autonomy not only diminished white men's authority over African Americans but threatened their dominion over their own households and women. Lynching was thus more than a white prerogative; it was a patriarchal duty through which white men restored their masculine dominance.[10]

Fears about moral and physical safety also account for why so many middle-class townspeople watched and participated in lynchings with such vehemence and enthusiasm. Lynch mobs, to be sure, included white southerners of varying classes and occupations, depending on the locality and the circumstances surrounding the event, and lynching persisted through the tacit support and participation of social elites. The mobs at mass spectacle lynchings, however, tended to be dominated by skilled laborers and white-collar workers — members of the rising middle class.[11] These were townspeople who were themselves newcomers to the southern economy, engaging in occupations related to industrial and commercial enterprise: managers, petty merchants, salesmen, mechanics, and other tradesmen. Usually young and recently transplanted from the country, they had much to gain from the changing economy of the New South. Although not wealthy, they were not under direct economic threat from black men, nor were they dependent on black labor. They were nevertheless anxious about their own financial well-being, especially amid the economic fluctuations of this period. Their social mobility was neither assured nor steady; their standing as respectable citizens was not yet firmly established. As with rising middle classes elsewhere, moral propriety and self-discipline, as well as a sense of authority over their households, came to define their social worth and assure their social ascent. These traits, after all, distinguished them from poor whites and, most of all, from African Americans. These were the southerners whom sociologist John Dollard in 1937 called "strainers," people who were "pressing forward and straining to get on in the world." According to Dollard, the middle classes "must stress sharply the differences between themselves and the lower-class whites and Negroes because they are none too sure that the differences are very important or permanent."[12]

Although not necessarily threatened economically by black men, many white middle-class townspeople did feel an intense personal and physical threat from them. They felt a keen investment in maintaining a strict racial hierarchy and ensuring that white male authority held sway in their communities. They were thus the most likely to express outrage over moral decline and the spread of crime, which they perceived as direct assaults on their integrity, their honor, and their homes. These fears about their own personal and social vulnerability ultimately led them to strike out viciously and excessively against the objects of their terror.

Amid these transformations, white supremacy, although it was powerful and long lasting, was by no means stable or fixed. The war and Reconstruction had disrupted the racial hierarchies and relationships established under slavery and had presented the possibility that African American men would be accorded social and political equality. A degree of political fluidity still existed after Reconstruction, when freedmen remained politically active and yeomen and poor whites flirted with interracial populism as a means to challenge planter and industrial power. By the turn of the century, white southerners were hardly a monolithic group, let alone a unified community. Localities across the South were teeming with class tension and disruption as the proliferation of rural tenancy and the rise of industry brought new labor arrangements, new occupations, and new class roles and standings. White supremacy and white solidarity were thus not certainties — they were ideologies that needed to be constructed and established and that required constant replenishing and constant reenvisioning. That is, they needed to be performed and witnessed.[13]

Lynching spectacles, in this respect, did more than dramatize or reflect an undisputed white supremacy or attest to an uncontested white solidarity.[14] Rather, they generated and even coerced a sense of racial superiority and unity among white southerners across class, generational, and geographic divisions. The rituals of lynching themselves, in their torturous dehumanization of black men, enacted and embodied the core beliefs of white supremacist ideology, creating public displays of bestial black men in visible contrast to strong and commanding white men. Lynching allowed white southerners to perform and attach themselves to these beliefs — to literally inhabit them. The crowds of spectators at the most public lynchings also literally created a community of white southerners united by a common interest and purpose. Not all spectators at a lynching witnessed the violence in

the same way, of course; many might have been disgusted, horrified, or dis-
engaged. Nevertheless, their very presence in the crowd helped constitute a
white public that lent legitimacy to the lynch mob's claim of white solidarity.
In these ways, lynching spectacles revealed the threads with which white
southerners stitched together an idealized white community.

Narrative representations of lynching—in news accounts, pamphlets,
popular stories, and ballads—reproduced these rituals of white dominance
and unity for a larger public, describing lynch mobs and their spectators in
language brimming with moral and class significance. Even as mobs perpetrated the most sadistic atrocities on the bodies of their victims, their
supporters insisted on their manly civility and self-restraint against the
purported criminal savagery of black men. Prolynching rhetoric commonly
portrayed mobs, a term that usually connotes unruly and chaotic irrationality, as methodical and orderly, acting out of righteous determination and
working with cool-headed deliberation. These men were accordingly "reputable" or "respectable citizens" carrying out their masculine duty to protect their women and their honor. Prolynching reports further noted that
mobs and crowds consisted of people from all walks of life. Yet, although
these accounts recognized that lynching crowds often cut across class and
community lines, they imagined them as cohesive groups, collective bodies
of citizens. These images of a forceful yet controlled white citizenry stood
against opposing images of brutish black men. The defenders of lynching
all too often described the lynching victim—the alleged criminal—as the
inhuman "prey" or "fiend" that white supremacist ideology purported him
to be. Reports made careful mention of his comportment at the moment
of his capture and death, as if his struggling, crying, and pleading revealed
his essential lack of self-control or mastery, the very qualities that characterized the mob. These kinds of narrative accounts were central to lynching's cultural power, especially as they spread from town to town and from
generation to generation. Through their often lurid and graphic detail, they
helped govern and standardize the practice of lynching. Their rhetoric of
white unity and moral superiority, which absolved individuals of any guilt
or responsibility for the violence, also helped make that violence appear
socially acceptable, even respectable.[15]

Representations of lynching in photographs and motion pictures, however, re-created the spectacle itself. They not only replicated, in starkly
visual terms, the ideological force of prolynching rhetoric but also literally
projected images that substantiated that rhetoric and allowed it to be continually reimagined. The remarkable mimetic quality of photography and

film—their capacity to simulate reality with uncanny accuracy—accorded them enormous cultural influence in modern life. Through their graphic realism, they came to alter people's perceptions of truth and their apprehension of the world around them. In other words, because photographic and filmic images ultimately blurred distinctions between reality and representation, spectators received them as transparent and truthful reflections of the objective world and, in turn, came to measure their own realities against them. Photography and film thus carried a particular power to animate feeling and shape understanding in ways that far exceeded narrative forms of representation. It was through this power that photographs and moving pictures of lynching, culminating in *The Birth of a Nation* in 1915, came to affirm and authenticate white supremacy. Indeed, they were central to its construction.

In this way, even as lynching represented a revolt against modernity and its effects, lynch mobs made use of new modes of spectacle to enact and perpetuate their violence. With the heightened sensationalism and publicity surrounding them and their masses of eager spectators, the most public lynchings resembled modern theatrical entertainment. The style of new, sensational journalism at the turn of the century exploited the violence by paying lurid attention to the pain and suffering of both the violated white woman and the lynching victim, making their torment palpable for readers. The melodramatic tone of prolynching rhetoric, with its tropes of helpless white women and villainous black men, itself pronounced lynching as theater. White southerners, furthermore, bought, sold, and circulated photographs and other souvenirs as consumer goods, and, in motion picture theaters, they watched scenes of lynching, projected as thrilling amusement.

Recent scholars have accordingly argued that lynching persisted through a web of modern consumer and media practices that reproduced and commodified white supremacist violence for a large public. In this view, these practices helped generate a national tolerance for that violence by making it appear to be a natural aspect of modern life—yet another distant and thrilling spectacle that could be consumed and then overlooked.[16] Modern spectacle arose in the United States and Europe at the turn of the last century as a category of social interaction marked by a heightened focus on visuality—that is, on thrilling visual displays, particularly through new technologies like photography and film, which had a unique ability to captivate and seduce viewers. The emergence of modern spectacle was also inescapably bound up with the growth of commercial capitalism and the rise of mass society. Photographic and moving images circulated nationwide and, through magazines, advertising, and the film industry itself, came to dominate the landscape of commercial capitalism. The modern spectator was always a consumer, nourishing and sustaining the market through his or her visual consumption. At the same time, individual spectatorship was always subsumed within the crowd, defined as that undifferentiated and passive body through which images and products were mass produced and mass consumed.[17]

Yet, although southern towns and cities were lurching into modernity in this period, they were by no means modern, urban places, and white southerners were hardly modern, urban subjects. These were people in the midst of social upheaval and disruption. The spectacle of lynching did not signify southerners' immersion into modern commercial culture as much as it embodied this moment of transition and flux. In fact, although the sizes of the crowds at lynchings expanded in the late nineteenth century and the tenor and ferocity of the violence certainly changed, there was nothing particularly new about the ritual of lynching itself. It did not invoke modern spectacle as much as it did older traditions of spectacle and ritual—not only vigilante practices but parades, theater, and, as discussed in the first part of this book, public executions and religious ceremonies. To restore a sense of order and stability in the face of transformation, white southerners turned to familiar practices and customs. By rooting their violence within these traditional practices, mobs made the torture and mutilation of black men appear to be a legitimate, even customary, response to crime and social disorder.[18]

Moreover, unlike the dominant image of the modern spectator, the crowds at lynchings were by no means passive or disembodied voyeurs. They cheered, hooted, clapped, grabbed souvenirs, and, at times, participated. Nor was the spectacle entirely dominated by visual sensation; lynching included not only the sight of black desecration but also other senses. Spectators heard the speeches of the mob, the shouts of the crowd, the confessions of the victim, and, most of all, his dying shrieks and cries. In cases where the victim was burned, to witness a lynching was also to smell it. And, in all instances, the feel and push of the crowd created the sense of belonging and commonality that sustained the violence. In this respect, spectators did not watch or consume a lynching as much as they witnessed it—that is, they beheld or experienced it with active engagement.

The sensational media surrounding lynching—the lurid narratives, the photographs, and motion pictures—also represented a reactionary impulse against modern developments, even as they spread through commercial markets and channels of communication. Rather than stemming from a particularly modern interest in cruelty and sadism, these forms of repre-senting or imagining lynching emerged from this same moment of transi-tion. Modernity, after all, was marked by increasing aversion to pain and suffering or, at least, to public displays of such suffering. The rise of Enlight-enment liberalism and urban society in the eighteenth century had led to a new, heightened sensitivity to and empathy for the physical afflictions of others, a sensitivity that was epitomized in the humanitarian and sentimen-tal sensibilities of nineteenth-century Victorian culture. Religious thought in this period absorbed these same values; a Puritan, Calvinist theology that placed emphasis on God's torturous wrath and retribution against human sinfulness gave way to a more liberal and romantic Protestantism that em-phasized Christian bonds of affection and heavenly grace. For Victorians, modern civilization hinged on a civil society in which citizens restrained their own violent impulses and sought the alleviation of others' suffering. They, in turn, considered cruelty and the desire to revel in the torment of others to be the province of savages. The modern state consequently moved to prohibit corporal punishment from the military, schools, and prisons and came to shield its citizens from the execution of criminals. The profes-sionalization of medicine, as well as the rise of the funeral industry in the late nineteenth century, further removed the sight of pain and death from people's everyday experiences.[19]

Urban life had certainly increased crime and had generated new forms of shocks and violence, such as industrial and traffic accidents, train wrecks, and riots. But, for the most part, Americans at the turn of the century — even those southerners who lived in smaller towns and cities — were more pro-tected than ever before from the violence and misery of human existence. It was precisely because Americans no longer witnessed death, pain, or bru-tality in their everyday lives that sensational literature and images, which abounded with scenes of cruelty and suffering, so titillated and fascinated them. These media pandered to fears, desires, and impulses that modern life had otherwise restrained or forbidden. For instance, newspapers began to provide detailed and lurid accounts of executions only once the state began conducting them behind prison walls, away from public view. The less direct access people had to pain and suffering, the more they saturated their lives with images of it.[20]

The desire to read sensational accounts of lynching and, especially, to view lynching in photographs and moving pictures derived from these incli-nations to witness and imagine primal experiences of punishment, torment, and death. Yet, whereas northerners may have gazed at lynching photographs or produced and watched motion pictures of lynching out of voyeuristic curiosity or for morbid thrills, white southerners brought a much more immediate knowledge to their spectatorship. To be sure, most southerners had not witnessed a lynching firsthand; nevertheless, they lived in places where stories about black crime abounded, where public executions still occurred, albeit less often, and where they were surrounded by an evangelical religious culture that had retained a more conservative, Calvinist theological outlook. Lynching photographs and moving pictures did not represent scenes that southerners could apprehend as simply thrilling amusement or entertainment. Rather, white southerners produced and received these most modern lynching representations through very personal and local terms. Through them, they rehearsed narratives of crime and punishment, of sin and retribution, that they already understood through the practices of public executions and from their religious traditions. Their racial fears about crime and the loss of white masculine dominance only made these narratives seem all the more pressing and relevant.

Lynching spectacles, in this sense, could alleviate many of the anxieties that modern life had generated, including a fear of the crowd itself. Modernity was, after all, also marked by a new cultural awareness and apprehension about crowds, about the gathering and congestion of vast numbers of people in the increasingly crowded spaces of the city. Urbanization brought together masses of strangers, across racial and ethnic lines, which appeared all the more frightening amid not only personal crimes but riots, civil unrest, and "mobbing." In this respect, whereas the posse belonged to a frontier or rural imaginary, the mob belonged to a decidedly modern one. Although they were not experiencing urbanization to the same degree that their counterparts in larger cities were, southerners in growing towns and small cities did share these anxieties and apprehensions about crowds and social mixing. New laws and regulations developed in these places to control crowds and mitigate disorder, not only through Jim Crow ordinances that separated the races but also through, for example, the prohibition of alcohol and bans on public executions.

Mass lynchings emerged from this consciousness about the crowd and fears about social disorder, primarily in places on the cusp of urbanization, even as they encouraged and depended on throngs of spectators. Lynching spectacles, however, inverted and thereby defused these fears. If urban life had threatened white authority by bringing whites and blacks together on streetcars, sidewalks, and markets, lynchings performed on city streets and courthouse squares reclaimed urban, public spaces as decidedly white spaces. What is more, lynching spectacles reimagined the urban mob as an idealized community, a unified body of righteous and triumphant whites; they, in turn, isolated the figure of the black criminal, making him appear powerless and defenseless.

The spectacle of lynching, in these ways, erupted and thrived along that fault line where modernity and tradition collided. In fact, the more modern that spectacle became — as images of lynching circulated to wider audiences and became more commercialized and more a part of national popular and political culture — the more it lost its power to affirm and substantiate white supremacy. That power depended on a limited and controlled spectatorship. Lynching spectacles were able to mobilize white southerners around white supremacy because viewers actively witnessed them, imposing their own beliefs and points of view on them. Their significance was not intrinsic to them, nor was it fixed or irrefutable. Indeed, once lynching images became detached from local settings and local sensibilities, they helped mobilize the antilynching movement, a shift marked, in many ways, by the NAACP's forceful campaign against *The Birth of a Nation*.

By the 1930s, lynching opponents effectively came to exploit the graphic realism of lynching photography, as well as the spectacle of Hollywood cinema, to play on the empathy of national spectators and engender in them feelings of outrage and disgust toward lynching. These activists recognized that the cultural power of lynching rested, in part, on visual representation. They thus waged the battle against lynching through images, putting the most excessive and sensational elements of lynching, as well as viewers' voyeuristic impulses, in service against lynching.[21] In doing so, they embarrassed white southerners, who found their own racial claims to moral superiority increasingly under scrutiny and attack, until they sought to disavow and renounce lynching.

THE CHAPTERS OF THIS BOOK are arranged thematically and chronologically, beginning with the height of lynching at the turn of the century and covering the shift in public responses to spectacles circulated from the 1910s through the 1930s. Any cultural history, however — particularly of an atrocity like lynching — risks falling into abstraction, especially if it focuses on the realm of symbol, image, and representation. To avoid this risk, this book pays close attention to the social landscapes in which those who perpetrated and supported lynching lived their lives and understood the violence they committed. Much of the research here is based on specific localities, each of which experienced one or more lynchings, ranging from towns to midsize cities to larger urban centers, in three Deep South states: Georgia, Mississippi, and Texas.[22] Each chapter begins with a vignette that establishes the chapter's central themes and offers a sense of social and cultural texture surrounding lynching and its spectacle. And just as lynching spectacles moved from the local to the national, so does the trajectory of this book.

PART I ◈ SPECTACLE

1

❖ ❖ ❖

THEY WANT TO SEE THE THING DONE
Public Executions

WHEN HENRY HODGES, his wife, and their three children were found brutally murdered in their home six miles outside Statesboro, Georgia, the white people of that town and surrounding Bulloch County were whipped into a frenzy of horror and fear.

On the evening of 27 July 1904, Hodges, a yeoman farmer of modest means whose wife had recently inherited a small amount of money, was knocked down and robbed in his yard. The culprits proceeded to murder each member of the family with an axe. They then piled the bodies in one room and set a torch to the entire house. Suspicion immediately fell on a black man, Paul Reed, a tenant on the land of Hodges's neighbor. When questioned, Reed's wife revealed that her husband had confessed the crime to her, saying that he had committed it with his friend, Will Cato, a laborer on another nearby farm.[1]

By the Saturday after the murders, thousands of white citizens had gathered in Statesboro, anticipating a lynching. Hundreds more gathered at the burned remains of the Hodges house. There, according to the *Statesboro (Ga.) News*, "They were met by the sight of the most awful scene that we have ever been called upon to witness. The smoke was still issuing from the smouldering ruins and the scent of the burning of human flesh filled the air."[2] Such a crime had never before occurred in Bulloch County, a relatively prosperous county in the Georgia pine barrens, populated largely by white yeoman cotton farmers and a growing middle class in the county seat of Statesboro. The county had grown considerably since 1889, when the railroad connected it to outside markets. Statesboro, which increased in population from 525 in 1890 to nearly 2,500 in 1904, boasted a new courthouse, new churches, electric lights, and new telephone and water systems at the time of the lynching. It was "distinctly a town of the New South," observed

Ray Stannard Baker, a northern journalist who investigated the lynching for *McClure's* magazine.[3] African Americans made up over 40 percent of the population, working mostly as farm laborers or in the growing turpentine industry, a key source of wealth and development in the county. But white residents, searching to place blame for the Hodges murders, pointed their fingers at the turpentine industry, which, since it required transitory labor, brought what they considered shiftless and disruptive young black men into the county.[4] Many of these men, like Cato and Reed, stayed on to work on local farms, and white residents believed they raised the level of vice and crime in the county. White residents were filled with terror that they might meet the fate of the Hodges family at the hands of black men who lived on or near their land. This was a "community of good farmers moving along the even tenor of their way," reported the *Statesboro News*, awakened "to the fact that they were living in constant danger and that human vampires lived in their midst, only awaiting the opportunity to blot out their lives by murder and the torch."[5]

Amid this climate of racial fear and outrage, a public meeting was called in the county courthouse to decide whether to lynch Reed and Cato before they were brought to trial. The few men who attempted to persuade against any unlawful vengeance, including the mayor and several ministers, were met with silence. Even the "best citizens of the county" reportedly showed "little sympathy for the effort to protect the set of red handed devils who had committed this, the blackest crime that ever blasted the good name of our county and state."[6] No lynching was attempted at this point, however, largely because people became convinced that more blacks were involved in the crime and that Cato and Reed could provide essential testimony. The prisoners were removed to Savannah for safekeeping and brought back to Statesboro for their trial under guard from the state militia. Special trains were chartered from Savannah to bring in out of towners, and hundreds crowded the courthouse to witness the trial, which lasted one day. Rumors that Reed and Cato were members of a secret organization of blacks called the Before Day Club, which was conspiring to murder white farmers and their families, only amplified the sense of alarm throughout the county and intensified public interest in the trial. Reports quickly surfaced that such clubs existed across the state and the wider South.[7]

Before the trial had even started, most white citizens had already deemed the accused men guilty beyond all doubt. They wanted to see Reed and Cato convicted and punished swiftly and openly. In fact, more than a week before the trial began, the *Statesboro (Ga.) News* had printed an editorial calling for a public execution of the "bloody devils who did the terrible crime" on the grounds that "the people not only are anxious to know that these murderers are hanged high and hanged until they kick out their bloody and criminal existence between heaven and earth, but they want to see the thing done." Although it conceded that such an execution would not "restore one of the unfortunate victims again," the paper purported that "it will be at least some satisfaction to an outraged people, to see the thing happen." Indeed, once Cato and Reed were convicted and sentenced to hang, the crowd in the courtroom almost immediately demanded that the presiding judge, Judge Daly, declare a public execution. Although Daly insisted that he lacked the power to authorize a public hanging, he assured the crowd that, as compensation, Cato and Reed would be held in Statesboro to await their sentence, keeping power in the hands of local authorities. But once it was rumored that the militia was arranging to send the prisoners back to Savannah, a mob of 75 to 100 men, aided by several local bailiffs, snatched Cato and Reed from the guards, whose weapons were reportedly unloaded. Almost 2,000 people watched as the mob led the two black men back to the site of the crime, the remains of the Hodges home. Overcome with the August heat, the mob stopped at a clearing in the woods two miles from town, chained the men to a tree stump, drenched them with kerosene, and lit them on fire.[8]

By burning them to death, the lynchers, in effect, reenacted the crime Cato and Reed had allegedly committed against the Hodgeses, performing a literal retaliatory vengeance on them. When some members of the mob had proposed hanging the men, the crowd had protested and demanded a burning, reportedly yelling, "They burned the Hodges and gave them no choice: burn the niggers!"[9] The mob thus re-created the scene of "smouldering ruins" filled with the "stench of burning flesh" that witnesses had experienced at the Hodges house. They could now see the death that haunted their imaginations projected onto the two black men, an event that eased their worst fears by making them visible. The event could, for this reason, be celebrated without restraint. A local photographer snapped pictures, and afterward, the spectators scrambled for souvenirs. The chains that held the men were broken and distributed, as were pieces of the burned tree stump and charred bones. In an especially assertive act of defiance against the state, one young man brought remnants of bone back to town as an offering for Daly, who reacted with disgust.[10]

The excitement surrounding the lynching lasted for weeks, in some measure because the rumors about the Before Day Club continued to fester.

Posses of white men charged through the county threatening and whipping suspects and even lynching three other black men.[11] Many white citizens sympathetic to the lynching of Cato and Reed thought this spate of vigilantism excessive, but many others saw it as an unfortunate but necessary tactic to rid the county of undesirable black men and to ensure the safety of whites. The violence subsided only when county farmers began to note that many black laborers were fleeing the county just before the cotton harvest.[12]

Soon after the lynching of Reed and Cato, a court of inquiry was held, partly because of the national exposure the violence had brought to Statesboro and partly because of the mob's obvious defiance of Daly's courtroom and the state militia. There, witnesses identified nine men who were directly involved in the lynching, but none were ever indicted. Three were farmers and neighbors of the Hodgeses: George Deal, a well-off farmer, who testified at the trial and was seen in the mob on the courthouse lawn, and Ben Mallard and Henry Mock, who served as bailiffs at the trial and helped the mob inside the courtroom. The other bailiff, John G. Mitchell, was a blacksmith who lived in Statesboro. The other alleged members of the mob were men in their thirties who also lived in Statesboro and worked as skilled laborers or in white-collar occupations: a brickmason, a bookkeeper, an auditor for the railroad, and a manager at the local ice company.[13] Except for Mallard and Deal, these were not men who had a close connection to the Hodges family or even knew them. Neither were they particularly poor or likely to have felt economically squeezed or displaced by black labor. Except for Mallard, who was struggling in tenancy on a rented farm with his mother and four siblings, all these men owned their own land or homes. Cotton prices had dropped slightly in 1904, but farmers still considered them reasonable, and people in Statesboro were generally optimistic about their economic future.[14]

The men who committed the lynching of Reed and Cato—whether they included these nine men or not—did so because they shared a vested interest in seeing the crime against the Hodgeses avenged. They were willing and eager to exact punitive justice themselves, as if the crime were a personal attack on them, not only as fellow residents of the county but as potential victims of what they saw as widespread, savage black criminality. As white men, they would have believed they had both a responsibility and a right to avenge such a terrible offense against their race. Many local residents also considered the law inadequate to punish such a crime, assuming that it would not give Reed and Cato what so many white citizens thought they deserved. As the *Atlanta Journal* wrote in defense of the lynching, "It is said by many that burning at the stake is barbarous, cruel and inhuman. Measured by the standards of law and morality, it is true, and yet there are crimes which go far beyond the law and punishments which the law is utterly incapable of administering adequately. Such a case is the murder of the Hodges family at Statesboro."[15]

Still, as enraged and as fearful as they were, the people of Statesboro acquiesced to the state's authority until the last moment. They initially held off from lynching the men and submitted to a trial. Presumably, had the judge authorized a public execution and assured the crowd that the prisoners would stay in Statesboro, the lynching would not have occurred.[16] The men who burned Will Cato and Paul Reed to death did so because they believed, with outraged indignation, that the state was denying them their right to witness justice enacted, to see the "murderers are hanged high and hanged until they kick out their bloody and criminal existence between heaven and earth." In fact, by defying the judge's orders, they were able to punish the men with a cruelty and vengeance that the state could not.

The demand for a public execution as late as 1904 was not as astonishing as it might appear. In many places in the South at the turn of the century, executions were still public affairs, drawing crowds of hundreds, if not thousands, of spectators. Legal executions had been made private in other areas of the country in the mid- to late nineteenth century as a means to impose efficiency, order, and the semblance of respectability on them. Southern states, however, tended to lag behind the North. Even when southern judges and sheriffs, concerned about the demoralizing effect of public hangings and the potential disorder of the crowd, did attempt to hold executions in private, enclosing gallows behind fences and walls, citizens often actively resisted by bribing sheriffs, climbing rooftops, and breaking down enclosures. Not incidentally, at the same time, lynchings were becoming more public, more ritualized, and more spectacular. Just as they resisted when local and state authorities prevented them from attending executions, white southerners resorted to lynching to guarantee their active involvement in and witnessing of criminal punishment, to satisfy their outrage and desire for vengeance by, as the *Statesboro (Ga.) News* put it, "see[ing] the thing done." Of course, Americans in other parts of the country had similarly protested the move to private executions, and yet they did not as frequently resort to public lynchings. There were clearly other reasons that white southerners felt compelled to torture and lynch black men publicly. But their frustration that the state was interfering with their right to witness punitive justice and to participate in the retribution of a crime was undoubtedly a significant factor. As in Statesboro, lynching was commonly performed in active resistance to the encroaching power of the modern state.

In this way, although lynching was often reinforced through the use of modern technology and media, it was, as spectacle and ritual, firmly rooted in the traditional social performance of public executions. At public executions, white southerners learned what hanging a person looked like and that watching such a spectacle was socially acceptable. Lynch mobs even appropriated many rituals of public executions—the declarations of guilt, the confessions, the taking of souvenirs and photographs—to confer legitimacy on their extralegal violence. They saw themselves not as criminals or defilers of the law, as their critics saw them, but as honorable vindicators of justice and popular sovereignty, fulfilling their rights as citizens to punish crimes against their communities.[17] When lynch mobs staged rituals of public executions, however, they did so in exaggerated and distorted forms, with a degree of sadism that far exceeded the most boisterous hanging-day crowd. Once mobs had wrested the power to punish from the state, they did so with a ferocious vengeance that the state could not grant.

Although the excessive brutality of many lynchings distinguished them from executions, their performative and symbolic value drew from the execution-day spectacle. To understand the significance of public executions in the South is to make sense of not only that excessive brutality but also the pleasure that so many white southerners derived from seeing it. In both executions and lynchings, spectators were central to the rituals of retributive justice that were performed. The crowds of people who gathered for execution day were present not simply as onlookers but as witnesses to the state's punishment on their behalf. Because the spectacle of hanging was meant to deter crime, it required a somber and fearful crowd of potential criminals who would identify with the condemned and tremble at his fate. But witnesses also gathered as united citizens to sanction the execution's rituals of repentance and retribution, through which the criminal was expunged and community order was restored. For these reasons, spectators at executions themselves became the objects of intense scrutiny and observation—the composition, the attitude, and the behavior of the crowd all mattered greatly.[18] News accounts and legal authorities regularly expressed concern over the comportment of the crowd: Were they properly solemn?

Were they too boisterous or rowdy? Were they paying attention to the condemned's final words or prayers? Spectators at lynchings held a comparable importance, especially as those witnesses came to stand as a unified community lending credence to the lynching ritual.

As with the lynching-day crowd, conceptions of the execution-day crowd were inextricable from white supremacy and its racially bound notions of moral superiority and social justice. African Americans were, as today, more likely to be sentenced to death for their crimes and, it appears, more likely to be hanged publicly for their crimes. Moreover, many southern states considered rape a capital crime well into the twentieth century, and at least two southern states specifically authorized public hangings in cases of rape. The overwhelming majority of those sentenced to die in rape cases were African American men convicted of raping white women.[19] When white southerners attended an execution of a black criminal, they would have differentiated themselves both from the condemned and from any African American witnesses present, whom they saw as most needing deterrence. These white spectators would have believed they were witnessing not so much the terrible consequences of crime but an inherently savage black criminality justly punished by white authorities. As protected and guiltless witnesses—as literal extensions of the state—they could feel a communal sense of white virtue and strength, particularly in contradistinction to the moral depravity of the condemned. These narratives of black culpability and white innocence learned and witnessed at executions were carried into the practice and witnessing of lynching.

LIKE THE CITIZENS of Statesboro, Georgia, countless southern defenders of lynching saw the violence as an inevitable and justifiable substitution for capital punishment, in particular because the legal system bestowed too many rights on black criminals and offered too little respect for white victims. Certainly the state provided little recourse for black criminals in the South—they were often inadequately defended, convicted, and sentenced by all-white juries in exceptionally hasty trials, and they were more likely to be sentenced to death than were white criminals. Nevertheless, white southerners who justified lynching regularly expressed frustration with the slow, bureaucratic wheels of justice. White citizens in Statesboro, for instance, expressed distrust that the courts could satisfactorily avenge the Hodgeses' murders, arguing that "the lawyers would get them off" or that "the case would be appealed and they would go free." These southerners believed they could more adequately serve justice and vindicate white supremacy than could the state, which was bound by its theoretical impartiality and color blindness. Even in a criminal justice system overwhelmingly slanted to the advantage of southern whites, the modern state imposed restrictions and limits that lynch mobs certainly did not.[20]

In the early twentieth century, many scholars and critics of lynching hoped that as the South continued to modernize its legal and social institutions and as its citizens developed greater deference toward the legal authority of the state to oversee criminal punishment, lynching would eventually become anachronistic. In this view, legal executions, more efficiently and frequently administered, could act as a necessary deterrence to and replacement for lynching. This argument was used in defense of capital punishment in the face of growing hostility toward it in intellectual circles. Political scientist James Cutler, for instance, argued in 1907 that "to abolish capital punishment in this country is likely to provoke lynchings," since "lynchings represent an attempt on the part of private citizens to inflict a penalty that in severity will be proportionate to the heinousness of the crime committed." He further contended that "whenever unusually brutal and atrocious crimes are committed, particularly if they cross racial lines, nothing less than the death penalty will satisfy the general sense of justice that is to be found in the average American community."[21]

The notion that legal execution came to substitute for lynching holds powerful sway even today, as evidenced by the popular term "legal lynching" to refer to the ways in which the legal system was consistently manipulated to ensure that black criminals received the death penalty more often than did white criminals. As will be shown, authorities in some southern localities consciously used capital punishment to placate enraged white citizens and deter lynching.[22] Yet there existed no consistent correlation between legal executions and lynching. States that had abolished the death penalty by the turn of the century were also the least likely to lynch, and, conversely, the states with the highest lynching records also had the highest execution records. What is more, in localities with the highest rates of lynching, the legal system was already disproportionately swift and severe in its punishment of African American criminals. Legal executions did not and could not simply replace or temper people's impulses toward lynching.[23] But the concern here is less with the relationship between lynchings and legal executions as a whole than it is with the relationship between the rise in spectacle lynchings at the turn of the century and the state's simultaneous attempt to abolish public executions.

By 1904, when the *Statesboro (Ga.) News* was calling for a public execution, executions in the North had been performed privately for some time. Until the mid-nineteenth century, condemned criminals were usually executed in public hangings before large, often festive, crowds. Execution days were mass spectacles that made very evident the state's and the church's authority. By the end of the 1840s, however, all the mid-Atlantic and northeastern states had passed legislation abolishing public executions, mandating that criminals be hanged behind jailhouse walls before a select group of witnesses. Public executions were abolished in the Midwest and West by the end of the nineteenth century. The movement to shield executions from the public arose not, primarily, out of humanitarian sentiment for the privacy and humanity of the condemned but, rather, out of an increasing anxiety over the crowd's potential disorder, particularly in growing urban centers. For the public execution to ratify state and religious authority and thus deter crime, it was necessary that the spectators identify with the condemned criminal, to believe that they, as potential sinners, were capable of the same crime and susceptible to the same punishment. By the early nineteenth century, however, civic leaders and other elites began to express concern that crowds were not observing the solemnity of such occasions and instead were treating executions as carnivalesque entertainment. Spectators, they feared, were not properly reflecting on their own sinfulness in these moments; in fact, in large cities where the condemned was a stranger to the crowd and more likely to be a minority or a foreigner, it was all too easy for spectators to disidentify with the condemned, to view his sin as far removed from their own culpability.[24]

These fears coincided with a growing conception among the genteel classes that watching an execution, or any other form of violence, hardened human sensitivities to violence and stimulated brutish impulses. In this view, public executions excited the crudest sensibilities of the public—always rhetorically configured as the lower classes—polluted their moral senses, and indulged their basest feelings; in short, rather than deterring crime, public executions encouraged violence, crime, and social disorder. Once public executions were perceived as chaotic displays of the crowd's unruly sensibilities, the upper and middle classes found public executions increasingly distasteful and intolerable. Some humanitarians began to focus on the suffering of the condemned, demanding that they be chloroformed before the hanging or that capital punishment be abolished altogether. (This sort of humanitarian sentiment was behind the movement away from hanging to the use of the electric chair in the 1890s.) But, for the most part, reformers were more concerned with the impact of an execution on its spectators, particularly on what sensitive, civilized eyes could and should not witness.[25]

In light of these views, the state sought to impose efficiency and order on executions, making them less ritualistic and more rational. Sheriffs and other local authorities began to build fences and enclosures to shield the gallows from public view, and execution-day speeches and prayers were eliminated. This transition, however, was neither uniform nor without resistance. Some authorities simply disregarded the law. When they did not, many people accustomed to execution-day spectacles climbed rooftops and walls to catch a glimpse of the gallows. In 1878, 15,000 people arrived for the execution of a black man, Sam Steenburgh, accused of murder and other crimes in Fonda, New York. Although the gallows was built behind a high fence, spectators perched on rooftops to view the hanging. As late as 1897 in Mansfield, Pennsylvania, the sheriff overseeing the execution of a white man convicted of murdering his wife was inundated with requests to view the hanging. Although he limited the witnesses to fifty, crowds gathered outside the fence that enclosed the gallows, peering through knotholes or pressing themselves against the fence to at least hear the sounds of the hanging. This kind of crowd behavior ended only when executions were brought under state authority, with all executions within a state occurring in one central location, usually the state penitentiary, a move that was contested by those who opposed state centralization of power.[26]

To satisfy the public's continuing desire to witness executions in the face of these changes, newspapers began providing excruciating details of the condemned's final moments, creating a vicarious spectacle that caused no end of concern for social elites. Some states went so far as to ban news reporters from the gallows and prohibit them from reporting salacious details of executions. These laws made little distinction between the act of viewing an execution and the sensational representations of it in the press; both were seen to have damaging effects on the moral sensibilities of the public. Newspapers protested these laws on First Amendment grounds and often outright ignored them.[27]

By performing executions behind prison walls and by removing state violence from public view, the state effectively reasserted its power over the people. Executions never became fully private, however; authorities only limited the number of spectators, a limiting based on gender, race, and class that removed any semblance of an unruly or impressionable crowd. Witnesses to executions were now almost entirely middle-class professional white men — journalists, doctors, ministers — who were considered to possess the proper respectability and moral strength to witness such an event.

It is also significant that while private executions strengthened state power, they arguably weakened religious authority. Ministers were still present at executions, but their role in mediating between the condemned and the public through prayer and song was vastly diminished.[28]

Although in the rest of the country, the transition to private executions was largely complete by the end of the nineteenth century, public hangings continued across the South well into the twentieth century, the last taking place in Kentucky in 1936.[29] It is difficult to ascertain exactly when executions became private in the South because executions were still administered and recorded on the local level long after they had been centralized in the North. Legislatures in most southern states did attempt to abolish public hangings in the latter part of the nineteenth century, but as they had in other parts of the country, local judges and sheriffs often disregarded these laws to satisfy the public's desires and to assert their own authority against state officials. Georgia, for instance, enacted a law against public executions as early as 1859, but local officials largely ignored it.[30] Whether an execution was deemed private depended on a number of factors, including the sensationalism of the crime and the preference of the sheriff. Authorities in larger cities, for instance, were more likely to shun public hangings because the threat of disorder from the crowd was larger and the relationship between authorities and the people more distant. Moreover, although executions throughout the South became increasingly private in the twentieth century, there was no consistency even in individual localities, for a sheriff from an earlier period may have preferred private hangings, whereas his successor allowed public ones. The process of making executions private was fully completed in the South only when states began to use the electric chair, held in a centralized location in each state. Because the electric chair stood indoors, within prison walls, with room available for only a select number of witnesses, there was no possibility of large crowds breaking through or climbing rooftops to see.[31]

When they were performed, public executions were exceedingly popular entertainments, mass spectacles of morbid amusement that drew thousands of spectators, who traveled long distances, collected souvenirs, and took photographs. That is, they were legal versions of the spectacle lynchings that took place in this same period.[32] Indeed, at the turn of the century, it was common for the northern press to denounce the southern penchant for public executions as a barbaric custom that was little more than lynching in legal disguise. In 1879, the *Chicago Tribune* bemoaned hanging days in the

South, which "seem to be devised for the entertainment of the people and to take the place of the circus and the dog-fight," a phenomenon that was only made more "atrocious" by the fact that "the gallows is intended only for the negro." When it came to black criminals, the paper opined, "the usual mode is to hang him and lynch him without the benefit of law," and even when he did stand trial, "the demand for justice is tremendous—if the prisoner is a negro—and he is hurried out of the world neck and heels."[33]

Although they would not admit to this racial imbalance except as a reflection of black proclivities toward crime, many southerners during the Progressive Era denounced public executions for many of the same reasons that they had become unacceptable in the North. "Such spectacles are brutalizing," asserted the *Atlanta Constitution*, one of the most vocal proponents of private executions, in 1891. "Most of the lookers-on are always of the very lowest class. It is not conducive to public order to draw so many people together. Their worst passions are gratified and stimulated by this scene on the scaffold." The *Macon County (Ga.) Citizen* concurred in 1893 that "public executions are demoralizing and hurtful and should be abolished. Let executions be private and they will be fewer," referring to the concern that public hangings, rather than deterring crime, only exacerbated it. The notion that public executions might "furnish examples for imitation and swell the volume of violence," as the *Atlanta Constitution* put it, had its own racial tinge, since African Americans regularly attended public hangings and were understood by whites to be the most impressionable members of the crowd.[34]

Despite the emerging elite opposition to public executions, many southern judges and sheriffs continued to authorize hangings held outside the jail yard to accommodate thousands of spectators, and the executions were often performed as a remarkable blend of solemn admonition and festive entertainment. The 1909 execution of Will Mack in Brandon, Mississippi, took place after a speedy six-hour trial in which Mack was convicted of raping a white adolescent girl. According to a local report, a "vast crowd" of more than 3,000 people, arriving on trains and buggies from the surrounding counties, witnessed the hanging, while vendors sold soda pop, ice cream, peanuts, and watermelon. As Mack's body dropped, the crowd let out a "loud shout," and hundreds rushed the gallows for souvenirs. The hanging rope was "quickly cut into small pieces and carried off by those who wished to keep a memento of the gruesome scene," while Mack's shoes were left on the gallows as a reminder of his crime and sentence.[35] Six thousand people attended the 1893 execution of Charles Johnston in Swainsboro, Georgia, where "flying jennies and fake shows were side attractions." And in Stark-ville, Mississippi, the gallows for a 1915 double hanging of two black men convicted of murder was erected in a pasture encircled by bluffs, creating a "natural amphitheatre" that provided the 5,000 "on-lookers an excellent view." Again, vendors sold pop and snacks, and many spectators brought their lunches, "making it a picnic."[36] For those executions conducted on flat-ter terrain, the gallows themselves created a staging area, so even those in the middle or back of a large crowd could see. These kinds of spectacles, in which vendors and grifters exploited the day for commercial gain—where the analogy of hanging day as circus was made literal—particularly shocked and distressed critics.

In some cases, the condemned was paraded through the center of town so that a maximum number of citizens could see him before the hanging. Henry Campbell, hanged in Lawrenceville, Georgia, in 1908, was taken to the courthouse square so he could address a large crowd before being taken to the gallows set up in a semiprivate yard behind the Baptist church (figure 1.1).[37] In other cases, sheriffs displayed the bodies of the condemned after the hanging to satisfy crowds who had missed the execution. The coffin holding Erastus Brown, hanged in Statesboro, Georgia, in 1897, was brought to the stockade yard, "where all that wished could go see him." Similarly, when the crowd waiting to see Tom Delk's 1897 hanging in Zebulon, Geor-gia, began to protest that they could not see, "the Sheriff sent out word that everybody would be given an opportunity later to inspect the corpse, and this seemed to satisfy the excited mob." Delk's body was removed to the courthouse and "placed on exhibition." There, "everybody saw it, the crowd coming in at one door in a steady stream and passing out at another." The act of witnessing the execution, in this regard, included being physically near the scene of the action and among a crowd of like-minded people. To wit-ness a hanging was also to hear the proceedings and perhaps the cries of the condemned, and to feel the push of the crowd, to sense that one was a part of something important or extraordinary. For some, surely the experience lay in being part of the crowd, amid the excitement, with the possibility of catching a glimpse of the execution. When John Williams was hanged in the tower of the county jail in Waco, Texas, a substantial "crowd" of witnesses was allowed in the room, but the *Waco Times-Herald* also reported that "an-other crowd had gathered in front of the jail to witness the proceedings from the outside."[38]

As noted above, even when authorities did attempt to conduct execu-tions behind fences or enclosures, they ostensibly became public when

FIGURE 1.1 Hanging-day crowd at the execution of Henry Campbell (standing center in black suit), Lawrenceville, Georgia, May 1908. Courtesy of Georgia Archives, Vanishing Georgia Collection, gwn010.

spectators climbed walls, trees, or rooftops to see the hanging. In the case of Delk's execution, according to one account, although the sheriff had enclosed the gallows, "the execution was not private, as it was easy for the several thousand of those who surrounded the enclosure to look through the clumsily strung rolls of bagging which shut the gallows." Will Gordon, like Henry Campbell, was hanged in Lawrenceville, in 1906, within an enclosure behind the Baptist church, but still twenty guards were needed to keep the enormous crowd back. On some occasions, people paid sheriffs for the privilege of witnessing a private hanging. Under one sheriff's jurisdiction in Waco, Texas, rooftops and second-story galleries surrounding the jail yard were rented; prices ranged from twenty-five cents to one dollar, according to location and vantage point.[39]

News reports of executions tended to point out that many women and children had attended, presumably because their presence contributed both to the sense of public spectacle and to the social legitimacy of the event.[40] The clear majority of spectators were white men, however, and certainly only men and boys climbed trees, walls, and fences to witness. Of the estimated 6,000 people at the 1901 execution of Will Jackson in Cartersville, Georgia, hanged for an assault on the "wife of a well-to-do farmer," only an estimated 500 were white women. Similarly, at Roy Mitchell's 1923 execution in Waco, Texas, out of a crowd of 4,000 to 5,000 people, reportedly only 500 were women. Yet, as was the case in many lynchings, white women were the most prominent members of the crowd, particularly when they were figured as the victims of the black man's crime. When Mathew Howell was hanged in Lawrenceville, Georgia, in 1907, for killing a local bailiff, torrential rains dampened the day, yet the *Lawrenceville News-Herald* made note that the bailiff's wife said "she would have walked all the way in the rain to see the Negro executed."[41]

In its account of the public hanging of Will Mack, the *Brandon (Miss.) News* reported that "some ladies were present" as well as "many little children." One mother "kept her eyes on the gallows," despite the "nursing infant" who "tugged at [her] breast," because "she didn't want to lose any part of the program she had come miles to see—to tell about to the neighbors at home who were unable to be at hand—to think about while awake; to doubtless see in horrible dreams, when asleep, and to never want to see again." This image of the nursing mother pilgrimaging long distances to witness the death of a black criminal speaks particularly to the cultural importance of these events, which went far beyond mere morbid curiosity. For one, being present at the hanging gave one the authority to narrate the event to others, "to tell about to the neighbors at home who were unable to be at hand."[42]

DESPITE THE FESTIVITIES that often surrounded executions, spectators also saw them as dramas that performed grave tales of crime and punishment, dramas that brought deep satisfaction to citizens fearful of what they perceived as increasing crime in their towns and counties. The executions followed a standard script, as the condemned, along with district attorneys, sheriffs, and ministers, imparted religion-infused narratives of sin, confession, and redemption to the witnessing crowd. These performances were meant to convey powerful lessons to spectators about the terrible consequences of crime, which they would then carry into their everyday lives. It was these performances, dramatizing both state and divine power, that rendered spectators, who may have been present merely for perverse amusement, into witnesses with a civic and spiritual responsibility to reflect on the gravity of the day.

Commentators, however, regularly made patent distinctions between the effects of witnessing on white and black spectators. Proponents of public executions were most concerned that these hangings stand as conspicuous warnings to potential black criminals. In its editorial calling for a public execution, the *Statesboro (Ga.) News* argued that the people of Bulloch County deserved to witness the hanging of Reed and Cato, and it added, "Let the example be given in public that all men of a criminal leaning can witness the fate that awaits them, if they engage in the crime of taking the lives of their fellow men." As so much of the public conversation in Statesboro at this time was focused on black criminality in the area, particularly the specter of the Before Day Club, it is clear what "men of a criminal leaning" the *Statesboro News* was hoping to target. Likewise, when authorities in Gainesville, Georgia, decided to hang convicted murderer Cassius Law privately in 1899, the local paper made special note that local blacks had wished for a public hanging because "they say it would restrain their race to have Law hanged in public, that all might see the awful punishment administered to him."[43]

For these reasons, the press commonly noted the presence of African Americans at public executions. For Will Mack's hanging in Brandon, Mississippi, it was reported that "probably one fourth, or maybe one third of the crowd were negroes" and that the "only good effect it can have on them is to see, that, even if one escapes death by mob by hanging or burning, that although the state might use soldiers to have him tried legally that, if convicted, the rapist must hang."[44] Although there is no evidence that proportionally more blacks than whites attended executions, their attendance was particularly conspicuous to white southerners in part because it justified the public execution as a socially necessary admonition. Their attendance was also conspicuous because of their decided absence from lynching crowds. The presence of several African Americans amid the almost all-white crowd at Henry Campbell's 1908 execution in Lawrenceville, Georgia (figure 1.1), is startling precisely because the image in so many ways resembles a photograph of a lynching crowd—until one sees the black spectators.

Indeed, despite the warnings against sin and crime that they were meant to convey to black spectators, executions were unquestionably less threatening than lynchings, not only because hanging-day rituals were bound by legal restraints but also, to some extent, because African Americans could witness these rituals and even participate in them. In most hangings of black men, the condemned directly addressed other blacks to warn them against sin and wrongdoing and exhorted the black spectators to sing and pray along with them. Before Burrell Parish ascended the scaffold to meet his death in Vicksburg, Mississippi, in 1891, he knelt to the ground and "commenced singing a familiar hymn, lining it himself, which was joined in by about 300 colored people in assembly." Similarly, Jesse Washington, executed in Waco, Texas, in 1906, asked to sing a song on the scaffold that was "familiar to the negroes."[45]

In instances like these, a substantive identification was created between the condemned man and black spectators—or, at least, white eyes imagined this relationship. When Ed Frey was hanged in Marietta, Georgia, in 1889, before a crowd of 3,000, Frey "recognized some friends" in the crowd and bowed to them. Frey's hanging was particularly fraught with emotion because, the *Atlanta Constitution* reported, he "feared that his sins had not been forgiven." As the minister led the gathering in a hymn, Frey broke down in loud sobbing, "and the negroes in the crowd began to moan," apparently in sympathy for his fate.[46]

Southern blacks, to be sure, might have attended executions to witness a remarkable event, just as many whites did. It was in the best interest of white reporters to assume that black spectators were identifying with the doomed fate of the criminal, but African Americans might simply have wanted to be part of a public moment in which a black man was the celebrated, though infamous, star. Many condemned men took advantage of this attention for what it was worth, taking their time on the scaffold to tell their stories and sing. In one execution in Georgetown, Texas, in 1896, the condemned began telling jokes to the crowd, "caus[ing] the people to laugh," and the news report of the hanging offered the headline "Hanging of a Humorist." When Charles Johnston, a black minister convicted of murder, was hanged in Swainsboro, Georgia, he "preached his own funeral sermon," inducing the crowd to sing, kneel, raise their hands, and pray along with him. According to one report, just before he died, Johnston "said he was happy and he seemed to feel that he was the hero of the hour." At the moment of their deaths, these men were probably accorded more status than they had ever before had. The condemned man received a last meal, a new suit of clothes, and the rapt attention of ministers and news reporters, and he frequently was led to the gallows with cigar in hand.[47]

Photographs of the condemned at a hanging indeed stand in poignant distinction to the ravished bodies of black men in lynching photographs. Most execution photographs do not show, at least in close view, the condemned after death; they depict, from afar, the scaffold just before the hanging or the crowd surrounding the gallows. The photograph of Seaborn Johnson shows him proud and defiant, face uplifted, in a suit, with a fat cigar planted in his mouth, despite his being handcuffed and chained to a bullish-looking sheriff (figure 1.2). Johnson's brother, who stands beside him in the photograph, accompanied him to the gallows. A drawing that appeared in the *Waco (Tex.) Times-Herald* of Will King, hanged in 1901, depicts the condemned man sitting in the jail with his mother, appearing as if in a respectable family portrait. In some instances, the condemned was offered authority over these images. Just before Jesse Washington was hanged, after he had been "placed in position" on the scaffold, he was handed a photograph that had been taken in the jail the day before, and "he was asked if he liked it." Washington "looked at it with a smile and said it was fine and hoped the pictures would be given to his friends."[48]

Critics of public executions bemoaned precisely this sort of glorification of the criminal, which they believed undermined any deterrent effect the execution might have. The *Atlanta Constitution* in 1871 fretted that "the worst elements of society are usually present at hangings," and "in their inflamed eyes, the man on the scaffold, the central figure of so vast a crowd, the victim of so terrible a tragedy, becomes a sort of hero and martyr, and inspires more emulation than fear." One proponent of electrocution echoed this judgment some forty years later in arguing that electrocution would be "swift" and "solemn," unlike hangings, which "often tended to make the subject a hero, permitting him to address the assembled crowd, forgive his enemies . . . and then go off in a blaze of glory." Such scenes, he added, were "actually attractive to certain classes of our population," since "a negro likes

FIGURE 1.2 Seaborn Johnson on the day of his execution with his brother and the county sheriff, Thomas "Papa T" Brown, Emanuel County, Georgia, 1923. Courtesy of Georgia Archives, Vanishing Georgia Collection, emn041.

nothing better than to be the central figure, be it a cakewalk or a hanging." Opponents of public hangings accordingly argued that private executions, in their invisibility, could stand as a more terrifying warning to potential criminals. "Let the jail walls . . . hide the operations of our law," proposed the *Atlanta Constitution*; "let the public stand in silent wonderment and know only when the dishonored coffin comes from the awful gates of the jail yard, that the law has avenged the wrongs of society." It was this concentration of state power, made all the more terrible because the mechanisms of its power were hidden from view, that proponents of public executions protested. It was also this dynamic of invisible terror that made lynching so horrifying for African Americans.[49]

Many white southerners undoubtedly shared an appetite for public glimpses into the lives and worlds of criminal celebrities, both white and black. For white audiences, however, the desire to see an African American criminal brought to death was based in something more than mere proximity to the infamous; white crowds wanted to witness justice enacted, particularly against black men who had harmed whites. As in Statesboro, Georgia, a public hanging could act as a surrogate for lynching. A public execution, contended the *Statesboro News* in its 1904 editorial, "will go a long ways towards appeasing and quieting the people who are ready and willing to take this matter in their own hands." Similarly, when Will Mack was hanged publicly in Brandon, Mississippi, the *Brandon News* reported that "public hangings are wrong, but under the circumstances, the quiet acquiescence of the people to submit to a legal trial, their good behavior throughout left no alternative to the board of supervisors but to grant the almost universal demand for a public execution." In cases like these, the state did not intend that the executions stand as admonishments to deter individual crimes; rather, in staging public executions, the state was deterring *mob* crime. Public executions were the reward to white southerners who refrained from lynching and yielded to the authority of the state.[50]

If a public execution was compensation to potential mobs that had let the law run its course, it could be celebrated to a greater degree than even the most public lynching. Indeed, whereas news reports often described lynching crowds as "determined" or "outraged," they commonly represented crowds at executions as festive. The *Brandon (Miss.) News* described the spectators at Mack's hanging as "good-humored," adding that "there was no reason to be otherwise for the law was to hang a criminal whose death every decent person in the world said should be the penalty of rope." Likewise, after some women's clubs and state organizations tried to make private the execution of two African American men, Dit Seales and Peter Bolen, in Starkville, Mississippi, local officials "decided that a public hanging would be the proper thing." The *Jackson (Miss.) Daily News* reported that authorities "did everything possible to make the hanging a gala event," at which "every vantage point was covered with spectators, all eager to see the mandate of the court carried out." Despite common perceptions that lynching spectacles were equally festive, southern reports on lynching never described them with this light-hearted tone, and they made no mention of vendors, side attractions, or other overtly commercial activities.[51]

BY ALLOWING WHITE CROWDS to witness the punishment of a criminal, to grab souvenirs, and, in some cases, to take photographs, public officials created a continuum between the state and the people; the people were not merely onlookers to the imposing power of the state's punishment but participants in the enactment of that punishment. The execution thus established a visceral identification between white spectators and the power of the state. The act of witnessing bestowed a sense of authority on the white spectator, as did his or her identification with the state's authority to judge and condemn wrongdoing.

Not only did public hangings make manifest the state's power to punish criminal behavior, but they were also elaborate religious ceremonies, dramas of sin, punishment, and redemption. The condemned, flanked by a minister, customarily gave an execution speech, which often read as a lengthy religious confessional, in which he testified to his own sin and accepted the suffering he must endure as a means to his salvation. Many offered public prayers and hymns, asked God for mercy, or warned the crowd against a life of wrongdoing and sin. These testimonials ensured that the condemned understood his crime and punishment, an understanding that was necessary to ratify the execution in secular terms.[52] Even more important, the confession justified the execution as divinely sanctioned, the rightful punishment for a life of sin. For instance, before Will Gordon was brought to the gallows in Lawrenceville, Georgia, for killing his girlfriend, he addressed a large crowd in the courthouse square for thirty minutes, speaking mostly about the ruin that liquor had wrought in his life and assuring the crowd that he had "made peace with God and would soon be in the glory world." The Lawrenceville News-Herald also noted that Gordon "said his punishment was just."[53]

That these rituals appeared to have been the same for black and white criminals is quite remarkable. Although, as noted, their words were often directed specifically to black spectators, African American criminals were afforded an exceptional—albeit confined—pulpit to command a mixed-race audience. Steve Allen, executed in Oxford, Mississippi, in 1889, before a crowd of 2,000 people, offered several speeches, both from his jail cell and from the gallows, in which he testified to his own "peace with God" and exhorted both black and white "to lead better lives, to keep working at the chariot wheels so they might meet him in heaven." Declaring that "Jesus died on the Roman cross for me; through his mercy all my sins are forgiven. I forgive all. I am anchored in Christ," Allen went to his death "without a tremor." At the 1915 double hanging of Seales and Bolen in Starkville, Mississippi, the condemned men asked the crowd to join in them in a hymn, "There Is a Land of Pure Delight," and confessed to their crimes just as the caps went over their heads.[54] Of course, white correspondents wrote all such accounts. But that white witnesses chose to remember and record black confessions in these ways is in itself significant.

White spectators would not necessarily have heard the condemned's confession as a sign of his redemption and salvation, as the minister and the condemned's prayers and benedictions anticipated. In identifying with the state's power and its right to punish, the white spectators would not have shared in the black criminal's confession of personal sin, nor would they have necessarily acknowledged their own sins at these moments. Instead, they would have associated themselves with those who had the right to condemn and punish sin—the already redeemed—especially because the condemned so often and so conspicuously directed their testimonials at black spectators. When Ed Frey refused to speak at his execution, it was "a disappointment to the crowd," for "nearly every one present thought he would have a great story of crime to tell."[55] To anticipate a "great story of crime" was to assume a considerable amount of detachment from the confession, as if one were not in the least implicated in the criminal behavior. A black confession of criminality could in fact simply reaffirm the crowd's beliefs in black inferiority, justifying whites' racial domination. Public executions as demonstrations of civic power were thus indistinguishable from the displays of white power that the crowd enacted.

The pleasure that white spectators experienced from an execution thus required a certain disidentification from the condemned and stemmed from a notion that the hanging not only established legal justice but also reaffirmed a larger social and racial justice. Seeing the pain and suffering of the condemned only intensified the crowd's enjoyment and sense of gratification. Newspapers reported faithfully whether the hanging rope broke the condemned's neck or strangled him to death; how long he suffered and how long it took him to die; whether his body jerked or shook; and whether he cried, fainted, or prayed. There was little humanitarian concern expressed in all this, except by certain reformers who wanted to promote the use of the electric chair as a "painless" alternative to hanging.[56]

Executions, as spectacles of white power and black culpability, also produced a sense of white solidarity among the crowd that was founded on a shared sense of white moral virtue and authority. The spectators could feel united in their shared act of witnessing something important, but they were also united in beholding a drama of retribution against sin and criminality that, as white people, they believed themselves removed and absolved from. There were, perhaps, white spectators who deplored what they were watching, who felt a sense of alienation or discomfort within the crowd. Nonetheless, their very presence in the crowd not only sanctified the state's authority but created a public image of white power and unity. Despite the sentiments and reactions of individual spectators, and even despite diversity in age, gender, and class, reports invariably figured the white crowd as a unit, sharing the same outrage at and condemnation of black criminality.

For this reason, as noted above, news accounts paid as much attention to the comportment and reaction of the crowd as they did to those of the condemned. Execution-day photographs commonly depict the throngs of spectators, as they were as much part of the spectacle as was the hanging itself. In the image from Henry Campbell's hanging (figure 1.1), some spectators are looking at Campbell, perched on a wagon before being brought to the gallows, while others are staring directly into the camera, as if aware of themselves as both observers and observed. The photograph projects an image of an orderly congregation, unmoving and staid. The spectators are wearing their Sunday best, presumably in recognition of the day's solemn importance. Despite the festive mood at so many executions, local news accounts often emphasized that the crowds at public hangings were unexpectedly respectful and well behaved. These reports were written defensively, since opponents of public executions were quick to criticize the rowdy atmosphere at these events. For these critics, the "holiday" atmosphere stood as evidence of the barbaric and perverse nature of public hangings and only confirmed their suspicions that public hangings fostered social disorder and violent impulses. The *Brandon (Miss.) News*, therefore, felt compelled to report that at Will Mack's execution, "there were very few under the influence of liquor and they did not get over the line of decency enough to be arrested." Similarly, the *Vicksburg (Miss.) Evening Post*, after the hanging of Sam Leflore in 1892, wrote that the sheriff "deserves credit for the fine order he kept," especially when accosted by a man holding a pint of whiskey. The man, who was sitting atop the jail yard wall, shouted to the sheriff, "asking him if he would allow the 'nigger to take a drink before he was hanged.'" When the sheriff told him to keep quiet or come down, the man replied, "You had better come up here and take me down." The sheriff sent two deputies to bring the man down, and "peace was restored once more."[57]

WHITE SOUTHERNERS, HOWEVER, were quick to engage in disorderly resistance to civic authority when sheriffs tried to block them from witnessing executions. Sheriff Tilley of Waco, Texas, attempted in vain to have Jesse Washington hanged privately, a decision he announced days beforehand; he enclosed the gallows, which previously stood "in plain view of the public," and permitted "only a few people . . . to see the hanging." But a crowd of 2,000 to 3,000 people arrived to witness the execution and promptly tore down "the veils that enclosed the scaffold," while others climbed trees, telephone poles, and rooftops or gathered in the courthouse to look out the windows. In a 1920 execution in Tupelo, Mississippi, a five-foot board fence erected around the gallows did not stop more than 5,000 people from attending the hanging. The deputies guarding the fence were forced "to draw guns to keep the crowd back." The citizens of Ellaville, Georgia, eager to watch Charles Blackman's hanging in 1889, went so far as to cut the town's telegraph wires to prevent the governor from intervening. For that hanging, the sheriff placed ropes around the gallows, and although "none but guards, reporters and physicians were allowed inside . . . fully five thousand people were present to witness the execution."[58]

Lynching was yet another way that white southerners wrested power from the state. For crimes committed by black men against whites, particularly white women, white southerners felt an intense investment in witnessing the enactment of justice and the restoration of the racial order, to the point of taking control themselves. White men tended to view these crimes as direct attacks on their racial and masculine authority, which only they themselves could restore. As noted, although the state was hardly a color-blind arbiter of justice in the Jim Crow South, white southerners believed that the modern state was inadequate to deal with black criminality. When writer Marcet Haldeman-Julius visited Little Rock, Arkansas, after the 1927 lynching of John Carter, who was accused of assaulting a white farmer's wife and his daughter, she questioned members of the mob as to why they did not have Carter arrested and tried in court for his alleged crime. She was consistently told that the law was "devious and uncertain," that guilty men too often were set free. "They's been too many of these damn niggers gettin' away. . . . It was time folks showed 'em somethin'," one informant told her.[59]

White southerners also resented the perceived leniency of state executions. Many of the most atrocious lynchings were defended on the grounds that the worst criminals deserved more than just a hanging. When a white mob in 1893 in Bardwell, Kentucky, lynched C. J. Miller, a black man accused of murdering and "mutilating" two white girls, they hanged him with a large log chain because "rope was a 'white man's death.'" Miller was also stripped of his clothes, dragged through the streets, and, after the hanging, "burned to ashes." In Statesboro, Georgia, Ray Stannard Baker reported that he "heard intelligent citizens argue that a tough negro criminal, in order to be a hero in the eyes of his people, does not mind being hanged. He is al-

lowed to make a speech, the ministers pray over him, he confesses dramatically, and he and all his negro friends are sure he is going straight to Para-
dise." The lynch mob stripped away these final dignities of the condemned,
and, as it stole these rights, the mob commanded the roles previously performed by sheriffs, hangmen, and ministers. Lynching thus extended the
role of witnessing at a public execution by allowing the spectators themselves to become the executioners.[60]

Despite lynchers' seeming dismissal of the law, theirs was not the attitude of a frontier, lawless society; these were men who otherwise respected
the law. Haldeman-Julius described the men who lynched John Carter as
acting "with much ostentation and self-righteous dignity," adding that "they
had meted out justice—thus their thoughts ran—they were no hoodlums or
villains." After Henry Smith was burned to death for the murder of a young
white girl in Paris, Texas, in 1893, one defender of the lynching wrote that
"the law had no punishment to fit such a deed, for law . . . never contem-
plated such a deed. The people who make the law sat in judgment on the
case, and rendered a verdict; the people who uphold and respect the law
executed the criminal." Because, in whites' eyes, issues of racial order went
beyond the law, infractions against that order were subject to a greater justice. The mob in Paris even scrawled the word "JUSTICE" on the platform
on which Smith was cremated.[61]

In these ways, the mass public lynchings that arose in the late 1880s and
1890s merged the tradition of vigilantism, previously performed privately
by small posses, with the spectacle of public execution. In merging these
two traditions, and transforming them in the process, lynch mobs created
a new social phenomenon. But this new practice of spectacle lynching was
made acceptable and justifiable through its associations with the older social practice of public executions. Early public lynchings, like that of Smith
in Paris, Texas, even conspicuously reenacted public executions by building
scaffolds or by allowing the condemned to make final speeches. Through
this association, mobs imposed an aura of legality on an extralegal practice
and an air of social acceptability on what were sadistic and horrific acts of
violence. Making a lynching public and spectacular rendered it more legitimate than an act of vigilante violence performed secretly, outside town.

Many white southerners also deemed the act of participating in and
watching lynching atrocities socially permissible—in fact, they encouraged
them—because they also conceptualized lynching through traditions of sin
and violent retribution rooted in Christian eschatology. Indeed, often the

higher law or greater "justice" to which white southerners appealed in a lynching was divine judgment. As rituals infused with religious meaning, lynchings did more than create a secular image of white superiority; they also offered white southerners a vision of themselves as morally pure and spiritually redeemed.

2

◈ ◈ ◈

A HELL OF FIRE UPON EARTH

Religion

ON A BRIGHT SUNDAY MORNING in July 1885, a white mob lynched Harris Tunstal behind the Methodist Episcopal church in Oxford, Mississippi. According to the *Memphis Commercial Appeal*, Tunstal, a black man, was hanged for a "diabolical" sexual assault on one of Oxford's "most highly respected young ladies." The alleged assault had occurred in the very early hours of the day, and Tunstal was arrested for the crime shortly after. By nine in the morning, crowds were gathering in town. The courthouse bell was rung and a "large body of citizens, composed of ministers, lawyers, merchants and planters, and, in fact, men from all walks of life" congregated in the town square. The young woman in question had identified Tunstal as her assailant, and a committee of "best citizens," quickly organized to investigate the matter, had determined that Tunstal was guilty.[1] At that point, the mob led Tunstal away from the courthouse to a tree behind the nearby church. He was there allowed a short prayer and a brief opportunity to say goodbye to family and friends who were present. Tunstal reportedly showed "remarkable coolness," praying that God show mercy on his soul. As for the mob surrounding him, its members showed themselves to be "orderly" though clearly "excited and indignant." The news report concluded with the stunning comment that the mob also "seemed to appreciate the fact that it was horrible work for the Sabbath day, and that they were sending a spirit illy prepared before his God, and realized that human life is sacred and a human soul divine, yet they knew that they had duties to perform and paramount to all others was the thought that *they must protect their women*."[2]

Tunstal's lynching is remarkable on several counts. Occurring in 1885, it was one of the first public lynchings in the post-Reconstruction period. It was committed openly near the center of town and involved a large number of spectators and participants from the town and surrounding county. The lynching is also remarkable for the way in which the mob organized, and the newspaper represented, the proceedings as both a quasi–criminal trial and execution and an evangelical church discipline. This mob felt compelled to impose the appearance of legality on the violence by including as part of the lynching ritual witness testimony, a twelve-member jury, and the final farewell and prayers of the condemned. That this lynch mob conspicuously retained aspects of public executions speaks to the ways in which, especially in the early postbellum period, mobs saw themselves as extensions of the state. It also explains why members of the black community were present that morning.[3] In addition, the lynching suggested the ritual of evangelical discipline whereupon the sinner is exposed, investigated, and finally—in this case violently and fatally—expelled from a sacred community of believers.

What is most extraordinary about this lynching is that the lynchers, consumed with the desire to bring immediate vengeance against a perceived criminal in their midst at the very time when the people of Oxford would otherwise be congregating in their churches, were confronted with the fact that they were overstepping sacred bounds. They were thus compelled to justify their unholy actions as just the opposite—the noble protection of an even greater sanctity, that of southern white womanhood. For this reason, the mob could not remain on the courthouse grounds. To do so would have been to contain the act of vengeance within the secular realm—an extralegal version of a criminal trial and execution—and to engage in such a secular activity on the Sabbath would have seemed overtly blasphemous. But to move to the church was to embrace the holy sensibility of the day, to merge symbolically the mob's act of vengeance with the divine justice enacted in the evangelical church. White womanhood was the most precious icon, the black man its "demonic" transgressor, and the mob the instruments of divine wrath and retribution.

As in most towns of the New South, religion permeated almost every aspect of life in Oxford. Most of the town's 2,000 inhabitants belonged to one of six Protestant churches, and revivals held at the Methodist campground just outside town drew crowds of people from all denominations, many of whom traveled from surrounding counties to camp there for a week at a time. Religious news, sermons, and lessons appeared regularly in the local papers, where Oxford evangelicals increasingly expressed concern that entertainments and social activities were threatening the town's moral and spiritual integrity.[4] In this context, it is not surprising that these southerners not only defended the lynching of Tunstal in spiritual terms but infused the

performance of it with Christian tropes and rituals.

Oxford, Mississippi, was also the hometown of William Faulkner, who, in *Light in August*, written some fifty years after Tunstal's lynching, imagined the lynching of Joe Christmas as a similar act of religiously inflamed vengeance. The lynching of Christmas was modeled less on Tunstal's lynching than on the 1908 lynching of Nelse Patton, which occurred in Oxford when Faulkner was eleven years old. Patton, an African American bootlegger and petty thief, allegedly raped and murdered a middle-aged white woman who lived outside town by slicing her across the throat, just as Christmas kills Joanna Burden in Faulkner's novel. According to the *Memphis Commercial Appeal*, upon Patton's arrest, "the streets were thronged with men and boys, all armed," and a lynching became "inevitable." Several county elites, including a local Methodist minister, pleaded with the mob to let the law run its course, but former U.S. senator W. V. Sullivan roused the crowd with a call for swift vengeance. The men, with much effort, tore into the jail, and, when Patton fought back like a "wild man," they shot him dead. The mob then dragged him through the streets to the courthouse yard, where they castrated him and hanged him from a tree. As the *Jackson (Miss.) Clarion-Ledger* reported, "The white people of the community were determined to avenge the victim of the black brute's lust, and they went about it in a businesslike way."[5]

Although news reports represented Patton's lynching as a secular, "businesslike" affair, Faulkner reconceived it through the lynching of Joe Christmas as something holier, both a Crucifixion and a Last Judgment, the expiation of southern racial sins. As Christmas is castrated, the faces of the mob "seemed to glare with bodiless suspension as though from haloes." In his determination to avenge white honor, their leader, Percy Grimm, is described as "prophetlike," with the "unearthly luminousness of angels in church windows." "Now you'll let white women alone, even in hell," he says to Christmas, who instead, as he lies dying, "seemed to rise soaring into their memories forever and ever."[6]

By 1932, when Faulkner published *Light in August*, white southerners had perpetrated thousands of lynchings, many of which evinced a degree of sadism grossly at odds with Christian convictions. To be sure, some southern Christians, like the minister who protested Patton's lynching, recognized the shameless hypocrisy of lynching. But, all too often, mobs and their defenders not only overlooked that hypocrisy but actively interpreted and justified their violence as the willful expression of God's vengeance, as in the lynching of Harris Tunstal. Defenders of lynching, however, typically did not need the backdrop of the church to characterize their actions in sacred terms, especially when the alleged crime involved any sort of sexual outrage against a white woman. It is rarely possible to determine the religious affiliations of lynchers, let alone spectators. Nevertheless, regardless of whether individual lynchers were church members, they lived in a culture steeped in evangelical Protestant beliefs and values. Christianity was the primary lens through which most southerners conceptualized and made sense of suffering and death of any sort. It would be unconceivable that they could inflict pain and torment on the bodies of black men without imagining that violence as a religious act, laden with Christian symbolism and significance.[7]

Many African American writers, activists, and artists also conceptualized lynching as a Christian act — more specifically as a Christian sacrifice — to confront the violence and oppression enacted against them. By imagining lynching as a Crucifixion and its victims as Christian martyrs, black Protestants could claim African Americans as the true inheritors of Christian salvation and redemption and their white oppressors as unholy savages. A handful of white ministers and writers likewise recognized the continuities between the sacrificial murder of Jesus and the lynchings of African Americans, as Faulkner himself did in his depiction of Joe Christmas's lynching. Moreover, more recently, some scholars have posited lynching as a form of ritual sacrifice, and African Americans the scapegoats, through which white southerners expiated their own sins and psychically restored a sense of communal purity and social order.[8]

Yet most white southerners in no way perceived lynching as a form of sacrifice and certainly not as a Crucifixion. To do so would have been to bestow on the black victim an elevated status utterly at odds with their own racism.[9] Instead, defenders of lynching commonly represented the violence as a terrifying retribution, ordained and consecrated by God, against the black man's transgressions — certainly not their own. In their view, made apparent in the language and tropes they used to justify lynching, mobs were messengers of God's wrath, summoning all the tortures of hell for the black "fiends" and "devils" in their midst. In short, their conception of lynching evoked not the Crucifixion but the Last Judgment. To recognize lynching in ways that would have made sense to those who perpetrated and defended the violence is to comprehend not only the reasons that mobs could commit public lynching in the so-called Bible Belt with impunity but also why they, and their spectators, so relished the torment and suffering of their victims.[10]

These notions of black sin and white righteousness were felt with particular urgency amid the profound transformations that southerners were experiencing in the post-Reconstruction period. Indeed, the same sense of social upheaval that brought a rise in lynching also led to a growth in evangelical religiosity and moral reform efforts.[11] The public defenses of lynching dovetailed with a rising evangelical concern that modern life posed a grave threat to traditional moral and sexual codes. Even the language that Protestants used to express their fears about sin and vice was remarkably similar to that used to justify lynching. They exhibited the same distress about moral and racial purity, and they evinced the same need to protect white women and children from moral and racial corruption. The evangelical alarm about moral disorder was thus inseparable from the broader distress that emancipation and urbanization had upended the traditional racial hierarchy. It was for this reason that white southerners so often conceptualized the threat of black enfranchisement and autonomy as, above all, a dire moral threat to white purity, literally a physical assault on white homes and white women. In the minds of many white southerners, black men came to personify the moral corruption that they believed to be the root cause of social disorder.[12] Evangelical moral crusades that interpreted social flux and instability in terms of sin and morality set the climate in which white southerners attributed racial conflict to an alleged black propensity toward immorality and licentiousness.

They unleashed the full force of their fury against these black "fiends" through the blood rituals of lynching, rituals that created a veritable hell on earth. Lynching, in this sense, acted as more than a form of political terror that restored white dominance against the threat of black equality. It became a divinely sanctioned retribution for black "sin," sin that threatened not only white authority but white purity and virtue. These rituals also did more than simply punish the black "demon" in their midst. Through their spectacular excess, they constructed a symbolic representation of white spiritual and moral superiority. Lynching rituals produced, in very stark and dramatic terms, dichotomies between black and white as damned and saved, sinner and saint, which came to define white supremacy. They gave visual form to white supremacist beliefs, allowing white southerners to both perform and witness them. Just as in evangelical practice, in which the act of witnessing conferred truth and sanctification on the convert's rebirth and his entry into a communion of believers, the public ritual of lynching offered white southerners a certainty of their own grace and a sense of belonging to a virtuous and consecrated white community.

"IT IS EXCEEDINGLY DOUBTFUL if lynching could possibly exist under any other religion than Christianity," wrote Walter White, an antilynching activist and NAACP leader, in 1929. For White, it was "no accident" that the states with the highest levels of lynching were those in which "the great majority of the church members are Protestants and of the evangelical wing of Protestantism as well." Not only had these churches "indirectly given [their] approval to lynching and other forms of race prejudice," but the very nature of evangelical worship, for White, created "a particular fanaticism which finds an outlet in lynching." Accordingly, White contended, "No person who is familiar with the Bible-beating, acrobatic, fanatical preachers of hell-fire in the South, and who has seen the orgies of emotion created by them, can doubt for a moment that dangerous passions are released which contribute to emotional instability and play a part in lynching." White's indictment of southern religiosity was exceptionally inflammatory, but a number of lynching opponents expressed similar disdain that southern white Protestant churches had not only remained relatively quiet about mob violence but had become vocal supporters of white supremacy. For instance, sociologist Arthur Raper, writing in 1933, rebuked southern churches for failing to take a more active stance against lynching and leaving "unchallenged the general assumption that the Negro is innately inferior and of little importance." For these critics, Christian leaders' acquiescence to southern racial prejudices and their unwillingness to condemn mob actions in their own communities made them ultimately complicit in lynching.[13]

Some church leaders did at times actively oppose lynching by either confronting mobs or deploring lynching in their sermons or written editorials. "Religion and lynching; Christianity and crushing, burning and blessing, savagery and national sanity cannot go together in this country. Good men must make choice [sic] between these," charged a 1904 editorial in the *Wesleyan Christian Advocate*, which served Southern Methodists in Georgia. "The Church does not need and cannot tolerate lynchers."[14] That same year, the Reverend Whitley Langston, a Methodist minister in Statesboro, Georgia, convened his church members to condemn the lynching of Paul Reed and Will Cato in that city and published indictments against the violence in the local newspaper and in the *Wesleyan Christian Advocate*. Langston and other members of the church then published a resolution in the paper requesting that any church members who participated in the lynching come forward and "withdraw without delay from our communion and membership" unless they made a "public confession of wrong" and expressed "penitence and contrition." Several members were in fact expelled—though a number of other members, in turn, quit the church in protest over the expulsion.[15]

These kinds of denunciations as early as 1904 were exceptional, however. During lynching's peak at the turn of the century, most southern churches were resoundingly silent on the issue. In places where lynchings had occurred, available church records made no mention of lynching, nor did preachers mention them in their Sunday sermons, even when news of a lynching dominated the local press.[16] It was not until the national mood began to shift against lynching in the 1910s and 1920s that ministers became more outspoken against lynching. By 1930, most church papers and official organizing bodies, such as the Southern Baptist Convention, had taken public stances against lynching. Even so, most ministers, especially in communities in which lynchings had just taken place, were reluctant to denounce lynching publicly. A 1935 questionnaire answered by some 5,000 ministers showed that only 3.3 percent had preached or worked against lynching in some way. As Raper noted, most simply felt that lynching was "inevitable" and that, in taking a stance, they would divide and alienate their congregations. For example, when Methodist minister the Reverend Schuler denounced a 1920 lynching in Paris, Texas, he did so "in the face of advice of friends that such a course is unsafe for him."[17]

Even when evangelical leaders did speak out against lynching, they largely assented to the worst of white southern racial views. Many, for instance, implied that lynching was an understandable, albeit unfortunate, consequence of black propensities toward crime and sexual violence. Methodist bishop Atticus Haygood, after the 1893 lynching of Henry Smith in Paris, Texas, denounced lynching as "a crime against God and man." Yet in the same editorial, Haygood asked for understanding of the "infuriated" mob faced with Smith's "demonical cruelty" against the little white girl who was tortured "in the mad wantonness of gorilla ferocity."[18]

This acquiescence to lynching, or at least to its mythologies, was due, to some extent, to the largely conservative, even reactionary, role that white Protestantism played in the South. To be sure, many church leaders in the New South considered themselves to be progressive and modern purveyors of God's word, and many, likewise, sought active roles in redeeming southern society from what they considered to be the worst effects of modernity. Nevertheless, their social outlook tended to enforce dominant social structures and beliefs—in particular, Jim Crow segregation—and, indeed, offer them religious legitimization. Moreover, their spiritual emphasis on personal sin and salvation ultimately meant that they abdicated any responsibility for alleviating widespread social inequalities and suffering—most glaringly in the case of lynching. As antilynching activist Ida B. Wells wrote, "Our American Christians are too busy saving the souls of white Christians from burning in hell-fire to save the lives of black ones from present burning in fires kindled by white Christians."[19]

WALTER WHITE AND OTHER LIBERALS did not condemn southern Protestants simply for their passivity in the face of lynching, however; they also saw evangelical worship and lynching as twinned expressions of the South's utter backwardness—as cannibalistic and primal rituals that placed the South far outside the purview of modern civilization. Even less provocative critics, like Raper, believed that once the South modernized—that is, once its people became more educated and less poverty stricken, its social institutions stronger, and its churches more liberal and enlightened—lynching would inevitably decline.

Yet lynching and religiosity both surged in the postbellum period not because the South was standing still but because it was experiencing the fits and starts of modernization. As southern towns and cities developed, largely because of industrial and commercial expansion, they produced new kinds of occupations, new social arrangements, and new forms of recreation that many emerging white working- and middle-class men and women embraced. Even so, these people feared many of the consequences of those changes, particularly those that threatened the social authority and advancement they desired. Above all, they feared that urban crime, as well as the consumption of alcohol—phenomena that were regularly racialized—placed white women and white homes in peril. Southerners embraced religion in this period, in large part, because it represented a form of stability and tradition—a safe haven—amid the political and economic turmoil around them. These anxieties likewise became the fuel that fed the rising success of moral reform efforts, especially Prohibition, in this period, as evangelicals increasingly attempted to stem the tide of moral change by imposing traditional standards of behavior on New South citizens.

For example, although Rome, Georgia, had been a center of cotton marketing since railroads entered the city in the late 1830s, the city was expanding its commerce and industry at the turn of the century, largely because of busy trade on the Coosa River. In 1900, the *Rome Tribune* boasted that the city's population had grown to 14,035, adding that "every one of these 14,035 people are a part of the commercial and industrial life of Rome." In the previous fifteen years, the city had seen the development of several industries, including cotton mills, a furniture factory, an iron furnace, and chemical works. In the 1890s, an electric trolley, an opera house, and a large park that housed a theater pavilion and a racecourse had been built. At the same time that white citizens in Rome celebrated the industrial growth that had brought wealth and development into the city, however, they began to worry about crime and vice, particularly among the young men who labored in these industries. The area near the river docks known as the "cotton block" was of particular concern. Most of the city's thirteen saloons were located there, and young men and disreputable women of both races congregated in the neighborhood.[20]

Church life thrived in Rome in these same years. Between 1890 and 1900, membership in the First Baptist Church had increased four times as much as had the city population. The established Baptist and Methodist congregations built new and elaborate church buildings, while new churches sprang up around the city, including eight other Baptist churches. Revivals and protracted meetings, lasting up to eight weeks, brought thousands of worshippers to the city, especially when the celebrated evangelist and noted antiliquor crusader Sam Jones, who had lived in Rome in the early 1870s, returned to town.[21]

This spiritual fervor was coupled with rising concerns about the impact of commercial greed and, most conspicuously, modern amusements on Christian virtue. Evangelical leaders shared and tapped into larger public anxieties about urban vice, and they attended to them through an alarmist rhetoric that urged fellow Christians to safeguard their homes and their souls against moral sin. Most young, middle-class whites, especially women, did not frequent saloons and pool halls, but some went to dances or played cards, activities that their parents deemed disgraceful and that evangelicals readily conflated with more licentious activities. As one Methodist minister intoned, "Petty problems, such as wine, cards, dancing, theaters, that arise to vex the soul . . . were lurking toward and finally led into the great world of unbridled license and sin."[22]

Because, like most white southerners, evangelicals tended to believe that African Americans were more likely to engage in immoral activities than were whites, they interpreted the threats that modern temptations posed as decidedly racial ones. Although both white and black men frequented the saloons in Rome's cotton block, it was considered a more scandalous and unseemly activity for white men, particularly since to visit a saloon, even a segregated saloon, in that neighborhood was to blur racial boundaries. These fears also energized an evangelically based crusade to cleanse the city of the "social evil" of alcohol. In 1902, after fierce public debates, a city referendum closed all saloons and replaced them with a dispensary operated jointly by the city and county, a solution to the liquor problem that left those reformers who wanted total legal prohibition unsatisfied. In 1907 the state of Georgia went dry, which, although it effectively ended the controversies over the dispensary in Rome, brought new concerns about moonshining and "blind tigers" in the county.[23]

Amid this turn-of-the-century turmoil, white Romans lynched three African American men within a fifteen-month period, all for purported attacks on white women. The last of these occurred in April 1902, on the same day that the liquor dispensary opened, and involved an attempted assault on a thirteen-year-old girl in the city center as she was walking home alone near dark. That night, a mob of 150 captured her alleged assailant, Walter Allen, a waiter at a local hotel, hanged him from a telephone pole, and riddled his body with bullets, all under the glare of an electric street light. The following day, the *Rome Tribune* justified the lynching on the grounds that "there is something in the southern heart that will not tolerate the mistreatment of women. . . . The purity and chastity of our women first, last and all the time, is now and ever shall be a southerner's foremost thought."[24]

Lynching and religiosity were, in this sense, twinned expressions not so much of southerners' rootedness in a primeval past but of their reactionary and conflicted responses to modern life. Indeed, evangelicals regularly imagined the "petty problems" of drinking and dancing as threatening to their sense of propriety—to their "purity and chastity"—as were criminal assaults. In other words, they perceived white integrity as under physical assault from particular moral behaviors in modern life, behaviors that stood as very personal and visceral dangers to vulnerable souls and bodies. Ministers again and again warned against the harmful effects of worldly pleasures that could lead to "spiritual death" and "wasted lives." One Roman minister, for instance, admonished that in sin "the soul became blinded—calmed, diseased, betrayed, deadened."[25] To describe a spiritual failing as physical suffering prepared believers to understand their individual conversion and salvation as a visceral transformation of the self. But to characterize sin as an assault on the body was also to raise the stakes for spiritual renewal not just for the individual but for society as a whole. Language that figured white southerners as under attack necessitated an aggressive defense. Evangelicals accordingly envisioned their spiritual mission to save individual souls as a physical salvation of bodies, most often feminine bodies.

Religiosity allowed many white Protestants to anchor their own sense of moral integrity against this onslaught of modern temptations. That sense of moral integrity was often rooted in a nostalgic vision of a simple and virtuous past—what evangelicals deemed "traditional" values or "old-time religion." Their nostalgia was manifestly tinged with white supremacy, especially as evangelical churches played a significant role in the public commemoration of Confederate heroism and glorification of the Lost Cause in this period. Evangelicals likewise interpreted and celebrated in decidedly spiritual terms the political "Redemption" of the Democratic Party, which restored white power after what were considered the gross injustices of Reconstruction.[26]

Faced with the erosion of their traditional authority and values, most white Protestants did not retreat to the church simply to firm up their own moral resolve; rather, they saw themselves at war with modern culture, believing that their own salvation demanded that they wage battle against not only their own sin but the immoral excesses of others. Although popular amusements had certainly represented a spiritual threat for evangelicals since the antebellum period, they initially countered that threat through a self-imposed exclusion from the secular world, governing only the moral behavior of church members, largely through the practice of church disciplines. But amid the rapidly changing world of the New South, churches found it increasingly difficult to discipline younger converts who, despite their evangelical devotion, refused to deny themselves pleasures that were accepted in larger society. Once church disciplines were no longer capable of containing the threat that secular amusements posed, evangelicals turned their focus to the moral welfare of secular society as a whole, spearheading ardent public crusades to regulate and legislate moral behavior. Evangelicals' new concern with the social world was as much about their own survival as it was about a sincere regard for what they perceived as a wayward society. Even so, evangelicals firmly believed that if religious faith and its claim to moral authority lost cultural force, then white southern society would be laid to waste. That is why they so fervently expressed alarm that individual moral misconduct—"petty problems, such as wine, cards, dancing, theaters"—spelled social disaster.[27]

Even as Protestants resisted what they saw as the harmful effects of modern life, they were nevertheless implicated in the process of modernization they eschewed. That is, evangelical devotion, like lynching itself, was not simply a primal reaction against social change; it was also in and of those social transformations. Churches and other religious institutions owed their burgeoning numbers to urbanization, since city people could more easily attend church and participate in reform efforts than could those isolated in the countryside. Churches in towns and cities were also expanding into large administrative centers that provided educational and recreational services for their congregations. Moreover, often as a means to attract and maintain larger congregations, church leaders adapted themselves to modern behaviors and assumptions, appropriating the language, styles of engagement, and amusements of secular culture even as they used them to strike back at secular institutions and practices. In many ways, the exhortations against modern amusements heard again and again in southern churches served as jeremiads that, in lamenting the changes in cultural values that modernization had wrought, provided psychological reconciliation to that very process of change.[28]

WHITE EVANGELICALS ALSO regularly expressed the sense that they were under siege and waging battle against the secular world in unambiguously gendered and racialized language—language that reverberated throughout the rhetorical defense of lynching. They, for instance, often interpreted the threat of losing their cultural dominance amid competing values as a collapse of masculine vigor within the church. In turn, the evangelical duty to save lost souls, usually imagined as young women whose virtue was wasted by worldly pleasures, translated to a patriarchal duty to protect the honor of white women. This moral reform rhetoric allowed individual white male believers to connect themselves both to a larger Christian identity and to a white masculine identity, just as it came to define and construct for them what exactly manliness and moral righteousness meant.

By using language associated with masculine power, strength, and vitality to describe church battles waged against sin and immorality, evangelicals were able to attract male converts and shore up their own sense of social authority, a need they especially felt in light of women's numerical domination in both churches and reform organizations. A masculine Christianity, in fact, justified evangelicals' social dominance, a dominance it could not have sustained if evangelicalism were associated with feminine weakness or docility. To this end, public reports commonly described preachers as "strong," "forceful," and "powerful," especially in their condemnations of sin. The Reverend Charles Forbes Taylor, arriving in Paris, Texas, to preach at a Baptist revival, was photographed in a boxer's stance, his hand clenched in fists. Sam Jones was a celebrated evangelist not only for his entertaining manner but also for his fearless attacks on the sinful. Jones was remembered in one, perhaps apocryphal, story as quelling some "prankish cowboys" who disturbed an evangelical meeting he was leading "with a single threat of eternal damnation." When Jones told the men that "he would hurl them out the window," they promptly "grew reverent." For Jones at least, saving souls was a contest over masculine dominance. Such public demonstrations of manly piety and faith were considered imperative precisely because of a supposed friction between evangelical virtue and masculinity. Southern evangelicals had long wrestled with the seeming contradiction between proscriptive Christian virtues, such as submissiveness, sacrifice, and purity, and virtues associated with southern white manhood, such as power and assertiveness. As one evangelical noted in Rome, Georgia, "If a young man has a good case of religion, he is generally known as a sissy in society."[29]

In what came to be popularized as "muscular Christianity," evangelicals described battles against sin in violent and aggressive terms. A Methodist preacher in Lawrenceville, Georgia, for example, devoted one Sunday sermon in 1904 to "the warlike or fighting propensies of the Christian." He asserted that the Christian should show the "ferocity and prowess" of a lion "when his honor is at stake and the cause of Christ is assailed. There should be no compromise with sin and evil." He then "attacked the Lawrenceville pool parlor." As concerns about modern temptations became more pressing, ministers frequently held "men-only" meetings in which "social concerns" were discussed. At one such meeting in Rome, Georgia, advertised for "RED BLOODED" men and as "a Challenge to every home-loving man in Rome," the preacher "handle[d] some life issues without gloves."[30]

For many white southern middle-class and working-class men, evangelicalism, fused with masculine authority, also offered class respectability and an assurance of their own upward mobility. Emmett Cole, who wrote a series of religious columns for the *Rome (Ga.) Tribune-Herald* throughout the 1910s, was representative of this sort of male evangelical. In his weekly columns, Cole regularly protested what he saw as moral lapses in southern society, lamented the "irreverence" and "ill-breeding" of the youth, and intoned against sin and vice of all sorts, especially the demonizing influence of liquor. At the same time, he repeatedly affirmed the masculine vigor of believers. He derided the "moral coward" as the "most contemptible man in the universe" and lauded those men who "stand for righteousness against the powers of darkness." While "the hell hounds are always turned loose on the man who takes his stand against evil," he noted, "they are helpless when it comes to any harm to the character of real manhood." These columns offered Cole a certain amount of prestige within Roman society, though he was not a member of the elite or professional class. Rather, he had begun his adulthood as a tenant farmer out in the county, and at the time he wrote his columns, he was a salaried furniture salesman in his thirties, living in a mortgaged home with his wife and children. Religious piety offered him a sense of authority and respectability to match his emerging status as a middle-class man, a status he was clearly anxious about, as his repeated assertions of his own propriety and manliness attest. At the same time, he bemoaned the class "factionalism" and "haughtiness" in churches that betrayed the "socialistic" message of Christianity. Evincing a belief in class solidarity through Christian fellowship was yet another means for Cole to ensure his own social authority.[31]

This evangelical concern for both masculine authority and the moral virtue of southern society was closely bound to white anxieties about racial dominance. The antiliquor crusades were especially infused with racially coded language concerning purity, integrity, and class respectability. Indeed, these crusades gained force in the South because drunkenness and alcohol- and drug-induced licentiousness were associated with the very worst of African American society. Stories of black bootleggers or owners of "blind tigers," intoxicated or "drug-crazed" black drifters, and drunken fights between African Americans filled small-town and urban newspapers.

Protestants repeatedly appealed to a sense of patriarchal duty in exhorting southern men to protect their women and their homes from such threats. Images of an evangelical masculinity waging war against sin coincided with and fueled prolynching rhetoric that similarly intertwined ideals of masculine aggression, duty, and moral righteousness. They, in fact, lent sacred force to that rhetoric. An editorial in Wiggins, Mississippi, for instance, denounced whiskey as a "monster" on a "march of deviltry and destruction" and as "the demon that has dug more graves and sent more souls unsaved to judgment." Like a predator, the piece continued, whiskey even "enters an humble home to strike the roses from a woman's cheek." Five months later, a black bootlegger, Will Moore, was lynched not far from Wiggins for allegedly killing a white lumber company superintendent, J. H. Rogers. Cole urged the Christian men of Rome to organize to "drive blind tigers from our midst . . . and certain other evils with which we have to contend." He asked, "Why should we as citizens allow such things to exist in the same community where our wives and daughters have to live?" Cole wrote this column days after, according to the *Rome (Ga.) Tribune-Herald*, a black man, "crazed with drugs . . . terrifie[d] [a] crowd of whites," and two other black men attempted separate assaults on two white girls in the center of town—assaults that almost precipitated lynchings.[32]

This hyperbolic language was the same used to describe black criminals, the "demons" and "beasts" who broke into homes to defile white women's purity. This rhetoric had particular resonance in the culture of Jim Crow segregation, a system arranged to keep white bodies pure and uncontaminated through the physical separation from black bodies. In this scheme, the white body, especially the female body, was accorded an almost sacred status, its boundaries and borders requiring protection against any violation.[33] Prolynching reports thus regularly set frightening images of dissolute black predators against the moral purity and Christian piety of their white victims. Charges of intoxication further inflamed white anger and provided an added justification for mob retribution. In his narrative of three-year-old Myrtle Vance's rape and murder and Henry Smith's subsequent lynching in Paris, Texas, P. L. James noted that the little girl was last seen singing "Jesus Lover of My Soul" "in her childish treble voice." He described Smith, in contrast, as "devoid of any humanizing sensibilities . . . a quiet, industrious servant when sober, a fiend incarnate when in liquor." Once the girl's body was found, James recounted, "all the energy of an entire city and country was turned toward the apprehension of the demon who had devastated a home and polluted an innocent life."[34]

Prolynching rhetoric also created an impression that all whites, despite their class status, were united in their moral superiority to the drunken and degenerate "fiends" in their midst. Nelse Patton was lynched in Oxford, Mississippi, for allegedly murdering Mrs. McMullin, the wife of a tenant farmer who was serving a sentence in the county jail. Yet local reporters described Mrs. McMullin as a "respected white woman" and assured readers that although "the family is poor, they bore a good reputation" and that Mrs. McMullin was "hard-working" despite Mr. McMullin's apparent criminality. On the other hand, Patton, a known moonshiner who was "in an intoxicated condition" when he allegedly committed the murder, held an "unsavory reputation" and was a "black fiend incarnate."[35]

IN THESE WAYS, the defenders of lynching borrowed the language of evangelical moral crusades to justify—and sanctify—their own crusades against black depravity. But the actual rituals of lynching also uncannily reenacted evangelical church practices, including confessions and testimonials, attention to torment and suffering, and the act of witnessing, practices that publicly rehearsed narratives of human sin and divine judgment. Lynch mobs were not necessarily replicating these rites self-consciously; nevertheless, the metonymic relationship between them imbued lynching with sacred meaning and even consecrated it as God's vengeance against moral and racial transgression.

Evangelical faith was, of course, not theologically dependent on or based in ritual. For liturgically based Christians, such as Episcopalians and Catholics, salvation rested on adherence to moral precepts and the performance of ritual sacraments, but for evangelicals, salvation rested on emotional submission to God's grace—the experience of conversion or "rebirth." Although evangelicals believed in living a morally pure life in obedience to scriptural command, moral virtue, in theory, did not ensure grace but rather flowed from the converted as a consequence and physical manifestation of his or her salvation. In turn, sin was primarily a reflection of the individual's rejection of grace. Evangelicals believed that God punished sinful behavior with such vindictive fury because it represented human disavowal of his power and his love. Similarly, the dominant sacraments and rituals within evangelical practice—baptism, communion, testimonial, and prayer—primarily acted as visible expressions of faith rather than as actions that shaped or brought about one's faith. In other words, the performance of sacraments did not lead to salvation but simply made manifest the believer's faith and state of grace.

In practice, however, ritual was still important, even intrinsic, to evangelical faith. It was through ritual that individual believers came to feel the transformative experiences of grace and salvation and to experience a sense of belonging to a sacred community of the faithful. The public performance and practice of faith were thus central to the believer's sense of himself as a saved and purified Christian.[36] For instance, the ritual of baptism, in which the minister submerged the newly converted underwater, was a symbolic act of purification, making visible the convert's absolution from sin. But the frightening act of being pushed underwater also replicated the surrender to God—and to the church—expected of the convert. The ritual, in this sense, not only represented the convert's spiritual transformation but produced a new social identity within the convert, as one who was now submissive to a higher authority and attached to a like-minded community of believers.

Because evangelical rituals established social identities in this way, they needed to be public in order to have larger social meaning beyond the individual's personal commitment to God. Large crowds of converted and unconverted alike commonly gathered to watch baptisms and revivals, where evangelicals gave public, and often very dramatic and emotional, testimonials of their conversion experiences, significantly called "witnessing." Within evangelicalism, "witnessing" referred to the speaker's relationship to the truth of God—he acted as a witness to divine grace—and was crucial to the evangelical's duty to proselytize nonbelievers. The spiritual truth revealed in the act of witnessing was reinforced because others, hearing and seeing it, were made witnesses as well.

Lynching rituals operated in comparable ways to these kinds of evangelical rituals. Just as evangelical rituals did more than simply reflect or make manifest belief, lynching rituals did more than merely dramatize white supremacist ideology or attest to white solidarity. The performance of lynching created a spectacle of virtuous and sanctified white supremacy and brought individual whites together into a communal devotion to it. In some extraordinary incidents, like the 1885 lynching of Harris Tunstal in Oxford, Mississippi, lynch mobs evoked religious rituals conspicuously, which lent the violence a more striking appearance of divine sanction. In 1897, a mob in Hawesville, Kentucky, lynched Raymond Bushrod, a black man accused of raping and mutilating the daughter of a prominent planter, on a Sunday afternoon while a revival was taking place. The lynching took place in the courthouse yard, not at the revival—though, according to one report, the mob did its work "in the broad opening glare of a Sunday sun" and "within a stone's throw of four churches." In recognition of the holy day, however, the "infuriated" mob paused so that Bushrod could confess his crimes and offer "a long and fervent prayer on bended knee."[37]

That Bushrod was allowed to pray and compelled to offer a confession was not unusual. Lynch mobs at times gave their victims time to pray and, more frequently, wrought confessions from them. The hearing of the condemned's last words and prayers was a central ritual of the public execution, one that was carried over into lynching rituals. As noted in the previous chapter, lynchings often conspicuously reenacted, in perverted and exaggerated form, legal rituals of public executions, which were themselves overtly laden with religious meaning—except that, in lynchings, any power or privileges given to the condemned in a legal execution were stripped away.

In most lynchings, the victim confessed after being beaten or tortured into admitting his guilt or as a desperate attempt to assuage the angry mob. Sam Holt, burned alive in Newnan, Georgia, in 1899, was pulled from the flames so that he would admit his guilt. Over twenty years later, in Nodena, Arkansas, the mob that burned Henry Lowry alive interrogated him as the flames scorched his body. According to one news account, as Lowry confessed, one man questioned him and another "wrote answers down in a notebook. It resembled a courtroom scene with prosecuting attorney and court reporter." As this example makes evident, confessions lent lynching the trappings of lawful punishment and served to justify the mob's violence as rightful and warranted, despite that confessions were forced and were often obtained after the lynching was underway and not likely to be aborted. Newspaper reports and prolynching narratives took pains, however, to assure readers that these confessions were true. As in legal hangings, the insistence on confession also compelled the condemned to sanction and participate in his own demise. In a 1905 lynching in Waco, Texas, for instance, the mob asked Sank Majors, accused of assaulting a white woman, not only to admit his guilt but to agree that he should be hanged for his crime.[38]

These confessions also contained significant religious undertones. According to Ray Stannard Baker, before the mob lynched Paul Reed and Will Cato in Statesboro, Georgia, they paused "to let the negroes kneel and confess."[39] Since Reed and Cato had already been convicted in a court of law, their confession at the lynching site undoubtedly had a function beyond establishing their legal guilt. Lynching victims often followed their confessions with pleas for mercy, if not from their captors, then from God, pleas that southern newspapers regularly noted for their readers. When William Gibson was burned alive for the murder of a white woman in Corinth, Mississippi, in 1902, before a crowd of 5,000, newspaper reports printed the speech he made to the crowd, in which he not only confessed to his crime but sanctioned the lynching. "Ladies and Gentlemen—I am up here this evening for this crime on me, and I am guilty of the crime," he declared. "I ask everybody to forgive me if they can. My heart has been troubled ever since the death of Mrs. Whitfield, and I deserve the punishment I am going to get." At that point, he began to pray: "Oh, my God, the time has come and I hope I will be able to meet you in heaven. Oh, God, I have prayed all night and all day long. I ask the Lord to be with me on this stand this evening and I thank Thee with all my heart."[40] Whereas in the secular realm, confession leads to conviction and punishment, in the spiritual realm, confession leads to salvation and deliverance. When lynching victims confessed and then begged for God's mercy, their confessions had spiritual meaning for them.

For white mobs and spectators, however, the black man's confession would not ensure his salvation, for it was assumed that, as a "fiend" and "demon," he was already a hellish creature. Rather, the confession only demonstrated the righteousness of the lynching. Indeed, prolynching rhetoric commonly sanctioned mob violence as an enactment of divine law and justice. Because lynching participants and their defenders believed that secular law was inadequate to deal with the enormity of black crime, particularly rape, they conceptualized lynching as the worldly invocation of a higher law and a higher form of justice. After all, in their view, human law could not possible prosecute "demons," "fiends," and inhuman "brutes." As P. L. James explained regarding the lynching of Henry Smith, "People wanted justice. The crime was beyond description in words borne in even our prolific language. Our statute books held in all their pages of fact and precedent, no law worthy to mete out justice in such a case." Once the lynch mob formed as "the solution of the problem . . . all the people resounded, 'Amen!'" In acting out divine law, lynchers could perceive themselves as God's messengers, sanctified and redeemed as such. After Smith's lynching, another defender wrote, "It was nothing but the vengeance of an outraged God, meted out to him, through the instrumentality of the people that caused the cremation."[41]

Because these southerners perceived the lynch mob's retribution against black transgression as God's retribution, they could also understand the tortures that the mob inflicted as bearing all the power of divine wrath. Mobs and their spectators insisted on extensive and prolonged tortures to ensure acute physical and emotional suffering—suffering that would have been audible, visible, and palpable to the watching crowd. When a member of the mob that lynched Lloyd Clay in Vicksburg, Mississippi, in 1919 wanted to shoot him dead, members of the crowd cried out, "Let him die slow!" Similarly, when Henry Lowry tried to hasten his death by swallowing the hot coals surrounding him, the crowd kicked them away. As a mob burned Dan Davis at the stake in Tyler, Texas, in 1912, the spectators apparently grew restless because the flames took some time before they started to scorch Davis's feet. According to one report, they "had waited so long to see him tortured that they begrudged the ten minutes before his suffering really began." Davis had "calmly" said to the mob as they led him to the stake, "I wish some of you gentlemen would be Christian enough to cut my throat," but "nobody responded." As the fire started, "he screamed, 'Lord, have mercy on my soul.'"[42]

For the lynching victim who prayed as he was strung up or as flames engulfed his body, his suffering was the physical manifestation of the spiritual tribulation that precedes salvation. He could thus interpret his pain and anguish as signs of his imminent sanctification. For the lynch mob, however, this process of sanctification was inverted, as the black victim's torment offered them, and the white crowd witnessing it, a sign of their own spiritual redemption. The physical torment and tortures inflicted on the lynching victim were, in this respect, crucial elements of the white crowd's own sense of moral and spiritual superiority. Prolynching reports and commentaries, for this reason, belabored the sufferings of the lynching victim, recreating for readers his cries of pain and unheeded pleas for mercy. Readers did not relish these sensational details simply out of voyeurism or sadistic pleasure; rather, the victim's suffering allowed them to feel their own spiritual elevation in contrast to the condemned's utter degradation.[43]

The victim's reaction to his suffering became further evidence of his moral inferiority and justification for his punishment. If he screamed, cried, or wept, his protestations were read as signs of his weakness, physical and moral, that sanctioned the violence against him. Descriptions of his pained frenzy also stood in counterpoint to the white men in the crowd, whom prolynching reports frequently characterized as calm, orderly, and determined. Alternatively, if he remained stoic or relatively calm, observers noted his brutishness, his fundamental inhumanness, which accordingly indicated the justness of the punishment. When Henry Smith kept repositioning himself on the burning scaffold to alleviate his suffering, James interpreted his movements as a demonic attempt to subvert death. "Any human being, unsustained by the genius of evil, must have been overcome ere this, but not so with Smith; with a tenacity unequaled, he clung to his unhallowed life," he wrote. An eyewitness to the 1895 lynching of Robert Hilliard in Tyler, Texas, recalled with astonishment, "Hilliard's power of endurance was the most wonderful thing on record! His lower limbs burned off before he became unconscious." The writer asked, "Was it decreed by an avenging God as well as an avenging people that his sufferings should be prolonged beyond the ordinary endurance of mortals?"[44]

The black man's suffering was measured against not only the grim composure of the mob but also the suffering of the white woman who had endured his alleged assault. It was her suffering, after all, that ultimately justified the excessive tortures the mob inflicted. If the sanctity of white womanhood had been violated, that sanctity could be restored only through the unbearable torment and suffering of the alleged violator. In his account of Henry Smith's lynching, James described in considerable detail the imagined sufferings of Smith's alleged victim, Myrtle Vance. Then, as he lingered over the gruesome details of the mob's violence, he added, "All this while the vision of the mutilated child was the actuating principle in these ominous proceedings." Smith begged the mob to shoot him, but, James noted, no one answered his charge, for "he had been merciless, and in like measure must it now be meted unto him." Similarly, according to Baker, some members of the Statesboro, Georgia, lynch mob at one point suggested hanging the two men, but "some one began to recite in a high-keyed voice the awful details of the crime, dwelling especially on the death of the little girl," Hodges's daughter. This narration of white suffering, spoken in a "high-keyed voice" as if to conjure audibly the little girl herself, "worked the mob into a frenzy of ferocity," and the men chose to burn Reed and Cato instead. As noted lynching advocate Rebecca Felton asked, referring to cases of sexual assault, "What is this death by rope, compared to the humiliation, ignominy and life-long suffering of the innocent victim" of the black man's outrage? Even if the black rapist were "torn by red-hot pincers, or burnt with slow fire, his fate would be elysian" compared to the white woman's torment, she reasoned.[45]

This vengeance against white female suffering was more than secular retribution or an avenging of honor between worldly subjects. Lynch mobs and their defenders envisioned themselves as Christian soldiers, battling the evil in their midst, much as evangelicals waged war against vice and moral transgression. In the hangings, shootings, mutilations, and burnings that far exceeded the social need to avenge a crime and punish a criminal, lynch mobs were re-creating divine judgment on earth, enacting the damnation they were certain the black criminal would be facing in death. After the Waco mob took Sank Majors from jail, a member of the crowd reportedly shouted out, "New trial granted, and change of venue from Waco to hell!" Or, as the *San Antonio Express* editorialized after Henry Smith's lynching, "The blood of the innocent has not cried to heaven in vain for vengeance. The black beast that ravished a white babe at Paris, Texas, has paid the penalty for his accursed crime—has perished at the stake, has passed through a hell of fire upon earth to the hotter flames of an eternal Hades hereafter."[46]

In imagining their victims as "demons" and sinners passing through hell on earth, the defenders of lynching were not simply resorting to Christian hyperbole to justify secular actions. Evangelicals, to be sure, also emphasized salvation and peaceful eternity, and religious experience was most certainly about joy, harmony, and comfort. But this reassuring language was regularly coupled with stern warnings about the wages of sin, eternal damnation, and God's inevitable judgment on humans' wicked and selfish denial of his grace. Indeed, a believer's salvation would offer such blissful reassurance only if the alternative was truly dreadful. Sermons that emphasized an eternal and torturous punishment for sinners indubitably inspired dread within believers, intensifying evangelicals' desire to perceive themselves as purified and saved by God's grace. Temptations that preachers so often associated with modern life — drinking, dancing, and other amusements — only exacerbated these fears, if not in terms of their own faith then in terms of the faith of less pious family members and friends. Lynching, however, could assuage these anxieties about white sin, since in re-creating a hell on earth for black "sinners," white southerners transferred onto black men that which they so feared themselves. Those whites, in contrast, could feel and appear sanctified, despite their individual moral behavior. The rituals of lynching, like those of evangelical practice itself, could make them feel transformed and cleansed of their own sins.

These elements of white sanctification — the confessions, the suffering — were performances that depended on witnesses. At a legal execution, when a condemned man on the gallows "witnessed" to the crowd surrounding him, testifying to his own sin and redemption, the reactions and responses of the watching crowd reinforced his sense of his own salvation. The act of witnessing substantiated his faith and his redemption by making it visible to others. The spectacle of a lynching served a similar purpose, yet, rather than testifying to the condemned's salvation, the confessions and sufferings of the black victims testified to the white mob's sense of its own divine righteousness. The spectators at a lynching were thus crucial to the social and spiritual transformation enacted in the lynching. Lynching reports paid particular attention to the composition and reactions of lynching crowds, noting their cheers as the victim suffered or their scrambles to get a glimpse of the mob's work. The *Waco (Tex.) Times-Herald* noted, for instance, that as Jesse Washington, lynched in Waco, Texas, in 1916, "commenced to burn . . . shouts of delight went up from the thousands of throats and apparently everybody demonstrated in some way their satisfaction at the retribution that was being visited upon the perpetrator of such a horrible crime."[47]

The same Waco reporter also observed, however, that "not all these [in the crowd] approved." This observation in the southern press was not unusual; reports at times did note that spectators at lynchings were repulsed, turning away in horror and disgust. Yet, although they at times noted that individual spectators were shocked by the visible sight of torture, these reports assumed that their presence at the lynching signified their complicity. As members of a crowd, individual spectators, regardless of their personal feelings, provided the lynchers with an audience, a public before which they could enact their rituals of white redemption. In this sense, the boundary between participants and spectators in a lynching was porous, often literally, as spectators jumped in to fire guns, stoke fires, or collect souvenirs, and figuratively, as a crowd of spectators created an image of a united white public before which lynchers could vindicate their actions.

As with evangelical rituals, the presence of witnesses linked individual members of the crowd to a larger community of believers, in this case an imagined community of white southerners of all classes and ages, united in their devotion to white supremacy. Lynching reports commonly focused on the diversity of the crowd at a lynching—including men from different occupations, from city and country, as well as women and children—not to highlight divisions within southern society but, rather, to accentuate the unity of that society. As noted in the Oxford lynching of 1885, "Men from all walks of life" congregated in the town square, becoming one "large body of citizens." The *Rome (Ga.) Tribune* remarked that the mob that lynched Walter Allen "was composed of citizens of high and low degree, without regard to friendship, politics or social standing." Despite its diversity, the mob was "not a wild and frenzied crowd at all," but "grim and determined," acting "quietly and in an orderly manner." Reports like this both created a public perception of white solidarity and served to accord those of "low degree" a sense of social respectability and equality.[48]

The performance of a lynching thus created a symbolic representation of white supremacy—a spectacle of demonic and wicked black men against a united and pure white community. That those images coincided with evangelicals' impassioned exhortations against sin gave lynching sacred force and justification. Indeed, the imprint of Protestant language and tropes on lynching rituals and defenses imbued the violence with divine sanction and made it appear familiar and recognizable to a people immersed in Christian beliefs and values. Mobs could thus conspicuously flout the law and perpetrate what otherwise would be considered aberrant and grotesque acts of sadism while considering themselves to be righteous and moral citizens.

The racial fears and anxieties that fueled both evangelical reform and lynching violence emerged from the disruptions and upheavals of traditional values and forms of authority that white southerners were feeling with grave intensity in the modern South. Religious fervency and lynching were accordingly reactionary attempts to reestablish an old order. In that sense, lynch mobs and their advocates had to impose the familiar Protestant notions of sin and retribution onto what were, in many ways, new forms of

racial violence and new conceptions of white supremacy. But white southerners also made abundant use of modern technologies of vision to represent the fictions of white supremacy. These technologies expanded the act
of witnessing to a broader public, creating a witnessing that not only offered
those fictions the aura of divine truth but also gave them the stamp of visual
certainty.

PART II ❖ WITNESSING

3

◈ ◈ ◈

THE SPECTATOR HAS A PICTURE IN HIS MIND
TO REMEMBER FOR A LONG TIME

Photography

WHEN HENRY SMITH fled Paris, Texas, after being accused of sexually assaulting and murdering Myrtle Vance, the three-year-old daughter of a former police officer, the city came to a standstill as a posse sought his capture. As one local man, P. L. James, reported with melodramatic embellishment, "Men scarcely stopped to eat, much less to sleep, women trembled and prayed, and the common heart of the whole community throbbed with a single impulse and that was to compass such retribution for the damnable outrage committed among us as the full measure of justice could demand." When word came that the posse was returning with Smith by train so he could meet his fate, the "streets of Paris were a busy spectacle." Schools and businesses closed. People from the surrounding county, nearby towns and counties, and places as far away as Dallas and Arkansas came by foot, horse, and train into the town. "Every highway leading into the city was an almost continuous cavalcade. . . . Every train that arrived from any direction was crowded to suffocation," enthused James. Men erected a scaffold ten feet tall near the railroad where Smith would arrive, in full view of the city center, in preparation for his "execution." By the time Smith and his captors arrived, over 10,000 people had gathered at the railroad depot to witness Smith's death. The mob paraded him through the city streets before bringing him to the scaffold, where men, including members of the Vance family, tortured him for nearly an hour before burning him to death. James described the spectacle of the day with such hyperbolic enthusiasm because, for him, the crowds flooding the town only confirmed the righteousness of the vengeance exacted on Smith. These spectators were not merely curious onlookers; rather, the sheer size of the crowd reflected that "common heart" and "single impulse" toward "retribution for the damnable outrage."[1]

The number of spectators for Smith's lynching was further expanded

FIGURE 3.1 The lynching of Henry Smith, Paris, Texas, 1893. Prints and Photographs Division, Library of Congress, Washington, D.C.

through the many photographs taken of the day's events. Local photographers had prepared to document each step of the violence, producing pictures both of Smith and his torturers on the scaffold and of the massive crowd of spectators (figures 3.1 and 3.2). James subsequently published some of these images in his pamphlet to "show . . . pictorially the last scenes in the passion-play of Texas." Another photographer, J. L. Mertins, sold his photographs, mostly crowd shots taken from a distance, at his office for fifty cents each. Other photographs were preserved separately and circulated across the region and country.[2]

In a 1901 antilynching pamphlet, black activist Samuel Burdett recounted coming across photographic images of Smith's torture, displayed on easel boards, on the streets of Seattle. The images were made audible through phonographic equipment that had supposedly recorded Smith's dying moments. A barker on a platform was enticing crowds to "enjoy" this new,

FIGURE 3.2 Henry Smith on the scaffold, Paris, Texas, 1893. Prints and Photographs Division, Library of Congress, Washington, D.C.

phenomenal "entertainment" "according to their individual relish for the awful—the horrible." Burdett explained that he too "took up the tubes of the phonographic instrument and placed them to [his] ears" only to find, "Oh horror of horrors! Here we are selling the dying groans and pitiful pleadings for mercy of a man as he suffers the awful agony of having his eyes burned out one at a time with hot irons." That Burdett used the phrase "we are sell-ing" suggests that he recognized his own collusion in this further violation of Smith's humanity, even as he expressed disgust that the sounds and sights of Smith's lynching were rendered into casual entertainment. The exhibi-tion was horrifying to Burdett because it reenacted the lynching, making it present and visceral even for distant observers. "His limbs writhe and twist for a minute, and then all that is left of the man, as God made him, is the limp, lifeless body," he recounted with a detailed clarity that far exceeded what the photographs and the recording could actually demonstrate. The images resurrected Smith only to torture and kill him once again. After encountering these images, Burdett noted, "the spectator has a picture in his mind to remember for a long time."[3]

Some years later, Smith's lynching was still being hawked as entertainment. In 1909, black theater critic Lester Walton was appalled to find several moving picture theaters in New York city enticing patrons in to see scenes of Smith "burned at the stake" and to "hear his moans and groans" for the price of only one penny. Although these theaters were normally reserved for moving pictures, the scenes advertised were most likely the same still photographs and phonographic records that Burdett witnessed; there is no evidence that moving images of Smith's lynching were recorded. Nonetheless, through these channels of promotion and profit, Smith's lynching appeared forever present, detached from time and place. Smith himself had become no more than an anonymous "colored man being burned at the stake" for the shock and marvel of perversely curious spectators.[4]

The sensationalism surrounding Smith's lynching—the vast crowds, the publicity, and the photographs and recordings that circulated across the country—have led some to consider it the first "modern" lynching.[5] Modern technology, including trains, cameras, phonographs, and the national media, transformed what was an act of mob vengeance into a larger, broader sensation that continued to capture public attention long after the lynching was over. As Burdett found, even those far removed from the actual event, geographically and temporally, could become complicit in the violence through their secondhand witnessing. The lynching of Smith, in this sense, gathered more cultural force through modern technologies that expanded its audience and through the commercial markets that made displaying and "selling" a lynching profitable.

Yet, in describing the photographs of Smith's lynching as "the last scenes in the passion-play of Texas," James characterized them not as products of modern media but as part of a much older visual tradition: the iconic representation of Christ's suffering and death. As noted in the previous chapter, James, who referred to Smith as a "fiend incarnate" and a "demon," would not have perceived him as a black Christ redeeming his race through his suffering. Rather, in James's view, Smith's torture and cremation were "the vengeance of an outraged God."[6] The "passion-play" envisioned not Smith's salvation but the redemption of the white girl's suffering and the consecration of white supremacy. The photographs were thus not simply secular mementos of a public spectacle but an iconography celebrating what were considered divinely sanctioned acts. As an iconography, the material manifestation of faith or belief, the images made visible and tangible the racial ideologies that the lynching purportedly defended: the black man as bestial, dehumanized "fiend," the white man as heroic savior of civilization.

Hundreds of images like the ones taken at Smith's lynching, in the forms of ghostly sepia and grim black and white snapshots, cabinet cards, and postcards, exist today in archives, in libraries, and on websites; perhaps even more lie in drawers and attics of private homes. These images shock present-day viewers precisely because they offer seemingly unmediated access to the horror of lynching—visual proof of the celebratory nature with which white southerners attended and accepted public spectacles of torture and death. As James's account suggests, however, for the white southerners who posed for, viewed, and preserved them, lynching photographs testified to something more. The photographs in James's pamphlet replicate the tone and pitch of his narrative hyperbole in starkly visual terms. In doing so, they render his vision of a heroic, unified white crowd wreaking vengeance on the demonic black brute both eerily immediate and eternal.

Lynching photographs assumed this ideological force because they were taken, distributed, and gazed at within a host of conventions and assumptions about photography at the turn of the last century. Photographing a lynching marked the occasion as special, worthy of the camera's view, but it also made what was an extraordinary event somewhat familiar, especially because white southerners would have posed for and interpreted these images through their experiences with other, more typical photographic forms and practices, such as portraiture and hunting photographs. Lynching photographs, in this sense, served to normalize and make socially acceptable, even aesthetically acceptable, the utter brutality of a lynching.[7]

White southerners would have also understood these images through popular notions that photographs reproduced reality with uncanny clarity. Since its inception in the mid-nineteenth century, photography had been vitally linked to modern rationalism and empiricism, which invested vision with an unquestionable capability to uncover truth and validate knowledge. The photograph, in its irrefutable, indexical representation of reality, came to embody modernity's scientific and objectifying gaze. Accordingly, whereas present-day viewers tend to be skeptically attuned to the possibilities of photographic distortion and manipulation, as well as the photographer's inherent subjectivity, turn-of-the-century viewers were more likely to believe that photography projected an unmediated or transparent reflection of reality. This sense of visual realism bestowed on the photograph a profound sort of proof, a capability of revealing and preserving in memory truths that the naked eye could perhaps not so accurately perceive.[8]

The ideological certainty that white southerners imposed on these images rested on these assumptions about photographic objectivity. The photographs provided seemingly indisputable graphic testimony to white southerners' feelings of racial superiority. In a lynching, the perpetrators, through their torture, took the black man's body apart piece by piece to obliterate his human and masculine identity, to make him into the "black beast" that their racial and sexual ideology purported him to be. The lynching victim was in this way himself a representation—a signifier of black inferiority and depravity and, in turn, of white male power and supremacy. To take a picture of the victim in this state of debasement reinforced this process by freezing the moment of representation in time. It created a fixed image of a united and orderly white citizenry in full mastery over supposedly savage and inhuman black men, an image that authenticated and reinforced the racist ideology that had justified and incited the violence. The subsequent public display and circulation of these kinds of images ensured that the lynching was visually remembered and repeatedly witnessed, that it was perpetually alive or in force.

Because they embodied principles of objective and scientific truth, as well as a heightened visual sensationalism, lynching photographs stand as one of the most significant markers of lynching's investment in modern spectacle. The images detached the violence from its horrific particularity in time and place as they became fodder for mass sensationalism and commercial enterprise.[9] Yet, although lynching photographs were in many ways conspicuously modern, the white southerners who took and collected them felt an intensely local and personal investment in them. They functioned in some ways like the other "souvenirs" of a lynching that were hoarded—the pieces of rope, body parts, embers, and charred remains that spectators eagerly collected and saved after a lynching, totemic relics that allowed the collector to feel an exclusive connection to the emotive power of the event. Or, as James suggested of the photographs of Henry Smith's lynching, they possessed a sacred aura. As souvenirs, they remained personal mementos, tied to the beliefs and values of specific places. In fact, their ideological significance was inextricable from the particularities of the lynching and the alleged crime that it avenged. The white supremacist ideals of white heroism and black criminality were not permanently imprinted in the photographs; rather, as many white southerners implicitly knew, they depended

on a controlled and limited viewership.

MOST LYNCHING PHOTOGRAPHS were taken by mob participants or those sympathetic to the lynching, either local professional photographers or amateur photographers who came to the scene with their Kodaks. The accessibility and popularity of amateur photography emerged in the 1890s, at the same time that racialized lynchings in the South were increasing. George Eastman's invention of the Kodak camera and roll film system in the mid-1880s revolutionized photography by making it possible for anyone who could afford a camera to take pictures.[10] Amateur photography quickly became a national fad, reaching even into the rural South. One existing photograph of Leo Frank's lynching in Marietta, Georgia, in 1915, reveals a portable camera in the hand of a man in the far left of the frame (figure 3.3). That same year, a news report of a lynching in Tennessee noted that "hundreds of kodaks clicked all morning at the scene of the lynching."[11]

In other cases, especially in the largest mass lynchings, local professional photographers took responsibility for recording the violence. As P. L. James indicated at Henry Smith's lynching, "preparations were previously made" by several professionals, including local photographers J. L. Mertins and Frank Hudson, who captured the event from different "points of vantage." One photographer climbed "high in a tree . . . so as to command an elevated view of the scaffold, and thus obtain the best possible views of the torture and final cremation." For the 1916 lynching of Jesse Washington in Waco, Texas, a local photographer named F. A. Gildersleeve, notified that the lynching would take place on the city hall lawn, arranged with the mayor to take photographs from a city hall window. Gildersleeve's Waco shots also included close-ups of Washington's charred corpse taken after the event (figures 3.4 and 3.5). Professional photographers like Mertins and Gildersleeve may not have participated in the violence directly, but neither were they recording events as outside journalists or commentators. They produced these photographs for profit, printing them in celebratory souvenir booklets of the lynchings or making them into postcards to be sent to sympathetic eyes.[12]

Despite the variety of people taking them, lynching photographs appear highly standardized, much as prolynching reports and narratives do. No significant distinctions can be made between images taken across various regions of the South or even across time. Over and over again, three types of images emerge: the lynching victim's hanging body, disheveled and limp,

FIGURE 3.3 The lynching of Leo Frank, Marietta, Georgia, 1915.
Frank, a white Jewish man, was lynched for the murder of Mary
Phagan, a worker in the factory he managed. Courtesy of Georgia
Archives, Vanishing Georgia Collection, cob850-84.

alone in the frame; large crowds of spectators, taken from a distance; and,
perhaps the most horrid, proud white men grouped around their lifeless
victim. Nevertheless, we must be cautious in making claims about the stan-
dardization of lynching photographs. The photographs that have survived
over time represent a small fraction of the total number of lynchings that occurred, and there is no way to determine how many lynchings were photo-

FIGURES 3.4 AND 3.5 The lynching of Jesse Washington, Waco, Texas, 1916.
Prints and Photographs Division, Library of Congress, Washington, D.C.

graphed. As the accounts from Paris and Waco, Texas, make evident, photographers took more images than we now have access to, and thousands of images could have been lost or destroyed, or have not yet been recovered.[13] All the same, the uniformity among existing photographs indicates that photographing a lynching was probably quite common. Furthermore, the apparent consistencies among the photographs that do exist, which cannot be attributed to any technological limitations of the camera, suggest that certain kinds of images were either more likely to be captured or more likely to be developed, sold, and preserved.

Especially in cases when professional photographers snapped the images and sold them for profit, photographs rendered the violence of a lynching visible and accessible to a wider audience. Although, as will be shown, the public for these images was imagined as relatively narrow or contained, they nevertheless seemed to punctuate the lynching as a public spectacle. Small posses that quickly lynched their victims outside town but paused long enough to take pictures intended their actions to be witnessed. In 1913, a mob of masked men in Leitchfield, Kentucky, abducted Joseph Richardson, charged with criminal assault on a young white girl, and hanged him from a tree in the public square. It was reported that "the mob worked quietly and most of the citizens of Leitchfield knew nothing of it until the body was found hanging from a tree early this morning. . . . A large crowd congregated . . . after the hanging was reported." A photograph of Richardson's hanging body was mounted on a card and peddled door-to-door by an unknown photographer. Similarly, in Gadsden, Alabama, in 1906, a group of four masked men covertly lynched Bunk Richardson, accused of rape and murder, from a bridge over the Coosa River. Pictures of Richardson's body, probably taken after the lynching by a professional photographer, were mounted on cabinet cards and imprinted with the mark of a local studio.[14]

As visual extensions of the lynching itself, photographs could at times assuage crowds that had missed the opportunity to witness and participate in the violence. In 1934, the posse that captured Claude Neal, accused of raping and killing a young white woman named Lola Cannidy, chose to lynch him in the woods outside Marianna, Florida, rather than bringing him to the Cannidy home, where a large crowd had gathered in anticipation of the lynching. When the waiting crowd discovered that the mob had lynched Neal privately, they were reportedly outraged. The mob finally arrived with Neal's body in tow, and the crowd, which included Cannidy's family, took out their vengeance on the corpse, kicking and shooting it, tearing it apart, and even driving their cars over it. Neal's mutilated, nude body was then hanged on the courthouse lawn in the center of town, and hundreds of photographs were taken. The next day, as people congregated in the square to see the body, the photographs were sold to those purportedly still incensed that the posse who lynched Neal had denied them the satisfaction and pleasure of witnessing Neal's lynching.[15] The images acted as visual replications of the actual spectacle, offering them vicarious access to the missed thrill of the lynching. The gratification local viewers derived from the images of Neal's lynched body was directly attached to their outrage over Cannidy's rape and murder, their fears of black criminality, and their desires to assert their racial power and superiority in the face of these threats.

Lynching photographs gathered further force and meaning in southern communities like Marianna because people tended to ascribe notions of visual accuracy and objectivity to them. Unlike the most detailed verbal account, photographs provided a chilling certainty of the lynching, the undeniable proof it happened because someone was there to record it. At the same time, a photograph abstracted the object of the gaze from the subjective perspective of the viewer or the cameraman and thus created the illusion of a detached, unmediated view, or a transparent reflection of reality. The camera, taken to be a neutral piece of technology, could compensate for the intrinsic subjectivity and fallibility of the human eye, providing empirical verification of experiences and events. Standard photographic conventions, such as taking images either directly level and in front of the object or above, from a bird's-eye vantage point, only enhanced these assumptions about the photograph's objective realism. What was more, whereas the photograph itself might age and deteriorate, its image remained stable. Unlike oral accounts or personal recollections, it was not modified through time, nor was its representation of the past contingent on a subjective recounting; the selectivity or subjectivity of the image existed in the moment the photograph was made, not in each showing or display. Photographs could, in this respect, appear more authentic and truthful than other forms of evidence.[16]

For these reasons, lynching photographs could expand the act of witnessing, and all the notions of truth and veracity wrapped into the act of witnessing, to viewers who did not directly experience the lynching and its enactment of brutal "justice." They could also serve to justify the violence or to prove its necessity after the fact. Despite popular perceptions that lynchers often chose their victims at random, selecting black scapegoats unconnected to the alleged crimes, lynch mobs and their defenders were very much concerned that their victims were indeed guilty of crimes. That is not to say that lynch mobs were never rash in assigning guilt; black men innocent of any wrongdoing were probably regularly lynched for others' crimes. But to justify the practice as a legitimate act of communal and sacred justice to outsiders as well as to themselves, lynchers had to believe they had condemned a guilty man. Mobs often bent over backward to establish the guilt of the man they had captured or had already lynched, often without the investigative techniques of a modern police department or the authority of a legal trial. The victim's confession, even when coerced, was accorded high value for this reason.

In cases of sexual assault, lynch mobs, in particular, relied on the eyewitness testimony of the violated white woman. The supposed violation of white womanhood, of course, stood at the center of prolynching rhetoric. For this reason, although lynching was in many ways a masculine ritual, it nevertheless depended on women's participation as accusers and witnesses.[17] Not only was the woman's cry of rape a galvanizing force in lynching, but the alleged black rapist was frequently brought before the white female victim for identification. In these instances, the eyewitness identification of the accused was a critical moment in the lynching process that endowed the white woman, even a poor woman, with a crucial, albeit circumscribed, amount of authority. When Mrs. Joseph White, "the wife of a respectable farmer" according to local news reports, was viciously attacked and raped in Rome, Georgia, in 1900, an outraged posse seized her neighbor, a twenty-year-old black man named Bud Rufus whose family were tenants of a nearby planter. As White lay near death, "in a semi-conscious state," the men brought Rufus to her bedside for identification. Despite her condition, the local paper assured readers, when Rufus was "ushered into her presence, some indefinable horror seized the dying woman, and, through her clouded brain consciousness of surroundings seemed to come for a moment." White's suffering incited the mob, "sworn to protect their mothers and daughters from undoing," to "expiate" her crime. Moreover, the "indefinable horror" that "seized" her became the evidence against the black man that "sealed [his] doom." Without delay, the mob hanged Rufus from a nearby railroad trestle and fired shots into his body.[18]

Yet the wronged white woman was a problematic witness. The emotional vulnerability and physical fragility for which white women were honored and protected were the same qualities that placed into question their reliability as witnesses to sexual or criminal assault, especially, as in White's case, when their suffering took the form of incapacitation or hysteria.[19] In some cases, photography served as a critical tool in resolving this dilemma. When Mrs. Locklear, assaulted in Rome, Georgia, in 1901 — not long after the Rufus lynching — was at first deemed unable to identify her assailant because of her "condition," lynching photography provided visible identification after the fact. Once George Reed was arrested for the crime, a large processional formed to take him to Locklear, the twenty-six-year-old wife of a tenant farmer and former bailiff, for identification. The mob processed through the main streets of Rome, before a throng of nearly 2,000 spectators, to reach the Locklear home in east Rome. There, the crowd, which included some of Rome's most "popular and prominent citizens," was asked to stay back, so as not to "frighten" Locklear, and assured that "if he is the right Negro we will bring him back and let you all see him hanged." The spectators became silent when Reed was brought inside to Locklear, who, after looking at him "long and intently," declared, "He is not the man."[20]

For Locklear, this must have been a daunting moment, with the fate of a man's life hanging on her testimony and a crowd of thousands showing her attention and "consideration" she might not have otherwise received in life. Reed immediately became "hysterical with joy," and a *Rome (Ga.) Tribune* reporter who had interviewed him earlier affirmed that he believed Reed to be innocent. Reed was taken back to jail and then released when the judge decreed that there was not enough evidence to hold him. A mob of about 150 men were still determined to lynch someone for the crime, however. They were convinced that Reed was guilty, claiming that he had confessed and "contradicted" himself several times. The men recaptured him and hanged him about a mile outside town, riddling his "struggling body" with bullets. In a curious reversal, the *Rome (Ga.) Tribune* reported the next day that "evidence" had accumulated that "George Reed was the man." Locklear also recanted, stating that "there was no doubt that George Reed, the Negro who was lynched, was the man who assaulted her." When asked why she did not identify him the day before, she explained that she "was very much frightened" because "they told me they would kill him in my presence." But "when told how the Negro looked dangling at the end of a rope," she "seemed gratified."[21]

In fact, she added that "she would like to see a photograph of the scene" — a photograph that could confirm for her that Reed "was the man." The morning after the lynching, local photographer C. W. Orr had taken "two excellent photographs of the ghastly scene" (figure 3.6).[22] Though Locklear was too frightened to witness the lynching in person, the photographs provided her with a safe, removed glimpse of the lynching. At the same time, they

FIGURE 3.6 The lynching of George Reed, Rome, Georgia, 1901.
Courtesy of Georgia Archives, Vanishing Georgia Collection, flo165.

allowed her to identify Reed now that she was no longer "frightened" and
was in a calmer frame of mind, furnishing visual proof of what the mob said
was its rightful vengeance. In other words, the presumed realist objectivity
of the photographs served to legitimize the lynching as the righteous expiation of a crime, the decisive "evidence" that "George Reed was the man."

THE CONFIDENCE THAT turn-of-the-century Americans invested in the
photographic image was not merely a secular trust in realist objectivity,
however. Lynching photographs acquired cultural power not only because

of the visual certitude they conveyed but also because more subjective notions of personal authenticity and moral clarity were ascribed to them. These notions were rooted in nineteenth-century assumptions about photography, which were inversely related to expectations of the camera's visual realism. Early viewers of photography believed not only that photographs referenced objective truth but also, particularly in the case of personal portraits, that they revealed deeper, moral truths that lay below the surface of the image. In a Victorian world that placed remarkable emphasis on exterior appearances and behaviors as markers of character, photographs were seen to have a mystical quality because of the camera's uncanny ability to freeze expressions, postures, gestures, and other indicators of states of mind that the human eye might not discern. The ghostly image of a photograph, it was believed, might disclose the sitter's soul. Even well into the twentieth century, Walter Benjamin distinguished portraits from other forms of photography because of the "aura" that "emanates . . . in the fleeting expression of a human face." Portraits, unlike other mechanically reproduced images, gain authenticity through their attachment to a unique existence and singular moment in time. In this context, images of confident, restrained white men beside bodies of debased black men could validate the racist convictions of the white southerners who gazed on them not only because viewers assumed the visual accuracy of the surface image but because they believed that photographs made manifest interior truths about the essence of racial character.[23]

Visual associations between lynching photographs and other turn-of-the-century photographic conventions only solidified and reinforced these assumptions. Common rituals and practices surrounding photography, indeed, served to substantiate the very ideals of white supremacy and white solidarity that the lynching itself effected. Rarely do lynching photographs depict the crowd in the process of hanging, shooting, or burning the victim. To be sure, early cameras required long exposures to take pictures, resulting in still, posed images. However, even in later photographs, when faster shutter speeds enabled cameras to depict action, crowds tended to stop and gather for the camera. Those few images that do show lynchings in process (see figures 3.2 and 3.4) suggest that such action shots were in fact technologically feasible. That most lynching photographs depict static posing was thus a factor of convention more than technical limitations. In most photographs, the action of a lynching was stopped for the photographer to snap the picture, suggesting that the photographing was an integrated part of the lynching ritual. In some cases, as in Paris and Waco, Texas, several stages of the lynchings were recorded, creating a stop-motion tableau of the event. By regularly stopping the action, the very act of picture taking prolonged the ceremony.[24]

In some cases, the lynching was paused for a picture of a still relatively intact body to be recorded. Although at times, especially when the lynching occurred at night, photographers returned the next day to take pictures of the hanging body in daylight, many photographs apparently depict the victim just after he was hanged, either alone or with a crowd of white faces surrounding him, often as an interrupted moment in the process of the lynching. In these images, none of the effects of a lynching, such as bulging eyes, burst blood vessels, and bloating, are yet visible, suggesting that the hanging had just taken place. Mobs often riddled these bodies with bullets or cut them down to be burned after the pictures were snapped. Black attorney and journalist R. C. O. Benjamin noted in an antilynching pamphlet that at the 1893 lynching of C. J. Miller in Bardwell, Kentucky, a photograph was taken just after Miller was hanged; then, after "his fingers and toes [were] cut off, and his body otherwise horribly mutilated, it was burned to ashes."[25]

These conventions of lynching photography—keeping the actual violence outside the frame, the mob's posing for the camera—became instrumental in creating and perpetuating images of orderly, respectable mobs. Lynching photographs, in this way, mirrored the rhetoric of southern newspaper accounts and other prolynching narratives, which, as we have seen, frequently assured readers that lynching crowds were organized, determined, and united in purpose. The photographs projected images of the lynch mob as neither violent nor chaotic but contained and composed within the frame of the picture. In recounting the 1904 double lynching of Paul Reed and Will Cato in Statesboro, Georgia, journalist Ray Stannard Baker described how the mob periodically paused the lynching to allow photographs to be taken. Once Reed and Cato were chained and their bodies "drenched with oil . . . the crowd stood back accommodatingly, while a photographer, standing in the bright sunshine, took pictures of the chained Negroes." Baker noted that "citizens crowded up behind the stump and got their faces into the photograph." Once the timbers beneath the two men were lit, "the crowd yelled wildly" and "threw knots and sticks at the writhing creatures." According to Baker, however, they "always left room for the photographers to take more pictures." Baker provided a telling contrast between the vision of "citizens" standing back "accommodatingly" for the pictures and the more brutal image of the crowd "yell[ing] wildly" and throwing "knots and sticks"

FIGURE 3.7 The lynching of Will Cato and Paul Reed, Statesboro, Georgia, 1904.
Courtesy of Georgia Archives, Vanishing Georgia Collection, bul070-84.

at their victims. The photographs taken at the Statesboro lynching, however, transmitted and made permanent only the images of a "civilized" and
"orderly" crowd. For example, in figure 3.7, the white mob stands casually
around the shackled figures of Reed and Cato before the burning, seemingly detached from the action. In this image, the black men stare almost
defiantly into the camera, weakened only by the ropes and chains securing
them. Another image shows the burning in progress, but the members of

the mob appear only in the distance, as if they are incidental to the violence. These scenes of white men posed with organized precision substantiated popular notions of white emotional restraint and command in contrast to the presumed savagery and moral depravity of their victims.[26]

The frozen and affected posturing of these men marked and replicated for the camera an ideal not only of white self-control but also of white unity and single-mindedness. By projecting these images of group cohesion, photographs of white mobs and crowds imagined the very solidarity that white supremacist ideology propounded. As people began to visually document family and social gatherings in the late nineteenth century, photographs served to project, to themselves and others, images of family and social harmony. Grouping everyone for a photograph soon became a ritual at most private and public occasions. The photograph acted not only as a sign of the celebration but also as a marker of the cohesiveness of the group.[27] In this respect, the act of posing with the mob or the crowd in a lynching would have facilitated or generated a sense of group identity among the participants. In the photographs, the white participants gather as one, pushing their bodies together, leaning forward, heads peering over shoulders so all are in view. In many images, men and women, young and old are apparent in the lynching crowds, and men in suits stand beside men in overalls — people from all walks of life presenting themselves as united in this moment. Their differences, albeit still visible, were obscured by their common purpose, and, more significant, by their sharp distinction from their black victim (see figures 3.5 and 3.11). For the middle classes who took part in and supported lynching, these images of white unity and restraint would have validated their own claims to respectability and social authority that placed them on par with southern elites. In other words, it was in their interest to present a unified white mob that crossed class boundaries.

The self-conscious posing of the white mob and the inverse, forced posing of the black victim also merged two of the most prominent conventions of turn-of-the-century photography: the bourgeois portrait and the criminal mug shot. Portraiture was one of the first uses of early photography, providing a relatively inexpensive and accessible means for middle-class Americans to emulate elite portraiture and make evident their respectability. Their social character was literally and figuratively inscribed in the image. The portrait itself, the presentation of self it conveyed, served as a sign of social status, while the image within the portrait ideally made the moral worth of the sitter manifest through facial expression and bodily comportment. For this reason, portrait photographers took enormous care to arrange their sitters with the proper lighting, backdrop, and pose to capture, in an instant of time, an imprint of character. The expression one bore in a portrait became one's public mask, the image of oneself that was presented to society.[28]

By the first decade of the twentieth century, even the smallest towns had local photographers, as well as itinerant photographers, who advertised their services for portrait sittings in newspapers.[29] Most catered only to white citizens, for although African Americans sat for portraits during this period, white southerners assumed that portraiture and the respectability it endowed were reserved for them. In Rome, Georgia, for instance, a news item from 1899 mockingly recounted a scene in which a photographer asked to take the picture of a black street preacher and the crowd of black listeners around him: "Hats were removed, cravats arranged, and hair smoothed. It is amusing to see each one moving forward to a prominent position in the crowd though none vied a young man whose appearance indicated a country dude and who stepped forward, put his hat on the back of his head, thrust his hands in his pocket and snap the deed was done. . . . Their picture had bin took [sic]."[30] For this white observer, the notion that African Americans would fashion themselves for a photograph was absurdly pretentious. This scene is made more poignant when one sees the photograph of George Reed's lynched body, outfitted in a suit, head jarringly uplifted, produced and circulated as a postcard in Rome in 1901 (figure 3.6).

The criminal photograph, on the other hand, developed in the late nineteenth century as part of the increasing professionalization of police work and the development of criminology as a social science. Along with fingerprinting and physiological records, criminal mug shots were organized in police files and public archives so that both police and citizens could come to identify not only individual criminals but generalized qualities of criminal deviancy. This latter purpose depended on the belief that a criminal's character and pathology were visible in his face and composure. The criminal photograph, in this sense, functioned as an inverse of the bourgeois photograph portrait. Both relied on a belief in the scientific objectivity of the camera and its simultaneous, almost supernatural, capacity to reveal deeper moral truths.[31]

In some well-publicized crimes that were avenged in lynchings, photographic portraits of the white victims were circulated along with the lynching photographs, making apparent to viewers their innocence and moral worth. They then served as visual justifications for lawless vengeance. An image of Myrtle Vance was included in P. L. James's pamphlet on the lynch-

FIGURE 3.8 The Henry Vance family, Paris, Texas, 1893. Prints and Photographs Division, Library of Congress, Washington, D.C.

ing of Henry Smith. (The image was edited from the family portrait shown in figure 3.8, taken by the same photographer who snapped some of the shots of the lynching.) The picture of this small, blond girl, always referred to as "Little Myrtle Vance," was set in striking distinction to the image of Smith's body (figure 3.2). Whereas James described Smith as bearing a "brawny muscular body, surmounted by a small head," which supposedly revealed his animal nature, Myrtle Vance appeared in her portrait as small and frail, with a child's oversized head and eyes.[32] Similarly, after the 1904 lynching in Statesboro, Georgia, postcards of the Hodges family were circulated along with photographs depicting both Reed and Cato and the lynching. Local photographer T. M. Bennett, who took both sets of photographs, advertised in the local newspaper that he was selling all of these images directly from his studio for twenty-five cents each. Bennett also fashioned a cabinet card in which he pasted together separate images of the members of the Hodges family into one family portrait. The photograph of Reed and Cato, with their ill-fitting clothes and harsh grimaces, makes them appear all the more threatening when juxtaposed with the mannered poses and innocent expressions of the Hodges children (figures 3.9 and 3.10). A full-length picture of Reed, his body looking misshapen and his trousers slightly

TALMAGE and HARMON, the Hodges infants who were burned alive in their home Ne r Statesboro, Ga., July 28 1904, by Cato and Reid. Copyright 1904 by T. M. Bennett.

FIGURE 3.9 Talmage and Harmon Hodges, Statesboro, Georgia, 1904. Paul Reed's name is misspelled in the original caption. Courtesy of Georgia Archives, Vanishing Georgia Collection, bul024.

unbuttoned, appeared on the front page of the *Atlanta Constitution* the day after the lynching.[33]

In his report of the Statesboro lynching in *Following the Color Line*, Ray Stannard Baker included the same images of Cato and Reed, edited to show only their heads and torsos, in a clear mimic of classic mug shots. Below them appear two pictures of black criminals taken in the Atlanta jail, with the caption "Negroes of the Criminal Type." With no explanation for this juxtaposition of images, the reader was evidently expected to make a visual association between the expressive character of the two convicts and Cato and Reed. The images only underscored Baker's argument that "worthless Negroes" like Cato and Reed—"ignorant and lazy" and prone to crimi-

Reid and Cato in Jail Yard.

FIGURE 3.10 Paul Reed and Will Cato, Statesboro, Georgia, 1904.
Reed's name is again misspelled in the original caption. Courtesy of
Georgia Archives, Vanishing Georgia Collection, bul043b.

nality—posed the greatest threat to the southern countryside, a threat that
ultimately led to the horror of lynching.[34]

The social hierarchies apparent in the bourgeois portrait and the criminal mug shot were subsequently represented in the lynching photograph.
In these images, the black "criminal" is exhibited as a captured body, his
criminality supposedly revealed in his distorted and disheveled frame. In
some cases, the corpses were even rearranged to ridicule the victim's degradation. In an unidentified lynching in Arkansas from the 1890s, someone
has replaced the victim's hat on his head in a gesture of mock respectability.
The white man to his right uses a stick or cane to prop his body, pushing him
forward so his torso is straight while his head flops to the side. In a postcard

of the corpse of Will Stanley, lynched in Temple, Texas, in 1915, his burned arms are contorted to make it appear that he is flexing his biceps. Although such a posture is more likely the physical result of the burning, it appears, within the frame of the postcard, as a gesture of mock strength and power, particularly in contrast to the unyielding stances of the white men beside him. The two men in the foreground, each posed with cocky sureness, form a triangle with Stanley's corpse at the apex; one, in shirtsleeves and hat, squints at the camera sideways, hands on his hips, while the other, in overalls and a cap, leans somewhat carelessly against the telephone pole, eyes closed, arms folded defensively against his chest.[35]

Unlike Stanley, these men posed themselves for the camera, as did the men grouped behind them, and in that self-presentation, they were accorded a measure of respectability. By their clothing, the men appear to cross class lines. The sender of the postcard was a young man named Joe Meyers, an oiler at a car company, who, before sending the card to his parents, distinguished himself in the picture proudly with a "cross." In this regard, the self-presentation of the white men in photographs further accentuated the class harmony exacted in the lynching.[36] Through these methods of presentation, photographs of lynching made visible to white southerners black depravity set against a united white superiority and civility. The image provided visible evidence of the white virtue and black criminality that legitimized the supposed social need for lynching.

In at least one case, a lynching photograph itself became a mug shot, used to identify an accused criminal across state lines. When John Crooms was lynched in Plant City, Florida, in 1893, a man in Albany, Georgia, recognized his name as that of a convicted murderer who had some years before escaped from that city's jail. On request, authorities in Plant City sent not only a description of Crooms but a photograph of his lynched body, "suspended . . . to the limb of a tall tree in a beautiful Florida forest." With the help of a magnifying glass, officials and fellow prisoners in Albany identified scars on Crooms's face that marked him as the missing prisoner.[37] This account illustrates the circulation of lynching photographs—even, at times, among municipal and county authorities.

The "proof" embedded in lynching photographs was never put to the service of the law, however. In one existing photograph of the 1904 Statesboro lynching, the faces of the white men have been scratched out (figure 3.7). Since this appears to have been done on the negative, the photographer himself may have tried to protect the mob. As discussed in chapter 1, several members of this mob were identified at a court of inquiry held after the lynching. Not surprisingly, none of these men were indicted, but this instance does make evident that some people were aware of the ways that forms of proof other than those originally intended could be placed on a lynching photograph. Although photographs were never used as legal evidence to prosecute lynchers, they could have been. Few lynchings were prosecuted, and if they were, as the Crisis noted regarding an Oklahoma lynching in 1911, "even with such proof [as the photograph], we are sure the jury would acquit." For instance, after the lynching of Charlie Hale in Lawrenceville, Georgia, a town with a population of about 1,500 at the time of the lynching, the Atlanta Constitution asserted that "no members of the mob were recognized, and no arrests have been made." However, a photograph of Hale's body surrounded by white men, staring intently into the camera, was made into a postcard (figure 3.11). Since the lynching took place at 12:30 A.M. and the body remained in the town square until the next afternoon, the photograph may have been taken the next day, and the men may have been merely onlookers. Even so, they chose to pose with hunting dogs borrowed from the county convict camp, which were used to track Hale down, and one man holds up, for the camera to catch, the mocking sign — "PLEASE DO NOT WAKE"—that hangs from Hale's toes. The photograph was undoubtedly taken in a spirit of pride and self-satisfaction, apparently without fear of rebuke.[38]

AS THE IMAGES of Hale's lynching make apparent, the photographic convention that the lynching photograph arguably most evokes is that of the hunting photograph. The image of white men posed next to their black victim bears an uncanny resemblance to the familiar snapshot of a hunter with his prey. We see the same confident posture and the same proprietary gestures (figure 3.12). As a contemporary black leader noted about one photograph he had seen, "The only thing I could think of as I glanced at this picture was a photograph I had seen of huntsmen returning with the animal that had been shot, proud of their achievement of marksmanship."[39] Hunting was an intensely masculine ritual in the South, distinctly segregated from feminine domesticity and virtue, often marking a boy's initiation into manhood. As one 1911 advertisement for shotguns and rifles in Paris, Texas, announced, "There is nothing more conducive to real manhood than shooting." For many southern white men, hunting was a ritualized performance, a ceremonial dance of power between man and animal and an outlet for white masculine self-assertion and self-indulgence.[40] The visual association between hunting and lynching photographs thus underscores the ways in

FIGURE 3.11 The lynching of Charlie Hale, Lawrenceville, Georgia, 1911. Courtesy of
Georgia Archives, Vanishing Georgia Collection, gwn277.

FIGURE 3.12 Hunters with deer, Jekyll Island, Georgia, undated. Courtesy of Georgia Archives, Vanishing Georgia Collection, jeko59. Original, Jekyll Island Museum.

which lynching photographs bore within them both white supremacist ideology and the gendered elements of that ideology. White southerners' conviction of their own moral superiority was, indeed, inseparable from their gender expectations and ideals—that is, notions that white men were, by nature, self-contained and tough, and that white women were delicate and defenseless, in need of white male protection.

Yet, although lynching was meant to reinforce these ideals against the threat of black male criminality and insurgency, the actual rituals of the lynching process contradicted them in significant ways. For a lynching to restore white male power and authority not only over black men but over white men's households and their women, it needed to be witnessed and appreciated by white women. But lynchings were brutal and sadistic events. Mobs performed extreme acts of violence and often exposed the naked bodies of the black men before the same vulnerable and virtuous eyes of white women that lynching was intended to defend. Lynching photographs, however, especially in their metonym with hunting photographs, could resolve this conflict because of the ways in which they sanitized and obscured the most horrific aspects of the violence.

Lynchings themselves often reenacted the hunt-and-kill ritual, adopting its methods and language, a fact that is not surprising in a culture that conceptualized black men as "beasts" and "brutes." A "manhunt" would be formed to search out and surround the "black beast," and, in some cases, as in that of Charlie Hale, hunting dogs were sent out to track the prey down. Once cornered and caught, the black man was often dragged through town before he was hanged or burned.[41] Finally, the trophy snapshot of the hunter with his "prey" memorialized the conquest. The word "snapshot" itself was a British hunting term denoting a gunshot that went off too quickly, a term photographers began using in the 1850s. Advertisements for cameras in southern towns sometimes made overt connections between photography and hunting. An advertisement for the Owl Drug Store in Hattiesburg, Mississippi, read, "Do your spring hunting with an EASTMAN AUTOGRAPHIC KODAK. No game laws to conflict with this fascinating sport." Another in Waco, Texas, for a company that rented "Guns and Kodaks" to the public, highlighted in large, bold type, "GO KODAKING . . . GO HUNTING." These verbal associations between hunting and photographing only accentuate the ways in which picture taking at lynchings was itself an act of violence that reenacted the objectification and physical degradation of the black victim. In this context, the camera, held and operated by white men, "shooting" and "capturing" their subjects, served as yet another weapon in what Susan Sontag has called "sublimated murder."[42]

Not only did framing a lynching as a hunt underscore the dehumanization of the black man that the torture and killing itself enacted, but, in a culture that deemed hunting the marker and privilege of white manhood, it also served to reaffirm the heroic masculinity of the lynchers. This heroism matched the popular image of lynch mobs as determined and restrained. As the Little Rock, Arkansas, sheriff, who watched as a mob lynched John Carter in that city, remarked, "I never saw a more orderly crowd of hunters in my life."[43] The photographic image re-created and further authenticated these ideological roles: white man as masculine hunter, black man as degenerate beast.

This process of dehumanization was more complicated, however, than might be assumed. For despite the utter desecration that a mob enacted on its victim's body, certain aspects of the black man's humanity were retained. Lynchings, especially those avenging alleged rapes of white women, often reenacted that crime on the black man's body. Mobs, in other words, felt compelled to desecrate the bodies of those who they believed had desecrated their communal bodies.[44] The black victim was often stripped nude, or at least partly undressed, and every part of his body was touched, dismembered, or molested in some way. On the one hand, to perform a lynching in this way was to dehumanize the victim, to gut him like a hunted animal. Yet, on the other hand, the black man's body needed to be recognizable as a human body in order to restage and avenge the crime against the white community, for animals cannot be held morally culpable for rape or murder. Hence mobs insisted on their victims' confessions and final prayers. In short, the figure of the "black beast rapist" was both inhuman brute (a "beast") and hypersexual man (a "rapist").

The act of genital dismemberment is a case in point. For obvious reasons, this act has haunted the cultural memories of both blacks and whites arguably more than any other aspect of lynching. One in three lynching victims was emasculated, a practice reserved for the worst alleged crimes and assaults. Because castration was performed routinely on farm animals, the act was commonplace for rural southerners in association with animals. But, in removing either the penis or the testicles of their victims, mobs also demasculinized them; that is, lynchers robbed their victims of their sexual and reproductive capabilities, removing the perceived threat to white womanhood and, by extension, to white masculinity. The lynchers did literally to black men what Jim Crow restrictions effectively achieved in rendering them economically and politically dependent and powerless. Cutting off his genitals rendered the black man a negation of white masculinity against which white men could define themselves. After the Jesse Washington lynching in 1916 in Waco, Texas, NAACP investigator Elizabeth Freeman reported that one white townsperson was carrying Washington's penis as a souvenir. In this case, the participant could literally possess that sexual power he found so fearful and despicable. Such actions depended on some recognition, albeit distorted, of the black man's humanity.[45]

Lynchings thus reinforced white masculine power ostensibly more than they did what they rhetorically aimed to do—that is, protect and defend white womanhood. For this reason, some southern women, like Jesse Daniel Ames and Lillian Smith, vigorously objected to what they perceived as a hollow chivalry that exploited an idealized and ultimately oppressive view of "pure" white womanhood to celebrate and condone a brutal form of masculinity. Smith, for instance, railed against "lecherous old men and young ones, reeking with impurities, who had violated the home since they were sixteen years old," using "sacred womanhood" as a "rusty shield" to condone their violent suppression of black men. These sorts of objections, it should be noted, however, were decidedly uncommon, particularly during the height of lynching.[46]

For many white southern men, lynching both defined and bolstered an idealized sense of manliness, one that merged competing models of masculine behavior. Prolynching rhetoric imagined white men as emotionally restrained, purposeful, and chivalrous, the epitome of Victorian genteel manhood. Yet the violence they committed against black men allowed them to engage in a hard, virile, masculine brutality. They then denied that brutality by projecting violence and savagery onto black men. They also denied it through the photographs they posed for. Images of white men, immobile and stalwart, surrounding the black corpse projected *only* an ideal of restrained and sturdy manhood. At the same time, for the male viewer, these photographs may have revived memories of the danger, depravity, and sheer masculine power of the event. In either case, the images functioned as a visible record through which white men could confront and assert their own masculinity. As the images passed between whites in town squares, barbershops, and general stores, they could also act as a bond between white men, creating connections across class lines.[47]

The photographs furthermore brought the masculine rite of lynching into the home and, in doing so, effectively domesticated the violence they represented. As noted earlier, southern news reports and prolynching narratives often made particular note that women and children were present at lynchings, especially the largest mass mob lynchings, since their presence indicated that the event was socially acceptable and respectable. In cases of alleged sexual assault, the female victim frequently played a prominent role in the lynching. Her presence was crucial to legitimize the violence and make manifest that the lynching was a direct act of vengeance. According to one account, when Edward Coy was burned to death for allegedly assaulting a white woman, Mrs. Jewell, in Texarkana, Texas, in 1892, someone in the crowd of 5,000 people yelled, "Let his victim apply the torch." When Jewell emerged, escorted by male relatives, the crowd "cheered." "Pale and determined," she identified Coy as her assailant and then "set a match to his body where kerosene had been poured." Antilynching crusaders, on the other hand, pointed to the presence of white women and children as further indication of the moral depravity of lynching. Describing the 1919 lynching of Lloyd Clay in Vicksburg, Mississippi, the *Chicago Defender* sardonically noted that "the dainty hands of young girls, who will represent the future mothers of Vicksburg, Miss., were seen with guns pointing at the victim, eager for a chance to be a party in furthering this grewsome [sic] method of cannibalism."[48]

Reports like this only made evident the embarrassing contradiction that lynch mobs desecrated black male bodies in the name of white feminine purity often before the very virtuous eyes they were meant to protect. Arthur Raper noted that at Raymond Gunn's 1931 lynching in Maryville, Missouri, "One woman held her little girl up so she could get a better view of the naked Negro."[49] In Vicksburg, Mississippi, in 1919, when the mob stripped Lloyd Clay before hanging and burning him, the *Vicksburg Evening Post* reported that "the sight of the nude body rising above the crowd increased the excitement." But because the lynching took place in the front yard of a "respected" white elderly widow and grandmother, Ida Keefe, a number of people protested that such brutality was committed in the presence of white women. Keefe herself told the *Vicksburg Evening Post* that she tried in vain to persuade the crowd to leave her yard. "I felt so absolutely helpless . . . and in order to not be compelled to witness the horrible scene [I] went into the home and locked the door," she explained. "It was distressing to me to see so many women and girls in the mob and I can't understand how they could bear to stay and witness such a terrible scene." Her choice of words posited her as the white female victim—helpless, distressed, locking herself within her house—that the lynch mob was supposedly defending. Likewise, another woman angrily wrote to the *Vicksburg Herald*, "There is an innate feeling in most women that causes them to experience horror at the thought of witnessing such a scene. . . . In stripping the clothes from the body of the negro and exhibiting it and burning it at the very doors of women who were horrified at the sight, did that mob exhibit a spirit of chivalry?" On the other hand, another white woman, Emily Shaw, the wife of a local real estate agent, asserted in a letter to the editor that "those women who shut themselves away from the atrocious sight of the lynching were physical cowards." What seemed to be at issue here was not that the mob avenged the assault on white womanhood by lynching Clay but that white women were forced to view the event.[50]

Yet, although they were often present at lynchings, women do not appear in most lynching photographs, with several notable exceptions. We can presume, however, that they did look at these photographs. Mrs. Locklear in Rome, Georgia, was "frightened" at the idea of witnessing George Reed lynched in her presence, but she eagerly anticipated seeing the photograph of his lynched body, in part to see that her violation had been avenged. In this respect, if women were not present at the lynching, a photograph could provide a bridge between these masculine acts of violence and the protected and sanctified domestic sphere.

Significantly, lynching photographs almost never reveal the black man's genitalia, whether dismembered or not.[51] In some instances, it is clear that the lynching victims have been covered for the photographs—burlap sacks tied around their waists, pants clumsily pulled up (figure 3.3). In the 1930 double lynching in Marion, Indiana, the clothes of one victim, Abe Smith, were torn off as he was dragged around town, and at one point his genitalia were visible. Yet, for the photograph, a towel and a feed sack were tied around his waist (figure 3.13). For many white southerners, the "savagery" of the black man, with his uncontrollable sexual appetites, was signified, above all, by the imagined virility and size of his penis. That member came to embody the black man's supposed moral weakness, intellectual inferiority, and animal nature. Even when, during the lynching, the penis was uncovered and molested or severed, there was evidently something forbidden about showing it in fixed detail in a photograph. It was the black man's naked body, after all, that served as a visual reminder of the alleged crime against white womanhood. As James noted in his description of Henry Smith's lynching in Paris, Texas, once Smith was stripped naked before the crowd, "the brawny form stood revealed, gigantic in brute force, and then was felt the full thrill of horror as the thought of such a force being applied to such an ungodly purpose as he had consummated, rushed through the minds of

FIGURE 3.13 The lynching of Thomas Shipp and Abe Smith, Marion, Indiana, 1930.
Prints and Photographs Division, Library of Congress, Washington, D.C. Courtesy of
the National Association for the Advancement of Colored People.

those present." Smith's nudity is not visible in any of the photographs, however. As an abstruse symbol, the imaginary signifier of black "beastliness,"
bolstering every defense of lynching, the black man's penis could never be
revealed in a photograph for what it actually was.[52]

Covering the black victim for the photograph also imposed a sort of
genteel morality on the violence, or at least on the preserved public representation of that violence. By concealing the black man's genitalia, the
photograph allowed white women to gaze on black male bodies without

compromising the very purity that the lynching was purported to defend. Moreover, because the violence itself was elided in the image, white women could safely view the lynching without having to witness white male brutality and thus could retain their own sense of feminine propriety.

IN CREATING THESE IMAGES and allowing them to circulate, immune from incrimination, lynchers ensured the continuation of their violence, at least in the visual imaginations of others. The black criminal was thus not ritually expunged from the community in some sort of scapegoat fashion. Rather than exorcising the black "beast" and the threat his blackness represented, the photograph functioned as a souvenir, a portable memory, ensuring that the now dismembered black body was continually remembered. This is perhaps one reason that the victim was often photographed while his body was still intact, so he could be recognized and defined as a criminal deviant. The image redramatized the violence, allowing the victim to be tortured and killed once again in the viewer's memory.

Although there is much more to be discovered about the circulation and private use of lynching photographs, we do know that at least some of these images were advertised for sale in city newspapers, sold openly in stores, sent through the mail as postcards, and presumably displayed openly in homes.[53] Photographer Claude Jackson hawked photographs from Sam Holt's 1899 lynching in Newnan, Georgia, for fifteen cents each in the *Newnan Herald and Advertiser*, and, as noted, T. M. Bennett did the same in the *Statesboro (Ga.) News* after the 1904 lynching in that city. In August 1893, the *Charlotte (N.C.) News* reported that photographs from a recent lynching in South Carolina of three black men had reached the city and were "the most salable items that have struck this market lately." According to one account of a 1915 lynching in Tennessee, photographers "reaped a harvest in selling postcards showing a photograph of the lynched Negro." In this case, photographers had set up a portable printing plant at the scene of the lynching to produce and sell postcards almost instantaneously. The violation perpetuated in these images was intensified when they circulated to surrounding towns to be sold on streets and in stores for weeks after the lynching.[54]

Stereographic reproductions were another means through which lynching violence was commercialized. Stereographs or stereo views, a popular late-nineteenth-century parlor amusement, were made by placing two almost identical photographs side by side on a card, so that, when viewed through a stereoscope, a single three-dimensional image appeared. In their three dimensionality, these cards reproduced lynching with remarkable

FIGURE 3.14 "And speedily the punishment fits the crime," stereograph card, 1901. Prints and Photographs Division, Library of Congress, Washington, D.C.

realism, even, as appears to be the case with figure 3.14, when the scene was a fictional representation. In this stereograph, made by a company in Philadelphia for a national audience, a man of perhaps Mexican or mixed-race descent is hanged in a typical "frontier" setting. In at least one instance, stereographic views were made to represent an actual lynching. In 1897, a couple of entrepreneurs in Tyler, Texas, produced a set of sixteen stereograph cards that depicted the murder of a local woman and the subsequent search, capture, and lynching by burning of Robert Hilliard, who had been lynched in Tyler two years earlier. The cards were advertised and exhibited in Tyler and perhaps elsewhere, and they accompanied a sensational account of the lynching written by an eyewitness, printed by a local publishing house. In their graphic realism, these stereographs brought that eyewitness account to life for spectators. "These views are true to life. . . . Don't fail to see this," exclaimed an advertisement for them. The producers of the images even tinted some of them red to simulate blood. In this case, the pleasure of viewing the cards derived from seeing not just the torture and death of the black "criminal" but also the crime against white womanhood, in all its gory detail, that precipitated and justified the lynching. These images redrama-tized not just the lynching itself as a sort of momentary morbid thrill but the entire narrative surrounding it, a narrative that gave the mob's violence meaning and force.[55]

This kind of commercialization draws attention to the most modern elements of lynching. Through the sale and circulation of photographs, lynching was transformed into a mode of consumer excess and leisurely recreation, especially through the associations between the photographs and new forms of image-based advertising and tourist souvenir collecting that arose at the turn of the century.[56] Yet turn-of-the-century viewers might not have apprehended these images as modern spectacle in the way we conceive of the term, nor would they necessarily have associated postcards with casual leisure and amusement as we do today. After all, white southerners invested their racial convictions not in the mass culture of consumerism but in older photographic and iconographic traditions that could provide both objective and moral certainty to those convictions.

Furthermore, although white southerners did buy and sell images of lynching, most such transactions were confined to relatively local economies and interactions. For although some lynching images, like those from Paris, Texas, circulated nationally, most did not, especially as the antilynching movement gathered steam in the early twentieth century. There is also little evidence that white southerners welcomed this nationwide public display of their violence. For one, lynching photographs rarely appeared in the mainstream press or in southern newspapers before the 1930s, and then only under exceptional circumstances, even though large, urban newspapers had the technology to do so beginning in the 1890s. A Memphis journalist in 1892 reported, for example, that he had been given a photograph from a recent lynching in Mississippi only under the "express pledge" that he neither publish the image nor identify the men in the picture. Although this reporter deemed the lynching legitimate under "unwritten law" because of the ghastliness of the black man's alleged crime, he still "thought [it] best to preserve the secrecy of the transaction."[57]

This circumspection about publishing images stemmed not just from a desire to protect the identities of mob members. In 1895, the *Atlanta Constitution* was horrified that the *New York World* published a photograph of the burning of Robert Hilliard in Tyler, Texas, presumably the same image that Texas residents later reproduced in stereograph cards. Although the paper agreed that Hilliard was a "criminal monster" who committed a "diabolical crime," it objected to the display of the photograph because it "pander[ed] to a base taste" of those "readers who delight in everything that is exceptionally horrible." The *Atlanta Constitution* further expressed concern that such images only fueled the national perception that "the South was a land of barbarians." To publish the lynching photograph was, in this sense, a form of "pictorial libeling" against the good people of the South. The *Dawson (Ga.)*

News met with similar objections when it published a photograph of the hanged bodies of five men, lynched in 1916 for their alleged involvement in the murder of a sheriff in a nearby county. The editor consequently apologized in print for his "bad judgment" and expressed "regret" for "having offended any one's sense of propriety."[58] These protests undoubtedly stemmed from elite and middle-class concerns about decorum and reputation. Much like the women of Vicksburg, Mississippi, the respectable classes might condone, encourage, and even participate in a lynching, but they did not want that violence put on public view, even as other working- and middle-class people used those images to acclaim their solidarity with social elites.

For similar reasons, although white-owned newspapers often lingered over the graphic details of lynchings, they almost never chose to publish photographs of the actual lynchings, even when they had access to them. For instance, the *Dallas Times-Herald* printed a number of uncredited photographs related to the lynching of Allen Brooks in 1910, including shots of the courtroom where he was captured and street scenes after the lynching was over. If the paper had access to these images, it presumably had access to pictures of the lynching itself, at least one of which had appeared on a postcard, but opted not to print them. The *Atlanta Constitution* likewise had access to a copy of a photograph from Leo Frank's 1915 lynching, but it did not include the image in its lengthy and detailed news stories about the lynching. It instead printed images of the woods near where Frank was hanged and of the crowd that came to view Frank's body, which was laid out for public viewing at a local funeral home. A photograph of Frank's lynched corpse surrounded by the men who hanged him would have been too volatile to publish on the pages of the city paper, especially considering the national condemnation the lynching had generated, even as thousands of Atlantans lined up to view Frank's corpse and "mercenary photographers" sold copies of Frank's lynching photograph for twenty-five cents each. As the antilynching newspaper the *Columbia (S.C.) State* glibly reported, "The heroic Marietta lynchers are too modest to give their photographs to the newspapers."[59]

Mob participants wanted to retain control over lynching photographs, presumably to govern both what images were recorded and where they were circulated. As discussed in chapter 6, this control became even more important as the antilynching movement sought to acquire and publicize these images to protest lynching throughout the 1920s and 1930s. Indeed, there is evidence that when outsiders, including journalists, attempted to photograph lynchings, they were thwarted. When it was announced that Raymond

Gunn was to be lynched in Maryville, Missouri, on 12 January 1931, the *St. Joseph (Mo.) News-Press* sent a reporter and staff photographer to cover the scene. Gunn, who was accused of raping and murdering a white school-teacher, was abducted from police custody as his trial was set to begin and taken to the schoolhouse where the crime took place. There, before a crowd of over 2,000 people, Gunn was chained to the roof, and the whole building was set on fire. Several times throughout the course of events, members of the mob confronted the *St. Joseph News-Press* photographer, yelling, "No ko-daking, no pictures. . . . That's our orders." Although the photographer was forced to open his camera and destroy his film, he evidently was able to take some pictures of the mob surrounding the building and pulling Gunn to the roof and to hide the film in his car. One of these images appeared on the front page of the *St. Joseph News-Press*. According to one report, however, once the fire had begun, members of the mob proceeded to take their own photographs of the scene.[60]

Even if newspapers concealed lynching images from public view, the pro-duction of lynching images for sale, especially through postcards, facilitated their dissemination. Yet photographs and postcards, perhaps even more than other kinds of commodities, acquired meaning not through mass con-sumption but through individualized expression and sentiment. The mor-bid popularity of lynching postcards actually coincided with a larger post-card craze in the United States between the late 1890s and World War I. Postcards advertised consumer products and tourist destinations, as they do today. But because many newspapers did not have the technology to print high-quality images until the 1920s, postcards also presented for the public a visual record of newsworthy events. Most Americans witnessed sig-nificant events, places, and people through the production and circulation of postcards. In this period, for instance, postcards of natural disasters like hurricanes and earthquakes were commonly produced and sent around the country. The sale of postcards declined only as newspapers began printing more photographs in their pages.[61]

Americans also commonly used postcards as a convenient and inexpen-sive form of everyday communication, a use that was facilitated by rural free delivery, which the U.S. Postal Service instituted in 1898, allowing small-town and rural inhabitants to receive their mail at their homes. That same year, the postal service began offering a reduced rate for privately printed cards (as opposed to commercial trade cards). Soon after, the private post-card began to flourish as a form of personal correspondence; it declined only as telephones came into use. By 1902, Kodak had issued postcard-size

photographic paper on which images could be printed directly from negatives, and it subsequently offered to print postcards from a photographer's
negatives for ten cents a card. Professional photographers routinely created postcards of local scenes and events to be sold not only to tourists as
souvenirs but also to local residents who wanted personal images to send
to friends and relatives. Amateur photographers could also have their own
snapshots made into postcards. While they were undeniably commercial
products, postcards, in these ways, were also extensions of private photographs, a visual form of connection and communication between loved
ones.[62]

Although, within this context, lynching postcards appear grotesque, they
testify to the sense in which spectators of lynchings deemed these events
both customary and spectacular, much in the way they would find other special community events significant enough, both socially and personally, to
make into postcards. Moreover, by writing on the card, often directly on the
image, the spectator could render a communal and commercialized event
personal and intimate. As noted above, Joe Meyers marked the postcard of
Will Stanley's charred body to show his parents where he was in the crowd.
"This is the barbeque we had last Saturday," he wrote. After witnessing the
1910 lynching of Allen Brooks in Dallas, Texas, one man, who was apparently
visiting Dallas, sent a postcard to a doctor friend in Lafayette, Kentucky, on
which he wrote, "I saw this on my noon hour. I was very much in the bunch.
You can see the negro hanging on a telephone pole." He drew an arrow on
the front to mark the body of the lynched man, which is almost obscured by
the large crowd. For this man, witnessing the lynching—which, amid that
large crowd, he probably did not see clearly—was less significant than being
part of a big city gathering. Some postcard senders noted for the recipient
a personal connection to the lynching. "He killed Earl's grandma. She was
Florence's mother," wrote Aunt Myrtle to her niece or nephew regarding the
lynching of Lige Daniel in Center, Texas, in 1920. Spectators at lynchings
presumably also bought these cards to keep as personal souvenirs, since
they provided a portable and tangible memory of an event they witnessed
or participated in themselves.[63]

The marking and sending of postcards thus transformed what was a
mass social event into something individual and meaningful, even as the
cards were mass produced and sold by the dozens. Indeed, the ideological
significance of these images—that is, their capacity to substantiate white
supremacist views—depended on this specific contextualizing or personal
signification. As antilynching advocates well knew, once these photographs

were removed from these contexts, entirely new meanings could be imprinted on them.

The transmission of lynching photographs became increasingly controversial precisely because people began to recognize that these images could produce all sorts of unintended consequences. In 1908, the U.S. postal laws and regulations were amended to forbid the mailing of "matter of a character tending to incite arson, murder or assassination," a prohibition that included lynching images, since, as will be discussed in later chapters, authorities feared they could incite racial strife or violence. This ruling did not stop the production of lynching photographs, as the many postcards of post-1908 lynchings attest, but they were now sent in envelopes or circulated locally. On the back of a postcard of a quadruple lynching in Russellville, Kentucky, the sender wrote, "I bought this in Hopkinsville. 15c. each. They are not on sale openly. . . . A law was passed forbidding these to be sent through the mail or to be sold anymore." According to the *Atlanta Constitution*, when the assistant postmaster in Hopkinsville attempted to send the same postcard through the mail, he received a notice on behalf of the U.S. attorney general that such material was "not mailable." This news story itself suggests that southerners were taking note of both the circulation of lynching photographs and the governmental attempt to suppress them.[64]

Images from early lynchings, like that of Henry Smith in Paris, Texas, in 1893, were thus more likely to circulate across the country than were later images, reaching places as far away as New York and Seattle. Even in these instances, those Americans who consumed these images casually, as entertainment, did so because they were relatively detached from the crimes and racial fears that gave rise to lynchings. To be sure, many white Americans would have derived satisfaction from these images out of their racist sensibilities about innate black depravity and their own fears about black crime. But their encounters with these images were less fraught, less weighted. For these Americans, a photograph of an actual lynching might have borne no more meaning than representations of fictional lynchings they encountered in motion pictures or in pictorial magazines—as a gory and thrilling but distant "local custom."

In 1898, Frank Sweet, a teenage amateur photographer in West Mansfield, Massachusetts, staged photographs of his own "lynching," with his father and a friend serving as the vigilantes (figures 3.15 and 3.16). Lynching was long outmoded in Massachusetts by 1898, suggesting that these men were re-creating an event that was far removed from their own everyday experiences as New England farmers and businessmen. These men did not

intend merely to "play" at lynching, which the camera happened to capture; rather, they sought to create their own lynching photographs. In doing so, they mimicked the popular iconography of lynching that they had gathered either from narrative accounts or from images that they had seen. For instance, by dressing themselves in ragged overalls — clothing that other family photographs make evident they did not normally wear — they reproduced the widespread notion that lynching was a rural and backwoods practice. As alarming as these images are, they also suggest that lynching, for them, had become quite detached from the ideological significance it bore for

FIGURES 3.15 AND 3.16 Frank and William Otis Sweet feign a lynching, West Mansfield, Massachusetts, 1898. Courtesy of John Wood Sweet.

the white southerners who produced and circulated lynching photographs. After all, the Sweets could very well have been copying imagery not from southern, racialized lynchings but from older traditions of western, frontier-style lynchings that held sway within American popular culture well into the twentieth century. Indeed, these images resemble the stereograph scene shown in figure 3.14. What is more, these images, taken in sequence and then juxtaposed, do more than simply re-create lynching photographs; they effectively form a two-frame moving image. In fact, by 1898, these men may have first encountered lynching images through motion pictures.[65]

4

❖ ❖ ❖

THEY NEVER WITNESSED SUCH A MELODRAMA

Early Moving Pictures

ON A SPRING EVENING in 1911, a mob of about fifty white men in the small city of Livermore, Kentucky, lynched Will Potter on the stage of the local opera house. Potter was the black manager of a segregated poolroom where Clarence Mitchell, a young white liveryman, and a friend had come to play. When they refused to pay, Potter asked them to leave, explaining, according to one local report, that "a negro poolroom is not the place for white men." A fight ensued, and Mitchell left the poolroom, "cursing" Potter and daring him to come out. Potter "walked to the door with a pistol in his hands and fired two shots." The city marshal almost immediately arrested Potter and brought him to the theater, securing him in a dressing room behind the stage. As news of the incident spread throughout the town, a mob of "infuriated citizens" formed and broke into the opera house, overpowering the marshal and his deputies. The men then took Potter to the center of the stage, tied him down, and turned on the footlights. Arranging themselves in the orchestra pit, they, on cue, began to shoot.[1] "Of about 200 shots fired, nearly half entered the body of the black man," reported the *Louisville (Ky.) Courier-Journal*. "The remainder tore to shreds the woodland scenery, arranged for the presentation of a more mild drama." Recognizing that the lynching itself was theater, the news account went on to exclaim that "the little Operahouse at Livermore . . . never witnessed such a melodrama."[2]

The lynching of Will Potter was not a mass spectacle lynching; that is, there were no crowds of spectators there to witness a mob of fifty white men avenging an attempted murder. But if photographing a lynching staged for the camera exaggerated images of white virtue and black degeneracy, the lynching of Potter placed in macabre relief the ways in which white southerners perceived lynching as a staged performance, a "melodrama" in which white righteousness triumphed over black villainy. That Potter was lynched in an opera house may appear to be an unfortunate coincidence, except that the mob did not simply shoot Potter where it found him. The lynchers evidently saw the dramatic potential of their violence; even without a crowd of supporters and spectators, they chose to turn on the "glaring footlights" of the stage and position Potter center stage. And by placing themselves in the orchestra pit rather than on stage with Potter, they positioned themselves as both performers and audience—spectators to their own drama.[3]

News reporters made much of this "melodrama" at the opera house, so that an otherwise all too typical lynching became national, and even international, news. The story, for instance, appeared in a Paris newspaper, Le Petit Journal, along with a drawing depicting the scene. "Whatever else may be said about the inhabitants of Livermore, Ky., it cannot be denied that in them the dramatic sense is strongly developed," opined the New York Times, "for, when they deemed it expedient to lynch a negro, they managed to do the familiar deed in a way not only entirely, but highly picturesque in the literal meaning of that much-abused word." Other accounts exaggerated the event, reporting that the mob had seized Potter from the jail and taken him to the opera house. According to these reports, the mob charged admission to the lynching and allowed those who had purchased orchestra seats to empty their guns into Potter, while those in the gallery were permitted only one shot each. This sensational attention ultimately led the "better elements" of Livermore to "deeply deplore the action of the mob" and support a legal indictment against "the members of the lawless band" to, according to the county attorney, "erase the blot on the fair name" of the county.[4]

This turn of events was also undoubtedly influenced by the fact that the whole affair began in an amusement hall of ill repute associated with African American men—the poolroom where Potter and Mitchell fought. The "better elements" of Livermore could easily abandon their support for a mob that rallied after a brawl in a poolroom operated for blacks. After all, according to the Owensboro (Ky.) Daily Inquirer, the fight began because Potter attempted to uphold Jim Crow segregation by telling Mitchell that "a negro poolroom is not the place for white men." Nevertheless, despite Mitchell's occupation as a liveryman and his presence at the pool hall, most papers initially represented him, as they did most white victims in these cases, as a "prominent citizen of the little town" who showed restraint against Potter's aggression. The lynchers, the ones who were indicted at least, were not the poorest in town—several of these men were able to, or had friends who could, post their bonds of $500 or $1,000—but neither were they well established or well respected. They were skilled laborers, like Mitchell, or small business owners, all "well-known" young men, except for W. N. Davis, a sixty-year-old man engaged in the "restaurant business." Two of the "leaders" were Clifton Schroeter, the proprietor of a "floating" photography studio, and Jesse Schroeter, also a photographer.[5]

By choosing to lynch Potter in the opera house, these men were in some sense recognizing the ways in which entertainment was bound up with violence, as well as the ways in which violence itself was a source of visual amusement. At the turn of the century, most southern cities and towns, even small towns like Livermore, had an opera house where white townspeople of all classes watched high dramas, vaudeville acts, minstrel shows, and, at times, motion pictures. In lynching Potter in the opera house, therefore, these working men were acclaiming their act of vengeance as respectable drama in a way that the poolroom brawl was decidedly not.

As audience members, the men who lynched Potter had very likely witnessed scenes of hangings and shootings on that same opera house stage. Between 1897 and 1905, in the early years of motion pictures, a number of short, one-reel films were made that depicted lynchings and extralegal hangings. In addition, several films reproduced the legal executions of notorious criminals; two rendered on-screen live executions.[6] These films were the extension of the spectacle created when showmen hawked the photographs and sounds of Henry Smith's 1893 lynching in Paris, Texas, discussed in the previous chapter. The producers of these films, who were white, urban, and northern, intended to seduce viewers by offering the sadistic thrill of watching another's violent death and satisfying a perverse curiosity about executions and hangings. Advertisements in trade periodicals and catalogs for these films described them as "thrilling," "exciting," and "ghastly," as well as "realistic," "accurate," and "detailed." The filmmakers in this sense appealed to sensational and sadistic desires that were aroused in modern, turn-of-the-century urban life, an appetite for morbid thrills that cinema both exploited and satisfied.[7]

White moviegoers in the South, however, saw these films at a time when it was still possible to witness executions and lynchings firsthand. This is not to say that the lynching in Livermore's opera house would not have happened without these films. But the reception of these pictures in the South underscores that white southerners understood lynching as a theatrical spectacle that dramatized and made publicly manifest their notions of white supremacy. Southern audiences for these films even, at times, replicated the crowds at a lynching, and they were similarly imagined as a racially unified and restrained group. Determining the reception of these films is unquestionably difficult; most films in this period were not reviewed, and descriptive accounts of audiences' reactions are rare. Nevertheless, the catalogs that advertised the films for potential exhibitors, as well as the films themselves, do reveal an intended spectator. We can thus ascertain how moviemakers expected viewers to respond. Actual response, of course, may not have matched the intended reaction, as different spectators inevitably brought their own cultural experiences to bear on what they saw on-screen and interpreted these films based on their particular social and historical positions, imposing their own assumptions and experiences on what they were viewing.[8]

These films were primarily what have been called "cinema of attractions," a term coined to describe particular characteristics of early cinema that distinguished it from the classical narrative form that emerged later. Rather than presenting a story with complex plot and character development, "cinema of attractions" emphasized acts of display and exhibition presented expressly to the camera and intended to shock and thrill the viewer. These included tourist scenes, panoramas, fires and other disasters, circus scenes, and sexually suggestive scenes, as well as lynching and execution films. These films engaged and excited viewers through the presentation of an "attraction," marking the extraordinary by its very presence on the screen. They addressed the spectator directly, as if to say, "Look at this!" thereby foregrounding the act of voyeurism that is a constitutive element of film spectatorship. Spectators were not absorbed into the seamless fictional world of a narrative, as later classical Hollywood cinema insisted, but instead viewed the moving picture as onlookers or voyeurs, standing outside the action and looking onto it.[9]

Spectators, however, did not necessarily experience "cinema of attractions" as mere voyeurs. These films, despite their brevity and their emphasis on visual appeal, did encompass a logical progression of action across space and time, such as in a chase scene. In fact, the attraction and thrill of these films were inseparable from the stories they told. The filmmaker himself, in choosing what action to film and in framing it for the camera, acted as a silent narrator, directing the viewer's gaze and response to the action. In addition, exhibitors often provided audiences with context and narration when exhibiting the pictures. Exhibitors in this period had enormous amounts of control and flexibility in what films they showed, in what

order, and how often. Acting as early editors, exhibitors could construct
narratives from a series of one-shot films when deciding the arrangement
for film programs, and they would often rearrange or reexhibit certain films
based on audience preferences. For this reason, although spectators in different localities saw the same films, they did not receive them in the same
contexts.[10]

The scenes displayed in early cinema further acquired meaning through
audiences' foreknowledge. These films referenced stories, plays, and news
events that were already familiar to turn-of-the-century viewers. Spectators,
therefore, would have understood and received what might appear today
as simple, momentary shocks through larger, more complicated narratives.
Accordingly, white southerners who viewed lynching and execution films
would have brought their knowledge of and experiences with lynchings and
hangings to their viewing. Film audiences derived pleasure from these films
as entertainment, but they did so much as the spectators of lynching did, by
interpreting the film as a narrative of sin, crime, and the righteous avenging
of that crime.

Audiences would have, in this way, understood these films as abbreviated
melodramas that, like Will Potter's lynching, brought visual clarity to what
were otherwise messy and morally ambiguous acts of violence. It is thus
not insignificant that the *Louisville (Ky.) Courier-Journal* understood Potter's
lynching as "melodrama," which at the time was a popular theatrical form.
It was also one that translated easily to the cinema screen. In fact, by 1910,
cinematic melodrama had largely overtaken theatrical melodrama in popularity. Melodrama was an imprecise genre that encompassed a wide range of
elements, but most Americans at the time understood it primarily as a sensational and action-packed form of drama. The stories typically represented
virtuous and innocent victims under assault from rapacious, cruel, and often
dark-skinned villains. The form itself had emerged in the early nineteenth
century as a response to the moral and social upheavals of modern life, in
which people's understandings of authority, character, and their own social
position suddenly seemed up for grabs. Within this cultural climate, melodrama had particular appeal. It rendered the differences between good and
evil absolute and unmistakable, and, with the killing or punishment of the
villain, it then restored social and moral order.[11]

Prolynching narratives, of course, relied heavily on these tropes of melodrama. Spectators would have thus brought their familiarity with these
tropes to their viewing of lynching films. Indeed, in a critique of melodrama's gross excesses, critic Ludwig Lewisohn, writing for the *Nation*, com-

pared the "tribal passions" unleashed in melodrama to "the motive of a . . . lynching party." He lamented that "the melodrama . . . brings into vicarious play those forces in human nature that produce mob violence in peace and mass atrocities in war," especially since these plays represented the dark-skinned or foreign villain as an "unscrupulous rake" who "attacks the honor of native women."[12] Lynching films, in this sense, served to sensationalize and "bring into vicarious play" prolynching narratives. As cinematic melo-dramas, they also projected moral clarity and relative restraint onto both lynching violence and the sadistic pleasure of witnessing that violence. To be sure, early cinema, and melodrama more specifically, was marked by its sensory and emotional excess. The scenes depicted not only were highly sensational but were meant to agitate viewers emotionally and physically. All the same, these films, like lynching photographs, abstracted and con-tained the most morbid and ghastly aspects of lynching in silent, black and white images.

Although these films make evident the ways in which lynching, and the act of watching a lynching, gained cultural force and acceptability through modern sensationalism and commercialism—and southern audiences re-ceived them as such—audiences also enjoyed these pictures because they represented practices of popular justice that in many ways were at odds with the process of modernization. These films deployed modern visual technology and its sensationalistic and objectifying capacity in order to up-hold antimodern forms of social power. In a sense, they enabled people to use modernity against itself.

WHITE SOUTHERNERS RECEIVED execution and lynching films not only through their preconceived notions of and experiences with lynching but also through their newly formed conceptions of motion pictures. Because of their relative isolation, southerners were less likely to see motion pic-tures than were other Americans. There were fewer projectors and, later, fewer theaters per capita in the South than in any other section of the coun-try. Southerners therefore saw pictures less often, saw more second- and third-run pictures, traveled farther to see them, and viewed them in smaller venues.[13] Nevertheless, despite these obstacles, motion pictures were intro-duced quite early in the South. In fact, it is surprising just how accessible motion pictures were to southerners, even in small towns. Moving pictures had appeared by 1897 in large cities, like Atlanta and Dallas, and in medium-size cities, such as Vicksburg, Mississippi, and Rome, Georgia. Southerners in smaller cities and towns such as Statesboro, Georgia; Paris, Texas; and

Oxford, Mississippi, had opportunities to view motion pictures by the turn of the century. Before nickelodeons (small theaters that specifically exhibited motion pictures) arose, pictures were most often exhibited at the local opera house or a similar theater and presented between acts of vaudevillian and other theatrical productions. Moving pictures were also frequently presented at fairs and carnivals as sideshow attractions. Most rural and small-town southerners were introduced to cinema at these kinds of venues. The people of Lawrenceville, Georgia (whose population was 858 in 1900), for instance, were offered special train rates to attend the Georgia State Fair in nearby Atlanta, where Edison's Vitascope was being exhibited. Trains also regularly took people from Statesboro to Savannah to view various urban amusements.[14]

When moving pictures appeared in southern towns and cities, they were considered both an extraordinary marvel and a potentially troubling new form of amusement. Like other modern amusements emerging in the New South, southerners greeted motion pictures with a certain amount of trepidation, in part because theaters brought together different groups of people, huddled in the dark. Jim Crow seating, already in place in opera houses and other theaters, was of course imposed on cinema spectatorship. But white southerners also evaluated motion pictures in terms of moral and class respectability, especially since the pictures themselves projected images that might threaten traditional mores and values. In these early years of cinema, moving picture audiences would have thus been aware of themselves as spectators in a way that even ten or twenty years later they would not be. To watch a moving picture, whether in an opera house or at the park or carnival, was to position oneself socially and morally within the larger community. Indeed, much like other crowd activities, cinema spectatorship helped to construct and solidify people's class and racial identities. When white southerners encountered a lynching or execution film, they did so through these larger social conceptions of themselves within an unsettled and changing world.

Southerners did have opportunities to view these lynching films, though because newspapers rarely noted which motion pictures would be shown at any presentation, it is very difficult to determine which specific films audiences viewed. But the first showing of Edison's Vitascope in Dallas, Texas, in 1897, included both a "hanging scene" and a "lynching scene." These were probably Edison's *Lynching Scene*, described as "a lynching of a horse thief by a band of cowboys," and *Lynching Scene: A Genuine Lynching Scene*, which was also distributed in 1897 by the International Photographic Film

Company. Similarly, Edison's *Lynching Scene*, also known as *Lynching of a Horse-Thief*, played at the first picture showing in Vicksburg, Mississippi. This program of Edison pictures traveled through the Deep South, showing in cities like Jackson and New Orleans, as well as, most likely, some smaller cities. Several years later, the lynching film *Tracked by Bloodhounds* (Selig Polyscope, 1904) was shown at carnivals and fairs in Waco, Texas, and other southern cities.[15]

These films would have been viewed by a large cross-section of southern white society. Except for the largest cities, most southern towns had only one theater, where a wide range of productions, such as high dramas and vaudeville and minstrel shows, were shown. So, unlike theatergoers in large cities of the urban North, where theaters were largely segregated by class because of their neighborhood locations and the kinds of productions they presented, white southerners of various classes would have frequented the same theaters. To be sure, at opera houses and larger theaters, a class structure was established in the seating, with tickets ranging from seventy-five cents for orchestra seats to ten cents for the balcony. At parks and carnivals, however, audiences would have been less divided, and ticket prices for these venues tended to be cheaper. In places other than standard theaters, it was also easier for people to sneak viewings. In Rome, Georgia, for instance, moving pictures were often shown on the second floor of the old city hall, and young boys climbed trees to peer through the windows.[16]

That everyone, from the roughest young men to the most genteel ladies, viewed the same pictures in the same spaces caused a certain level of unease for some southerners, especially because early pictures frequently depicted scenes of sexual flirtation, dancing, boxing, and other troubling activities. Exhibitors thus took pains to assure their potential audiences that moving pictures were respectable, not only for the elite but for evangelicals of all classes, by advertising them as "high-class" or "clean and wholesome" entertainment. To dispel the particular notion that motion pictures might be unseemly for women, they encouraged women to attend by offering special matinees for ladies and children or by admitting for free any lady accompanying a gentleman with a higher-priced ticket. When a moving picture program was shown at the Vicksburg Carroll Hotel in 1897, the exhibitor advertised that "this is a place where the ladies of our city can freely go and be entertained in the most interesting manner." In 1904, the *Waco (Tex.) Herald-Tribune* reassured spectators that a visiting carnival that was showing moving pictures was "first-class, instructive as a rule. It is one show that the pulpit, press, and laity can endorse."[17] Such announcements clearly had

the pragmatic aim of widening ticket sales, but they also allowed spectators, particularly those in the middle and lower classes, to feel that what
was entertaining them was respectable and worthwhile. In turn, audiences
could believe that they themselves were genteel and virtuous.

Although audiences brought their conduct and expectations as spectators of theater to the moving picture show, cinema also required new habits
and assumptions. As southerners learned cinema spectatorship, they also
came to understand themselves, to some degree, as savvy and sophisticated
viewers. For example, early cinema spectators often found moving pictures,
not just the content but the technology itself, thrilling and wondrous for
the ways they captured reality and rendered the figures on the screen so
lifelike. A few films accordingly parodied the spectator who mistakes the
screen images for reality. These films implicitly congratulated the viewer
for his or her own sophistication in knowing better. Predictably, these films,
such as *The Countryman's First Sight of the Animated Pictures* (Paul, 1901) and
Uncle Josh at the Moving Picture Show (Edison, 1902), depicted the unknow-
ing and foolish spectator as a southern rube. Thus, to derive pleasure from
the southern rube's ignorance, southern viewers would have had to adopt
a northern, urban position and perceive themselves as knowing, modern
subjects.[18]

For white viewers, this sense of their own sophistication would have been
intensified by both the racial segregation in theaters and the racial domination exhibited on-screen. African Americans in smaller cities and towns
had less access to motion pictures than did whites, as they were usually restricted from smaller theaters that did not have balconies or space to cordon
off the gallery section. The opera house in Rome, Georgia, for instance, allowed African Americans to attend the theater only for minstrel shows, sitting in the balcony or the gallery. Racially segregated seats and ticket prices
were never publicized for other productions or exhibitions. Black southerners might have witnessed motion pictures at carnivals, street fairs, or open-
air theaters in parks, but their presence was never conspicuous enough to
warrant mention in the white press. Newspaper reports assumed film audiences were not only genteel and sophisticated but also white.[19]

A sense of white superiority was also made explicit within the content of
films. Some of the more popular pictures in this period included minstrel
comedies and other scenes of African Americans engaging in racially caricatured behaviors, like stealing chickens, dancing, and eating watermelon.
Regularly set in idyllic rural settings, these kinds of films projected distinctly
nonthreatening images of African Americans as docile, happy, and bound

FIGURE 4.1 *The Watermelon Contest*, Edison, 1896.

to the plantation, images that stood in sharp distinction to the perceived menaces of black mobility and autonomy in new urban environments. Particularly popular throughout this period, for instance, were films of African American men devouring watermelons, in which the eaters appear ravenous and animalistic, juice and flesh running down their chins. Though they present simple caricatures, the scenes captured white fears of black sexual bestiality but neutralized those fears by placing them in the comic setting of a plantation feast. The Edison Company's version of this subgenre, *The Watermelon Contest* (1896), was, incidentally, shown in Dallas in the same program with the hanging and lynching films, and audiences undoubtedly viewed them in relation to each other.[20]

Like Jim Crow segregation itself, these kinds of films affirmed and made manifest racial differences and hierarchies. Indeed, the heightened realism of cinema made those differences appear especially natural and fixed. Another popular "plantation" scene depicts a black mother who tries with comic frustration to wash her young child, who, because she is not white, never appears clean. Audiences in Jackson and Vicksburg, Mississippi, saw Edison's *The Morning Bath* at the first Vitascope showing in 1896. The *Vicksburg Evening Post*, which mistitled the film *Washing the Pickaninnies*, stressed that the film was "humorous" and, remarking on this new form of visual comedy, added that it "requires to be seen to properly enjoy it as the colored mother seems to do." This comment impelled the spectator to identify with the mother, but clearly, for the white viewer, the comedy of the film derived from a comic distance from the mother and her racialized "problem." White viewers' pleasure stemmed from their knowledge and satisfaction that, of course, this baby could never become white.[21]

IT WAS IN THIS CONTEXT that white southerners viewed lynching and execution films, and they would have carried to their viewing the same sense of themselves as racially and morally superior. These films also allowed white southerners to view cinematic representations of what in some localities could still be witnessed firsthand. In watching such a film, spectators could replicate the experience of witnessing an actual hanging, transferring the thrill they experienced there to the theater. That thrill was predicated on a sense of white superiority and unity, a sense that was constructed through watching, as a group, the punishment of a criminal and the restoration of social order.

Execution films were particularly significant because they allowed people to witness through the camera's eye what the state was denying them. Although these films represented state-sanctioned executions rather than lynchings, they offered viewers a thrill comparable to that which lynching films offered. In both types of films, viewers would have experienced pleasure in observing the deserved punishment for a terrible crime enacted and moral and racial "justice" exacted. Many of these pictures were associated with the Spanish-American War and the Boxer Rebellion and depicted the executions of foreign others.[22] There were also several early fictional renderings of a criminal's life and punishment that concluded with execution scenes. These were conspicuous morality tales that demonstrated for audiences the terrible consequences of leading a dissolute life of drinking, womanizing, and gambling.[23]

But more relevant here are several films that reproduced the private executions of actual criminals, which in effect made public what state authorities had deemed too ghastly for most people to witness. Although they were certainly sensational, particularly because people perceived them as authentic renderings of another's death, these films nevertheless both sanitized that death and neutralized the threat of the crowd, confining both to the relative acceptability of the theater. As discussed in chapter 1, many white southerners were actively resisting making state executions private at this time. While many state officials deemed public executions archaic and uncivilized, many people still felt a vested interest in seeing and participating in the enactment of punitive justice, particularly when the condemned were black and accused of crimes against whites. When white southerners tore down barriers and fences and climbed walls, trees, and rooftops to witness executions — and when they committed lynchings and gathered to watch the violence — they were wresting control over punishment and justice from the modernizing state.

Moving pictures that showed executions were exhibited at the very moment when many southerners were, in these ways, going to great lengths to witness them in person. In making these films, the producers effectively exploited this popular desire to view executions. Much like photographers, they offered modern technology as a viable surrogate for the act of witnessing firsthand. Advertisements accordingly stressed the authenticity of these films and attributed the thrills they would induce in audiences to their realism. The attraction that cinema offered, therefore, was a sensation based on the accurate eye-witnessing of the camera, even if the execution presented was a reproduction and the so-called realism of the scene was produced through trick photography.

For early cinema viewers, the realism of film was the most significant aspect of the new medium. These spectators expressed amazement not only at the events depicted on-screen but at the technology itself that could render those events with such lifelike precision. Commentators regularly celebrated cinema as the latest feat of modern science, calling it the "greatest marvel of the age" and a "triumph of man's intelligence." The *Jackson (Miss.) Clarion-Ledger* reported with awe that "all the figures [are] life size, and move around, walk, run, jump and dance as natural as real people." The *Dallas Morning News* exclaimed that "this marvelous electric machine gives to the figures on the canvas all the naturalness of movement of real life. The figures seem to be real, breathing, living personages." The objective realism of modern technology, in this respect, allowed audiences to experience a simulation of actual events. At the same time, cinema's attraction also lay in the notion that it dislodged people from reality and allowed them otherwise inaccessible experiences. Even several years after the debut of cinema, one writer marveled that trick photography offered the viewer the experience "of doing the most stunning things. You ride on a train, you go to war, you see a Paris hotel fire, and you see a battleship in action."[24] You could also witness an execution.

Certainly most viewers would not have comprehended the technology behind cinema. To these viewers, the realism of moving pictures appeared more wondrous and magical than it did rational or scientific. Modern vision was thus predicated on a very premodern relationship to spectacle. Edison himself was named the "Wizard Edison," and commentators deemed his Vitascope a "supernatural thing." As the *Vicksburg (Miss.) Evening Post* observed, "It is difficult to realize that the pictures cast on screen, which 'move and have their being,' are not really endowed with life." Audiences were described as being "held spell-bound by the wonderful spectacle," and one reporter deemed it "practical hypnotism." For people steeped in a spiritual and religious culture, this supernatural quality would only have intensified the power that cinema embodied and the access to truth and knowledge it presented.[25]

In these ways, the realism of cinema offered spectators immediate access to execution, itself a premodern spectacle laden with a spiritual and awesome power, at a time when public authorities were deeming them unsuitable for modern, "civilized" eyes. The marvel of film technology, however, provided a distance—it appears real, but it cannot be real—that allowed executions to become respectable viewing, even as technology allowed for the immediacy of the moment. Several pictures, in fact, recorded on film live executions that were otherwise private or restricted. *An Execution by Hanging* (American Mutoscope and Biograph Company, 1898) showed the execution of a black prisoner in Jacksonville, Florida. The film company's catalog describes the film as "a very ghastly, but very interesting subject." The prisoner climbs the gallows with several clergymen. The executioner then "adjusts the black cap and the noose about the prisoner's neck. The trap is touched and the body is seen to shoot through the air and hang quivering at the end of the rope." This description appears in the 1902 catalog, suggesting that the film was still popular enough with exhibitors to keep in their inventory.[26]

The condemned in this film was most likely Edward Heinson, who was convicted for "criminal assault" on a fourteen-year-old white girl. His execution was meant to be private, but, according to one local paper, many people, especially soldiers who were stationed in the city, "clamored for admittance." As a result, "the crowd filled the entire jail yard." When Heinson's body dropped, "there was no holding back of the mass of humanity that swayed forward," to which a policeman reportedly responded, "Gentlemen keep back, you are in the presence of death. One would think by your actions that you were seeing an ox killed." Although the crowd unquestionably enjoyed this execution because they had disidentified with and dehumanized the condemned, presumably the killing of an ox would not warrant this kind of attention. Indeed, what the film could not show was Heinson's final speech, in which he declared his innocence but stated he was "perfectly willing to hang" because "my soul is saved and I am free of all my sins."[27]

An Execution by Hanging abstracted this moment of penance and death, allowing viewers to project their own narrative of black crime and white retribution onto the picture. Since Heinson evidently took fifteen minutes to die of strangulation, the picture must have ended before he died. Viewers would thus have projected his death onto the film as well.[28] For the thousands of viewers not from Jacksonville, Florida, who might have seen this picture, Heinson was an anonymous black criminal meeting his death. Some exhibitors might have contextualized the film for viewers, explaining that this was an execution in Florida, but most probably did not, and viewers would have witnessed this brief picture amid a number of other scenes. They would then have contextualized it for themselves, based on their own knowledge and concerns about black criminality and public punishments.

The film, in extending the witnesses to this hanging to thousands of others from all parts of the country, allowed people who would not have been admitted to the jail yard to watch the execution on film. A young woman, for instance, had requested to see the execution. Yet, although she claimed "she had witnessed executions in many foreign countries, and desired to see a hanging," the sheriff refused. There was only one woman allowed in the yard, Heinson's young victim, "who was determined to witness the execution of her assailant, despite the efforts of Sheriff Broward to get her not to do so." Her presence was considered "an unusual feature of the hanging," and the paper was careful to report that she was accompanied by a male relative. Whereas women were not allowed to attend the execution, they would have been able to watch it as part of a moving picture show.

In this respect, despite the "realism" and "accuracy" that cinema offered, it also created a detachment that allowed spectators to view subjects they would consider unbearable or unacceptable to witness live. For instance, although many Protestant groups considered Passion plays and theatrical reproductions of Christ's life and crucifixion sacrilegious, these groups embraced cinematic Passion plays as a popular means to edify and evangelize the public. Their relative comfort with religious films as opposed to religious theater stemmed in part from the fact that cinema, particularly silent, black and white film, abstracted the flesh and blood from the production. In what one scholar has called the "absence of presence," early cinema made real beings appear almost unearthly and supernatural, in effect, more spiritual. The term "absence of presence" recalls Walter Benjamin's thesis that photography and cinema "emancipate" the work of art from its "aura," or its basis in sacred ritual. Cinematic representations of Passion plays thus detached Christ's story from its sacred origins in a way that theatrical representations could not, which ultimately rendered the former more acceptable to American Protestant audiences. Yet this detachment from the "aura" was also what supposedly enabled Christian viewers to find spiritual meaning in Passion films.[29]

Similarly, boxing matches were illegal in most states in the 1890s, but moving picture exhibitors routinely showed them as parts of their programs. The film of the famed heavyweight match between Jim Corbett and Bob Fitzsimmons, filmed in 1897 in Nevada, where boxing was legal, was one of the most popular early films and attracted much attention in every town and city where it played. When the film came to the Dallas opera house in 1897, the *Dallas Morning News* marveled that "the triumph of the photographic science represented in the 'living pictures' as it were, is incomprehensible to the lay mind. Every movement of the numerous figures appearing in the kaleidoscope scene is absolutely true to life. . . . The blood on Fitzsimmons' face, brought in evidence by the terrible punishment inflicted by Corbett in the early rounds, can be recognized." Yet, despite this gruesome realism and despite that no respectable lady would have attended a live boxing match, the paper reported that, at an earlier showing of the film, there were "quite a number of ladies in attendance and while they were not as interested as the men, they found nothing but the most genteel could witness." Once boxing films became legitimate entertainment, boxing itself was gradually legalized in many states.[30]

A comparable dynamic was at work in execution films. Although the catalog description emphasized the "ghastly" nature of *An Execution by Hanging* and highlighted that the film made visible the distortions of the condemned's body, the film's silent abstraction of Heinson's suffering and death abated the power of that moment. Moreover, the presentation of the film as part of a program along with other films, as one of many spectacles on display, made the execution less extraordinary than actual executions were for southerners. By removing the execution from its place in very local and communal rituals of racialized punishment and justice, it rendered the execution merely sensational spectacle and entertainment. But in doing so, the execution film, like the Passion play, could offer new meanings for viewers. The execution could appear more ghostly, or even "ghastly," in its abstraction. And, though the execution, now commercialized for national audiences, was detached from its local meaning, individual viewers would have projected their own local and personal narratives onto the cinema screen, much as they did with lynching postcards.

The only other known film of an actual execution from this era is *The Hanging of William Carr*, which similarly presented for the public an execution that local authorities had attempted to make private.[31] There is evidence, however, that this film, although it was highly popular, met with some resistance because it sensationalized Carr's execution. Carr was a white laborer convicted of murdering his own three-year-old daughter in Liberty, Missouri, in 1897. Both the crime and the trial, in which Carr confessed to drowning the girl in a river for being "quarrelsome," received prominent attention in Kansas City and St. Louis. The *St. Louis Post Dispatch* included large sketchings of Carr committing the murder, as well as a detailed narrative of his conversion to Christianity on the day before his execution. His crime apparently so outraged people in Liberty that Carr was removed to Kansas City to prevent a lynching. Unsurprisingly, crowds of spectators arrived to witness his execution in December 1897, even though the sheriff had arranged for the gallows to be enclosed with a fence. The sheriff did sell tickets to the hanging, but he turned away many others. One man tried in vain to bribe the sheriff with five dollars. A near riot broke out when the trap was sprung before hundreds of people waiting outside the fence could gain entry.[32]

Carr's execution is a prime example of the ways in which the state's goals and the people's desires were becoming increasingly at odds. The sheriff, wanting the execution to be performed as quickly, cleanly, and orderly as possible, pulled the lever releasing Carr as soon as Carr said he was ready. The crowds waiting to see, however, wanted a slower hanging and were outraged that the execution had taken place so quickly, before they had a chance to enter the gallows yard. According to one news account, within the yard, the crowd, "as if moved by a single impulse, nearly all rushed forward, calling, crying, shrieking and laughing as they surged under the gallows and packed close around the grotesque thing. . . . The crowd scrambled and pushed and shrieked. It would not be satisfied. Men were angry and cursed one another and blasphemed." Hundreds outside the yard pushed to get in: "They cried and hooted at the Sheriff. Finally, in their excitement, they attempted to bear down the barricade." The sheriff threatened the crowd to stay back, but "they swept back the guards at the door and burst their way through the frail stockyard." Once able to see Carr's swinging form, the crowd quieted and quickly dispersed.[33]

This incident prompted an editorial in the *St. Louis Post-Dispatch* calling for an end to public executions on the grounds that certain groups of people should not witness such a "horrible scene." Claiming that the crowd consisted of "young girls, children, and, perhaps, mothers," the paper asked, "What man of refined instincts would wish his children, his wife, or his mother to attend a public execution?" Arguing that "public executions are a survival from the times when the carrying out of the law's sentence was looked upon as an act of revenge," the editorial suggested that "only those necessary to carry the sentence into effect and report the result should be present on such an occasion," positing a clear distinction between the people's desire for revenge for a crime in which they had a vested interest and the state's need for social control. Notably, the issue was not the white men who wanted to see Carr's hanging but those men who lacked "refined instincts" who would allow their womenfolk to witness such a scene.[34]

This newspaper described its position against the crowds who wanted to see Carr's execution in terms of class and moral sensibilities, but the people who wanted to witness the execution made the same moral distinctions between themselves and Carr. Although Carr was a white man, reports described him as illiterate, un-Christian — until his dramatic conversion — a "fiend," and a "demon in human form." As with the lynchings and executions of black men, the crowds of spectators clamoring to see his punishment disidentified with Carr, seeing themselves as rightful agents of his punishment. The white men who dominated the crowd were also claiming their masculine prerogative to protect white women and avenge their suffering, a prerogative Carr abandoned when he killed his daughter.[35]

Amid all this controversy, one entrepreneur was able to secure a moving picture of Carr's execution. Frank Guth was a manager of the Kansas City branch of the American Phonographic Company, which had previously made a phonographic recording of Carr telling his story from jail. For the execution, Guth secured permission to set up a camera just outside the enclosure, protected by a "little house." He cut a hole in the fence and recorded Carr's execution from the moment preparations began to the moment he was hanged. Guth had hired Percy Arnet, a professional cameraman, to film the hanging, but Arnet "weakened" at the last minute, "saying he wouldn't see the hanging if he were paid at the rate of $100 for every picture he should take." Arnet's concern was apparently not with filming the event — he had presumably agreed to it before he arrived in Liberty — but with seeing the hanging.[36]

Guth, who took over camera duties himself, harbored no apparent qualms about witnessing the hanging, although one reporter commented on the eerie juxtaposition of the somber mood of the hanging and the "merry clicking" of the camera. Yet, as noted, the crowd gathered for the hanging was hardly somber. As soon as Carr dropped, Guth explained, "the mob then tried to break down the stockade and shake it so I stopped the cinematograph and left. I'd like to have had a picture of that mob, though, but I was afraid they would smash my camera if they saw it, so I slid out." Unlike the lynching photographer, Guth saw himself as an outsider, attempting to record both the hanging and the mob as a spectacle for other outsiders. So although the crowd evidently did not mind that the hanging itself was filmed, Guth believed that those mobbing the gallows would not want their behavior recorded. Unlike a still-image camera, which, as noted in the previous chapter, people would have recognized as a personal and relatively localized technology, a motion picture camera would have appeared unfamiliar, and the images themselves would unavoidably be produced for audiences far beyond Liberty or even Missouri.[37]

Guth cleverly premiered the pictures of Carr's execution in Kansas City and St. Louis, places where Carr's name and crime were notorious and where audiences had a connection to and investment in the film. Indeed, the film allowed those who knew of Carr but had not seen his execution to do so. Advertisements for the film promoted it as not merely a reproduction but as real as the actual event. One report called it the "second hanging of William Carr." In Kansas City, the film was initially scheduled to be shown at the Academy of Music, with prices for admission ranging from fifteen to fifty cents. There were to be thirty other "interesting views" playing on the program, but *The Hanging of William Carr* was advertised as the feature.[38]

The exhibition of the film in Kansas City, however, brought the same reaction from elites as the hanging itself had. It did not play at the Academy of Music, as planned, but rather at a local phonograph shop. The presence of "loud-voiced" barkers outside the store, as well as outside Guth's company, prompted several people to protest. An editorial in the *Kansas City Star* denounced the film's promoters for having "exceeded the limits of decency," claiming that the film "possesses no features that can possibly appeal to civilized and enlightened people." Despite that Guth boasted in national trade advertisements that his picture was playing to "standing room only" crowds in Kansas City, the *Star* reported that attendance was lacking at the showing. "Timid people shudder as they pass by and hear the hideous story of the hanging exploited," the report noted. Only two women were present at the showing; the audience was dominated by boys "who should be protected by the law against such demoralizing influences." In addition, a restaurant manager next door to the theater complained to the police that the showing of the film "was a nuisance and had driven business away." The police responded by forcing the "barkers to stand inside the door." In this case, the public spectacle of the hanging, as opposed to the hanging itself, was considered more than what respectable people should witness. It is impossible to know whether other execution films, particularly *An Execution by Hanging*, met with the same resistance, or whether Carr's race made the public exploitation of his death less acceptable. What is more, *The Hanging of William Carr* might not have brought any protest at all if it had been shown at the more respectable Academy of Music, inserted within a larger program, as planned, rather than as the feature at a phonograph shop with barkers shouting the story as if at a carnival. In any event, Guth was successful enough with the film in Kansas City to promote and distribute it nationwide.[39]

In addition to these two live executions films, at least two prominent films reenacted the private executions of notorious criminals whose crimes and punishments were reported extensively by the press. These films served in some respects as early newsreels, visualizing for theater audiences the most sensational news of the day. In fact, audiences would not have necessarily realized they were viewing reenactments. The American Mutoscope and Biograph Company produced two related films in 1905, *Reading the Death Sentence* and *An Execution by Hanging* (reusing the title from its 1898 film of the hanging of Edward Heinson) to dramatize the hanging of Mary Rogers, a young Vermont housewife convicted of killing her husband. Both films, each comprising only one shot, recorded the actual death chamber in which she died but replaced Rogers and the hangman with actors. Rogers's lawyers had unsuccessfully appealed her case to the U.S. Supreme Court and were hoping the governor would offer her a reprieve at the last moment. Thus when American Mutoscope and Biograph made the films, over a week before the execution was scheduled, it produced an alternate version, titled *Reprieve from the Scaffold*, in which a messenger arrives at the last moment to stop the hanging. Evidently, both versions were released to exhibitors about a week after Rogers's execution. Presumably exhibitors were able to choose which ending to show. This series of films is thus a perfect illustration of the ways in which exhibitors acted as film editors in this period, creating narratives for their audiences through the films they selected and the order in which they showed them.[40]

Several years before American Mutoscope and Biograph reproduced Rogers's hanging for the camera, the Edison Company released *Execution of*

Czolgosz, a "realistic imitation" of the electrocution of President McKinley's assassin, which had occurred in October 1901 at Auburn Prison in New York. Because of the obvious notoriety of this case, this film was a popular moneymaker for Edison's company, especially since many Americans had a very real desire to see Czolgosz brought to justice for his crime. The film also allowed audiences to marvel at the electric chair as a wondrous and efficient method of killing. Both northern and southern audiences, however, would have understood this film not merely as a momentary look at a spectacular event but as the climax of a longer story about McKinley's death and Czolgosz's criminality. Even more than other execution films, *Execution of Czolgosz* was not simply a thrilling attraction; it was encoded with a more complicated narrative.[41]

The trial of Leon Czolgosz, an anarchist of Polish descent, had drawn national attention, including in the South. In Savannah, Georgia, for instance, special train rates were offered to people traveling north to the trial. The execution, however, was performed privately, with only twenty-six people in attendance. People around the country were nevertheless eager to see the assassin put to death. As Czolgosz arrived at Auburn Prison to receive his death sentence, crowds of people surrounded him, hooting and yelling, some shouting, "Kill him, kill him, throw a brick at him!" In at least one town, in Long Island, a mob hanged Czolgosz in effigy before a crowd of over 1,000 people. Newspapers included drawings and detailed descriptions of Czolgosz's dying moments, which apparently were so horrid that "witnesses fled from the chamber, many of them visibly affected."[42]

Less than two weeks after the execution, Edison presented a "detailed reproduction" of the execution for American audiences, "faithfully carried out from the description of an eye-witness." It consists of four shots, beginning with a panoramic panning shot of Auburn Prison. A train then passes in the foreground, and the camera follows. This shot not only establishes the scene for the viewer but also puts Auburn Prison, already nationally known as one of the first modern state prisons and the first to house an electric chair, on impressive display. The moment of Czolgosz's death itself appears painless, as the actor shows no visible signs of distress. He merely breathes in and falls slightly limp. A doctor takes his pulse with a stethoscope and motions that he is dead.[43]

The film in this way presents electrocution as a clean and humane triumph of modern technology, even though it was in fact not necessarily less horrid than hanging, as the witnesses who fled the execution could attest. What was, for some, unbearable to see in person could, through cinematic

FIGURE 4.2 *Execution of Czolgosz*, Edison, 1901.

representation, become not only tolerable but wondrous. Electrocution was still a novel technology, which promoters, including Edison himself, insisted stood as a modern, civilized alternative to the barbarity of hanging. *Execution of Czolgosz* was thus a "cinema of attractions" where the attraction on display was not just Czolgosz's death but also the act of electrocution itself, as well as the ability of modern technology to reproduce this act on film. Advertisements, for instance, made much of the film's use of "dissolving effects," the latest advance in film photography.[44]

Despite that the film abstracted Czolgosz's execution, however, audiences would undoubtedly have projected all sorts of preconceived understandings of Czolgosz and his crime onto what they were watching. For many Americans, including many southern whites, their moral condemnation of Czolgosz became infused with racial and religious superiority. Czolgosz was a laborer and a follower of Emma Goldman, who said he assassinated McKinley because of the president's neglect for the poor. News reports made much of his foreign origins, his radical political beliefs, and his lack of Christian belief, integrating all three characteristics into a general portrait of moral culpability and weakness. For instance, even though Czolgosz was born in Detroit, reporters expressed surprise that he spoke "perfect English."[45]

Southern newspapers, in particular, made much of Czolgosz's atheism. Czolgosz refused the ministrations of a Catholic priest, who nevertheless maintained that the anarchist had become a Christian. Popular opinion in the South, however, declared him "unrepentant," showing "no signs of sorrow for his heinous crime." The *Statesboro (Ga.) News* scoffed, "The good priest thinks he will die 'A Christian,' but the world will remember him only as an anarchist and an enemy of law and order and mankind." The writer was surprised that Czolgosz "reviled the Christian religion and denied its power to comfort and save" considering "what the very near future holds for him, what the great and unknowable beyond may hold for him." Although, to these southerners, Czolgosz's rejection of Christianity seemed his greatest crime, their condemnation of his religious and political views also became entwined with nativist and racist sentiments. For example, a brief editorial item in the *Statesboro (Ga.) News* sharply quipped, "It is hoped that Buffalo will attend to Czolgosz in short order. A man with such a name ought to be killed on general principle anyway." The writer added, tellingly, "The North has the anarchists, she is welcome to them, and with the anarchists and Filipinos on hand, they can let the South alone," no doubt referring to northern criticisms of southern lynching practices.[46]

FILMS THAT REPRODUCED extralegal lynchings offered audiences the same vicarious thrill that these execution films offered. They allowed viewers to witness a vengeance against crime and the restoration of social—and racial—order. Most early lynching films tended to be fictionalized reenactments of western "frontier" or southern-style vigilantism, produced as stock "attraction" scenes that could appeal to adventure-seeking northern and urban audiences. The catalog entry for *Avenging a Crime; or, Burned at the Stake* (Paley and Steiner, 1904), for example, described the mob's cries for vengeance as a "typical southern scene," and *Lynching Scene* (Edison, 1897) was advertised as "a typical frontier scene."[47] Southern audiences would presumably not have watched these films with distanced curiosity, however. Rather, they would have brought their own experiences with lynching, either as defenders or as witnesses, if not participants, to bear on their spectatorship of these films. Northerners would also have brought their own assumptions about race, crime, and social order to their viewing, but northerners—particularly the urban, immigrant, and working-class northerners who made up a large portion of motion picture audiences—would have had little, if any, personal experience with lynching. Indeed, lynching films might have introduced first- and second-generation immigrants to a "typical" American phenomenon. White southerners, on the other hand, were observing on-screen what they could witness firsthand. Lynching films, even those representing "frontier scenes," offered southern viewers more orderly and more sanitized renderings of mass, spectacle lynchings, renderings that could be repeated again and again.

The earliest of these pictures, like early execution films, were very brief, capturing only the hanging itself on film. As "cinema of attractions," they not only allowed audiences to witness an extraordinary event but also demonstrated film's ability to capture that event on-screen. For this reason, producers promoted them for their realism and accuracy. One of the first pictures, *Lynching Scene: A Genuine Lynching Scene* (International Photographic Film, 1897), was touted as revealing an actual lynching in Texas. The catalog entry called it "the most thrilling and realistic subject ever offered for sale" and revealed that "by contract with the authorities, names of party and place cannot be given," insinuating that the film depicted a real lynching. This clause, along with the word "genuine" in the title, was probably merely a ruse to make the film appear authentic and thus "a most impressive and stirring subject." Although the race of the victim was not identified, the catalog entry for the film further described it much the way many southern, racial lynchings were portrayed: "This scene shows an angry mob overpowering the sheriff, storming the jail, and dragging their prisoner to the nearest telegraph pole, from which he is immediately swung into eternity as bullet after bullet is fired into his writhing body." If the man were white, there would almost certainly have been some cue intimating that fact, as there were for other films.[48]

Although films like this one were exceedingly short, focusing on the momentary shock of the hanging, audiences would have imposed narrative meaning onto them. Viewers may have enjoyed the scenes out of morbid curiosity or gratuitous sadism, but they very likely derived satisfaction from watching the lynching victim's death because they had already made assumptions about that victim's moral culpability. In Vicksburg, Mississippi, Edison's Vitascope films, which included *Lynching Scene* (listed as *Lynching of a Horse-Thief*), were exhibited for one full week in the local opera house to sold-out and standing-room-only crowds. The "regular programme" consisted of sixteen films, including scenes of a Jim Corbett prizefight and the famous on-screen kiss between May Irwin and Johnny Rice. Although the *Vicksburg Evening Post* reported that all the scenes were "much admired" and "gave unlimited satisfaction to the audience," the paper made special mention of the lynching scene, which was "so realistic that people of sensitive natures were somewhat shocked by [it], but [it] elicited hearty applause." The audience was, to be sure, applauding the "realistic" spectacle that the Vitascope was presenting them, just as they did for other scenes. But we must also consider that in the ten years preceding this showing, there had been thirteen lynchings—eleven of African American men—in the county and that an unidentified black man was lynched just four months later, in April 1897. The picture audience could very well have been applauding that the horse thief was caught and hanged, that the movie camera was able to capture this moment for them, and that they were able to witness it.[49]

Unlike an actual lynching, however, the cinematic lynching of the horse thief and the reenactment of "justice" that it represented could be witnessed repeatedly. As with a lynching photograph, in a film the condemned is put to death, only to be resurrected and murdered again on each viewing. Although the exhibitor in Vicksburg changed the program daily, bringing in new films from New York, he repeated the most popular films, even within the same showing. The lynching scene, in particular, was one that was "heartily encored" and would have been repeated for audiences.[50]

By 1904, filmmakers were producing short narrative films that used multiple shots and continuity editing to present a story unfolding over time. The three lynching films that appeared in that year represented lynchings as spectacular melodramas of crime and punishment. More directly than other lynching and execution films, these pictures visually reenacted prolynching narratives about brutish black men assaulting helpless white women and the determined, orderly mobs that exacted vengeance. In this respect, despite their spectacular excess, they projected onto lynching a degree of moral clarity and restraint. Indeed, in watching these films, audiences could experience the physical and emotional thrill and agitation that witnessing a lynching would spark while still inhabiting the relatively constrained and respectable position of cinema spectator.

All of these films were most likely shown in the South. Producer William Selig sent *Tracked by Bloodhounds* across the country on the carnival circuit or, as he claimed in a 1920 article, "for a long 'run' under what we used to call the 'black tops,' the dark-hued tents which were familiar to all devotees of the county fair." The more renowned film, Edwin Porter's *The Great Train Robbery* (Edison, 1903), went out on the same circuit. Both films appeared at a carnival in Waco, Texas, in October 1904 and were the "big hit" of the fair. Moving picture exhibitions featuring pictures from other production companies that also made these sorts of lynching scenes were common

FIGURE 4.3 The black criminal assaults his victim, *Avenging a Crime; or, Burned at the Stake*, Paley and Steiner, 1904.

entertainments at carnivals, outdoor theaters, and opera houses through-out the Deep South in these years.[51]

Avenging a Crime; or, Burned at the Stake was the only film in this period that explicitly portrayed a southern, racialized lynching. The film, as well as its narrative description in the distributer's catalog, represented black criminality and lynching in strikingly similar terms to the lynching accounts reported in many southern newspapers and much prolynching discourse, despite its being produced in the North. It made visual the very worst of white southern fears and then extinguished them through the filmic spec-tacle of the lynching. The film depicts a man in blackface assaulting a white woman, grabbing her pocketbook, and strangling her to death (figure 4.3). Even before this shocking scene, the viewer is given clues to the criminal's general depravity and moral corruption in the opening shot, when he is shown joining two black men playing craps in front of the "village tavern." He loses his money to them, and it is to make up for his loss that he robs the woman. His assault on the white woman was thus contextualized within a larger narrative of perceived black drunkenness and vice. Negative stereo-types continue through the film. The criminal is shown "sneaking" away, stealing a horse to escape, so that when he is finally caught, the lynch mob and the audience alike would have received his "begging for mercy" as a hollow, self-serving cry.[52]

The film's use of caricatured blackface is of particular interest. Early film-makers tended to use black actors only when they wanted to accentuate the authentic, documentary quality of the picture, such as idyllic plantation scenes of black people dancing or eating, as seen in *The Watermelon Contest* (figure 4.1). When they expected white audiences to sympathize with the character, or, as in this case, when the character was a criminal, they used white actors in blackface. To show an actual African American man murdering a white woman on-screen, even a simulated murder, would have been far too shocking to white audiences. The use of exaggerated blackface in this film and its evocations of the minstrel tradition also herald the lynching scene as theater, as a source of amusement and pleasure. Just as blackface minstrelsy played on cross-racial desires, white audiences may have experienced a perverse delight in watching a white actor perform transgressions they associated with African Americans. In the context of this film, however, the minstrelesque figure is not the happy, simple Sambo of the plantation but rather his nightmarish, urban inverse. There is no evidence that white southerners would have reacted with anything but horror at the sight of a black man—even one so blatantly caricatured—assaulting a white woman. The use of blackface in this instance served primarily as a mask to dramatize what was otherwise unrepresentable through a relatively safe and familiar theatrical form.[53]

Whereas the film represents the black criminal as unruly and degenerate, it offers an idealized representation of the mob and the lynching. The white mob is shown to be determined and orderly, pursuing the murderer as a cohesive unit throughout the elaborate chase scene. Although in many actual lynchings, the mob worked slowly and methodically, this mob exacts its vengeance quickly. Burning at the stake is a terrible torture to inflict, but it appears in the film's narrative as an expedient and efficient, albeit climactic, finish (figure 4.4). "Lashing him to a tree, they gather brushwood, and stacking it around him, set it on fire. He is soon enveloped in flames, the angry mob fire shot after shot at him and the vengeance is complete," reads the catalog description. The form of the cinematic image facilitated this idealized representation by abstracting the torture and death of the victim into one black and white, silent moment.[54]

The film further presents the vengeance of the mob as pure and just through the presence of a white female witness, once again mirroring many prolynching accounts. The crime itself, the violation of the white woman,

FIGURE 4.4 The mob prepares the lynching pyre, *Avenging a Crime; or, Burned at the Stake*, Paley and Steiner, 1904.

is witnessed in the film by a little white girl, who then runs to tell a farmer, who gathers the lynch mob. Before the men pursue the killer, however, they run to where the woman has fallen, and after viewing her violated body, they "swear dire vengeance on the one who committed the deed." While the women tend to her body, the men take off in pursuit, a separation of responsibilities that amplifies the gender roles lynching both exaggerated and defended. But as they "start out on the hunt for the murderer," the men are "led by the little girl." Although she is not seen in the chase scenes and could not have possibly kept up, she is present when the men finally wrestle their victim to the ground. As discussed in the preceding chapter, the female witness, either the white woman whose assault inspired the lynching or other white women, legitimized the terrible violence of the lynching. The white woman's violated purity acted as the motivating force behind the vengeance, and, in addition, the presence of that purity at the lynching site veiled the violence with righteous innocence, absolving the lynch mob of guilt.

Although the other two lynching films produced at this time have western settings, they present similar scenes of communal justice and vengeance on a racialized other that white southern audiences would have recognized and applauded as both morally satisfying and sensationally entertaining. *Tracked by Bloodhounds* depicts a man with a dark complexion and a large black beard—the catalog described him as a "tramp"—attacking a white woman in her home. *Cowboy Justice* (American Mutoscope and Biograph, 1903), a two-shot film that depicts one man killing another after losing a game of cards in a saloon, and then a mob avenging that crime, announces its lesson in its title. Although the condemned man appears white in the film, he is distinguishable from the other men by his Native American clothing. These pictures projected images of mobs punishing criminals and establishing moral justice with speed and precision, providing a thrill for audiences who feared crime in modern life and were frustrated by the slow wheels of judicial bureaucracy. In fact, because of the constraints and structure of the technology itself, the films presented the enactment of accountability at an even greater speed than that with which an actual lynching would have occurred.

The Selig Polyscope Company promoted *Tracked by Bloodhounds* for its authenticity, claiming it was produced at the site of an actual lynching in Cripple Creek, Colorado. In doing so, the producers expected that audiences would feel a personal, or at least an informed, connection to the subject of the film and would desire to see on-screen events they had previously only heard or read about. Hailing the film as "one of the most sensational pictures ever made," the catalog entry implied that the cameraman caught the actual lynching on film: "Our photographer was in Cripple Creek ready for business when the exciting events occurred. The negative was made in the great gold camp. Dozens of prominent miners and citizens who have since been involved in deportation troubles can easily be recognized in the picture." The entry further assured exhibitors that the film was a "sensational money-maker" and that "the advertising Cripple Creek has had during the past few months will make people extremely anxious to see a picture actually made in the Cripple Creek district." It represents the lynching—the hanging and shooting of a depraved criminal—as more swift and organized than it possibly could have been.[55]

The hanging in *Cowboy Justice* is brief; we do not see the hanging itself. The mob places a noose around the condemned's neck and then moves in front of the camera, blocking the scene as the man hangs. The mob then moves back out of the frame, and we see only the hanging man's body, writhing and struggling, his head cut off at the top of the frame (figure 4.5). The film ends when the men come back into the frame and shoot at the hanging body. The filmmakers may have elided the hanging itself only because they did not have recourse to trick photography, but the effect is to create an image eerily similar to many lynching photographs, as the camera's focus remains not on the violence committed but on the condemned's dead body.

FIGURE 4.5 *Cowboy Justice*, American Mutoscope and Biograph, 1903.

That his face is not visible at this moment allows a further transference of his racial identity.

Tracked by Bloodhounds also ends with a relatively still image, what the catalog entry described as a "life-size portrait of the bloodhounds and their keeper" (figure 4.6). In the shot, the frame of the screen acts as a photographic frame as the keeper gazes out to the camera, staring intently, much as in a portrait, at the audience. This shot provides the counterimage to the hanging body of the condemned, much as in lynching photographs, the self-fashioned poses of the white men stand sharply against the images of the black man's body. This image of the keeper allowed audiences a direct, steady intimacy with the hero of this western drama, thereby establishing a connection between the avenging mob and the film spectators.

This closing shot also bears significance when viewed in juxtaposition to the famous closing shot of *The Great Train Robbery*, in which one of the bandits, facing the camera directly in a medium close-up shot, shoots his gun at the audience (figure 4.7).[56] As noted above, *Tracked by Bloodhounds* was released alongside *The Great Train Robbery*, and exhibitors often showed them together, as was done in Waco.[57] Whereas the latter film depicts a gang

FIGURE 4.6 Closing shot, *Tracked by Bloodhounds*, Selig Polyscope, 1904.

of bandits holding up a train and escaping into the woods, *Tracked by Blood-hounds* shows the resolution and punishment of a criminal act. The closing shots in this sense complement each other. Both indicate the ways early cinema broke the fourth wall, creating a direct relationship between characters and audience in a way later classical Hollywood cinema eschewed. The bandit shooting at the audience in *The Great Train Robbery*, however, establishes an antagonistic relationship between the film and the audience; faced with the bandit shooting directly at them, viewers at this moment were to identify with the frightened and wounded passengers. The shot furthermore highlights the ways the film spectators were positioned as immobile, passive, and vulnerable. The shot of the bloodhounds and their keeper, on the other hand, establishes a contrasting identification between the audience and the lynch mob, the avengers of crime. Making direct eye contact with the keeper, the audience is not passive or vulnerable in the same way, as the control of the audience is mirrored in the posed stillness of the keeper.

As those in Vicksburg, Mississippi, did with Edison's *Lynching Scene*, we can assume that white southern audiences applauded these films. The pictures expected viewers to sympathize with the lynch mob, acting much like those spectators at actual lynchings who condoned the mob's violence and made it socially acceptable. Even those spectators of "sensitive natures,"

FIGURE 4.7 Closing shot, *The Great Train Robbery*, Edison, 1903.

shocked by what they were seeing, were providing the cinematic lynch mob with a confined audience that justified their violence. Movie viewers, seated closely together in the seats of the opera house or crowded under a carnival tent, would have, in this sense, replicated the crowds of spectators at mass lynchings. As the report of the Vicksburg audience makes evident, responses to these films were visceral, especially since audiences of silent film were more verbal and demonstrative than later film audiences. Audiences regularly clapped, gasped, hooted, and cheered at the screen. These responses were also communal. Applause, in particular, is a group response, as the act of clapping connects the individual to the larger group while subsuming any individual reaction. Cinematic spectatorship certainly differed considerably from that at a lynching, as cinema imposed a degree of restraint on the bodies of its spectators. Unlike those in the crowd at a lynching, who could direct their gaze where they wished, who could hear and smell the lynching, and who could choose to participate and intervene in the action, cinema audiences were for the most part confined to their seats only as observers, albeit vocal and animated ones. In this sense, just as these films presented idealized representations of the lynching itself, they likewise ensured a model image of lynching spectatorship—a controlled and appropriately awed crowd of witnesses.

MELODRAMA AND ITS MANIFESTATION in "cinema of attractions" were, in many ways, products of a modern, urban environment, which abounded in visual distraction and attraction and visceral shock and sensation. As early theorists of cinema like Walter Benjamin and Siegfried Kracauer posited, the thrill and sensationalism of film simulated for viewers the frenzied aggression of modern life while immunizing them against it by conditioning them to it. In particular, early sadistic films, like execution and lynching films, eased spectators' anxieties about the fragility and alienation of the body in modern life by displacing those fears onto the cinematic subject. Cinematic acts of sadism excited and titillated viewers by projecting physical assault and diminishment onto the bodies shown on-screen, all while guaranteeing the spectators' own physical safety.[58]

The popularity of *Execution of Czolgosz* is a perfect example of this dynamic. For turn-of-the-century Americans, electricity was an amazing phenomenon that changed daily life in profound ways, a testament to the ways in which modern people could harness and dominate the power of the natural world. But, all the same, that awe was tinged with a sense of dread and horror, especially as reports abounded of people being accidentally shocked and even electrocuted in their homes and on city streets. The electric chair, in this context, stood as a way to exploit electricity's lethal power for a beneficial purpose, that is, the humane and efficient execution of criminals.[59] Edison's film not only advertised the chair as a painless alternative to hanging but eased popular anxieties about electric power more generally by projecting visually the fear of electrocution onto the despised and reviled Czolgosz.

Southerners, to be sure, shared this sense of wonder and apprehension about the technological transformations of modern life. At the same time, the South was still relatively rural, and most southerners were not experiencing the attractions and stimuli of urban life to the same degree that many of their northern counterparts were. In this context, lynching and execution films were not so much simulating the shocks and thrills of modern life as they were representing for public consumption older, traditional rituals of popular justice and vengeance that were, in fact, at odds with practices of modern life. Cinema itself, especially before the advent of motion picture theaters, was not an isolated form of commercial entertainment, for it was predicated on and merged with other, older forms of amusement: melodrama, vaudeville, minstrelsy, carnivals, and circuses. Lynching was likewise not a distinct phenomenon, for it overlapped with other facets and events in southern life, including cinema.

Furthermore, these films reasserted traditional hierarchies of power and authority that the social and political transformations of modernity were threatening, particularly for white men. As men increasingly moved from farm to industry, and as both women and African Americans began to claim political equality and autonomy, white men found not only their dominance but their own sense of manliness under assault. Cinematic acts of sadism projected the physical diminishment and fragility of the body that white, middle-class men feared from modern life onto the bodies of people lacking in social power: African Americans, the poor, or foreigners. The white, male spectator in turn regained a sense of strength and authority through his objectifying gaze. He also experienced a sense of power, in part because, as a spectator, he was somewhat disembodied; that is, the relatively motionless act of watching another's action made the spectator less aware of his own body's vulnerability, especially as he witnessed the violation of another's body.[60] He had a command over his body that the victim clearly did not. White female viewers would also have experienced this sense of physical and social assurance while watching a cinematic lynching, especially in light of the ways that prolynching discourse commonly represented white women as fragile and helpless. At actual lynchings, they might have felt particularly vulnerable amid the push and thrust of the crowd. The theater, however, provided a comparatively safe and controlled venue through which to experience, vicariously, scenes of white female violation and vengeance against that violation.

These films thus intensified the sense of dominance that witnessing a lynching bestowed on spectators, both male and female. Their viewing of these films would have taken place against the backdrop of actual public executions and lynchings, in which white southerners of all classes made manifest their racial and moral supremacy against black inferiority and criminality. A similar kind of disidentification with the condemned took place for the spectator of these films, so that the sadism of spectatorship incorporated reactionary claims to moral authority and social power. Ultimately, spectators took pleasure in these filmic spectacles of lynching because they allowed them to enact, if only vicariously, this power in the face of modernity's most threatening transformations. After all, each of these films represents lynching or execution in a rural, almost idyllic setting, in which the community avenges the crime swiftly and orderly. Lynchings are performed as melodramas without any moral ambiguity or messy resolutions. These films were thus precursors to the most infamous cinematic lynching melodrama, D. W. Griffith's 1915 film *The Birth of a Nation*. It was in *The Birth of a Nation* that lynching as a national spectacle of white supremacist "justice," filmic performance, and sacred ceremony was most fully and popularly realized.

5

◈ ◈ ◈

WITH THE ROAR OF THUNDER

The Birth of a Nation

WHEN *THE BIRTH OF A NATION* opened in Atlanta on 6 December 1915, it caused a sensation throughout the city. Long lines at the Atlanta Theater were continuous from morning to evening, as crowds swelled to view the production, some coming back three or four times. Response was so great that the theater extended the film's run by two weeks, closing it on Christmas night. Atlanta audiences received *Birth*'s majestic tale of the white South's torment and redemption with a passionate degree of devotion and awe. At the film's first showing, the *Atlanta Constitution* reported, "cheer after cheer burst forth," as "never before . . . has an Atlanta audience so freely given vent to its emotions." When the Klan begins its heroic ride to avenge the torment of the white South, "the awful restraint of the audience is thrown to the wind. Many rise from their seats. With the roar of thunder a shout goes up. Freedom is here. Justice is at hand! Retribution has arrived!" Ward Greene, reviewing the film in the *Atlanta Journal*, was equally effusive, declaring that the film "swept the audience at the Atlanta Theater . . . like a tidal wave." Gushed Greene, "A youth in the gallery leaped to his feet and yelled and yelled. A little boy downstairs pounded the man's back in front of him and shrieked. Here a young girl kept dabbing and dabbing at her eyes and there an old lady just sat and let the tears stream down her face unchecked."[1]

Reviews of *Birth* consistently felt compelled to do more than comment on the film itself. Reviewers insisted on detailing the emotive responses of the spectators, as if these ecstatic reactions made evident the brilliance of D. W. Griffith's "masterly genius." White southerners saw *Birth* as, in many ways, a direct address to them, a spectacular vindication of their sectional pride and their sense of racial honor. In his review, Greene hailed the reader directly to prompt the most fitting response to the film: "Your heart pulses

. . . you are wrung . . . your throat chokes . . . you are lifted by the hair and go crazy."

By the time it reached Atlanta, *Birth* had been in release for nearly nine months, and its reputation as a racist and incendiary film had become notorious, a reputation that undoubtedly drew more viewers to the film. Reviews and notices in the Atlanta papers, however, reassured readers that *Birth* was a historically accurate film that did nothing to promote racial prejudice. It, in fact, according to Greene, did "credit to the negro race." He also, nonetheless, stressed to readers that on witnessing the film, "loathing, disgust, hate envelop you, hot blood cries for vengeance." Objections notwithstanding, the waves of emotion that swept over Atlanta audiences as they witnessed the Klan's retaliation for their suffering under black rule bore a remarkable resemblance to those experienced by lynch mobs and spectators. The film aroused the same impulse toward revenge and the same sense of racial triumph and offered those sensibilities force and credibility through the spectacle of cinema.

Birth opened just a few months after the infamous lynching of Leo Frank just outside Atlanta in Marietta, Georgia.[2] Frank, a Jewish factory manager, was lynched in August 1915 for the murder of one of his female workers, Mary Phagan, after the governor commuted his death sentence. The murder of Phagan, Frank's arrest and trial, and the lynching had dominated local news for months, inflaming sectional pride and defensiveness in the face of northern intrusion and criticism. Atlanta spectators could not have put that recent memory aside as they watched *Birth*. Frank's case was itself rendered on film in a documentary, *Leo Frank and Governor Slaton*, produced by playwright Hal Reid and released in the summer of that year. What is more, a news film of the lynching, a prototype of later "newsweeklies," was released soon after the lynching in September 1915, and apparently included photographs from the lynching. It omitted pictures of Frank's corpse and revealed only shots of the crowd at the lynching. Nevertheless, censorship boards around the country suppressed the film. There is no evidence that it was prohibited in Atlanta, however. In fact, it is possible that just three months before *Birth* hit the Atlanta Theater, Atlantans witnessed the projection of a lynching crowd before them in nickelodeons around the city.[3]

The fiction that *Birth* projected on-screen further merged with reality when the Atlanta Theater hosted 100 Confederate veterans from the local Soldiers' Home at a matinee performance. According to the theater's report, the "realism" of the picture "was enhanced almost to reality itself" as

the veterans' rebel yells rose above the orchestration. "This audience LIVED
the picture! This audience KNEW!" the account raved. Indeed, the theater
used the testimonies of these men to promote the film's accuracy, including
one man's recollection of "the day I went to the polls, and they wouldn't
let me—me, a white man—vote." Recounted another, "I ain't saying I was
a Ku Klux, because we're not allowed to tell, but I saw how the Ku Klux
worked."[4]

The film's impact spilled out onto the streets of Atlanta with the reemer-
gence of the Ku Klux Klan that fall. William Joseph Simmons, a former itinerant Methodist preacher, was apparently inspired to reorganize the Klan as
a nativist, Protestant fraternity in anticipation of Griffith's picture. Ten days
before the film was to premiere in Atlanta, on Thanksgiving night, Simmons
gathered thirty-four men and conducted an elaborate initiation ceremony
atop Stone Mountain, just outside the city. He subsequently advertised his
new organization on the back of all the publicity *Birth* was receiving. On
the night the film opened, Simmons and his followers created their own
terrifying spectacle when they paraded down Atlanta's main thoroughfare
and stopped before the Atlanta Theater to fire their rifles. With this display,
white Atlantans' identification with and glorification of the Klan in *Birth*
found literal embodiment.[5]

With *The Birth of a Nation*, the spectacle of lynching as a sensational melodrama was most fully realized. The film was based on Thomas Dixon's play
The Clansman, which had won a welcome reception when it toured the
country ten years earlier.[6] *Birth*, however, achieved a level of success and
critical acclaim far beyond that of Dixon's play, largely because professional
critics and audiences alike marveled at the spectacle of Griffith's cinematic
vision. With *Birth*, Griffith pieced together newly developed elements of
cinematic technique in such a way that he brought film to what was considered the epic height of graphic realism. Critics consistently attributed the
tremendous thrill of the film to the notion that it brought the past to life —
that it was, as one southern paper deemed it, "history in motion."[7] Yet the
film resonated so strongly with audiences not only because it represented
the history of the war and Reconstruction with unprecedented realism but
also because it visualized that history through white supremacist and prolynching imagery that spoke to white audiences' fears and sensibilities in

the present. It then consecrated that imagery as both historical truth and modern cinematic marvel.

Griffith was able to achieve this visual consecration of white supremacy through a successful communication with white audiences, as the reception of the film demonstrates. In this respect, the spectator was as crucial to Griffith's ideological purpose as cinematic techniques were. Griffith promoted the film as a truthful representation of history, conveyed through a medium that could provide lifelike authenticity to that history. But the film also gained credibility as "truth" and as spectacle through audiences' spirited engagement with that history. As the reports from Atlanta show, spectators of the film saw themselves not simply as consumers of entertainment but as active witnesses to history.[8]

Nowhere was audience reaction as strong as in the South. The images that the film projected of black sexual assault against white women and the Klan's vengeance for those assaults imparted immediate and familiar meanings for viewers already well acquainted with and deeply invested in pro-lynching rhetoric and images. Moreover, spectators' strong emotional and visceral responses to these scenes evinced the same mob spirit, united in a sense of white superiority, that *Birth* itself depicted and celebrated. Watching the film, in turn, legitimated that crowd sensibility. In other words, as with early lynching films, *Birth* transformed audiences into lynching spectators and made their spectatorship of violence respectable, even righteous.

It was precisely the anticipation of this kind of reaction that ignited a storm of controversy around the film. African American critics and activists, as well as some white allies, protested *Birth* on the grounds that it misrepresented historical truth and that, in doing so, it incited racial antagonism and could provoke lynching itself—a protest that undoubtedly only drew audiences to the film and intensified white southerners' defensive embrace of it. Those who campaigned against *Birth* believed, with unquestioning intensity, that the distorted and offensive representations of black desire that the film flaunted were inseparable from the actual terror and oppression that black Americans faced. Their protests, in this sense, were based on the same presumptions about the cultural force of film that sustained *Birth*'s popularity—that cinema, as moving images, held both an uncanny mimetic power and a very real animating power. Because film could so vividly represent behavior, it could also stimulate it. Although the spectacle of *Birth* may have activated white audiences to embrace its white supremacist message as historical truth, it also activated audiences against it. In doing so, it galvanized a larger movement against racial injustice and lynching in America.

FIGURE 5.1 The lynched body of Gus, *The Birth of a Nation*, David W. Griffith Corporation, 1915.

THE SECOND HALF of *The Birth of a Nation* rests entirely on a visual dramatization of prolynching discourse, one that validates mob violence as the necessary and righteous defense against black political and sexual insurgency. Yet lynching appears in only one scene, in which the Klan "executes" the former slave Gus (Walter Long) for his would-be rape of the virginal Flora Cameron (Mae Marsh). That single scene, however, which occurs midway through the film, assumes enormous symbolic value. It is the first act the members of the Klan perform, and it presages their victorious rescue of Elsie Stoneman (Lillian Gish) from the lascivious mulatto Silas Lynch (George Siegmann), their liberation of the Cameron family from black rule, and ultimately their redemption of the South and the nation.[9]

The killing of Gus, however, although it is implied, is not shown in the film. The Klan chases and captures Gus and holds a "trial" in the woods; an intertitle reads "Guilty," and in the next shot, Gus's body is placed on a horse. In the following scene, a Klansman drops the body, pinned with a note bearing a skull and crossbones and the letters "KKK," on the porch of Lynch, the lieutenant governor (figure 5.1). Although one film critic alleged that Griffith originally filmed a lynching scene but excised it after the NAACP objected, there is no corroborating evidence for this claim.[10]

More likely, Griffith chose to omit Gus's lynching for the sake of cinematic decency, recognizing that reproducing a lynching on-screen would ensure that his film was banned. In fact, it is unlikely that any filmic depiction of a lynching was produced after 1905, since motion pictures were coming under closer scrutiny from reformers concerned about the lack of moral decency in pictures. Scenes of extreme violence were considered particularly controversial. The nation's first motion picture censorship ordinance, passed in Chicago in 1907, prohibited exhibition of any film that "purports to represent any hanging, lynching or burning of a human being," a prohibition that was surely repeated in cities across the country.[11]

Some spectators, no doubt, filled the elision of Gus's lynching by inserting their own images of his death into the film, based on their viewing of lynching photographs or earlier films. For instance, in a letter to the *Portland (Ore.) Journal*, a local NAACP officer protested that the film "shows the pursuit and capture of the girl's assailant, his trial by the clansmen, and the scene ends with the glowing embers of the fire where he has been burned." Her account may have been based primarily on rumor or imagined from other lynching images or from Dixon's 1903 novel *The Leopard's Spots*, in which a white mob burns alive the black rapist of the young woman named Flora, a scene that was reconfigured for Dixon's play *The Clansman*. On the other hand, some distracted viewers apparently missed the lynching scene altogether and, in a bewildering confusion of reality and representation, wrote to Griffith's studio expressing hope that Gus had been jailed "because white women would not be safe with him at large."[12]

In any event, by not showing the actual violence against Gus, *Birth* cleansed the act of lynching of any gruesomeness or impropriety, just as lynching photographs and some earlier lynching films had done. By omitting the actual scene of violence, the film visually projected for spectators prolynching rhetoric, which itself imagined white men not as bloodthirsty and frenzied mobsters but as determined, stoic heroes. Without seeing the brutality or bloodshed, the viewer could imagine the Klansmen as righteous avengers of the honor of Flora, that virginal "flower" of southern womanhood, and, by extension, the honor of the white South. Indeed, the lynching is presented as an act of efficient and honorable justice, "a fair trial in the dim halls of the Invisible Empire," as the intertitle reads. The film further justifies the Klan's vigilantism because the state, governed by "carpetbaggers" and former slaves, is presented as illegitimate, "a veritable overthrow of civilization in the South." The Klan is introduced as the rightful surrogate for a corrupt and failed government, military, and judiciary. In this regard, the Klan does not "lynch" Gus at all; rather, it places him on "trial" and "executes" him.

Although his actual death is eclipsed, Gus's corpse comes to bear enormous ideological value in the film, much as photographs of black bodies contained and signified the racial ideologies enacted in lynching. Gus's lifeless body comes to stand in for the lynching itself. The shot lingers on his corpse, much like a lynching photograph (figure 5.1). The Klansmen drop Gus's body on Lynch's doorstep as a warning, ensuring that his punishment for transgressing racial boundaries is visible to the black leadership. The note they pin to his shoulder, reading "KKK," in a sense inscribes their power onto his body. Lynch comes out and sees Gus's body with a gasp and then orders that it be taken to the home of the Republican leader, Austin Stoneman (Ralph Lewis), supposedly to inform him of and protest the Klan's action. In the next shot, at Stoneman's home, Lynch and Stoneman look together at the body lying on the parlor floor. In this respect, although neither these characters nor the film audience witness the lynching, they do, in looking at Gus's corpse, bear witness to its terrible effects.

Birth does more than envision lynching as a legitimate exercise of secular power, however; it also sanctifies it through the use of Christian imagery. The Klan's leadership is endowed with religious authority, most conspicuously through the image of the burning cross, which first appears in the shot titled "The Trial."[13] With their white robes and crosses, the Klansmen, in this scene, resemble angels of judgment and death more than a secular judiciary. The film ends with the image of Christ projected over a jubilant crowd, representing, as the intertitle explains, the victory of "peace" and "brotherly love" over "bestial war"—that is, the victory of white supremacy and the spiritual redemption of the nation.[14]

At the moral center of this story is the violated and suffering white woman, a figure that not only coincided with prolynching discourse but also operated within the images and expectations of stage and film melodrama. *Birth*, for all intents and purposes, translated the history of Reconstruction into a melodrama, with black villains and white women in distress. This trope of melodrama, of course, already existed in prolynching rhetoric, which repeatedly interpreted the political and economic threats of emancipation through a similar kind of moral polarization. Griffith merely appropriated this script, visualizing it as the melodrama it already was, that is, as black "fiends" pursuing chaste white women. The film drew emotional power to its defense of lynching by eliciting the sympathy and engendering the outrage of white audiences across the country, who were overcome with

FIGURE 5.2 Silas Lynch's assault on Elsie Stoneman, *The Birth of a Nation*, David W. Griffith Corporation, 1915.

pathos for both the southern Flora Cameron and northern Elsie Stoneman as they desperately attempt to resist black men's assaults on their virtue. Indeed, whereas the suffering of Gus remains off-screen, the anguish of both Flora and Elsie is shown in excessive detail. Silas Lynch's extended lustful and drunken attack on Elsie would have been particularly shocking to audiences unaccustomed to witnessing such an explicit and graphic scene of sexual aggression, especially between the races (figure 5.2).[15]

In counterposing the white woman's and the black man's sufferings in this way, the film made manifest how defenders of lynching understood white women's suffering as the outrageous price paid for emancipation and black enfranchisement. As Ben Cameron (Ben Walthall) holds his dying sister, he wipes the delicate blood from her mouth with a Confederate flag, which he later uses in an elaborate Klan ceremony as an icon to the racial purity that the Klan must defend. Cameron dips the flag in a basin of water and, holding it aloft, proclaims, "Brethren, this flag bears the red stain of life of a southern woman, a priceless sacrifice on the altar of an outraged civilization" (figure 5.3). He then lifts a "fiery cross" and "quench[es] its flames in the sweetest blood that ever stained the sands of Time." That "priceless

FIGURE 5.3 The Klan's ceremony, *The Birth of a Nation*, David W. Griffith
Corporation, 1915.

sacrifice" was thus imagined as a decidedly Christian sacrifice, a martyrdom
made on behalf of white supremacy and southern honor.[16]

It is important to note that *Birth* never represents black lust as rape. Instead, Gus and Silas Lynch are presented as wanting to marry Flora and
Elsie—albeit crudely and animalistically. Although a proposal of marriage
does not temper the women's horrified responses, it does impose some Victorian respectability on what was a most unseemly subject. Viewers would
have immediately understood this euphemism, however, and imagined
for themselves the sexual implications, a projection the film encourages
through the depiction of Gus and Lynch as overly aggressive and lascivious.
These proposals of marriage also parallel the film's representation of black
enfranchisement and leadership; both are portrayed as hollow calls for immediate equality, with no history, no experience, no courtship.[17]

This dramatization of white supremacist ideology was only enhanced by
the medium in which it was conveyed, for rendering this story on film bestowed on it an unparalleled air of immediacy and authenticity. Griffith made
brilliant use of newly developed camera techniques by moving the camera
out of the studio and into wide open spaces, depicting masses of people

and horses in one shot, and, communicating human subjectivity through close-ups and point-of-view shots—techniques that created the illusion of a vibrant and self-contained cinematic world. Whereas early cinema expected viewers to remain outside the story, looking at the "attraction" on-screen as an observer, *Birth* represented the shift to what would become the classical Hollywood style, in which the viewer is absorbed emotionally into the cinematic narrative, supposedly oblivious of the artifice of the representation. Despite that the camera represented reality in a way that no one actually perceived it—not only was the picture silent and flickering, but it was projected larger than life onto theater screens—audiences consistently marveled at just how true to life motion pictures were. Griffith liked to quote one social critic who claimed that "the most beautiful picture ever painted on canvas, the finest statue ever carved, is a ridiculous caricature of real life compared with the flickering shadow of a tattered film in a backwoods nickelodeon."[18]

Through this cinematic illusion of realism, Griffith lent visual authenticity to his highly charged narrative of white innocence and black depravity. For this reason, *Birth*'s cinematic achievements cannot be separated from its white supremacist content. For example, although Griffith's novel use of lighting has been praised, he used it most effectively in the film to accentuate the racial polarization of his characters, to glorify whiteness and to demonize blackness. In this same manner, he innovatively appropriated techniques of photographic portraiture to frame and highlight the faces of his white actresses to give them an aura of respectability and virtue. Ben Cameron, in fact, becomes enamored of Elsie Stoneman when he gazes on her in a photographic miniature. The beauty and innocence of white womanhood are, in this instance, made visible and elevated to iconic status through photographic portraiture.[19]

Whereas white women needed only to be illuminated for their purity to be revealed, white men were not so innocent, as the sad fact of miscegenation made embarrassingly clear. In prolynching ideology, white men were redeemed through protecting and avenging the honor of white women; in the film, they are literally draped in white. The Klan costumes provide a stark visual contrast to Gus's blackness and reestablish a racial hierarchy based on discernible differences, differences that miscegenation and Gus's desires for Flora threaten.[20] The film, in this way, paralleled the many lynching photographs that similarly perpetuated a racial hierarchy based on visible distinction between white and black bodies.

FIGURE 5.4 The death of Flora, *The Birth of a Nation*, David W. Griffith Corporation, 1915.

Griffith was able to intensify the emotional impact of the lynching scene for white viewers through a masterful and effective use of cross-cutting. Just before the Klan finds Gus guilty and kills him, the film cuts to a shot of Flora on her deathbed. Through parallel editing, Griffith could thus represent, in place of the actual lynching, the image of wronged white womanhood that, according to lynching rhetoric, dominated the imaginations of lynching participants as they tortured and hanged their victims. The suffering of the black man's body is literally replaced, in this instance, with that of the lifeless white woman (figure 5.4). This juxtaposition of images is repeated later when the scene of Lynch assaulting Elsie in his office is cut against the Klan's heroic ride to the rescue. Parallel editing, which, incidentally, Griffith had first experimented with in a lynching scene from his 1908 film *The Greaser's Gauntlet*, served a number of narrative purposes. It not only conveyed two concurrent actions but implied a relation between those actions that went beyond mere simultaneity. As in the cutting between the Klan's ride and Lynch's assault on Elsie, it created suspense and tension by holding time and delaying the resolution of the action. But it also implied a moral contrast between the two scenes. By cross-cutting an image of Flora with that of her attacker, Gus, or an image of the lascivious Silas Lynch with the valiant white Klansmen, Griffith made visually conspicuous the moral polarity of the story's melodrama.[21]

Griffith confused the very racial distinctions that the film insists on, however, by using white actors in blackface to portray both Gus and Lynch. The custom of using white actors in blackface to play criminal black roles far predated *Birth*, as seen in *Avenging a Crime*, discussed in the previous chapter.[22] This convention arose in part because using actual black actors to play these deviant roles would have been far too threatening to white Americans, since it would make visible their greatest racial fears. But what is interesting about *Birth* is that while other white actors playing black characters in the film wear the caricatured blackface of minstrelsy, the face of Gus—and that of Lynch—is merely darkened in tone. Griffith presumably did not want to represent Gus as a comic, minstrel-like figure. He may also have wanted audiences to believe Gus was black. If he had wanted them to know that Gus was a white actor masquerading as a black man to ease their racial anxiety, he would have made the actor's race more obvious by using standard techniques of caricature. In fact, according to one account, many spectators did mistake Gus for a real black man, an oversight that only heightened the emotional power and terror of the rape scene for white audiences.[23] Ironically, putting white actors in blackface to play these deviant black characters only made apparent the notion that race exists simply as a facade, a premise that white supremacist ideology entirely rejected. Both Gus and Silas Lynch stood as exemplars of the idea at the heart of many black freedom struggles of the time—that black men were, after all, the same as white men, only with darker skin.

THE VISUAL ELEMENTS of the film not only sustained the ideological underpinnings of the narrative but were vital to its popularity. Indeed, *Birth* created crowds of devotees that neither Dixon's best-selling novels nor his play *The Clansman* could ever match. To be sure, audiences had received *The Clansman* enthusiastically when it toured the South and the rest of the country ten years earlier, but the play did not elicit the degree of awe and approbation that *Birth* did. *The Clansman*, in fact, met with a tepid critical response, even from southern critics, for its ugly and rabid negrophobia. The racially moderate *Richmond (Va.) News Leader*, for example, called it about as "elevating as a lynching."[24] The same paper, however, praised *Birth* as a "magnificent production" with "powerful appeal" for "southern audiences." The account noted that that the "tremendous volume of enthusiasm" evinced during the film's first showing in Richmond made it seem at moments as if "the roof was going to be blown off and sent sailing into the middle of the next block." Far from comparing *Birth* to a lynching, the reviewer asserted that "the drama conveys a powerful message for universal peace."[25]

This difference in response is somewhat puzzling. Scenes of lustful and crazed ex-slaves—in particular the scenes of Gus's pursuit of Flora and her horrifying leap to her death—as well as the Klan's retribution against Gus, remained from Dixon's play. Griffith even amplified the scene in the play in which Lynch asks for Elsie's hand in marriage by transforming it into an extended, lascivious attack on her.[26] Yet, unlike in the play, these scenes appear in *Birth* within a larger context of Lost Cause ideology, including poignant images of war, suffering, and loss, as well as nostalgic visions of loyal and happy slaves—images that resonated emotionally with white audiences nationwide. Griffith, in this sense, did not temper the negrophobia of Dixon's play so much as render it respectable by couching it within a larger, sentimental melodrama.[27]

Even more, the sheer spectacle of cinema overwhelmed the responses to *Birth*, leading many white spectators to accept its vision of history and racial discord with unquestioning reverence. Newspapers regularly called it "The World's Mightiest Spectacle" and "The Miracle Movie" rather than simply a "photoplay" or "motion picture." Commentators asserted that nothing had ever been visualized as brilliantly, that the production was "more than a mere moving picture." Reports on the film also expressed awe at the size of the production, enumerating how much it cost ($500,000), how many scenes it contained (5,000), how many actors appeared in it (18,000), and even how many horses were involved (3,000). It was the scope of the production, after all, that distinguished the film from what had come before, and certainly what distinguished it from theater.[28]

For many viewers, the spectacle of the production lent a particular aura of authenticity to the narrative. Griffith was able through the medium of film to convey a reactionary racial fiction more successfully than Dixon had because audiences carried their assumptions about the documentary nature of filmic vision to their viewing; they then celebrated this vision as modern marvel. These viewers unquestionably accepted Griffith's representation of lustful black brutes because this representation appeared, within the production of the film, less like artifice and more like fact. Indeed, Griffith defended his film by asserting that it was a work of art with momentous historical importance—because it could, with unprecedented accuracy, represent history as it had actually happened. According to Griffith, *Birth* was under attack by the "witch burners" who wanted to censor it only because motion pictures were now able to depict "the evils of a vicious past" with frightening and vivid realism.[29]

Reviewers time and again echoed Griffith's own promotion of his film as history brought to life. One Dallas reviewer, for instance, commented that because Griffith "pictorialized [the] action of thousands of players in the great outdoors," he offered a "realistic picture of history in the making." The reviewer further marveled that the film represented "the supreme achievement of modern histrionism in its new guise untrammeled by the limitations of the theater." The modern achievement of film, its ability to portray events "with lifelike realism," as one review asserted, thus authenticated as historical truth what was, as its critics pointed out, a very biased and distorted portrayal of the past. The film's intertitles, which claimed that certain scenes were "HISTORICAL FACSIMILES," as well as Griffith's use of historians' testimony to promote the film, enhanced these claims to pictorial accuracy.[30]

Such hyperbole, repeated throughout the film's promotion, was also, of course, a strategy to attract large crowds, particularly crowds who might have eschewed motion pictures as an unsophisticated form of amusement. Whereas cinema initially had captivated all classes, by the early twentieth century, elites and the respectable middle classes, especially in northern cities, tended to disdain moving pictures as unrefined entertainment. Middle-class people certainly attended nickel theaters, or nickelodeons, but the bulk of audiences were working-class people and immigrants who flocked to neighborhood theaters for cheap entertainment. Middle-class reformers were in turn becoming increasingly anxious about the negative impact that they perceived moving pictures were having on the moral values and conduct of these audiences. Cinema did not develop such a seedy reputation in the South, especially in smaller cities where downtowns were not divided by class. Evangelical leaders did object vigorously to the sinfulness of the motion picture houses, but their vehemence stemmed, in part, from the fact that so many of their constituents, especially younger ones, went to the movies regularly. Most churches concentrated their energies on censoring certain kinds of films or attempting to force movie houses to close on Sundays. These disputes assumed that evangelicals were attending the cinema; the controversies simply involved when they were going and what they were seeing.[31]

Griffith, however, pointedly sought to attract elite and middle-class audiences, as well as appease reformers, by creating a respectable and moral attraction, an epic spectacle that was "more than a mere moving picture." For this reason, Griffith avoided nickelodeons and other strictly motion picture houses to exhibit his photoplay. He insisted that the film play in opera houses and other upscale theaters. In its first run, nine prints traveled the country with a company of fifty people, including a thirty-piece orchestra. Ticket prices ranged from two dollars for front orchestra seats to fifty cents for the gallery, prices more in line with theater tickets, which far exceeded the ten- or twenty-five-cent price of the nickelodeon. *Birth* was, in these ways, promoted and exhibited more like a refined theater production than a moving picture, which was, in part, why promoters described it as a "spectacle" and an "attraction" rather than a film. The success of *Birth* both represented and fostered a larger industry shift in which producers and exhibitors in the 1910s sought to refashion motion pictures into respectable entertainment that crossed class lines. By creating three- or four-reel "features" and "photoplays" and, eventually, by building elegant picture "palaces" that mimicked the grandest opera houses, the industry actively solicited middle-class and elite patrons, making motion pictures the most successful mass entertainment of the modern age. *Birth* proved instrumental in this transformation. In promoting the film, Thomas Dixon, in fact, lauded motion pictures as "a universal language of man . . . equally resistless to an audience of chauffeurs or a gathering of a thousand college professors."[32]

By attracting audiences from all classes, *Birth* achieved a class unity that muted any elite critique of its most salacious and violent scenes, including, especially, the rapes and Gus's lynching. Although the film brought white spectators together across class lines, however, it did so in part by aggravating racial divisions. The reception of the film, in this sense, reenacted the vision of white interclass solidarity that white supremacist rhetoric propounded and that the film itself imagined. In the picture's climactic finish, the Cameron family takes refuge in the small cabin of Union veterans, and together, former slaveholder and yeoman, southerner and northerner, they fend off the encroaching black mobs. The southern home under siege is not a planter mansion but the humble cabin of the yeoman farmer, where elites and ordinary folk unite against their common enemy.[33]

The popularity of the film collapsed not only class divisions but sectional borders as well. The nationwide enthusiasm for *Birth* echoed the call for national reconciliation that the film itself envisioned, a reconciliation that demanded that white northerners commemorate the Confederate Lost Cause and consent to the South's white supremacist social vision. *Birth* was not extraordinary in this matter. Leading up to the semicentennial commemoration of the war's end, scores of films were released in the 1910s that similarly celebrated the South's noble defeat and projected wistful images of an idyllic Old South. For the previous twenty-five years, at least, white northerners had been indulging in this sort of nostalgia, largely as a response to their own Victorian anxieties about the erasure of traditional authority and morality in modern life, as well as to class and ethnic conflicts surfacing in northern cities at the same time. Many also had accepted the white southern mythology that black men, emancipated from the civilizing chains of slavery, represented an enormous criminal and sexual threat not only to the South but to the nation, even as many white northerners also objected to lynching as a lawless and dangerous practice. Popular books, plays, advertisements, and films commonly fed fantasies of picturesque and peaceful plantations where white masters and black slaves interacted with grace, good manners, and good cheer—a vision of national reunion that came at the expense of African Americans.[34]

Birth epitomized this national reunion; in fact, audiences came to represent this reconciliation incarnate, especially as white northern spectators regularly embraced a southern point of view in their enthusiasm for the film. Chicago film critic Percy Hammond, for instance, expressed surprise that crowds in his city "cheered the Stars and Bars" while remaining unmoved "by the Stars and Stripes." These spectators, he moaned, "applauded 'Dixie' and greeted 'Marching through Georgia' with silence." Similarly, the Moving Picture World reported that the applause was "spontaneous and frequent" at the film's premiere at the Liberty Theater in New York. "It was evident that the audience felt the grip of the story and sympathized with the work of the Ku Klux Klan battling against negro domination," the account remarked. In some southern cities, Union and Confederate veterans were invited to screen the film together, acting out within the theater the reconciliation between former enemies that the film itself imagined.[35]

Not all northern white viewers accepted the film, of course. Many white liberals supported African American protests over the film's damaging portrayals of freed slaves and black politicians. Some also disputed its sanctification of the Lost Cause. Chicago mayor William Thompson declared his intention to prohibit Birth in that city not only because it was objectionable to black citizens but also because, according to the Chicago Tribune, it gave "the impression that northern statesmen . . . committed great wrong against the South in the years immediately following the war."[36] Hammond similarly objected to the southern "propaganda" in the film, especially as it depicted Sherman's army as a "drunken mob, addicted to murder and rapine." Likewise, another northern viewer, in an incensed letter to the *Boston Herald*, contended that the film was "a gross libel upon the Union cause, upon its public leaders, Lincoln only excepted, upon every soldier, living or dead who fought for it, and upon the whole people who supported it." He then added, with a derisive slap, "In the South, with conditions reversed, such a show and its perpetrators would be lynched. This is not the Massachusetts way."[37]

In the South, however, there was a relatively unquestioned reverence toward the film. Although *Birth* broke box office records in both sections of the country, southern responses were more emotional and fervent, with less room for dissent. Certainly, African American civic leaders did object to the film in cities across the South, sometimes with the support of white allies. In Atlanta, for instance, the Evangelical Ministers' Association was sympathetic to black concerns that *Birth* would incite racial prejudice against them and sought, unsuccessfully, the help of newspaper editors to suppress the picture. A group of white ministers there also asked the mayor to prohibit its showing, although the Atlanta censorship board ultimately found nothing unacceptable in the film. Similar objections were raised in other southern cities, but it does not appear that the film was ever banned in the South. The *Elizabeth City (N.C.) Independent* was one of the few southern white papers to come out against the film, condemning it, with unrestrained paternalism, as "a cruel slander of a weak and helpless race" and "a cowardly attack upon a people who are not strong enough to hit back." Nevertheless, the paper advised southern blacks to "let the picture alone," since any opposition would be "in vain."[38]

In most southern cities and towns, however, those who opposed the film were given little public voice. Most white southerners embraced the film as one with direct bearing on their lives, with a passion unmatched in the North. As film critic Seymour Stern recalled, they "poured into the theatres, breathless with anticipation, excitement, superiority and wonder" and "beheld [the film] with hungry eyes." He concluded, "in effect, to the southern people, the *Birth of a Nation* came as a religious experience." The United Daughters of the Confederacy and other southern civic organizations, as well as teachers and ministers throughout the South, endorsed the film publicly. One minister in Wytheville, Virginia, used his Sunday sermon to express his gratitude "to the creator of such a picture" and to say he "hoped all his people had seen it." Reporters and reviewers, furthermore, by consistently representing the film as a deeply meaningful event, groomed viewers to have an emotional and visceral response to it. As one Georgia paper told its readers, "Griffith does not just tell you about [the South's history]. He employs an art that makes you see it; feel yourself a part of it, and while it is being enacted before your eyes the blood tingles with the heroism and the marvels of it."[39]

Although *Birth* played only in larger cities, a surprisingly large number of people in the South were able to see it. Papers regularly reported that it played to standing-room-only crowds, and theater owners frequently extended engagements to meet audience demand. Rome, Georgia, with a population of around 14,000 in 1910, was one of the smallest cities in which the film played, a fact that the city paper proclaimed proudly in its advertisements as a marker of Rome's sophistication and legitimacy. The Nevins Opera House, which was all but closed in 1915, reopened to screen the picture, which was reportedly "witnessed by more people than have ever attended an amusement offering in Rome."[40] Many people viewed *Birth* more than once and related the story to those who could not attend. Moreover, in many small towns where the film was not shown, local papers still advertised it. Residents in these outlying areas made special trips to cities to see the production, and, in some cases, trains were commissioned to take them there. The *Charlotte (N.C.) Observer* reported that the local theater had received mail and telephone orders for the upcoming exhibition of the film from towns as far away as seventy-five miles. And for those who missed the production in its 1915–17 run, it toured the country a second time in 1921 and again in 1930. By one estimate, 90 percent of southerners had seen the film by 1930.[41]

These audiences consumed the picture actively, responding demonstratively and even, at times, inserting themselves into the action. In Dallas, "the large audience . . . was from tears to cheers and from laughter to throat-choking tenseness" throughout the production. In Asheville, North Carolina, the "large crowd experienced successive thrills, several people becoming excited almost to the point of hysteria." Spirited displays of emotion were not unusual for early film audiences, who commonly interacted with each other and the screen well into the sound era. But what is remarkable is just how boisterous *Birth*'s spectators were and how consistently reviews of the film reported on their reactions, as if the spectacle drew its strength not just from what appeared on the screen but from what transpired in the theater itself.[42]

A central feature of *Birth*'s cinematic spectacle was its capacity to represent large, epic crowds, a feature that reviews regularly remarked on:

the onslaught of soldiers in battle, the audience at Ford's Theatre, and,
of course, the train of white-robed Klansmen riding to the rescue. These
crowds, celebrated and marveled at within the film, were mirrored in the
spectacle of animated theater crowds. As poet Vachel Lindsay, writing on the
new medium of moving pictures in 1915, contended, "While the motion picture is shallow in showing private emotion, it is powerful in conveying the
passions of masses of men." In other words, although silent pictures could
depict the inner lives of individuals only in crude pantomime, they could
make visibly apparent the emotional sway of a crowd. Audiences became
yet another crowd whose behaviors helped generate the emotional power
of the film. Although individual responses would certainly have varied depending on taste, mood, and perspective, reports on the film more often
than not portrayed audience responses as unanimous reactions. Spectators
clapped, cheered, hooted, and stamped their feet, all responses that bear
more weight when performed as groups. As one critic has noted, according
to legend, southerners came to the theater "as one folk, one people," united
in their passion for the film. These crowds were, of course, always imagined
as white. As will be shown below, black southerners did see *Birth*, sitting in
galleries and balconies, and sometimes protested it, but reports in southern
papers rarely noted their presence.[43]

The excessiveness of white audiences' responses stemmed, in part, from
the dramatic effect of melodrama, which was predicated on emotional in-
dulgence and sensationalism; that is, in melodrama, the characters' extraordinary conflicts and heightened emotions were meant to arouse a visceral
sympathetic response in audiences. Southern audiences felt the response
to *Birth* with added intensity because the film's melodrama was so closely
tied to their own sense of history and loss, as well as to their very deep fears
about black enfranchisement, criminality, and sexuality. Reports often commented that spectators' responses, particularly their cheers and rebel yells,
drew from their sense of sectional pride and honor. The *Rome (Ga.) Tribune-
Herald* reported that "old war shouts are heard in the audience from the lips
of veterans who momentarily forget that it is only in the play." Likewise, the
Charlotte (N.C.) Observer exclaimed, "Never was a scene more truly lived
than that of the southern soldiers leaving their loved ones." As the soldiers
"marched away to the tune of 'Dixie,' the house was fairly lifted to its feet
by the enthusiasm displayed." Accounts like these not only described audience responses to the film but projected the spectators into the narrative
itself.[44]

These representations of ardent, united spectators, inflamed with racial

and sectional pride, also evoked images of impassioned and unified lynching crowds. As Lindsay observed, "*The Birth of a Nation* is a Crowd Picture
in a triple sense. On the film, as in the audience, it turns the crowd into a
mob that is either for or against the Reverend Thomas Dixon's poisonous
hatred of the Negro." But much as prolynching rhetoric regularly insisted
that lynching crowds were orderly and respectable, reports assured readers
that *Birth's* audiences, though passionate, remained controlled and self-
possessed. As the *Asheville (N.C.) Citizen* recounted after a showing in that
city, "Cheering and 'cat-calls' were sustained for several minutes at various
periods, but there was not the slightest approach to disorder." Just as the
film rendered lynching an efficient and honorable act of justice, it also managed to contain lynching spectatorship within the refined confines of the
opera house or other high-class theater.[45]

Reviews of the film tended to pay particular attention to audiences' reactions to the attempted rapes of Flora and Elsie and to the Klan's heroic
ride to avenge their honor. "As that audience of southerners sat at the
Academy of Music watching the huge Negro brute, Silas Lynch, make love
to the white daughter of Austin Stoneman . . . their blood fairly boiled in
their veins," reported the *Charlotte (N.C.) Observer*. "But as the thousands of
white-clad clansmen came swinging through the fields on the white-robed
chargers, bent upon suppressing the Negro and saving the South, the cheers
went through the roof." Similarly, in Waco, Texas, the sight of Flora leaping
to her death to save "her most priceless possession . . . took the house by
storm." And in Richmond, Virginia, an audience of veterans, who cried "the
old Rebel Yell" throughout the picture, were "particularly please[d]" at the
scene in which "the Klan place[d] the dead body of Gus, the renegade negro,
at the porch of Silas Lynch."[46] The rape scenes would have been especially
disturbing for white men to witness, for they made visible images of black
lust they had previously only imagined or had relied on female witnesses to
describe. Some men were so overcome by these scenes that they moved to
intervene and lynch Gus themselves. As one historian notes about a showing of the film in Spartanburg, South Carolina, "Men who once wore gray
uniforms, white sheets, and red shirts wept, yelled, whooped, cheered, and
on one occasion even shot up the screen in a valiant effort to save Flora
Cameron from her black pursuer." In at least one case, fiction did collapse
into reality: a Kentucky man left the theater after seeing the picture and
proceeded to shoot and kill a fifteen-year-old African American high school
student.[47]

The cinematic spectacle of white-robed avengers further spilled over into real life when, in some Deep South states, Klan regalia and souvenirs were sold in theaters and ushers were costumed in Klan garb. Some theater managers even promoted the film by having horsemen dressed as Klansmen march through town in advance of the screening. As noted in the beginning of this chapter, the film also played a crucial role in the formation in 1915 of the second Klan, which by the early 1920s boasted a national membership nearing 5 million, with a scope and power that far exceeded its original Reconstruction incarnation. Throughout the 1920s, the Klan capitalized on showings of the film, appearing in costume and distributing pamphlets and flyers to spectators, as well as using the film as a recruitment tool in its own meetings and ceremonies.[48] The founder of the second Klan, William Simmons, himself credited the film for giving "the new order a tremendous popular boost." As film critic Terry Ramsaye wrote in 1926, "The picture *The Birth of a Nation* and the K.K.K. secret society . . . were sprouted from the same root. In subsequent years, they reacted upon each other to the large profit of both. The film presented predigested dramatic experience and thrills. The society made the customers all actors in costumes." In other words, by joining the Klan, spectators could literally project themselves into the fantasy of white heroism and righteousness that the film envisioned.[49]

IT WAS PRECISELY this overidentification with the film, this slippery boundary between audience and player, that worried many critics of the film. From its premiere in Los Angeles in February 1915, a chorus of African American and white liberal civic leaders, journalists, and writers, dominated by the NAACP, sought to restrict exhibition of the film on the grounds that its misrepresentations of Reconstruction and of the black race posed not only a hindrance to black advancement but a real and present threat to black safety. By confirming all the worst stereotypes of black lust and crime, the film would, in the words of many of its critics, "enflame race hatred" and "incite racial violence"—they claimed that it would, in fact, have real-world effects on the lives of African Americans. Indeed, the NAACP's popular slogan for the picture—"assassination of a race"—denoted it as a weapon, collapsing any distinction between the murders of African Americans onscreen and murders that the picture might provoke.[50]

In doing so, the NAACP and others bestowed on *Birth* a degree of visual power and influence that Griffith and the film's supporters also acclaimed for it. The black press had waged a similar campaign against Dixon's *The Clansman* when it toured the country ten years earlier, but the outcry against *Birth* was more vociferous, in part because the protest against *Birth* had a central organizing body in the NAACP, formed in 1909. But it was also more fervent because critics perceived that there was more at stake; not only would more people see *Birth*, but a motion picture opened a greater possibility that spectators would confuse the picture with reality. "'The Clansman' did us much injury as a book. . . . It did us more injury as a play," wrote James Weldon Johnson. "Made into a moving play it can do us incalculable harm." For Johnson, the film was an exponential threat because "every minute detail of the story is vividly portrayed before the eyes of the spectators." Focusing on the near-rape scene, he asked, "Can you imagine the effect of such a scene upon the millions who seldom read a book, who seldom witness a drama, but who constantly go to the movies?"[51]

Not all critics of the film moved to censor it, however. While most bemoaned the negative representations embodied in the characters of Gus and Lynch, some African American leaders, along with a number of white liberal critics of the film, found the efforts to ban *Birth* futile and counterproductive. Others, like Booker T. Washington, sought to stem the protests for fear that the consequences of direct action would be far worse for blacks than any harm the picture itself might do. But public demonstrations against the film in places like New York and Boston, and the NAACP's persistent campaign to pressure mayors, city councils, and censorship boards across the country to prohibit screenings or cut inflammatory scenes, garnered the most attention nationwide. They were also somewhat successful. Some key scenes were excised or shortened for exhibition in a number of northern and western cities, and other places, including Ohio and Kansas, prohibited the film.[52]

The NAACP based its campaign on the premise that the film would, in Johnson's words, do "incalculable harm," in particular, that the sight of black men chasing white women on-screen would justify and even incite racial violence. "The production is . . . designed to palliate and excuse the lynchings and other deeds of violence committed against the Negro," insisted the NAACP. "It is an appeal to violence and outrage." As Mary Ovington, who spearheaded the protest for the NAACP, recalled, "If I could show . . . that the [film] might injure the Negro in the city where it was shown, if it was bestial as to create antagonism, even violence, then it should not be produced." The NAACP, for this reason, focused attention on what it called the film's "rape scenes," rather than the lynching of Gus, and demanded they be cut or, at least, shortened. According to Ovington, Gus, with "his great clutching hands repeatedly pictured," was rendered so hideous and threatening that it "was enough to make a Bostonian on Beacon Hill double-lock his door at night."[53] The concern here was not that white spectators would imitate what they saw on-screen but that certain scenes would excite their most racist fears and their "bestial" natures, which they would unleash on exiting the theater. The NAACP thus included in its pleas to various mayors and city councils frightening stories of viewers' reactions to the film, including an anecdote about one young southern man who, on exiting the theater after a New York showing, said to his companion, "I should like to kill every nigger I know." The *Crisis*, as well as other black newspapers, regularly included reports of lynchings and others acts of racist violence in addition to its coverage of the protests against *Birth*, and it made much of the incident, mentioned above, in which a man killed an African American teenager after seeing the picture.[54]

The NAACP's push to prevent the film's exhibition took place within a larger cultural climate in which motion pictures were routinely subject to censorship. In the early 1910s, cities and some states across the country began to pass ordinances and establish censorship boards. The National Board of Censorship, formed in 1909, acted as the leading private organization that advised the film industry about what was appropriate and inappropriate for audiences to see. In fact, the NAACP had unsuccessfully appealed to the board before taking its case against *Birth* directly to exhibitors and public officials.[55] Reformers who advocated for censorship laws did so because they believed that motion pictures had a particular potential to do harm, since they constituted a form of amusement unlike any before — not only because of their popularity but also because they could depict a full range of human behavior with vivid realism. These reformers, in particular, feared the moral impact of scenes of sexuality and vice on impressionable audiences, but they were just as concerned that pictures not incite civic unrest of any sort, including racial discord or violence. As noted earlier, censorship laws in at least one city prohibited the depiction of lynching and other scenes of interracial violence. The National Board of Censorship also regularly rejected films that represented "the criminal passion and rough handling of a white girl by Negroes."[56]

These concerns were given legitimacy with the Supreme Court's landmark decision in *Mutual v. Ohio*, a decision handed down in February 1915, just as the NAACP began its battle against *Birth*. In that decision, which upheld the Ohio state legislature's right to create a state censorship board regulating motion pictures, a unanimous court deemed that motion pictures did not constitute protected speech under the First Amendment because they were just entertainment, "mere representations of events . . .

originated and conducted for profit" and not "organs of public opinion." Yet the decision also made clear that the state had a legitimate public interest in regulating motion pictures that went beyond what it might need to do for other kinds of amusements. Motion pictures posed a unique threat because of "their attractiveness and manner of exhibition." Although they could amuse or educate, they could also incite the most prurient and dangerous thoughts, especially since pictures gave those thoughts visual form and credence under the guise of simple entertainment.[57]

The NAACP thus felt nothing but frustration and anger at the racial hypocrisy evinced by the board and by so many public officials across the country, especially in the South, who refused to prohibit or edit *Birth*. After all, when black boxer Jack Johnson became the heavyweight champion in 1908, films of his bouts, especially that against "the great white hope" Jim Jeffries in 1910, were banned in cities across the country and everywhere in the South, on the grounds that they might incite racial violence and unrest. Many towns and cities instituted statutes that forbade any showing of a motion picture that was "calculated to provoke racial prejudice and create disorder," as a local ordinance passed in Dallas just days after the fight stated.[58] Those African Americans who had tolerated the ban on films of Johnson's fights in their cities at the expense of their own feelings of racial pride now felt betrayed by city leaders who would not uphold the same principles when African Americans expressed fear that *Birth* would similarly foment racial violence.[59]

Both Griffith and Dixon took to the stage and the press to defend *Birth* against its critics and the threat of censorship, no doubt relishing the publicity that the protests were bringing to the film. They did so not by downplaying the film's cultural effects but by touting its cinematic and historical importance. On the one hand, Griffith claimed his film was a production that was owed the same "fair reception and treatment" that theater productions received, especially because it played to the same reputable class of people. On the other hand, he put forward loftier claims about motion pictures as the most vivid and expressive art form in the world, capable of chronicling the tragedies of history with vibrant clarity—arguing that cinema was, as Woodrow Wilson was said to have remarked about *Birth*, "like writing history with lightning." In this respect, Griffith could not argue that the film was harmless fiction; instead, he painted his critics as suppressors of historical truth who sought to distort the plain facts of the past.[60] The battle over *Birth* thus became a battle over historical authenticity, with the NAACP countering Griffith's claims with statements from historians and other experts testifying to the film's inaccuracies. The NAACP also attempted to squelch Griffith's claims to cultural significance by reminding potential allies that the film was a commercial product, and a lascivious and immoral one at that. While the group recognized that *Birth* had "artistic qualities," it likened these qualities to the "lavish decorations of a gambling den or the luxurious boudoir of a courtesan" and denounced the film as no more than "an attempt to commercialize the evil passions of men."[61]

Protests against the film were understandably more demonstrative in northern cities, where the NAACP concentrated most of its efforts. At times, the picture animated audiences against it to the same degree that it roused devoted audiences in the South. At screenings in New York and Boston, protestors rallied outside the theater, and spectators hissed at the black caricatures on-screen and even threw eggs at the screen. The NAACP was able to campaign against the film forcefully in these cities and others across the Northeast and Midwest because of larger changes in African American life, including black migration to northern cities, and the concomitant rise of sustained and organized civil rights activism. In places like New York and Chicago, African Americans began to see themselves as active consumers of media and popular culture, through which they could act out and make evident their own sense of social advancement.[62]

Although protest against the film in southern cities was muted, African American leaders and their white allies did attempt to prevent its exhibition in a number of places in the South, including, as mentioned, Atlanta. These attempts were initially without success, as no southern city banned the film or cut offensive scenes from it in its first run. Nevertheless, because news of protests in the North had traveled south, a fear of racial unrest hung over every screening. One theater manager, in Biloxi, Mississippi, banned African Americans from seeing the picture because "a number of white citizens objected" to having them in the theater. Supported by the mayor and the chief of police, the manager based his decision on the fear that "animosities might be engendered, which would result in trouble."[63]

In other southern cities, civic leaders assured the public that screenings of the film were absent of racial discord and promoted that absence as a sign of peaceful race relations in their locales. "We had not the semblance of trouble," asserted the chief of police in Asheville, North Carolina, where several civic groups had attempted unsuccessfully to suppress the film. "I have heard no pronounced criticism from the colored people who witnessed the performance." Likewise, the *Charlotte (N.C.) Observer* praised local blacks who had seen the film for being "well behaved and conservatively critical."

The paper then blamed the problem the film was facing in the North on "white people of mistaken friendship for the negro — a manifestation of the same mistaken policy that led the negroes in the South into so much trouble in the past." In other words, the *Charlotte (N.C.) Observer* perceived the conflicts that arose over *Birth* as a reenactment of the past racial conflicts that the film dramatized.[64]

Although southern blacks had remained more "conservatively critical" than their northern counterparts, they nevertheless interpreted the film as a direct assault on them, one that, though set in the past, had a real impact on their lives under segregation. "When they showed that lynching, the whites were cheering. I tell you, we were suffering in the balcony," remembered Milton Quigless, a teenager living in Port Gibson, Mississippi, when the production passed through. Whites, he wrote, "praised" the film "to no end." He added, "Everybody was talking about it. . . . You could tell a difference in things for about six months after it was gone. They weren't exactly hostile, but you could sense a strange feeling."[65]

In later showings of the film, some southern blacks did become more demonstrative in their opposition to the film, creating the very scenes of racial discord that so frightened southern whites. According to the *Chicago Defender*, "a near riot was precipitated" at a showing of the film in Salisbury, North Carolina, in the 1920s, when black spectators in the balcony applauded and cheered at what the white spectators deemed inappropriate moments. Although no violence broke out, whites in the audience threatened "vociferous" blacks that they would "come up there and get you," to which some black spectators replied, "Come on up." When the film played again in Salisbury several years later, the theater did not advertise it "until the last minute" so that protestors would have no "time to form an organization or opposition." All the same, city officials, fearing further disruption, urged black citizens to stay home and "blacklist" the film, in effect exploiting black protest against the film for their own desires for civic peace.[66]

Black spectators, like those in Salisbury, who cheered at "inappropriate" moments were engaging in a rereading of the film that must have been startling to those whites who had accepted the film's white supremacist perspective without question. After all, those protestors who had sought to censor the film recognized its point of view, even as they denounced it as false and damaging. But these African American spectators, though they too certainly understood the film's white supremacist perspective, disrupted that perspective by imposing their own reading on it through their cheers and hollers. According to a local patrolman, a riot nearly broke out at a 1931 showing of the film in Memphis, Tennessee, because "the Negroes had been cheering every time a Negro killed a white man." Rather than boycotting the film, these spectators reinterpreted it as a picture of black revolt. The patrolman further related that "when the picture started killing Negroes the whites down below got up an applause of their own." The police subsequently shut down the balcony, barring African Americans from the screening while allowing white spectators to carry on. The officer's use of the phrase "the picture started killing Negroes" is itself telling, as if he wanted to reassert the film's point of view; that is, black men may have killed white men in the film, but it was "the picture" — as an active force — that killed black men.[67]

That these kinds of conflicts arose in later years, rather than during the film's initial run in 1915 and 1916, is not surprising. Blacks would have felt more emboldened to respond vocally in the theater, not necessarily because southern racial constraints and strictures or the fear of reprisal had lessened, but because the film's power had waned. To be sure, most white southerners still considered Birth a masterpiece, but they did not approach it with the same degree of reverence and awe, in part because the novelty of its spectacle had diminished. Moreover, as will be shown in the following chapters, after World War I, white elites throughout the South increasingly turned against lynching and, in particular, expressed discomfort with public images of lynching and racial violence.

For these reasons, protestors had more success in convincing civic authorities to ban Birth's exhibition when it was rereleased. In 1918, the NAACP launched another campaign against the film and received support from many governors and mayors in northern and western states, as well as from state defense councils and the National Council of Defense. After a delegation of African American leaders tried to suppress the picture in Columbia, South Carolina, on the grounds that black citizens had evinced loyalty and patriotism during the war, the chairman of the South Carolina Council of Defense recommended that the film not be shown in that state. "There is no excuse for showing it in the South at this time against the protest of the leaders of the negro race," the chairman told the Columbia State. "This was especially true since the negro has cooperated so heartily in all patriotic activities since the beginning of the war." Local authorities in Winston-Salem, North Carolina, called off a screening of the film for similar reasons. Many southerners were still committed to the film, however. Mississippi governor Theodore Bilbo, known for his vitriolic white supremacy, responded to the NAACP's plea that he ban the film by boasting that it "has been presented in every picture play house in the State" and had not met with any objection from black Mississippians. In fact, he asserted, the film had "caused no friction between the races" at all.[68]

By 1930, however, when Griffith rereleased *Birth* with synchronized music and sound effects, white voices against the film in the South were louder and more abundant. Various religious groups, missionary societies, and other civic organizations, including the Commission on Interracial Cooperation, sought to suppress the picture on the grounds that it would, as one prominent minister explained, only "stir up irritation and friction between the races." These groups were especially worried because, after a slow decline throughout the 1920s, lynchings had suddenly increased in 1930. The Woman's Missionary Council of the Southern Methodist Church accordingly expressed concern over "particular scenes which show the mobs, reproducing the crisis and all such gruesome effects," which they believed would have "a dangerous and demoralizing influence, stirring up the passions, rousing the spirit of defiance of law and unreasonable hatred." The focus of their fear, however, was not the African Americans who might be the victims of those "passions" and "unreasonable hatred"; rather, they insisted that "it is a terrible thing to subject white children to the influence of pictures that arose such racial prejudices and hatreds"—a point of view that, as will be shown, dovetailed with many white southern liberal objections to lynching in these years.[69]

W. E. B. Du Bois reportedly once professed that, "while the NAACP failed to kill *The Birth of a Nation*, it succeeded in wounding it," by which he meant that although the film continued to garner not only profit but critical acclaim for its cinematic brilliance, the NAACP had forever tainted it with the stain of racial prejudice. By 1938, the NAACP claimed it had suppressed the picture in eighteen states and even more cities, and, in many places where it was shown, enough scenes had been cut to make the film incoherent. More significant, the NAACP had won the publicity war. Many white Americans by the 1930s had come to accept that the film's caricatures of African Americans were offensive, even harmful.[70]

In the battle over *Birth*, the NAACP placed images at the forefront of its struggles against white supremacy and racial oppression, a focus that might appear curious and even counterproductive, considering the very real subjugation and violence that black Americans experienced on a daily basis. But the NAACP did so because it saw a continuum between the representations of racial violence on-screen and the prejudice and terror that hampered black advancement. Images were not incidental, especially because people were so willing to understand cinematic and photographic images as truthful reflections of reality. They shaped perceptions, understanding, and behavior. For the NAACP, they were the building blocks of racial prejudice and violence.

For this reason, the NAACP and other black leaders used their outrage against *Birth* to energize a burgeoning black film industry with the aim of generating images and representations of black life that could counter the damaging stereotypes prevalent in mainstream American cinema. The first black-owned production company, the Lincoln Motion Picture Company, had formed in 1913, making films that championed black advancement, but *Birth* made the need for such pictures more urgent. The years following *Birth*'s release saw the emergence of a number of black-owned studios and the production of several films that served as direct rebuttals to Griffith's film, including *The Colored American Winning His Suit* (Frederick Douglass Film, 1916) and *The Birth of a Race* (Photoplay, 1918). The latter film, which attempted to chronicle black achievement from slavery to emancipation, received the most public attention because it had backing, at various points in its production, from the NAACP and the Tuskegee Institute, as well as leading black and white philanthropists, and was shot by a leading studio, the Selig Polyscope Company. The finished product, however, was a disjointed and embarrassing failure. More successful cinematic rejoinders to *Birth* were Oscar Micheaux's antilynching films, *Within Our Gates* (1920) and *The Gunsaulus Mystery* (1921), the latter pieced together from elements of the Leo Frank lynching. Black filmmakers, like Micheaux, relied on the same expectations about cinema's abilities to act as a direct reflection of historical and social reality and, in turn, to shape social behavior and action. These filmmakers thus sought to produce films of racial uplift that projected positive images of black independence and upward mobility on-screen, images that stood in direct counterpoint to the racist caricatures of *Birth* and other mainstream fare. The hope was that these positive images would stand as the new reality of black life and uplift their audiences.[71]

Arguably the greatest success of the NAACP's battle against *Birth*, however, was that it brought an enormous amount of publicity to the organization and its antiracist agenda. It also set the stage for its antilynching campaigns, which gained momentum the year after *Birth*'s release. In those campaigns, the NAACP well understood the power of images to activate people against prejudice and racial violence. Indeed, as the next chapter addresses, lynching photography became a crucial element of them. The spectacle surrounding *Birth* gave visual credence to white supremacist beliefs, projecting them as authentic historical truth. Audiences did not merely soak in these images but brought them meaning and significance through their active engagement with them. But that spectacle also activated black audiences, who were able to shape an alternative meaning from the same images, one that ultimately undermined the authenticity that *Birth* purported. Although the NAACP sought to suppress *Birth*'s images of lynching, locked as they seemed to be within Griffith's white supremacist narrative, it soon came to recognize that the spectacle that offered so much force to prolynching rhetoric could be used against it.

PART III ◈ BEARING WITNESS

6

❖ ❖ ❖

WE WANTED TO BE BOOSTERS
AND NOT KNOCKERS

Photography and Antilynching Activism

THE 1916 LYNCHING of Jesse Washington in Waco, Texas, stands as one of the most widely known and scrutinized lynchings because it, in many ways, typified the grotesque excess of spectacle lynching. Just over two months after *The Birth of a Nation* played in Waco, an estimated 10,000 people watched as a mob mutilated, strangled, and burned Washington to death on the grounds of the city hall. The mayor and the chief of police watched from a window above. Washington was a seventeen-year-old African American who lived about eight miles from Waco, in Robinson, with his parents and several siblings on the farm of George Fryer. When Fryer's wife Lucy was found dead on the farm, her skull smashed with a hammer, authorities promptly arrested Washington and brought him to Waco, where he confessed to murdering and raping her. On the day of the trial, thousands of people poured into the city, and, though most assumed Washington would be convicted and hanged quickly, talk of lynching filled the air. Indeed, just moments after the jury, which had deliberated for only four minutes, read its guilty verdict, the crowd in the courtroom surged forward and seized Washington. Local businesses promptly closed their doors as spectators— men, women, and children—swarmed the city center, climbing trees and standing on rooftops to get a better view. A local photographer, Fred Gilder-sleeve, who had been notified that Washington would be lynched, captured the events on film from a window in city hall. Afterward, his images were sold on the streets of the city along with body parts and other grisly remnants from the day's events (figures 3.4 and 3.5).[1]

The lynching of Washington is also noteworthy because it represents a defining moment in the history of lynching, an instance when the spectacle of lynching began to sow the seeds of its own collapse. Newspapers across the country covered the lynching, generating national attention, which gave vital fuel to the NAACP's antilynching movement and embarrassed not only Waco's political and business leaders but white elites across the South. The northern press swiftly condemned the savagery of the lynching as a shameful stain on the South's, and America's, reputation. "What the [citizens of Waco] did . . . brings disgrace and humiliation on their country as well as themselves," read a *New York Times* editorial, "for wherever the news of it goes—and the news of it will go far—it will be asserted that in no other land even pretending to be civilized could a man be burned to death in the streets of a considerable city amid the savage exultation of its inhabitants." The NAACP also took notice and, within days of the lynching, hired Elizabeth Freeman, a white northern suffrage activist working in Texas at the time, to travel to Waco to investigate.[2]

When Freeman arrived in Waco, she found a thriving city that belied the assumption, widely held outside the South, that lynchings were confined to backward and impoverished communities. Lying on the Brazos River in central Texas, Waco in 1916 was a substantial city of about 35,000 people, a quarter of whom were African American. A booming retail and railroad center, it was considered a progressive city. In the previous five years, the city had come to boast the construction of Texas's then tallest building (the twenty-two-floor Amicable Insurance Company building, built in 1911), an interurban railway connecting Waco to Dallas, and the introduction of electricity and streetcars. Residents also expressed pride in the city's numerous churches and educational institutions, including the state's oldest college, Baylor University. The city's religious conservatives, however, chafed against the vitality of the new urban center and expressed growing alarm about numerous saloons and a flourishing red-light district. In the spring of 1916, a heated public debate was under way over whether local movie theaters should be permitted to open their doors on Sundays. And, despite that the city had a relatively sizable black middle class and was home to two black colleges, Waco newspapers focused on stories of "Negro crime." Waco and its surrounding area had a long history of vigilante violence, including lynching. In 1905, a lynch mob had hanged Sank Majors, an African American man accused of assaulting a white woman, from a bridge near the city center—an act that Jesse Washington's lynchers briefly considered mimicking before deciding to burn him instead. What is more, several months before the lynching of Washington, photographs of a lynching by burning of Will Stanley in Temple, Texas, including images of Stanley's charred corpse, were sold on the streets of Waco for ten cents each.[3]

Although the murder that Washington allegedly committed took place out in the county, Freeman found that the mob and spectators of Washington's lynching consisted primarily of Waco residents, most of whom presumably had little personal connection to Lucy Fryer.[4] After some digging, she discovered the names of six supposed mob leaders, including a bricklayer, a saloonkeeper, and several men who worked as clerks and drivers for a local ice company. These men acted with the full complicity of city leaders, who evidently considered lynching to be of "political value" to the sheriff and other county officials who were running for office that year. Neither the presiding judge in Washington's trial nor the mayor made any effort to stop the mob. In fact, Freeman concluded, the mayor had arranged for Gildersleeve to take the photographs from city hall as part of a "cooked business" between the men.[5]

Yet, soon after Freeman arrived, Waco residents began to cover up the spectacle, scrambling to undo the damage to their reputation that national attention had wrought. "Suddenly everyone became silent about the lynching," reported Freeman, particularly when they became suspicious about her purpose in town. Local estimates of the crowd's size shrank from 15,000 to 500. Believing she was a journalist, the former mayor of the city asked Freeman to "fix it up as well as you can for Waco, and make them understand that the better thinking men and women were not in it." Several city elites, including both a former railroad entrepreneur from the North and a wealthy businessman who had been the foreman of the jury that had condemned Washington to death, told Freeman privately that they had wanted to protest the lynching publicly. But ultimately the men retained an embarrassed silence, as did the *Waco Times Herald*, which reported the lynching as the work of a frenzied and "mad" mob but refrained from making any editorial comment. A number of local pastors, led by the minister of the First Presbyterian Church, C. T. Caldwell, did speak out, but stressed that the mob's actions represented the "sins of the few" or, as one Baptist resolution indicated, "the lowest order of society." The faculty of Baylor University also issued a public renunciation of the lynching, condemning it in part because they recognized "that the incident will evoke from the outside world reproaches unmerited by the majority of the people of our fair city and county." These responses from Waco's elite reveal a conspicuous fault line within the white community that belies the sense of class unity that the lynching supposedly enacted and that is so boldly represented in Gildersleeve's photographs.[6]

As might be expected amid this atmosphere, Freeman had a particularly difficult time obtaining copies of the lynching photographs. She made numerous attempts to buy them from the mayor and from the sheriff, who told her he did "not dare" sell them. The photographer himself eventually agreed to sell some, but then "he got cold feet" and let her have only three at fifty cents apiece. Gildersleeve later wrote to the NAACP explaining that "we have quit selling the mob photos; this step was taken because our 'city dads' objected on the grounds of 'bad publicity,' as we wanted to be boosters and not knockers, we agreed to stop all sale." For "city dads," that these images might circulate outside their community was particularly troubling, for what were consumed as celebratory souvenirs of white triumph in Waco would most certainly become icons of disgrace, "bad publicity," outside it. Waco elites recognized that new contexts changed the meaning and significance of the images entirely.[7]

For the NAACP, the photographs served as much needed publicity. The organization printed a special report based on Freeman's investigation in a supplement to the July issue of its magazine, the *Crisis*. It sent the report, titled "The Waco Horror," to NAACP supporters, as well as to President Wilson, his cabinet, and members of Congress, with the aim of raising money and support for a large-scale antilynching campaign. The *Nation* predicted that the NAACP fund-raising drive would "raise double the amount it asks if it would circulate with its appeal the pictures of the burning at Waco," something the organization had already done. The *Nation* also hoped, in vain, that the pictures would be used to identify and indict the ringleaders of the mob. In addition to placing advertisements in the *Crisis* asking readers to "read the shame of Waco" and "back us with your dollars," the NAACP sent Freeman on a speaking tour to publicize both her investigation of the Waco lynching and the NAACP's antilynching efforts. By the fall, these efforts had raised over $10,000, which the association used to support more lynching investigations and to establish the foundation for later campaigns for federal antilynching legislation.[8]

"The Waco Horror" not only emboldened the NAACP, but also led whites across the South to recognize that such "bad publicity" could threaten their New South economic ambitions and their sectional reputation. In an editorial several months after the lynching, the *Atlanta Constitution* expressed concern that the NAACP pamphlet "now being circulated throughout the United States" reflected badly not just on Waco but on Georgia and "any other southern state." It called for the Georgia legislature to take firm action against lynching not just for the "commercial future" of the state but for the "self-respect" of all Georgians. "It is more for the sake of ourselves, of our own flesh and blood and the civilization it represents, that we should stand so emphatically for law enforcement," the paper insisted. This editorial was part of a larger trend, as Georgia officials had begun to express strong anti-lynching sentiments after the lynching of Leo Frank in 1915 brought negative publicity to their state. Indeed, as news and images of lynching circulated through the national media and through antilynching publicity campaigns, white southerners increasingly found they could no longer openly support or defend mob violence with impunity.[9]

The aftershocks of Washington's lynching did not bring an immediate end to lynching—it was not the last lynching even in Waco—but the reaction to it epitomized a significant shift in the history of lynching, when the most visible excesses of mob violence, so vital to the construction and persistence of white supremacy, came into the service of antilynching activism.[10] From the mid-1910s through the 1930s, the NAACP and the black press's concerted efforts to disseminate and publish lynching photographs rendered the South, along with what were perceived as its backward and degenerate punitive practices, the object of a critical national gaze. In doing so, these activists created an alternate form of lynching spectatorship, one that impelled viewers both outside and within the South to bear witness to white injustice and brutality. By removing the photographs from the context of their white southern localities and by bringing them into national consciousness in far broader and more lasting ways than postcards and prolynching pamphlets had done, activists undermined their power to substantiate white supremacy and to act as yet another weapon against black autonomy. They bestowed on them an entirely different kind of authority.

Antilynching activism had emerged much earlier, in the 1880s, as a loose, disparate movement of organizations, ministers, and journalists who saw lynching as the most egregious hindrance to black advancement. Antilynching activism gained more cohesive political force with the founding of the NAACP in 1909. The association put opposition to lynching at the forefront of its agenda and devoted a large portion of its resources to investigating and publicizing as many lynchings as it could. It was aided in these efforts by the rise of the black press, especially as newspapers like the *New York Amsterdam News* and the *Chicago Defender* circulated nationwide. An escalation in racial violence during and after World War I, in particular, led the NAACP to focus its efforts on lobbying the U.S. Congress to pass antilynching legislation. Recognizing that southern authorities would rarely prosecute mobs or enforce state antilynching statutes, the NAACP sought to make lynching a federal crime, which would allow the U.S. government to penalize local authorities and communities that failed to stop mob violence. In this respect, the NAACP made lynching a national, rather than a local or regional, issue, and it appealed to a national audience to do so.[11]

Lynching photographs became crucial tools in these political campaigns. The horror they displayed with graphic realism—in short, their sensationalism—could capture attention and sway sentiment to a degree unmatched by text. To this end, the NAACP collected lynching photographs whenever possible and reproduced them in the *Crisis*, as well as in antilynching pamphlets and posters. By the 1930s, the association had its own archive of images, which it frequently lent to other activists, teachers, writers, and publishers.[12] Black newspapers also increasingly published lynching photographs when they had access to them, especially as, by the 1930s, developments in halftone reproduction made the printing of photographic images less burdensome and expensive. Activists, in these ways, made ample use of modern visual technologies, as well as the tropes of sensational media, to shock and incite outrage in the American public.

Lynching opponents also sought to challenge the original intention of these photographs by inverting the racist assumptions of black bestiality and propensities for violence that undergirded the defense of lynching. They instead represented white mobs as savage threats to American civilization, a representation that held particular force in light of the United States' international role as a beacon of democracy. In turn, the black media projected themselves, and by extension all African Americans, as the true defenders of American law, order, and justice. For many African Americans, the power of the lynching image helped to construct an alternative social identity that not only defied prevailing stereotypes of black men and moved beyond passive victimhood but also rendered them active critics of white hypocrisy and rightful participants in American democracy. In these ways, most antilynching activists aligned themselves with the values of modern liberalism and its commitment to human rights, a commitment that downplayed racial differences in favor of a universalist vision of equality and individual value. They insisted that racial prejudice and violence were at stark odds with civic ideals of progress and human advancement, and they relied on both the power of moral persuasion and government intervention to further these ideals.[13]

In this light, activists usually refrained from attacking lynching as a violent expression of race prejudice or a gruesome mechanism to ensure white power. Rather, they posited lynching as a universal and primeval form of criminal retribution that no civilized and modern nation should condone. In doing so, they aimed to appeal to white liberals and moderates who might harbor fears about black criminality but who would sympathize with the goals of social order and progress. They thus sought to convince white Americans that lynching was damaging and destructive not to black communities but to the nation as a whole. Accordingly, antilynching rhetoric increasingly shifted attention away from the black victims of lynching and onto the perverse brutality of white lynch mobs and spectators. The selective use and placement of lynching photographs in the press and in political propaganda did much to represent and accentuate this rhetoric.

As happened in Waco, the proliferation of lynching images in the media brought unwelcome attention to the South. For many white southerners, the growing national perception that lynching was a barbaric custom became a regional embarrassment, particularly for those "boosters" who wanted to promote economic and social development in their cities and states. In response, these southerners sought to prevent the widespread circulation and display of lynching photographs—that is, to conceal lynching as much as possible from public view. At the same time, many white southerners adopted the rhetoric of antilynching activism, especially as its deflection away from racial prejudice allowed them to denounce lynching without challenging racial segregation or undermining their claims to white supremacy. The national attention on lynching thus solidified growing sentiments across the South that lynching was a shameful practice that not only damaged the South's reputation but harmed civil and moral order, sentiments that ultimately rendered the public torture and killing of African Americans indefensible.

WITHIN TWO YEARS of its founding, the NAACP began publishing lynching photographs in the *Crisis* and in antilynching pamphlets, where they served as graphic testimony to the terrible wrongs that white mobs were inflicting on black Americans. In doing so, the organization relied on viewer expectations that a photograph represented a transparent and truthful reflection of reality, that it could, in fact, provide visual corroboration of what were incomprehensible acts of atrocity.[14] Yet the images were also horrifying because they represented a point of view—that of racist and sadistic mobs—that was embedded in the very taking of the photograph. In other words, because viewers assumed that the camera did not lie, the photographs stood as irrefutable evidence of lynching's reality, that it took place at all. At the same time, the photographs testified to a larger moral truth that to make and celebrate such an image was itself a grotesque and brutal act. Viewers were thus impelled to read the images oppositionally, that is, against their intended point of view, and to distance themselves morally from those who had taken and posed for the images.

Ida B. Wells pioneered this political reappropriation of lynching photographs when she published a postcard from an 1891 lynching in Clanton, Alabama, in her 1894 antilynching pamphlet *A Red Record*. She used this image in the text and in her public lectures to convince skeptical readers that the atrocities she narrated were true.[15] In an 1894 interview, Wells recounted that a white gentleman at one of her lectures protested that a pen and ink illustration of the Clanton lynching printed in English newspapers was "demoralizing," and he "expressed the greatest astonishment" once she "assured him that the picture was an absolute reproduction of a photograph, and proved it by showing him the photograph."[16] A photograph, in this sense, carried an authority that an artistic rendering did not.

The use of photographs to protest lynching, however, was still rare enough in the early 1910s that the NAACP had to prepare its audiences to view the images against their intended purpose. When the *Crisis* started printing lynching photographs, it explained to readers that photographs were taken at lynching scenes as an aspect of the violence. In 1912, it published a speech by New York minister and lynching opponent John H. Holmes, in which he mentioned the recent lynching of John Lee in Durant, Oklahoma, and excoriated the mob's decision to pose for photographs with its victim like hunters with their prey. Beside the speech, the *Crisis* reproduced a lynching postcard from Andalusia, Alabama, most likely from a 1906 lynching, which had been sent to Holmes with a menacing message: "This is the way we do them down here. . . . Will put you on our regular mailing list. Expect one a month on the average." (This postcard, figure 6.1, suggests that white southerners were paying attention to the actions of lynching opponents in the North.) But by positioning this postcard against Holmes's speech, the *Crisis* directed viewers' interpretation of the image so that they would disidentify with the writer of the postcard and the white spectators posing beneath the victim. Its placement, in this respect, predetermined viewers' disgust and horror at it—just as white spectators' hungry consumption of similar images was shaped by their knowledge of, spectatorship of, or participation in the lynching itself.[17]

By reproducing the image in this way, the NAACP punctured its threat for viewers and for Holmes himself. In March 1912, the *Crisis* printed a note

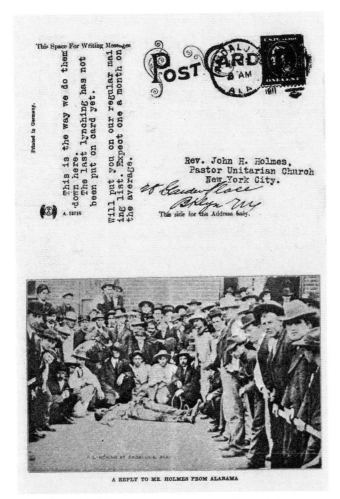

FIGURE 6.1 Lynching postcard, Andalusia, Alabama, *Crisis*,
January 1912.

from one of its readers that included a lynching postcard from Georgia that
had "so aroused" the reader that he "purchased the entire supply, with the
purpose of enlisting your aid in preventing the publication of such cards."
The journal ignored its reader's plea, however, and reprinted the lynching
image beside the note, broadening the audience further.[18] By buying the "entire supply," the writer had perhaps stopped its circulation in the lynching
locale. Yet the *Crisis* ensured that its publication continued beyond it, and
in doing so, it thwarted the terrorizing power of the image.

The NAACP thus transformed the ideological significance of these photographs by detaching them from their specific localities and recontextualiz-

FIGURE 6.2 "Jesus Christ in Georgia," *Crisis*, December 1911.

ing them. On the pages of the black press, these images no longer served as visual testimonies of white unity and superiority but instead as graphic and indisputable symbols of white brutality and racial injustice. In December 1911, within a year of its inauguration, the *Crisis* printed its first lynching photograph, an uncaptioned, cropped image of an unidentified lynching, to accompany a short story, "Jesus Christ in Georgia," by editor W. E. B. Du Bois. The photograph appears as part of the title graphic, which is dominated by a wooden cross with an image of Jesus' face at its intersection and flanked on one side by the story's title and on the other by the photograph (figure 6.2). Jesus gazes down in sorrow at the hanged body of the black lynching victim, a juxtaposition of images that mirrors the ending of the story, in which a crucified Christ appears "heaven-tall, earth-wide" beside the body of a lynched black man, his gaze "all sorrowful . . . fastened on [his] writhing, twisting body." But the title graphic did more than simply illustrate the story's ending; because the photograph depicted an actual lynching, it literalized the story's lynching, bringing it from the realm of fiction to that of truth. Within this context, the photograph had literally become iconic, a material representation of the divine.[19]

In this fashion, most lynching photographs shown in the *Crisis* remained unspecified, displaced entirely from the local circumstances and sentiments that had produced them. These images indeed served as interchangeable symbols of racial atrocity, one lynching image standing for all white brutality and black suffering. When the *Crisis* chose to illustrate John Holmes's antilynching speech about John Lee's lynching in Oklahoma with the post-card from Andalusia, Alabama, for example, this was not because there was no image of Lee's lynching. In fact, later in the same issue, the magazine reprinted a photograph from Lee's lynching, in crude halftone. It situated it, along with the image that had appeared with "Jesus Christ in Georgia," beside a poem by Leslie Pinckney Hill, "Vision of a Lyncher," which, as an inverse of "Jesus Christ in Georgia," represents the lynching scene as a vision from hell. As illustrations to the poem, the photographs, each depicting white men enveloping their victims with proprietary gestures, provided visual verification for Hill's ghastly image of "the burning plain" where "the tortured swarm" prepared for the lynching. In turn, Hill's poem would have guided viewers' understanding of the images as representing hellish and "soul-wrought pain." When these photographs appeared in an NAACP antilynching pamphlet, they bore different captions, recontextualized once again.[20]

As readers became more accustomed to seeing these kinds of images in the black press, explanations of how mobs photographed lynching—why lynching photographs existed at all—grew less necessary, presumably because viewers now understood the intrinsic violence of the images. Indeed, the fact that, in the mid-1910s, the *Crisis* felt impelled to explain to its readers that lynch mobs took and circulated lynching photographs at all indicates that most such images had not circulated far beyond the South until the black press began to publish them in greater numbers.

By the 1930s, lynching photographs had become almost entirely iconographic.[21] Some photographs, to be sure, were used to illustrate specific lynching reports. But, presumably because editors were not always able to obtain an image until after the relevant story had run, they often printed images days or even weeks after lynchings and provided readers with little or no context. For example, in 1934, the *Baltimore Afro-American* reprinted a cropped version of a 1930 photograph of George Hughes's lynched body in Sherman, Texas (figure 6.3), beside an antilynching poem by Esther Pope that had previously appeared in *Opportunity* magazine. With the title "Blasphemy—American Style," the poem derides lynch mobs' hypocritical claims to piety; beside it, the photograph of Hughes's burned and crumpled hanging corpse seems to signify both Christlike martyrdom and iconic effigy. Although a caption beneath the image reads "Sherman, Texas, Lynching," it misstates the date, and Hughes remains anonymous.[22] A "News Note" above both the poem and image refers to a Kentucky lynching in which the mob had its victim recite the Lord's Prayer before hanging and burning his body.

FIGURE 6.3 The lynching of George Hughes, Sherman, Texas, 1930.
© Bettmann/CORBIS.

Hughes's lynching became further abstracted when, in 1934, artist Isamu Noguchi modeled a metal sculpture, *Death (Lynched Figure)*, on the image of Hughes's corpse (figure 6.4). The piece appeared in the NAACP's 1935 art exhibition held in New York to garner public support for federal antilynching legislation. The power of the photographic rendering of Hughes's unnamed, abstracted body derived not from any understanding that it was represented through the perspective of the white mob; rather, as an icon, it took on a hallowed quality that stood outside time and place.[23]

In this respect, lynching photographs became visible touchstones for antilynching agendas, developing their own abstract power in the process. In fact, to present-day eyes, these photographic reproductions hardly seem realistic. The halftone process, which made it possible to print photographs beginning in the 1890s, broke the photograph into a series of black dots to convey the full range of photographic tone on the newsprint page, in a sense tricking the eye into seeing a photographic image from a series of etched dots. Larger newspapers perfected this process so the images appeared real and seamless, but in smaller papers, some photographs appear almost like drawings. At times, even the authenticity of the original image seemed to matter little, as is apparent in the *Chicago Defender*'s printing of a "composite photograph" in which several images were melded to depict

FIGURE 6.4 Isamu Noguchi, *Death (Lynched Figure)*, 1933.
Photograph by Shigeo Anzai. © 2008 The Isamu Noguchi
Foundation and Garden Museum, New York/Artists Rights
Society (ARS), New York.

"the actual lynching" of John Carter in Little Rock, Arkansas, in 1927 (figure
6.5). Such alterations of images were common in the tabloid press, and the
tabloids bore much criticism for it, but the *Chicago Defender* clearly was not
using the photograph to illustrate with graphic realism the report of Carter's
lynching. Rather, the photograph served to highlight the paper's opposition
to lynching, much like an editorial cartoon. The caption described how "the
most prominent white citizens" burned Carter at the stake, and it censured
officials for making "no attempt to check the mob and save the city and state

HOW WHITE CITIZENS OF LITTLE ROCK BURNED JOHN CARTER

FIGURE 6.5 "A composite photograph depicting the actual lynching and burning at the stake of John Carter by a crowd of the most prominent white citizens of Little Rock, Ark., on Thursday night, May 5." *Chicago Defender*, 21 May 1927. Courtesy of the *Chicago Defender*.

from the disgraceful exhibition of cannibalism." The photograph could thus encapsulate both a complex narrative of lynching and the argument against lynching in one image.[24]

On the other hand, lynching opponents were well aware that photographs, as accurate documents of reality, could provide the legal identification of mob participants. Lynching photographs thus held the potential to act as witnesses in the most literal, legal sense. Several weeks after it published the composite "photo" of Carter's lynching, the *Chicago Defender* published another view of Carter's hanged body showing a police officer standing several feet away. The headline read, "And They Can't Identify This Policeman!" accompanied by a caption that noted that "the picture . . . shows quite clearly, one of the stalwart guardians of Arkansas law" who had apparently played "an important role" in the lynching. Yet, the caption stated with dismay, officials in Little Rock claimed they could not identify members of the mob, and it added, "If this policeman cannot be identified, with a face like the one exposed in this picture, there is something wrong with the identifiers." Similarly, the *Chicago Defender* published a photograph of the lynched body of Lint Shaw, hanged and tortured in Royston, Georgia, in 1936, surrounded by a group of white men, with the headline "These Can Be Identified." Although the photograph was taken the day after the lynching and the men pictured could very well have been curious spectators, the caption argued, "The above men, whose identity cannot be questioned, must surely possess information which would lead honest officials to arrest and convict the murderers responsible for this human outrage." Lynching opponents, indeed, regularly expressed a frustrated sense of disbelief that the irrefutable "proof" of a photograph was so casually ignored in lynching communities, even as they themselves regularly altered these images and dislodged them from their local specificity.[25]

WITH THESE KINDS of dramatic editorial commentary and emotional appeals, the display of lynching photographs in black newspapers often became indistinguishable from their use as propaganda in NAACP pamphlets and advertisements for antilynching legislation. Lynching, it should be noted, was already on the decline as antilynching activism gained political force in the 1930s. The outcry against lynching in this period was in many ways more a response to a relatively small number of extraordinarily sadistic lynchings than to any sense that lynching was a consistent problem. For activists, the issue was that lynching was still happening at all in modern America. In this context, lynching photographs played a critical role in activists' efforts to incite outrage in a public that might otherwise wish to believe that lynching was a waning practice. In short, lynching photographs were particularly well suited to sensationalize the already sensational. Throughout the 1930s, both the NAACP and black newspapers thus continued to print these images primarily to keep the ugly specter of lynching at the forefront of readers' minds and to persuade them to commit energy and money to antilynching campaigns.

They adopted the tools of modern advertising and modern tabloid journalism to do so. In publishing lynching images, the black press and the NAACP made use of the very developments in modern photographic technology that caused a great deal of apprehension among other newsmen. By the first decades of the twentieth century, not only were newspapers able to reproduce images more cheaply and accurately, but photographers were able to take pictures at night and to wire photographs to news outlets across the country. Photojournalism quickly developed into a competitive and lucrative profession. These changes enabled the print media to compete with radio and led readers to expect photographic illustrations of the news. Many editors and cultural critics in the early twentieth century bemoaned these changes, believing that photographs appealed to base emotionalism and aliterate sensibilities at the expense of reason and complexity. More austere papers like the *New York Times* used photographs sparingly, and the decisions in the 1930s of magazines like *Time* and *Fortune* to compete with the most sordid tabloids by illustrating the news with photographs met with controversy. While defenders of the practice argued that photographs augmented the credibility and realistic depiction of the news, critics comprehended that photographs were hardly neutral conveyors of reality but were highly manipulative and titillating.[26]

To their critics, the print media were collapsing the boundary between news and entertainment, a sentiment felt with particular force since the advertising industry in this period was increasingly relying on photographic imagery to appeal to viewers' emotions. Modern advertisers recognized that photographs could encapsulate and freeze a host of feelings, sensibilities, and ideas into one schematic. In doing so, they created a mental association between the feelings the image stirred in the viewer and the product that was being marketed. This process rested on the assumption that consumers were impressionable and easily manipulated, that they were ruled by passion over reason. Photographs, in their graphic realism, not only could more readily attract consumers' attention than could text or even drawings but were also more likely to stimulate viewers emotionally. At the same time, because viewers assumed photographs to be factual, advertisers enhanced the credibility of their products when they used photographs to market them. That is, viewers could suppose that their emotional choices were rational ones.[27]

The NAACP and the black press relied on these dynamics in using lynching photographs as pleas for antilynching support. Because of their symbolic clarity, photographs could summarize for readers the antilynching position of the press with far more immediacy and accessibility than reportage or editorials could. At the same time, their stark realism would create a sense of disgust and agitation in readers that would sway them in support of that position. That realism would also lend credibility to antilynching advertisements or editorials as indisputable fact. When viewers encountered these images in the black press, the violence of the image very well could have horrified them, compelling them to turn away in revulsion. But the conventions of tabloid journalism and of modern advertising had already prepared them to accept photographs, even shocking photographs, as both news and propaganda.

As early as 1912, the NAACP created its own version of a lynching post-card when it produced a promotional postcard using the photograph of John Lee's lynching in Durant, Oklahoma, with a caption that included the NAACP's address and encouraged viewers to write to the association if "you are interested in joining our protest." The postcard ingeniously defused the white supremacist power imagined in the image and, in its place, called for an alternative community of lynching protestors. Several years later, in April 1916, John Ross, a reader of the *Crisis*, wrote to Du Bois urging him to use a lynching photograph from Georgia that the magazine had recently published to raise funds against lynching. Stating that "a number of my white friends" were shocked to see the photograph, "express[ing] astonishment that such atrocities are occurring in the United States today," Ross suggested the NAACP launch a chain letter campaign and include a copy of the photograph with each letter. "This I am sure would make every Negro interested in his race be willing to comply to the conditions, viz. contribute one dime and send five letters," he affirmed, implying that the photograph bore a particular power to incite action and build a sense of communal purpose. Acting secretary of the NAACP Roy Nash courteously responded to Ross that he had already "struck off" 1,000 copies of the images and was "going to give serious consideration to your idea." Several months later, of course, the NAACP began to use the images from Jesse Washington's lynching to great effect.[28]

By the 1930s, the NAACP regularly relied on image-based promotional materials. According to a 1935 publicity report, it sold and distributed 100,000 copies of a pamphlet featuring an image of the lynched body of Rubin Stacy for "25 cents a hundred, to permit maximum circulation" to NAACP branches, churches, women's groups, and other organizations, creating a network of exchange that far exceeded the original circulation of lynching photographs (figure 6.6). Similarly, when the photograph of Lint Shaw's lynched body appeared in the *Chicago Defender* in April 1936, NAACP secretary Walter White asked the paper to "lend" the NAACP the image, with the possibility of, as one friend suggested to White, "flooding the country with it." The NAACP also aided glossy pictorial magazines like *Look* and *Life* in obtaining lynching photographs to accompany stories about antilynching legislation efforts.[29]

Indeed, the most horrific aspects of lynching spectacles invigorated attempts to pass federal antilynching legislation. After the failure of Repre-

Do not look at the Negro.

His earthly problems are ended.

Instead, look at the seven WHITE children who gaze at this gruesome spectacle.

Is it horror or gloating on the face of the neatly dressed seven-year-old girl on the right?

Is the tiny four-year-old on the left old enough, one wonders, to comprehend the barbarism her elders have perpetrated?

Rubin Stacy, the Negro, who was lynched at Fort Lauderdale, Florida, on July 19, 1935, for "threatening and frightening a white woman," suffered PHYSICAL torture for a few short hours. But what psychological havoc is being wrought in the minds of the white children? Into what kinds of citizens

FIGURE 6.6 NAACP antilynching pamphlet, 1935, showing the lynching of Rubin Stacy, Fort Lauderdale, Florida. Courtesy of the National Association for the Advancement of Colored People.

doned its lobbying efforts until a terrible upsurge in lynchings in late 1933.
The national attention these incidents garnered made a new campaign seem
both necessary and opportune. Activists also redoubled their efforts after
the high-profile, spectacular lynching of Claude Neal in Florida in 1934. The
New York Amsterdam News, for instance, published a photograph of Neal's
lynched body next to an image of President Roosevelt, along with an open
letter to Roosevelt beseeching him to prosecute the members of the mob
under federal kidnapping statutes, since the mob had crossed state lines
with Neal before lynching him.[30]

In at least one instance, a ghastly lynching and congressional debates
over antilynching legislation brought attention to each other. As Congress
debated the Gavagan antilynching bill in April 1937, two men in Duck Hill,
Mississippi, Roosevelt Townes and Robert McDaniels, accused of murdering a local white merchant, were gruesomely lynched. A mob of 200 men
beat them and scorched them with gasoline blowtorches to extract their
confessions before shooting McDaniels and burning Townes alive. Although
it was shocking, the lynching might have escaped national notice if federal
antilynching legislation had not been pending. Unlike other high-profile
lynchings in the 1930s, the Duck Hill lynching was attended by a relatively
small crowd and occurred outside town, in the woods. But someone took
what became infamous pictures of McDaniels and Townes chained to trees,
in the midst of their suffering (figure 6.7). Lynching opponents seized on
the lynching as further evidence that federal legislation was necessary to
stop this kind of atrocity. Both the lynching and the congressional debates
made front-page news across the country, and some newspapers and magazines reproduced the Duck Hill photographs. According to *Time*, when the
Associated Press report of the lynching was read on the House floor, "debate
rose to a furious crescendo," and the bill subsequently passed the house by
a vote of 277 to 120, with 17 southerners voting for the bill. That fall, while
the Senate debated its version of the bill, supporter Senator Bennett Clark,
a Democrat from Missouri, displayed a poster on the wall of the Senate
chamber that included two images of Townes and Roosevelt's lynching. The
poster read, "These blow torch lynchings occurred while the Wagner-Van
Nuys Anti-Lynching Bill was Pending before Congress. There have been NO
arrests, NO Indictments, NO Convictions, of any one of the lynchers. This
was NOT a rape case."[31] The symbolic use of this particularly spectacular
lynching mirrored in some ways the symbolic nature of federal antilynching legislation. Many proponents of these bills knew that enforcement

FIGURE 6.7 The lynching of Robert "Bootjack" McDaniels,
Duck Hill, Mississippi, 1937.

would be weak, just as antilynching statutes in southern states were routinely ignored. But they also believed that a federal antilynching law would
send the national and international message that lynching was anathema to
American ideals.[32]

Despite their iconic use in the service of antilynching politics, lynching photographs held such power to move the public because viewers not
only accepted them as factual but also recognized that they were not im-
partial documents, that they were, in fact, bound up with the violence of
the scene. Editors often gave lynching photographs captions that spoke to
this indistinguishability between the lynching and the visual record of the
lynching by marking the photograph with the violent language of the mob or
by making no distinction between those posing for the photograph and the
perpetrators of the violence. For instance, the *Crisis* used the photograph of
Lint Shaw's lynching in a clever advertisement commenting on the Senate's
decision not to vote on an antilynching bill. It positioned the lynching on a
full page with the headline "Mobs Act, While—" next to a page titled "U.S.
Senators Talk," which featured the relevant extract from the *Congressional
Record* (figure 6.8). This juxtaposition set the activity of the mob against the

passivity of the Senate. But since, as discussed above, the photograph was taken the day after the lynching, the NAACP knew that the men posing for the photograph may have been not members of the mob but merely curious bystanders. Still, the caption assumed that to pose for a lynching photograph was to join the mob, a mob that continued to "act" even after its victim was dead. In this context, the photograph represented a continuous act of violence, one in which the Senate, through its failure to act, participated.[33]

The violence and exploitation embedded within the images denied viewers any aesthetic or emotional distance from the photographs. In this sense, lynching opponents relied on the most sensational qualities of these images—their use in the service of white supremacy—to stimulate shock and revulsion in the viewer, literally to produce sensation. They added dramatic captions and headlines to appeal further to viewers' emotional sensibilities and to jar them out of their complacency or voyeuristic curiosity. For activists, the spectator's revulsion became a political necessity and an ethical imperative. In publishing photographs of the lynched bodies of John Holmes and Thomas Thurmond, hanged in San Jose, California, in 1933, the *Atlanta Daily World* wrote that it was the paper's "duty to print these photographs, as horrible as they are, in the hope of causing public sentiment to surge against this most terrible of all American crimes." Despite that the images were crude halftone reproductions, the press asked, "Is there any human who can see this picture without fully realizing how revolting a crime lynching is?" To look at these images and to respond with horror was to move from the position of spectator to moral witness.[34]

It is this sense that lynching photographs are implicated in the violence, that the subjugation of African Americans is bound up within them, that has given rise to present-day concerns that displays of lynching photographs might reproduce the dynamics of lynching itself, positioning the viewer of the photograph as yet another spectator of lynching and reifying black victimhood.[35] Such concerns did not trouble antilynching activists, however. They were more likely to be uneasy about the possibility that lynching images would intensify racial prejudice and provoke antagonism against them. In 1937, the *Crisis* printed a letter from a reader who criticized the magazine's decision to publish the photograph of Shaw's lynched body. "Such publicity tends to increase race hatred," averred the letter writer, echoing the arguments made against *The Birth of a Nation*. For this viewer, the photograph was so tied to the white supremacist narrative that he imagined that viewers would see not a victim but a black criminal deserving of his fate. The editors responded that they believed that "the sheer horror of lynching serves to

Mobs Act, While —

This is a picture of the lynching of Lint Shaw, killed by a mob near Royston, Ga., April 28, 1936, eight hours before he was scheduled to go on trial on a charge of attempted assault. There was another lynching in Georgia on April 29, 1936 and still another in Arkansas on May 3, 1936.

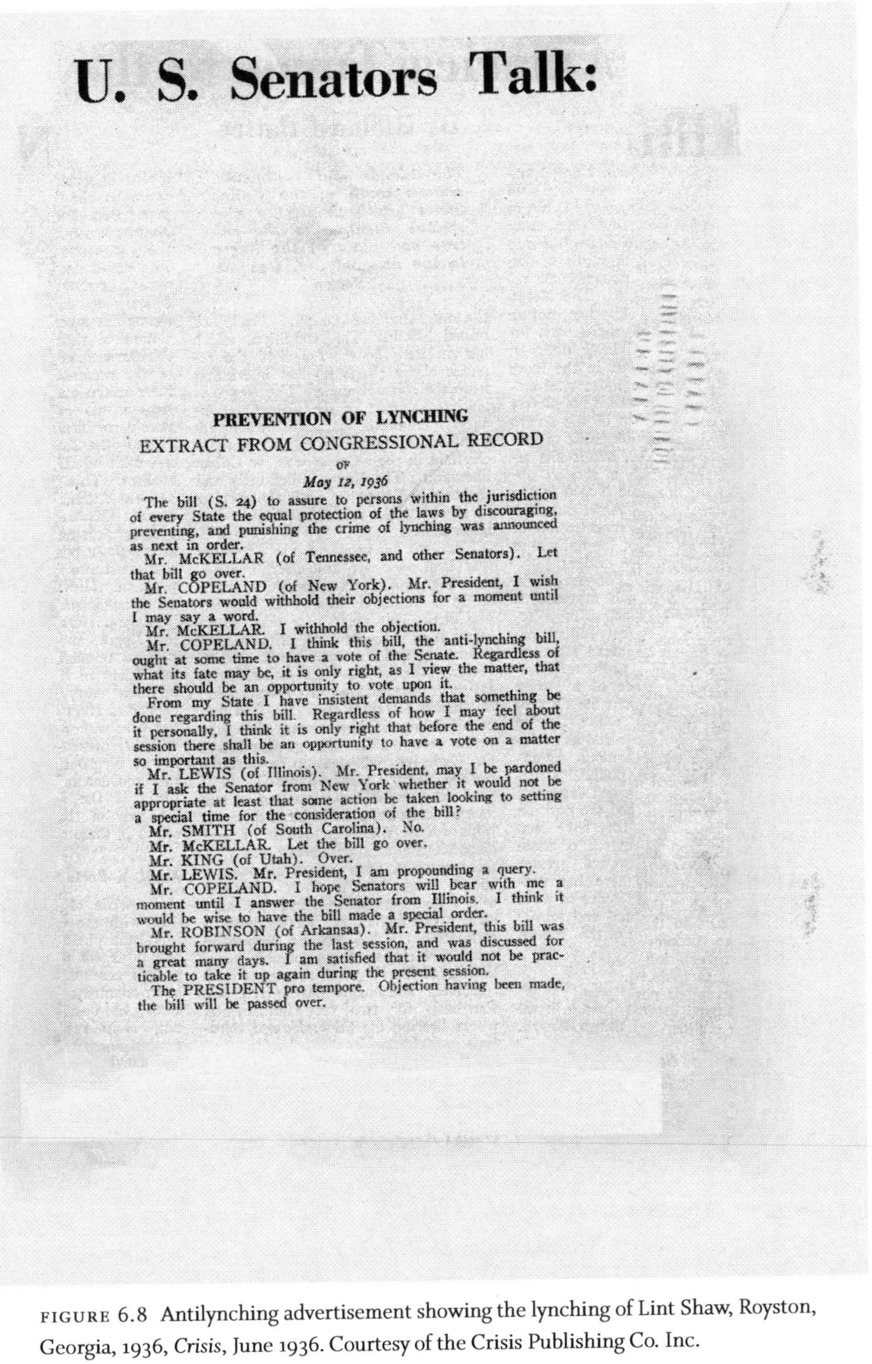

U. S. Senators Talk:

PREVENTION OF LYNCHING

EXTRACT FROM CONGRESSIONAL RECORD

OF

May 12, 1936

The bill (S. 24) to assure to persons within the jurisdiction of every State the equal protection of the laws by discouraging, preventing, and punishing the crime of lynching was announced as next in order.

Mr. McKELLAR (of Tennessee, and other Senators). Let that bill go over.

Mr. COPELAND (of New York). Mr. President, I wish the Senators would withhold their objections for a moment until I may say a word.

Mr. McKELLAR. I withhold the objection.

Mr. COPELAND. I think this bill, the anti-lynching bill, ought at some time to have a vote of the Senate. Regardless of what its fate may be, it is only right, as I view the matter, that there should be an opportunity to vote upon it.

From my State I have insistent demands that something be done regarding this bill. Regardless of how I may feel about it personally, I think it is only right that before the end of the session there shall be an opportunity to have a vote on a matter so important as this.

Mr. LEWIS (of Illinois). Mr. President, may I be pardoned if I ask the Senator from New York whether it would not be appropriate at least that some action be taken looking to setting a special time for the consideration of the bill?

Mr. SMITH (of South Carolina). No.

Mr. McKELLAR. Let the bill go over.

Mr. KING (of Utah). Over.

Mr. LEWIS. Mr. President, I am propounding a query.

Mr. COPELAND. I hope Senators will bear with me a moment until I answer the Senator from Illinois. I think it would be wise to have the bill made a special order.

Mr. ROBINSON (of Arkansas). Mr. President, this bill was brought forward during the last session, and was discussed for a great many days. I am satisfied that it would not be practicable to take it up again during the present session.

The PRESIDENT pro tempore. Objection having been made, the bill will be passed over.

FIGURE 6.8 Antilynching advertisement showing the lynching of Lint Shaw, Royston, Georgia, 1936, *Crisis*, June 1936. Courtesy of the Crisis Publishing Co. Inc.

rouse ordinarily lethargic people to action," indicating that their intention was to incite an emotional response. They called on their readers to offer their own opinions and published a selection of responses in the following issue. The readers in that selection unanimously agreed with the magazine's decision to print lynching photographs, confirming the *Crisis*'s own argument that the pictures were gruesome but necessary tools to arouse the national conscience. According to these readers, photographs provided a truthful depiction that could capture attention and educate the "indifferent" and "uninformed." One reader, identified as the chair of the public relations committee for the American Federation of Teachers, wrote that "to fight lynching, every available means of publicity must be employed." Another female reader noted that "a picture seen or described gets under the skin as no argument can."[36]

THESE READERS' REMARKS attest to the fact that, by 1937, lynching opponents had successfully erased the white supremacist narrative imprinted in the photographs and, by reframing the images, had replaced it with an antilynching narrative. This antilynching narrative focused attention not on black victimhood or suffering but on the savagery of white mobs, mobs that stood as abominations to American democratic ideals. In doing so, activists effectively used lynching photographs to overturn the rhetorical claims of white supremacy and to position African Americans and their allies as the true defenders of civilized morality.[37]

The use of captions and headlines did much to impose this new ideological truth on the images. Editors' use of text, in many ways, mirrored the signs white spectators displayed beside lynched bodies and the personal reports they scrawled on the backs of lynching postcards. Editors, for instance, commonly juxtaposed images with language that derided white southerners' claims to moral superiority, often by using the words of lynch mobs or their defenders against them. In the *New York Amsterdam News*, the headline that accompanied a front-page photograph of the 1938 lynching of C. C. Williams in Rustin, Louisiana, consisted only of a quote from one witness: "Then We Rammed a Red Hot Poker into Him." The caption below the image quoted the witness in full while noting that the picture depicted "300 blood-mad white American citizens" perpetrating America's "GREAT-EST SPORT." The witness's "gleeful" words were thus recontextualized to indict the perpetrators. Similarly, in its caption of a photograph from the 1933 lynching of Freddie Moore in Labadieville, Louisiana, the *Chicago De-fender* drew readers' attention to the sign white spectators were holding up to the camera: "Niggers, let this be an example." In doing so, the *Chicago Defender* transformed the implication of the word "example" so that it stood as a message of white injustice and hypocrisy. In fact, a sardonic headline above the image read "What Louisiana Worships." With the same acerbic irony, the *Pittsburgh Courier* included in its caption of a photograph from the 1930 lynching of George Hughes in Sherman, Texas, the lines "Texas Justice Has Its Fling" and "The Southern White Man's Glory . . . Pictured as Texas Mob Turns Savage."[38]

Activists often tied these critiques of white supremacist claims to larger nationalist claims of American superiority, particularly in light of U.S. foreign policy. They regularly pointed out that, although the U.S. government felt entitled and obligated to indict other nations for their blatant disregard for human equality and their undemocratic principles, it had denied African Americans full citizenship and had systematically refused to protect them from lynching violence. Soon after the 1916 Waco lynching, the *Chicago Defender* printed an editorial drawing of several black men hanging from trees with a caption that read, "Shall the American Republic be pointed with scorn by the foreign powers as a barbarous nation? . . . Why Mexico? Why bother about Germany or Japan? No civilized nation has disgraced itself with the above scenes in the past fifty years." In 1930, the paper echoed this rhetoric in its caption accompanying a photograph of George Hughes's burned corpse. First, in a deft racial twist, it questioned the "decent people, the churchgoers, those who belonged to civic clubs and the Y.M.C.A." who "resorted to cannibalism unknown even in the most remote part of Congo. Suddenly they became beasts, worse than any savage." Turning to American anticommunism, it asked, "Why raise the hue and cry about Godless Russia? Nothing in Russia equals the above. . . . Godless Russia? No! Godless America!" Likewise, in a 1934 advertisement for the NAACP campaign for antilynching legislation, the *Crisis* gave an unidentified photograph of a lynched black man the sardonic headline "My Country, 'Tis of Thee, Sweet Land of Liberty." Beneath the image, the text read, "This is a picture of what happens in America—*and no other place on earth*."[39]

Lynching became a particular source of embarrassment to the United States when foreign newspapers published lynching photographs. In 1934, the NAACP sent its report on Claude Neal's lynching, including the photograph of his nude, hanged body, to 144 newspapers in forty countries, and at least one, *El Nacional*, Mexico City's leading newspaper, published the report and a scathing critique of U.S. racism on its front page. Throughout the 1930s, lynching accounts and photographs appeared in newspapers in

Nazi Germany as evidence of American barbarism and hypocrisy compared to what Nazis perceived to be their more civilized and orderly police state. Because the Nazi press felt sympathetic to America's racial caste system, it expressed outrage that the United States condemned Germany for its racist practices, and the press sought, in turn, to assert German superiority. One newspaper in Berlin, for instance, published a graphic account that denounced the Duck Hill lynchings and commented that "fairy tales of horror" about Nazism were regularly printed in the U.S. press. The liberal press in the United States also liked to point out this hypocrisy, recognizing, as the *New Republic* did just after the San Jose lynchings in 1933, that "Hitler and his cohorts . . . must have read the recent dispatches with wry smiles."[40]

In criticizing American lynching practices, black activists were asserting the human and citizenship rights of lynch mob victims and, in turn, positing themselves as rightful and patriotic defenders of American principles. In its post-Waco editorial, the *Chicago Defender* not only compared the United States unfavorably to Mexico, Germany, and Japan but also implored white politicians for help: "If our race is good enough to give you our votes, then as American citizens, WE DEMAND PROTECTION." A 1942 cartoon in the *Chicago Defender* crystallized this sentiment in its rendering of an iconic lynched black man, hanging with flames lapping his feet and flanked by two other hanging figures — "National Unity" and "Democracy" — reminiscent of the three figures of the crucifixion. The hanged black man is labeled "Lynched American," bestowing on him the citizenship he was otherwise denied (figure 6.9). In these ways, antilynching activists reconfigured the prolynching narrative to construct a patriotic African American identity against white brutality.[41]

This commentary represented a larger rhetorical shift in black activism. After World War I, rather than explaining lynching as an outcome of deeply rooted racist structures and institutions, as had, for instance, Ida B. Wells, African American activists increasingly attacked lynch mobs, in their primal savagery, as disgraces to democracy and modern civilization. In doing so, they characterized lynching as an American, rather than a particularly southern, form of injustice — even though most lynchings still occurred in the South. White lynching opponents since the late nineteenth century had accentuated this argument, positing lynching as a barbaric menace to law and order rather than a historically or regionally specific tactic within a larger system of racial oppression. As federal antilynching legislation came closer to passage in the 1920s and 1930s, black lynching opponents adopted this rhetoric to appeal to white liberals and moderates in both the North

"He Never Dies Alone"

FIGURE 6.9 Antilynching cartoon, *Chicago Defender*, 7 February 1942.
Courtesy of the *Chicago Defender*.

and the South, who often expressed sympathy for white fears about black
criminality even as they criticized the lawless violence of lynching. To be
sure, in more detailed, analytical denunciations of lynching, these activists explained lynching as a mechanism to ensure white racial and economic domination over African Americans. But their political rhetoric,
and imagery, made surprisingly little mention of race or racial prejudice. In
fact, the black victim—a too visible reminder of black criminality—became
largely eclipsed, while the members of the mob, as defilers of justice and
law, moved to the center of antilynching discourse.[42]

Editors' decisions about how to contextualize lynching photographs mirrored, and even shaped, this discourse. Photographs, in their two-dimensionality, were particularly well suited for a simpler, more schematic argument that could unify lynching opponents, who often differed on the tactics and goals of the antilynching movement, in their collective shock and horror. Rarely did captions and lynching reports provide information about the victim beyond his name and age, although editors frequently commented on the lack of information about the white participants. What is more, although editors most likely had very little control over the photographs they had access to, it is striking that photographs depicting only the lynched man's body were exceptional in the black press. But even in images that foregrounded the lynched man's body, captions regularly drew focus away from the corpse and onto the white perpetrators. The NAACP antilynching pamphlet noted above that reproduced a photograph from the 1935 lynching of Rubin Stacy in Fort Lauderdale, Florida, included text that read, "Do not look at the Negro. His earthly problems are ended. Instead, look at the seven WHITE children who gaze at this gruesome spectacle." The caption compared the physical torture Stacy endured "for a few short hours" to the "psychological havoc . . . being wrought in the minds of the white children," as if to imply that the real victim of lynching was white society itself (figure 6.6).[43] As noted in earlier chapters, pointing out the women and children among lynching spectators was a common rhetorical device, since it cut into white supremacist claims that lynch mobs were protecting the most vulnerable members of their communities.

The discourse that figured mobs as savages beneath the veneer of civilization coincided with popular understandings in this period of civilization as a fragile institution restraining humans' primal impulses. Lynching, accordingly, was primarily an expression of a natural human reaction to crime that legal institutions otherwise inhibited. In 1935, for instance, the Crisis published short analyses of the Claude Neal lynching by several psychologists, who described the violence as "an orgiastic celebration" and a form of "sexual perversion" performed by "primitive sadists" similar to that "practiced by savage and semi-savage peoples." In the late nineteenth century, white supremacists had based their claims of racial superiority on the same Darwinian and Freudian conceptions of civilization, believing that whites represented a more advanced race, further removed from and better able to control their primitive desires. This thinking still had currency in the 1930s, especially as both psychoanalysis and evolutionary theory had been popularized in the 1920s. By this time, however, Americans were accustomed to conceiving of savagery as a universal concept rather than one specific to a racial group—after all, World War I had introduced them to the specter of the savage "Huns." This thinking also reflected an intellectual interest in the social psychology of race hatred and mob behavior, as manifest not only in U.S. racial structures but also in colonialism and fascism. The persistence of racist feelings and violence in the modern world flew in the face of liberal trust that modern progress and development would inexorably lead to more rational and enlightened sensibilities. Race hatred and mob violence thus came to be studied and understood as antimodern and irrational, symptoms of psychological sickness and degeneration. Antilynching activists were shaped by, and took keen advantage of, this thinking, positioning themselves in opposition to lynch mobs as orderly, civilized, and modern.[44]

IT IS STRIKING that in printing lynching photographs, the black press was transforming its largely African American readership into spectators of an act of violence that, though intended to terrorize them, was not necessarily performed *for* them. After all, despite the threats and warnings that white crowds sometimes held up for the camera's view, African Americans were not expected to be the primary witnesses to the spectacle of lynching. As has been shown, lynching photographs were primarily messages to other whites that amplified and solidified their own power and unity. Indeed, African American spectators and bystanders, the purported recipients of those menacing signs, are conspicuously absent from most lynching accounts and images. Whereas at legal executions, the presence of African Americans was well noted—the family of the condemned, the clergy who read him his last rites, and the black spectators who witnessed his final moments—lynching accounts in the white press resounded with their disappearance: the family members who decline to claim the body, the townspeople who hide behind closed doors, the absence of coverage of black resistance or protest. Thus when African Americans do appear in lynching photographs, their presence is jarring. In the photograph of Rubin Stacy's lynching, a black woman, dressed in uniform and most likely a nanny accompanying one of the young children in the photograph, appears behind a spectator, her face obscured by the young man in front of her (figure 6.6). She stands sideways, the only figure in the crowd who is gazing at neither the camera nor Stacy's corpse. "Do not look at the Negro," the NAACP's caption commands, further obscuring her reaction. Her presence is easily overlooked, reproducing the ways in which the mourning, fear, and anger that African Americans in these localities experienced was largely invisible in both pro- and antilynching accounts.[45]

For many African Americans, especially those in large northern cities, seeing lynching images in newspapers and NAACP pamphlets might have been their only direct visual encounters with lynching. The photographs may have satisfied any morbid curiosity they had to see the invisible terror, one that was perhaps more terrifying precisely because it was shrouded from view. In instances when bodies were left in public spaces for days after the lynching, local blacks certainly viewed them—they could not escape from viewing them—much like the woman in the Rubin Stacy photograph. There are also instances in which the lynched black body was brought before black communities as a warning and a threat. A representative from the NAACP described in a telegram to the governor of Tennessee one particularly frightening act of terror. A lynch mob in Erwin, Tennessee, in 1918 forced "the whole Negro population" to "line up and witness [the] burning" of Thomas Devert. The previous year, the severed head of Ell Person, burned to death in Memphis, Tennessee, was apparently thrown onto Beale Street, a location dominated by black-owned businesses. The local edition of the *Defender* carried the photograph of Person's head, making note that the atrocity was "not the work of the Germans, but the South." In printing the image, the paper extended and reconceptualized the African American witnessing that the mob intended on Beale Street.[46]

We know lamentably very little about how African Americans responded to or felt about these acts of witnessing, whether they unconditionally received them as messages of intimidation or treated them as sites of mourning. Similarly, much more needs to be known about the ways in which African Americans privately reappropriated lynching photographs. Although they most likely lamented the local circulation of lynching photographs, they at times collected and circulated them as tokens of mourning and memory. Legal scholar Patricia Williams has written that her aunt owned lynching photographs and that these pictures were commonly passed around African American communities to memorialize specific victims. Similarly, in Laurens County, South Carolina, black members of the community preserved the photograph of Richard Puckett's lynching to remember his murder. As memorializations of lynched corpses, lynching photographs eerily replicated postmortem memorial photography, a photographic convention that persisted, particularly in rural communities, well into the twentieth century. Preserving likenesses of loved ones produced just after they died, or laid out in coffins, was a popular means for Americans of various classes and ethnicities to grieve for lost family members. The realism of the photograph, by providing a lifelike portrait, aided the bereaved in their grief and provided a tangible memory of the deceased.[47]

For white southerners, the production of lynching images seemed to mock postmortem photography's sentimental memorialization of the dead. In the photograph of Charlie Hale's lynching (figure 3.11), the mob placed a sign on his body that read, "PLEASE DO NOT WAKE," a sign that takes on more meaning when understood within popular turn-of-the-century conceptions of death as an eternal, peaceful sleep. The image of death as sleep was made manifest in funeral photography, particularly in the 1890s and after, that depicted the deceased as if at tranquil rest in bed or in a coffin replete with cushions and pillows. For the lynchers to place this sign on Hale's body was to impose, with satire, the sentimentality of late Victorian notions of death on the distinctly unsentimental figure of a lynching. For black southerners to reappropriate these images as mourning photographs was, in some sense, to reimpose sentimentality on them, framing the deceased as someone with loved ones who mourn his death; he is thus conferred with dignity through them.[48]

Considering that these practices happened locally, it is significant that some black-owned papers in the South were more circumspect than those in the North in publishing lynching photographs. Lynching photographs undoubtedly assumed a more immediate terrorizing power in Georgia and Virginia than they did in New York and Chicago. For example, after the lynching of Thomas Shipp and Abe Smith in Marion, Indiana, African American residents were reportedly furious that local whites had produced and distributed a photograph of the lynching (figure 3.13). Local NAACP representatives protested and even interrupted its sale in both Marion and nearby Terre Haute. Although the NAACP as an organization regularly sought out and publicized lynching photographs, within and around the lynching locality, the photograph still bore the weight of its terror against African Americans, and its sale in the community commodified that violence. The image could not stand as an icon against racial injustice because it was too tied to a specific incident. Indeed, in lynching localities, fears that photographs might incite "racial antagonism" were felt with an urgency that did not exist in a national context.[49]

In this respect, as much as southern black papers like the *Atlanta Daily*

World and the *Richmond (Va.) Planet* took firm stands against lynching, to publish images that white southerners wanted to retain control over would have been to take too great a risk. The *Atlanta Daily World* did print a photograph of John Holmes and Thomas Thurmond, lynched in San Jose, California, but it did so only with the apologetic explanation that it was a "duty," one surely made easier by the facts, as noted below, that Holmes and Thurmond were white and the lynching occurred outside the South. The newspaper did not, however, publish photographs of the most sensational and public lynchings of African Americans throughout the 1930s. When Lint Shaw was lynched in Royston, Georgia, in 1936, the paper covered the incident heavily because of its relative proximity to Atlanta but did not print the image of his lynched body that circulated through the International News Photo Agency and appeared in several other black papers in the North — even though presumably it also had access to the photograph.[50]

The paper instead chose to publish photographic portraits of Shaw and his family, images that are surprising for their rarity. As noted above, although it did sometimes offer more personal details about victims, certainly more than the white press did, the northern black press tended to render victims emblems of American barbarism to promote antilynching legislation. Photographs of victims when they were still alive — images that resurrected lynched corpses — did at times appear in the pages of black newspapers, but in the forms of mug shots and images of the men in police custody flanked by white officers, images that marked them as dangerous and criminal while reminding viewers that the lynching had thwarted the law.[51] But the *Atlanta Daily World* printed a photographic portrait of Lint Shaw, dressed in suit and tie and sitting in a tall chair, his legs spread open in manly confidence. The caption described him as a "handsome, 225-pound, 45-year old father of eleven children and pioneer resident of Danielsville, Ga." Both the image and its description belied the larger headline printed above, which described Shaw as a "helpless victim." In the next day's issue, the paper printed more "interesting glimpses into the life of Lint Shaw," which a staff photographer had taken after the lynching: an image of his home, a portrait of his wife and eleven children — their names and ages provided — and a close-up of his wife holding their youngest child. Though their faces, in the conventions of portrait photography that persisted in rural communities as late as the 1930s, are stoic and inscrutable, they provide a rare view into the violence lynching continued to exact long after the event itself. In humanizing Shaw and his family, the *Atlanta Daily World* may have done more to subvert the intent and significance of the lynching photograph than reprinting it as part of an antilynching message would have done.[52]

WHEREAS ANTILYNCHING ACTIVISTS began printing photographs in pamphlets in the 1890s and in the wider black-owned media by the 1910s, white-owned papers in both the North and the South were more reluctant to adopt the practice, in part because they believed the images would be distasteful to readers. For instance, although the photograph of Thomas Shipp and Abe Smith's lynching circulated through a wire service, the *Marion (Ind.) Chronicle-Tribune*, as well as larger Indiana newspapers, chose not to print the photograph because editors deemed it "revolting" and not in "good taste."[53] Yet newspapers regularly printed sensational photographs of natural disasters and civic unrest with less concern for "good taste." Their circumspection about lynching photographs more likely reflected a deeper discomfort with racial violence. Lynching photographs were too graphic, too capable of inciting volatile and unmanageable emotional responses, including white guilt and shame. When viewed in light of opposite editorial choices made by the black press, these decisions to suppress lynching photographs appear only to soften the impact of lynching's horror.

In choosing not to print these images, editors concealed from public view the victims of lynching, a fact that was made more conspicuous in instances when editors did choose to print lynching photographs. These editorial choices mirrored and buttressed popular antilynching rhetoric, which increasingly sought to draw attention to lynching's negative impact on white society rather than on black personhood. Some papers that held strong antilynching positions did reproduce some photographs of lynching scenes, but rarely did they show the lynched body of the black victim. They more commonly printed images of people and places that obliquely gestured toward the lynching, visual metonyms that viewers' imaginations could fill in: local officials, the white victim of the black man's alleged crime, the site of the lynching, or the county courthouse or jail. The *Memphis News-Scimitar* printed three "exclusive photos" taken moments before J. P. Ivy was burned alive in Rocky Ford, Mississippi, in 1925, but the images depict only the white crowd surrounding Ivy. The series of photographs abruptly ends before the crowd committed any crime and before Ivy's suffering began. Other papers showed only the aftermath of lynchings, in many cases because photojournalists had not reached the scene until the next day. Photographs of national guardsmen on duty, for instance, appeared in the *Wash-*

ington Post after the Marion, Indiana, lynching and in the *Chicago Tribune* after the 1934 lynching of Claude Neal in Marianna, Florida. But neither paper reproduced the photographs of the lynching crowd or of the black men's corpses, which had appeared in several black-owned papers.[54]

Even when they did publish photographs from the scene of a lynching itself, white-owned papers were more likely to focus on the white crowd, enacting a displacement of the black body similar to that which the black press sought. Yet, unlike the black press, they erased the black body altogether. In doing so, they reflected the dominant thrust of antilynching opposition that placed the rhetorical focus on the lawlessness of white mobbers rather than on the wrongs committed against their victims. In a most telling instance, the *Chicago Tribune*, which had adopted a fierce, nationally recognized antilynching stance in 1892, when it began publishing yearly lynching statistics, published a photograph of the 1919 lynching of William Brown in Omaha, Nebraska. The photograph, which depicts a large group of white people leaning into the camera's view, grouped behind the sight of Brown's body being incinerated on a bonfire, also appeared in the NAACP's 1920 pamphlet *An Appeal to the Conscience of the Civilized World* (figure 6.10). Because this was one of the few lynching photographs that revealed a lynching in process—the action momentarily stopped so the photographer could snap a picture—it stood as a dreadful and vivid "appeal to conscience." But rather than reproduce this image in its entirety, the *Chicago Tribune* chose to crop Brown's burning body from it, on the grounds that it was "too revolting for publication." What remained was an amorphous mob of whites, an image that required clarification to have any meaning. "It is unique in the clearly defined faces of people at an actual lynching," the caption explained. "The expressions on the faces . . . are . . . a study in humankind in the mood of taking law into its own hands." Similarly, the *New York World* printed the photograph of the Marion, Indiana, double lynching but cropped it to depict only, as the headline read, "the spectators and participants in killing of negro boys." The text surrounding both these images called on viewers to scrutinize the mob to unlock the mystery of its brutality, when, in fact, what is most harrowing about these photographs is how normal the crowds appear—without the caption that denotes their purpose, they could be any crowd.[55] Not until 1937 did the body of a lynched black man appear on the pages of the mainstream press, when, amid congressional debate of the Gavagan bill, photographs of Robert McDaniels's and Roosevelt Townes's tortured bodies appeared in *Time* and *Life* magazines—a remarkable instance in which the struggling

THE BURNING OF WILLIAM BROWN, OMAHA, NEBRASKA, SEPTEMBER 28, 1919

FIGURE 6.10 The lynching of William Brown, Omaha, Nebraska, 1919.
Prints and Photographs Division, Library of Congress, Washington, D.C.

black body was made the center of antilynching discourse. These images later appeared in the *Chicago Tribune* as part of Senator Clark's antilynching poster. For the most part, however, white Americans were reluctant to witness the sight of lynched black men.[56]

Indeed, when two white men were lynched in San Jose, California, in 1933, all the rules regarding what could and could not be represented in the press changed. The case received a tremendous amount of attention—arguably more than any other lynching—and was the catalyst for the recrudescence of antilynching activism in the 1930s. The photographs of this lynching and their treatment in newspapers and magazines throughout the country confounded editors' previous claims that they declined to print lynching photographs out of decency. John Holmes and Thomas Thurmond had been the lead suspects in the kidnapping and murder of Brooke Hart, the son of a wealthy San Jose storeowner. For weeks, coverage of the crimes had dominated the local news, stirring the city populace into a frenzied desire for vengeance. Once authorities apprehended Holmes and Thurmond, a mob stormed the county jail, abducted the prisoners, took them to a nearby park, and hanged them before a crowd of thousands. Soon after the lynching,

California governor James Rolph issued a statement praising the lynching as "the best lesson that California has ever given the country" and promising that "if anyone is arrested for the good job, I'll pardon them all." Yet, although Rolph's assertion was stunning and the lynching itself was brutal, there was nothing exceptional about this chain of events within the history of lynching, except that they took place in California and the victims were white—facts that certainly startled those who otherwise dismissed lynching as a southern problem of race hatred.[57]

The lynching in San Jose also became a national spectacle because, for the first time, large mainstream presses chose to print lynching photographs. Since the lynching was announced beforehand, a number of news photographers were at the scene to document the entire event on film, despite that some members of the mob tried to stop them. Pictures of the crowd outside the jail, men battering down the jailhouse door, and crowds in the park where Holmes and Thurmond were hanged were emblazoned across the pages of almost every major newspaper in the country. Photographs were also made into postcards, and several were compiled in a "souvenir booklet" of the lynching, along with quotes from Governor Rolph's inflammatory defense of the mob. Some newspapers also printed pictures of Holmes and Thurmond while still alive. The *New York Journal* published photographs of Holmes's young children, who, according to the caption, would now have a "life clouded by sorrow and shame." Although the *New York Journal* was known for its sensational tabloid style, the images humanized the lynched man in a way that no white-owned papers ever did for African American victims.[58]

Remarkably, many newspapers across the country chose to print photographs of Holmes's and Thurmond's hanged bodies (figure 6.11). Because the mob had stripped Holmes nude and had removed Thurmond's trousers, these images were particularly indecent. For one postcard, a photographer manipulated the image to elongate Holmes's penis and make it appear semierect, a salacious alteration that would never have been made to a photograph of a black man's lynched body—to the contrary, as noted in chapter 3, black men's genitalia invariably were covered up for the camera. Most newspapers, however, managed to reproduce the photographs of Holmes and Thurmond without revealing their genitalia. Some, including *Time* magazine, published an image of Holmes's body turned so his backside faced the camera, while other papers altered the images to conceal the nudity. Several papers drew underwear or trousers on the men's bodies.[59]

These photographs were, understandably, deemed incendiary near San

FIGURE 6.11 The lynching of Thomas Thurmond and John Holmes, San Jose, California, 1933. This postcard was constructed from two photographs of the men. Prints and Photograph Division, Library of Congress, Washington, D.C. Courtesy of the National Association for the Advancement of Colored People.

Jose. A special edition of the *Oakland Post-Enquirer* had featured images from the lynching, including one that depicted Holmes's and Thurmond's nude bodies. The chief of police, however, seized all copies of the paper and, in addition, forbade the selling of lynching photographs in the city because he deemed them "indecent." City officials in San Francisco similarly banned the images, although entrepreneurs continued to sell bootleg copies of the *Oakland Post-Enquirer* for a handsome profit. The *San Jose News*, on the other hand, announced to its readers, with smug self-congratulation, that although it would publish no pictures from the lynching, it had not been "scooped." It simply had chosen, in "good taste," not to print the "gruesome and horrible pictures" so as not to shock "children and sensitive women." Yet, while it found the photographs of the lynching "gruesome and horrible," the paper's editorial on the lynching refrained from condemning the mob, deeming them a "vigilante committee" that had simply "demanded what they and the general public believed to be justice."[60]

Most news editors, politicians, and other officials around the country, however, spoke out with unparalleled vehemence against the San Jose lynching and Governor Rolph's flimsy justification of it. With no violated white woman or frightening black criminal to contend with, San Jose put the crime of lynching into sharp relief as a travesty of justice and of due process, as a cold, thirsty act of savage vengeance. The photographs made this conception of lynching, one that obscured race and assuaged white Americans' sense of guilt and collective responsibility, visually evident—their circulation accentuated that some victims of lynching were white. Much like the eager spectators shown in one image from San Jose, straining for a better view, they could witness a lynching without having to bear witness to racial injustices. Antilynching activists seized on the moment, calling for the impeachment of Rolph and renewing efforts to enact federal antilynching legislation. Indeed, the expediency of the San Jose lynching to their cause was not lost on black lynching opponents. "As long as Negroes were the victims, it was nothing for the nation's leaders to get worked up about. But now the show begins to squeeze the other foot," wrote the editors of the Atlanta Daily World. They added, "If black men are mobbed and nothing is done, it means that eventually there will be white victims. So we have the San Jose massacre. Already sentiment in the right places is beginning to crystallize for federal anti-lynching laws." Not only did the San Jose lynching coincide with antilynching rhetoric that deflected attention away from race and characterized lynching as a barbaric attack on civilization itself, but it helped cement those arguments in the national consciousness.[61]

Corresponding to the dominant rhetoric of black-led antilynching activism, white opponents of lynching regularly conceptualized the primary victims of lynching as legal institutions and American democracy. As Representative Hamilton Fish, a Republican from New York, stated in defense of the Gavagan bill just after the Duck Hill lynching, "[Lynching] amount[s] to a rape of justice, liberty, civil rights, equal rights, human rights, human lives, and the Constitution itself." (The cartoon in figure 6.9 echoes this rhetoric.) This language, which stunningly inverted the prolynching defense, had the added effect of creating a sense of disidentification between white lynch mobs and white lynching opponents, a distance that could relieve opponents from feelings of culpability. In other words, although lynching opponents conveyed great shame that such atrocities were committed in America, their rhetoric simultaneously expressed a sense that a vast gulf existed between the "sadistic barbarians" who made up lynch mobs and themselves as upholders of American civilization.[62]

Southern liberals, who, through organizations like the Commission on Interracial Cooperation (CIC) and the Association of Southern Women for the Prevention of Lynching (ASWPL), led by Jesse Daniel Ames, became the most organized and outspoken of white antilynching activists in the 1930s, echoed much of this same language. The official declaration of the Georgia chapter of the ASWPL, for example, stated, "The real victim in the crime of lynching, we affirm, is not the person done to death, but constituted and regularly established government." Similarly, the CIC's Southern Commission on the Study of Lynching declared in its 1931 report that "lynching makes a mockery of courts and citizenship. The state itself has been lynched." In their literature, white southern intellectuals and activists, like Ames, certainly recognized lynching as principally a southern problem and a southern disgrace, and they analyzed it as a practice that derived from the interplay of socioeconomic conditions and cultural attitudes concerning race, gender, and sex. But they also felt that lynching could best be opposed by persuading the potential participants in lynch mobs that lynching was to their own detriment, that they and their communities were lynching's primary victims. Their rhetoric thus stressed that lynching not only threatened law and order in southern communities but also corroded individual ethics and psyches.[63]

Although such rhetoric dovetailed with that of the NAACP, the organizations' goals and tactics were decidedly different. While the NAACP targeted African Americans and white moderates and liberals, mostly in the North, to garner support for federal antilynching legislation, the CIC and ASWPL primarily sought to change southern attitudes and behavior. Accordingly, while they did publicize lynchings, both the CIC and the ASWPL avoided using lynching photographs, since they did not want to alienate their southern audiences, who might deem this material incendiary. In this respect, Ames and her allies mirrored the circumspect rhetoric of southern journalists, who expressed shame about lynching by abandoning any sensational treatment of the topic. Indeed, the ASWPL sought to undermine lynching by convincing southern news editors to change the language and tone of lynching coverage to give less credence to mob violence.[64]

In this way, southern lynching opponents frequently expressed a sense of shame not for the blighting of national ideals but for the dishonor that lynching had brought to the South. Lynching "cheapens human life and lessens respect for human liberty and personality. It defeats the ends of justice," wrote sociologist and later CIC president Howard Odum in the *Nation* in 1931. "It violates all the better traditions of southern honor and ideals. . . . It negates the South's claim for excellence and genius in the science of politics." These arguments were repeated in editorials throughout the

South, as southern elites, like those in Waco, increasingly recognized lynching as a stain on the reputations of their states and communities. These voices became more frequent and amplified as the threat of federal anti-lynching legislation intensified throughout the 1930s — legislation that most southerners, including southern liberals, resisted as an attack on both states' rights and their honor.[65]

Although race and white supremacy were largely omitted from these discussions, most Americans in the 1930s would have been well aware that African Americans were the primary victims of lynching. As Ames stated at one early ASWPL meeting, "The word 'lynching' suggests race because one race almost exclusively is the victim of lynchers." This rhetorical shift was made possible in part because of the work of early activists like Ida B. Wells, who had successfully transformed the term "lynching" from one that, in the nineteenth century, denoted extralegal punishments to one that, by the twentieth century, denoted a mechanism for enforcing white supremacy.[66] Yet the consistent rhetorical absence of the black victim — and, in fact, his displacement by the "victimhood" of American ideals — together with the conspicuous absence of lynching photographs in the white-owned press, suggests that many white Americans preferred to keep race in the shadowed background of public discussions about lynching.

Southern news editors seemed to welcome the San Jose lynchings for precisely these reasons, especially because they drew attention away from the South and its "race problem." A number of southern newspapers broke with their standard visual suppression of lynching and, like their northern counterparts, printed photographs of Holmes's and Thurmond's lynched bodies.[67] To be sure, although they condemned the lynching, some editors did offer the familiar defense that the lynching occurred because most Americans were frustrated with the inefficiency of the legal system and outraged by the crime of kidnapping, which, as the *Jackson (Miss.) Clarion-Ledger* noted, aroused "passions . . . as strong as — and . . . akin to — those aroused by rape." But most southern editors denounced the lynching and Rolph's defense of it with an almost palpable relief that the South was not, this time, the object of national scorn. "Alabama has had its lynchings, but our governors have not condoned them," crowed the editors of the *Birmingham News*. The *Meridian (Miss.) Star*'s editorial on the San Jose lynchings likewise asserted almost gleefully that they had occurred "not in Mississippi or some other section of the country which eastern, northern, and western press delight to describe as the 'benighted south.'" Rather, "this so-called 'travesty on law' is perpetrated in the highly educated, well-behaved 'cultured' and smug complacent San Jose in California," the editor wrote, adding that he hoped Californians would now be more tolerant of "occasional rope outbreaks throughout the South." Overall, he concluded, the lynchings in San Jose demonstrated that "primal feelings know neither section, creed nor boundary line. All of us are in measure savages beneath a thin so-called veneer." In editorials like these, editors did backbends to denounce lynching as "savage" and a "travesty" while defending the national reputation of their section.[68]

The San Jose lynchings allowed many white southerners to adopt the rhetoric of the national antilynching movement without feeling attacked as a region. By the mid-1930s, southern editors and politicians regularly condemned lynching as a barbaric and outmoded custom, one that threatened the social and economic progress of their states and communities. While they still at times attempted to explain why mobs felt compelled to lynch, as the above editorials did, they no longer openly applauded the violence, nor did they consider mobs to be members of an orderly and restrained citizenry.[69] By focusing on the language of lawlessness and civility, these southerners also could distance themselves from lynching without abandoning their white supremacist convictions, including the belief that African Americans were, by nature, less civilized and more prone to crime. In fact, these convictions gave antilynching rhetoric added force. The notion that whites were more restrained and law-abiding than blacks only made images of frenzied, lawless white mobs more embarrassing.

Coverage of lynching accordingly became more circumspect in the southern press, as editors recognized that sensational accounts, including the printing of photographs, would only compound the shame. Some smaller papers in the South stopped covering lynchings — even the most spectacular lynchings warranted no mention in small-town and county newspapers. Just as lynching opponents were appropriating media sensationalism to make lynching atrocities as visible as possible to the nation, southern papers that had previously lingered over the most grotesque details of lynching violence began to cloak that violence in a veil of invisibility. Images that were tolerable, even celebrated, on a local level became unacceptable when they were transferred beyond local boundaries.

Consequently, as lynching photographs were increasingly used in the service of lynching opposition, they became harder for opponents to obtain. As the remark in Waco that the photographs might bring "bad publicity" reveals, white southerners were well aware of the ill consequences when photographic recordings of their actions circulated outside their localities. They thus became more protective about whom they showed and gave images to. (These concerns, surprisingly, did not stop them from posing for such pictures.) As noted in chapter 3, photojournalists at times met with resistance from mobs who physically attacked them or broke their cameras. Although some lynching photographs made their way to national wire services, the majority of images were taken by local photographers and remained in the lynching locality. After the 1917 lynching of Ell Person in Memphis, Tennessee, the *Chicago Defender* noted that, although photographs of Person's decapitated head were hawked on the streets of Memphis for twenty-five cents each, they were "sold only to whites." The paper boasted, "No one had a picture, but the combined efforts of the *Defender* force landed the above."[70]

In this climate, the NAACP and the black press obtained photographs through the resourceful practices of investigators, like Elizabeth Freeman, and from local sympathizers. In one instance, a traveling salesman—an outsider—took a photograph of a lynching in Florida and gave a copy to an African American police officer, who sent it on to the NAACP.[71] The photograph of Rubin Stacy used in the 1935 antilynching pamphlet shown in figure 6.6 was obtained, according to assistant secretary Roy Wilkins, through "a round-about way" from a staff photographer, H. Willoughby, at the *Miami Daily Tribune*. A Chicago man had written to Willoughby for a copy of the photo and then passed it on to the NAACP. Presumably the photographer would not have given the image directly to the organization. In 1937, the NAACP tried in vain to obtain the images of the Duck Hill lynching, but it was stymied by the national attention the lynching had received. The photographs of Townes and McDaniels's lynching were distributed by Campbell's Studio in Grenada, Mississippi, the largest town near Duck Hill. Yet the NAACP was told it could not purchase any. *Life*, which did print the photographs, wrote to the NAACP that "the pictures which we had were taken by someone who does not care to become a storm centre and has accordingly instructed us to refrain from giving his name to anyone." In fact, no pictures of the Duck Hill lynching ever appeared in the black press.[72]

That white southerners went to such great efforts to control the circulation and display of lynching photographs makes evident just how successful activists were in transforming their meaning. By the 1930s, these images came to represent, with iconic power, the most grotesque and egregious aspect of lynching, substantiating the notion that lynching was more than crude vigilantism—it was an atrocity. In this respect, the very spectacle of lynching, so vital to the construction and perpetuation of white supremacy, carried with it the tools of its own dismantling. Yet, just as many white southerners were attempting to obscure this spectacle as much as possible from public view, Hollywood turned its cinematic gaze on lynching, making a series of liberal attacks on extralegal violence that dramatized and popularized the rhetoric of antilynching activists to a degree that the news media could not begin to match.

7

✤ ✤ ✤

BRING HOME TO AMERICA WHAT MOB VIOLENCE REALLY MEANS

Hollywood's Spectacular Indictment

IN THE EARLY SUMMER OF 1936, in the midst of the NAACP's arduous campaign to pass both a resolution calling for a Senate investigation of recent lynchings and the Costigan-Wagner antilynching bill through Congress, executive secretary Walter White attempted to arrange a White House screening for the MGM film *Fury*. White had just previewed the film, a sensational dramatization of a near lynching, and had written to the studio to thank it enthusiastically for the "superb effectiveness" of the film. "More than I have ever seen it done before has the medium of the moving picture been used to bring home to America what mob violence really means," he cheered, adding that the film deserved "as wide acclaim as possible." The following day, White wrote to Eleanor Roosevelt, enclosing a synopsis of the film and asking her to view the film herself. Throughout the first week of June, White sent insistent letters and telegrams to the first lady in hopes that if she endorsed *Fury* and invited congressional leaders to view the film with her and the president at the White House, there might "arise out of this the stimulation" to ensure passage of the Costigan-Wagner bill before Congress adjourned. Meanwhile, the NAACP was sending members of Congress copies of its pamphlet on the recent lynching of Lint Shaw in Royston, Georgia, which included the photograph of Shaw's bloodied body surrounded by a stolid group of white farmers and townsmen. White, however, was much more enthusiastic about the potential for *Fury*'s fictional representation of lynching to spur congressional action.[1]

White also anticipated that *Fury* could help garner popular support for the NAACP's antilynching campaign, at least among African American filmgoers, and assured MGM that he would write all 404 branches of the NAACP urging members to see the film. Advertisements for the film in black newspapers publicized the NAACP's endorsement, and at least one theater, in

Washington, D.C., solicited contributions from patrons for the NAACP's antilynching fund.[2]

White praised, in particular, the film's objectivity and the way it "carefully steer[ed] away from propaganda," even though *Fury* took a clear stand against lynching, and he himself wanted to use the film for political purposes.[3] White suggested that, as a work of entertainment, *Fury* could serve as evidence of the horror of lynching more effectively than could nonfictional representations of lynching that were by then too associated with political rhetoric. That is to say, although billed as fictional entertainment, *Fury* would appear more real—more like document and less like propaganda—than a photograph. Because of its capacity to represent movement and sound, as well as both character interiority and multiple perspectives, cinema bore an authenticity and cultural power that could potentially persuade and stimulate action in a way that still images of lynching could not. In short, *Fury* could "bring home to America what mob violence really means."

Although his hope of a White House screening—what White himself called his "hare-brained scheme"—never came to pass, *Fury* was a box office success across the country, making $250,000 for MGM.[4] Critics in both the black and white mainstream press praised it for its truthful and technologically brilliant rendering of the terror and devastation that lynching wrought. Directed by Austrian émigré Fritz Lang, the film tells the story of a white working-class "Joe" from Chicago, Joseph Wilson (Spencer Tracy), who, traveling west to meet his fiancée, Katherine (Sylvia Sidney), is arrested and jailed in the fictional town of Strand for the kidnapping of a young woman. The people of Strand, whipped into a fury of vengeance, burn down the jail where Joe is detained. Unknown to the crowd, however, Joe escapes the fire and, in hiding, plots to avenge his own presumed death. When Strand's district attorney seeks indictments against twenty-two members of the mob, Joe surreptitiously aids the prosecution from afar. The second half of the film moves back and forth between the courtroom trial of these men and Joe's own descent into vengeful fury. In the end, Joe has a redemptive change of heart and appears in the courtroom to save his would-be killers from the death penalty, restoring his own humanity, his sense of justice and legal order, and, in a final embrace, his romantic union with Katherine.

In its sanitized depiction of lynching, *Fury* seems an unlikely tool for the

NAACP's antilynching campaign. The would-be lynching victim is white; he survives; the lynch mob is exonerated; and racism and white supremacy remain unexamined. In representing lynching as a crime detached from any explicit political and social context and in obscuring the black victims of lynching, the film seems to disavow the terrifying reality of racist violence in America. It posits lynching as a largely random act whose principal victim is law and order rather than as a mechanism and expression of white dominance. Some liberal white critics criticized *Fury* on precisely these grounds. As Otis Ferguson wrote in his review of the film for the *New Republic*, "There is no race angle, there is a dimly implied class angle, there is no mutilation and the man escapes," all because Hollywood needed to "make love, lynching and the Hays office come out even," referring to the Production Code that regulated the form and content of Hollywood productions. Nevertheless, black leaders like Walter White and critics in the black press uniformly commended the film for its realism, its objectivity, and its harsh indictment of mob mentality.[5]

Fury was followed by two other Hollywood releases that placed antilynching messages at their center. Together, these three pictures represented a turn in Hollywood during the bleak years of the Depression toward realistic and socially conscious films that reflected on the darker aspects of American society and that balanced the escapism and frivolity of the industry's popular fare of musicals, westerns, and romantic comedies. In 1937, Warner Brothers released *They Won't Forget*, a fictional representation of the 1915 Leo Frank lynching, directed by Mervyn LeRoy and starring a cast of relative unknowns.[6] Unlike *Fury*, *They Won't Forget* was set in the South and addressed the sectional prejudices that incited the lynching. Nevertheless, the film evaded the particulars of the Frank case and omitted any reference to anti-Semitism. In 1943, Twentieth Century–Fox produced its own antilynching story, *The Ox-Bow Incident*, a "prestige picture" that was not a box office success but was selected as the year's best picture by the National Board of Review and received an Academy Award nomination for best picture.[7] This film, based on Walter van Tilberg Clark's 1940 best-selling novel of the same name, was not set not in the contemporary South but in the mythical Old West, where a posse hangs three men—two white, one Mexican—accused of killing a local rancher.

Like *Fury*, *They Won't Forget* and *The Ox-Bow Incident* focused not on race or racial prejudice but rather on the irrationality and recklessness of mobs and their potential to corrode both democracy and civilized order. In this respect, the pictures reflected rhetorical trends in the wider antilynching movement, which, as noted in the previous chapter, had successfully deflected public attention away from black suffering and systemic racism and onto the ways in which lynching was a barbaric abomination to American democratic ideals. In doing so, the movement had won the sympathy of white moderates, who supported law and order despite their prejudiced assumptions about black criminality. If lynching opponents of the 1930s rhetorically posited white society and the white psyche to be the primary victims of lynching, antilynching films made them literally so. All three pictures, in this way, adopted activists' political interpretation of lynching and then popularized it. Indeed, through these films, antilynching principles became spectacular in the most modern sense, packaged and marketed to a mass audience as an evening's entertainment.

The modes and conventions of Hollywood cinema, or what has been termed classical Hollywood style, only served to advance the social message of these films. This style, which came into being in the late 1910s and 1920s and soon emerged as the prevailing model of cinema worldwide, was known for its naturalistic representation of lived reality that obscured or concealed the artifice of that representation. It depended on the spectator's immersion in the cinematic world; unlike the spectator of early cinema, the spectator was not meant to stand outside the world depicted on-screen as an observer aware that he or she was watching a staged display. Rather, the classical Hollywood style constructed a seamless visual world, a self-enclosed narrative that absorbed the viewer into it. Moreover, this style always interpreted and resolved larger social problems through individuals, that is, through the actions and reactions of the central characters with whom viewers were to identify. The technical aspects of film, including lighting, camera angle, and editing, were all geared to creating a visceral identification between character and spectator so that the spectator experienced the character's world as his or her own. This style, which remained dominant until about 1960, became so normalized that, to film spectators, the cinematic world Hollywood created could appear more real than reality itself. It could then serve as a means through which viewers evaluated and interpreted their own experiences.[8]

It was through this cinematic style that antilynching films proved to be forceful ways for Americans to confront lynching, as they were impelled to comprehend its damaging and traumatic effects through the characters' personal experiences, which commentators and reviewers largely understood as authentic ones. These experiences also included the act of watching a lynching. For even as these films themselves rendered lynching as mass spectacle, they also self-reflexively commented on the lynching spectacle and what it meant to witness it by focusing on the reactions and judgments of on-screen spectators and by calling into question the moral account-ability of those who eagerly and greedily consume scenes of suffering and cruelty. In doing so, the films obliged moviegoers to recognize and evaluate their own spectatorship of lynching. Viewers would, in turn, take the under-standing of lynching and its spectacle they garnered from the films back to their witnessing of lynching in the news and, in increasingly rare instances, in their lives.

Although antilynching films established a common language and imagery through which Americans could comprehend and reflect on lynching, re-ception of them was by no means uniform. Viewers invariably received these films through their own social positions, expectations, and assumptions. A viewer could not watch an antilynching film without being aware of his or her own social and spectatorial position in relation to lynching—as a white or black person, northern or southern, female or male. Accordingly, whereas the black press received these films enthusiastically, white southerners were generally uneasy about them, as publicity and reviews in southern papers make evident. Just as lynching itself was declining and most white south-erners were preferring that attention, especially visual attention, not be drawn to it, they were confronted with cinematic images of angry mobs and terrified prisoners, ineffectual officials and voracious spectators—the very images that, by the 1930s, had become shameful icons of southern barba-rism. *They Won't Forget* was not shown in the South. *Fury*, on the other hand, was relatively successful there, despite industry expectations that it would fail. Its success rested on the fact that it avoided any specific indictment of the South and white supremacy, or, in Walter White's words, it "carefully steer[ed] away from propaganda." White southerners' conflicted and frac-tious responses to these films, however, reveal much about their increasing discomfort with their own lynching practices, especially when those prac-tices were abstracted and reflected back to them as entertainment.

EVEN IF THEY HAD WANTED TO, filmmakers in 1930s Hollywood could not have represented lynching as what it was, certainly not as a racist act of vio-lence that constructed and ensured white power. In the 1920s, the film in-dustry's trade organization, the Motion Picture Producers and Distributors of America, pressured studios to adhere to a series of moral and social checks on the content of motion pictures. These checks were instituted to stave off local, state, and federal censorship and to appease various Protestant and

Catholic reform groups that were becoming increasingly vocal about what they saw as moviemakers' flagrant disregard for moral standards. Bolstered by the 1915 Supreme Court ruling that motion pictures did not constitute protected speech, legislators in nine states and in numerous towns and cities across the country had established censorship boards to regulate what was presented on movie screens in their localities. State and local censors either banned films entirely in their locations or required studios to make numerous cuts to render them acceptable. The trade organization's checks, tightened and formalized in 1934 under the auspices of the Production Code Administration (PCA), operated as both a public relations maneuver and a profit-saving device. Hollywood vowed to clean up its own image to mollify its critics while saving itself time and money by altering films to conform to censors' standards during production, rather than after.[9]

The PCA prohibited graphic depictions of violence, which included lynching, but it was just as troubled by the point of view the film might take about lynching, since the Production Code stipulated that all criminal activity be balanced by compensating moral values and that law and order be upheld at the end of every film. In particular, motion pictures were not to take a point of view that could be interpreted as inflammatory or propagandistic. In what the PCA euphemistically referred to as "industry policy," any group that might take offense at a picture and sue or lobby the industry had to be represented in the best possible light. This included religious groups, professionals, political officials, foreign nationals, and sections and regions of the country. For this reason, Hollywood was loath to release any pictures that would flout Jim Crow convention or impugn white southern character. On the whole, the PCA's concerns were based on the same principles that led Walter White and other African American critics to support these films — all believed that motion pictures, as entertainment, had tremendous power to shape popular consciousness, whether they would, as the code stipulated, "inspire others with a desire for imitation" or, alternatively, arouse repulsion. The PCA thus carefully monitored productions about lynching, since, as it wrote concerning *The Ox-Bow Incident*, "many political censor boards are very sensitive as to all stories dealing with lynching, especially when it is the basic theme of the story."[10]

Fury, They Won't Forget, and *The Ox-Bow Incident* were certainly not the only Hollywood fare to feature lynching in this period. But they were the only three to place an antilynching message at their center. Lynching and near-lynching scenes appeared in many Hollywood westerns as "local color" or stock scenes that helped define the region for viewers.[11] Lynching scenes played a similar role in a number of films set in the South, such as *Cabin in the Cotton* (Warner Brothers, 1932), though the depiction of lynching in these films was far more controversial, in part because lynching in the South was of the present, whereas 1930s viewers were more likely to perceive western lynching as an outmoded practice. Audiences would have also recognized the racial implications in any film with a southern setting. Only *Laughter in Hell* (Universal, 1933), a shallow indictment of southern chain gangs in the vein of the popular and harder-hitting *I Was a Fugitive from a Chain Gang* (Warner Brothers, 1932), was able to get a racialized lynching scene past censors. Four black prisoners are hanged from a tree while other prisoners look on. Presumably, the scene was allowed to pass because the PCA had not yet tightened its code and because the film was set in the past.[12] Furthermore, scenes of enraged mobs with pitchforks and torches gathering around a hapless white protagonist who is saved from the noose at the last moment appeared in southern melodramas like *Mountain Justice* (Warner Brothers, 1937) and *Among the Living* (Paramount, 1941). Both films represent the lynching crowd much as antilynching activists described it: a carnivalesque crowd of angry, determined men and boisterous women and children gathered around the courthouse eating ice cream and hotdogs while newsmen gleefully profit off the drama. But, unlike *Fury*, *They Won't Forget*, and *The Ox-Bow Incident*, these films backed away from any pointed commentary on or indictment of lynching.

The prevalence of lynching and near-lynching scenes in these kinds of films suggests that depicting lynching on-screen was not itself controversial but that doing so within a context that pointed an accusatory finger at the South most certainly was. Southern-born PCA representative Lamar Trotti objected to the graphic depiction of a lynching in the initial drafts of *Cabin in the Cotton* on the grounds that "the South is sensitive about the subject chiefly because such desperate efforts are being made to stop them altogether and because most southerners are as horrified by them as the rest of the country. I know I would I feel much better about the reception of the picture there were you to [cut the scene], leaving to the imagination what follows." The film, which centers on a class struggle between white sharecroppers in Mississippi and their greedy landowners, indicts lynching as a lawless expression of planter power; both the mob of planters and the sharecropping victim are white. Despite the absence of any direct racial angle, however, the depiction of vigilantism in the film was objectionable, according to Trotti, because any reference to lynching was a source of embarrassment for white southerners. Even those opposed to lynching did not want that lawless violence exposed or witnessed, especially when they were represented as the perpetrators. Based on these objections, the scene was eventually all but cut from the production of the film; it was moved from the climax of the film to a small episode within the film and was shot almost entirely in darkness.[13]

Fury, They Won't Forget, and *The Ox-Bow Incident* similarly underwent considerable studio and PCA scrutiny. In fact, after reading the first draft of the *They Won't Forget* script, PCA head Joseph Breen determined that the film was "utterly impossible" because "no political censor, anywhere, would allow such a picture to be publicly exhibited." The film went through numerous changes before meeting PCA approval. Even then, it ran into trouble in the South and was banned in Atlanta. That city's censor, Mrs. Alonzo Richardson, wrote to Breen explaining that a film "recalling one of the darkest pages of the state's history" would not be shown anywhere in Georgia for fear of "revisiting conditions which would be ghastly in the tragedy of results." It is not clear what tragic results Richardson had in mind, but some feared that the film could rekindle the sectional and ethnic hatred that gave rise to Leo Frank's lynching. According to the Jewish paper the *Southern Israelite,* Jewish leaders in Atlanta supported Richardson's decision "with great relief."[14] Evidently, the film was kept out of not only Atlanta but cities and towns across the South, even in places relatively removed from memories of Leo Frank. Although it did play in Louisville, Kentucky, the exhibitor pulled it after two nights because his audiences, apparently, hated it.[15] Other southern exhibitors and review boards very likely refused to show the film because they feared audiences would resist the film's unsympathetic exposé of sectional prejudices and practices, even when they themselves, like Trotti, might bemoan them—just as white southern news editors denounced lynching but refused to publish lynching photographs.

Fury was able to bypass many of these censorship problems, however, because its indictment of lynching was detached from both race and the South. Some reviewers from the leftist press complained that the film's setting in the Midwest and its avoidance of race were motivated by box office concerns. "Remember, we have to sell these pictures in the South," scoffed critic Kenneth Fearing in the *New Masses.*[16] But *Fury* was inspired by the 1933 double lynching of two white men, accused kidnappers John Holmes and Thomas Thurmond, in San Jose, California. As noted in chapter 6, the lynching of Holmes and Thurmond provoked considerable public condemnation not only because of its cruelty and California governor Rolph's pro-lynching statements, but also because the lynching happened to two white men, outside the South. Antilynching activists were able to draw on and exploit this condemnation to drum up support for antilynching legislation.

The publicity surrounding the San Jose lynching, in turn, influenced the filmmakers. Screenwriter Norman Krasna and producer Joseph Mankiewicz developed the initial story outline from the contours of the case, and when Lang was hired to direct the film, he researched the lynching through newspaper and magazine clippings. Lang borrowed a number of visual and narrative details from this lynching for the film, including the shot of the mob storming the jail with a battering ram that seems to replicate in moving form a similar image from the lynching that appeared in newspapers across the country. By constructing the film primarily from the details of this case, the filmmakers showed themselves to be more interested in a story of thwarted justice and the ruthless psychology of mobs than in a story of racial antagonism. That is not to say the filmmakers ignored race—as will be shown, references to race are encrypted in the film—but by displacing race from the main plot, they, like so many lynching opponents at the time, attacked lynching as an American, rather than a white man's or a southern, travesty.[17]

In doing so, they also ensured that the film conformed to the conditions and standards of the PCA. In August 1935, Mankiewicz presented the story outline to Breen's office, which responded with some restrictions before Lang and another screenwriter, Bartlett Cormack, sat down to write the script. As long as it included a "definite preachment against mob violence" and ultimately restored law and order, the film would meet with few objections. The PCA did caution against depicting any "undue gruesomeness or brutality" and asked the studio to "tone down" the far too "realistic" scenes of mob violence and treat them "from the standpoint of political censorship."[18] The filmmakers were also required to alter some details of the San Jose lynching, especially those that showed political officials in a bad light. Breen, for instance, objected to the appearance in the original script of a U.S. senator, "a typical western statesman" clearly modeled on Governor Rolph, named Will Vickery, who condones vigilantism and discourages the governor from sending troops to stop the lynch mob. In the final version of the film, Vickery plays only a minor role as an aide to the governor, who, like Rolph, does not attempt to stop the lynching. Unlike Rolph, however, he is overcome with remorse and shame for failing to do so. These constraints nevertheless ultimately contributed to *Fury*'s popular and political impact by assuring that the film reached the widest possible audience without causing offense.[19]

THE KINDS OF RESTRICTIONS that the PCA placed on filmmakers also unintentionally ensured that these antilynching films coincided with the rhetorical focus of the larger antilynching movement. The filmmakers picked up on conceptions and images of lynching formulated and sensationalized by the black and liberal press and then reframed them within a more unified dramatic spectacle. For example, to shock the public, antilynching activists placed both rhetorical and visual emphasis on the moral depravity of crowds, portraying them as soaking in the sight of another person's death with casual glee, much as they might attend a circus. *Fury* replicates these conceptions of unrestrained lynching crowds in its depiction of the townspeople's frenzied excitement as the mob storms the jail and sets it afire. One shot depicts a mother who lifts her child above the crowd to view the fire, a startling image that suggests an appalling degree of maternal degeneracy (figure 7.1). The shot mirrors a well-known drawing from 1934 by artist Reginald Marsh, "This Is Her First Lynching," which appeared in the *New Yorker* and in the NAACP's 1935 antilynching art exhibition in New York. It was also reproduced in the *Crisis* (figure 7.2).[20] Marsh's image represents the spectators at a lynching, presumably a burning at the stake, which takes place outside the frame. The light from the bonfire illuminates one woman who is lifting a little girl above the crowd to see. Marsh's image and the shot from *Fury* were both inspired by common antilynching rhetoric that drew attention to those lynching crowds in which women and children were present. In particular, they referenced a photograph from the San Jose lynching, published in several media outlets, in which a spectator is hoisting a young girl up for a better view (figure 7.3).[21]

The films not only borrow these kinds of tropes from antilynching activism but heighten and authenticate them through the modes of classical Hollywood style. As Walter White acknowledged about *Fury*, this style brought antilynching principles to life, making them appear less like political propaganda and more like lived reality. Antilynching films, for instance, depicted lynching through the experiences of the victim, the individual unjustly accused and punished without due process. Lynching opponents, as noted, had deflected attention from the victims of lynching, rendering them unidentified icons of mob injustice. They recognized that white Americans' racial prejudices would keep them from empathizing too closely with the black lynching victims, particularly given presumptions about black criminality and guilt. Antilynching films, on the other hand, made personal and real to audiences victims who would otherwise be nameless and remote statistics, especially by making those victims white. *Fury* encourages audi-

FIGURE 7.1 A mother lifts her child to see the burning of the jail, *Fury*, MGM, 1936.

FIGURE 7.2 Reginald Marsh, "This Is Her First Lynching," 1934. © 2008 Estate of Reginald Marsh/ Art Students League, New York/Artists Rights Society (ARS), New York.

FIGURE 7.3 Crowd at the lynching of Thomas Thurmond and John Holmes, San Jose, California, 1933.

ences to identify with Joe and experience with him his alarm as his terrible reality unfolds, an identification the film fosters by representing Joe as a likeable everyman. What is more, Joe's innocence is unassailable. He is presented as somewhat childlike—he mispronounces words; he rips his coat. Katherine behaves maternally toward him, correcting his speech and mending his coat. That the authorities and townspeople in Strand could think he was capable of any crime, and then terrorize him for it, only amplified for white audiences the injustice of lynching.

Because the first half of the film, in this way, comprises a straightforward condemnation of the mob's wrongheadedness, the second half of the film, in which Joe transforms into a vengeful character and the members of the mob are tried and then exonerated, appears confounding. A number of critics considered it a detour that detracted from the film's antilynching message. Although he did laud the film as "the most forceful indictment of lynch justice ever projected on a screen," critic Robert Stebbins in *New Theatre Magazine* criticized the second half of the film precisely for the sympathy it attempted to engender for the would-be lynchers. The *Nation* similarly felt that the film's ending, particularly when Joe enters the courtroom and "saves his lynchers," diverged from the "abhorrence" toward lynching expressed in the first half of the film.[22]

Yet it is within the second half of the film that *Fury*'s real argument against lynching lies. Indeed, these scenes parallel the wider thrust of the antilynching movement. The courtroom scenes allow characters to echo common antilynching rhetoric, which posited that lynching arose not from the particulars of America's racial and social structures but rather from natural human impulses that only law, as the cornerstone of civilization, could rescue us from. The district attorney (Walter Abel) informs the judge, the jury, and the courtroom spectators, as well as moviegoers, that "in the last forty-nine years, mobs have lynched 6,010 human beings by hanging, burning, cutting, in this proud land of ours, a lynching about every three days." Focusing attention on the corruption of justice that lynching entails, he declares that "the law is the only safeguard against 'an eye for an eye, a tooth for a tooth' and blind chaos. American democracy and its system of fair play for the rights of individuals under the law is on trial here."

Furthermore, the trial sequence spotlights the ways in which entire communities supported lynching by refusing to comply with any legal action against suspected mob members. In his speech to the jury, the district attorney indicts those "supposedly civilized communities [who] refused to identify [mob members] for trial, thus becoming as responsible before God, at any rate, as the lynchers themselves!" Frank Nugent in the New York Times praised the film precisely for revealing the "community hypocrisy" that lies at the "root of the lynch evil." They Won't Forget and The Ox-Bow Incident likewise comment on the ways in which social structures and community sanction perpetuated and enforced lynching. As noted, because of PCA limitations, none of the films could indict the legal authorities who regularly condoned lynchings or let them happen through inaction. Yet in none of the films are the lynchings committed solely by ruthless and renegade individuals. Although in both Fury and They Won't Forget the men who organize the mob are shown to be lower-class ruffians, town businessmen and elites implicitly condone their actions, and journalists hungry for sensational stories egg them on.[23]

But even more important, Joe's transformation from idealistic everyman to enraged vigilante contains a powerful, albeit subtle, indictment against lynching. After he survives the burning of the jail, Joe descends into his own fury of vengeance against the mob, a descent that drives him to wish death on twenty-two men for a crime they did not commit.[24] When Joe reveals himself to his brothers, he revels in the idea of retribution: "They'll hang for it. According to the law if you kill somebody, you gotta be killed yourself." Insisting that his brothers pressure the district attorney to press charges, he does bitterly allow that "they'll get a legal trial in a legal courtroom, they'll get a legal judge and a legal defense, they'll get a legal sentence and a legal death." Yet, although Joe's recourse to the law places him on a higher moral plane than his would-be lynchers, the mob, of course, did not actually kill Joe. The district attorney's charges against the mob are thus based on a lie. Joe, presumed dead, has to remain in hiding and becomes more and more alienated from those around him, especially as his brothers and his fiancée, Katherine, who has since discovered his lie, begin to feel sympathy for the men on trial. By the end, Joe is presented as being as vengeful and corrupt as the lynch mob itself. "You're as bad as them. You're lynching me!" screams his brother, tormented by guilt. Defending his duplicitous revenge, Joe says, "[I want to] let them know how it feels to be lynched." Cast out as not human and morally dead, Joe is left to wander the streets of the city alone, disheveled and broken, haunted by the sights and sounds of the people he has condemned to death, before coming clean in the courtroom to exonerate both the mob and himself. He has moved from lynch mob victim to lyncher, a figure beyond the pale of civilized society.

Lang was most interested in precisely that transformation—in the propensity of people to abandon the very things that make them civilized to satisfy their basest and most brutal impulses. According to production notes from the initial story conference, Lang envisioned Joe as a "terrific idealist," an honest man who believes in the authority of law and due process. He initially imagined Joe as a lawyer but rewrote the character as a factory worker to make him appear more ordinary. The producers, likewise, cast Spencer Tracy to play the part because he was considered a "typically American type." Enraged over the crime committed against him, however, this common man abandons his idealism. As Lang noted, "His philosophy breaks down. . . . He is weak and he betrays his philosophy. . . . He now has only one idea. He suffered unbelievably. He wants revenge. This is his guilt."[25]

Like antilynching rhetoric, *Fury*'s lens focused not on the tortured bodies of lynch mobs' victims but on the damaging effects of lynching on white psyches and white society. The film portrays the victims of lynching as not only Joe, nor even the twenty-two men falsely accused, but justice, law, and idealism. As Joe states in his closing speech in the courtroom, it was a "belief in justice, and an idea that men were civilized, and a feeling of pride that this country of mine was different from all others. . . . Those things were burned to death within me that night." Indeed, although Joe makes references to his mangled arm, we do not see any physical violence against him. Instead, the fire "burned to death" American ideals. As the district attorney announces in his opening statement, "When a mob takes it upon itself to identify, try, condemn, and punish, it is a destroyer of government." Furthermore, in his closing speech, Joe admits that he has not returned to save the lives of his would-be killers; he declares, "I don't care anything about saving them. They're murderers." Rather, he says, "I came here today for my own sake." In other words, to preserve his sanity, Joe must admit his own duplicity, thereby recommitting himself to American ideals and the sanctity of the legal system. Joe ultimately stands for America itself in the face of lynching, as the fury of mob vengeance repeatedly scorched patriotic notions of justice and civilized ideals.

Audiences were thus meant to identify with Joe not only as a lynching victim, feeling pity for his trauma and sitting in moral judgment against his attackers, but also as a potential perpetrator, a man with fallen ideals and a corrupted sense of right and wrong. The film impelled white audiences to recognize their own culpability and responsibility, just as Joe recognizes his. MGM marketed *Fury* as a "drama that stuns like the blow of a blackjack . . . because it could happen to any one of you."[26] But because the lynching of white Americans was exceptionally rare, the tagline makes more sense in reference to the descent into vengeful madness to which audiences, like Joe, were vulnerable.

Both *They Won't Forget* and *The Ox-Bow Incident* placed similar thematic emphasis on the importance of upholding law and order to defend against our most brutal natures. In what stands as *The Ox-Bow Incident*'s central sermon against lynching, mob victim Donald Martin (Dana Andrews) writes to his wife just before his hanging, explaining that he is not the mob's only victim because "a man just . . . can't take the law into his own hands and hang people without hurting everybody in the world." As law is the basis of all civilization and human morality, he continues, "law is a lot more than words you put in a book, or judges or lawyers or sheriffs you hire to carry it out. . . . It's the very conscience of humanity. There can't be any such thing as civilization unless people have a conscience." The men in the film who have unjustly sentenced and killed three men have abandoned civilization itself, out in the wild of the Ox-Bow Valley.

Such appeals had particular resonance in an era when many Americans clung to democratic civilization as the only bulwark against fascism and despotism. In focusing on mob lawlessness in such general terms, these films, in fact, invoked the same linkages between American lynching and European fascism that antilynching activists were making in the mid-1930s. Lang's experiences as a soldier in World War I and as a witness to the rise of Nazism in his homeland made him intimately aware of the human capacity for cruelty and the ugly and destructive power of the mob. Lang left Germany in 1934, apparently after Goebbels asked him to head Germany's film industry, and *Fury* was his first American film. Although Lang often insisted that *Fury* was his attempt to address the peculiarly American problem of lynching, he also at times characterized the film as an examination of a universal mob psychology drawn from his experiences in Europe. In a 1936 interview, for instance, he recalled his own encounters with mob mentality growing up in Vienna along the Russian front, fighting in World War I, and, of course, working in Berlin as Hitler came to power. These experiences taught him that a mob erases individual responsibility, that it has no conscience, a point that Lang made repeatedly during preproduction meetings for *Fury* and that Katherine mouths near the end of the film in defense of the twenty-two men Joe wants to send to death: "They're not murderers—they were part of a mob! A mob doesn't think, it hasn't time to think," she cries. As Lang told the *New York Times*, "'Fury' is the story of mob action. Lynching happened to be the result. People over the world respond in the same way."[27]

To represent lynching simply as a failure of human restraint might seem to excuse the violence, but it could also enable viewers to condemn lynching while sympathizing or even identifying with the rage that motivated it. Lang noted in one preproduction meeting that "people are innately sadists—they go to motorcycle races in hopes of seeing people hurt—they run to accidents—like all dangerous sports." This sentiment appears in the film when the deputy sheriff tells the clientele in a barbershop about catching Joe as the suspected kidnapper. The barber, wielding his razor at the neck of a customer, says, "People get funny impulses. If y' resist 'em, you're sane; if y' don't, you're on the way to the nuthouse, or the pen," and then explains his own desire to cut the throats of his customers at times. The scene reads as a curious intrusion, except that it prepares the viewer for the murderous rage of otherwise ordinary citizens. As Lang explained, "I've been through four revolutions and have made an intimate study of how people act. They often start out in the best of spirits. Suddenly you realize that humor has given way to hate and violence." *Fury* became his attempt "to picture that imperceptible line where the change comes."[28]

The filmmakers were certainly well aware, however, that lynching was not a universal phenomenon but a particularly American problem rooted in race prejudice and the specifics of American social structures. Indeed, racism provided white Americans the rationale to cross "that imperceptible line" with impunity, a fact to which *Fury*, as well as the two later antilynching films, alludes. All three films address the racial aspect of lynching obliquely, however, through codes and cues that signaled to knowing audiences the ways in which racism underpinned lynching and victimized African Americans. *They Won't Forget* and *The Ox-Bow Incident* include relatively complex black characters who act as witnesses to the chain of events unfolding on-screen, their presence reminding viewers of racial injustice.

Although there are no leading African American characters in *Fury*, black characters appear in the background of the film, subtly prompting the viewer to recognize that the film's subject of lynching is a racialized one: a laundress sings a spiritual outside Katherine's window; a shoeshine man in the barbershop polishes the shoes of a professor who defends the U.S. Constitution; a bartender serves a drink to a broken-down Joe at the end of the film. The black bartender, in particular, serves as a moral reminder to Joe that he is about to send twenty-two men to their deaths—that he himself has become a lynch mob of one. As the clock strikes midnight, the bartender accidentally rips an extra page off the day calendar behind the bar so the day reads "22." "Two pages must have gotten hanged together," he says. Horrified, Joe pops a pill and leaves the bar.[29] What is more, earlier in the film, in a long shot of the enraged mob as it rushes out of the barroom, heading for the county jail to confront the sheriff and ultimately to begin the lynching, a shoeshine man is shown listening at the door of the bar. As the mob exits the bar, he jumps up on his chair at the right of the frame, concealing himself from the mob (figure 7.4). In another context, the scene could be read as minstrelesque comic relief, but, considering the familiarity of the image of a determined mob heading toward a jail, the inclusion of a confused and frightened black man in the scene points to something more poignant. To be sure, sidelong inclusions of black characters who were both caricatured and physically segregated from the white characters in the film replicated the marginalization of African Americans from antilynching rhetoric and from American society itself. After all, the black shoeshine man jumps to safety while Joe, the white character, is the target of the mob's fury, thereby reversing the racist reality of lynching.[30] On the other hand, our vision is drawn to the very marginalization that the film inscribes; these almost indiscernible black figures were meant to be seen and noted. This kind of coding was not lost on contemporary African American viewers.

Just as antilynching activists inverted the racist defenses of lynching to denounce the savagery of white mobs, *Fury* sardonically observes white Americans' mistaken sense of their own racial innocence through pointed,

FIGURE 7.4 A shoeshine man jumps aside as the mob approaches, *Fury*, MGM, 1936.

caricatured references to "Indian savages" in the environs of Strand—references that accentuate the notion of lynching as anathema to civilized order. As Joe leaves Chicago to meet Katherine, his brother says, "Look out for the Indians out there!" and makes a stereotypical Indian call with his palm against his mouth. Later, as Katherine, waiting at a lunch counter, worries about Joe's whereabouts, the diner owner consoles her by saying, "Well I ain't heard o' anybody bein' tomahawked or scalped in the neighborhood for some time now." These lines make an association between the lynching Joe will face and racial strife and violence, albeit in racist stereotypes that posit white men as the victims of Indian savagery. But they are meant to be ironic—Joe is a victim of "savagery," but the savages are, of course, other white men, including, by the end of the film, Joe himself.[31]

ANTILYNCHING FILMS OF THE 1930s do not simply denounce the unrestrained brutality of lynch mobs, however; they also denounce the spectacle of lynching. Even as the films themselves re-create lynching spectacles for commercial entertainment, they impugn those spectators who consume the violence for vicarious thrill and amusement. *Fury*, in particular, repeatedly confounds distinctions between lynching spectators and moviegoers. References to movies and moviegoing appear throughout the film. In an early version of the script, the film opened with Joe and Katherine at the movies. The name of the town, Strand, itself would have been familiar to 1930s audiences as a common motion picture theater name.[32] Moreover, in the haunting scene of Joe's near lynching, the spectators who watch as the jail burns bear an uncanny resemblance to a movie audience. Once the mob has overtaken the jail and set it afire, Katherine arrives and comes into the crowd. There is no sound but that of the fire crackling, a sound that echoes the sputter of a silent film projector. The camera cuts to the spectators, who stare at the action before them silently, with gaping, frozen gazes, light flickering across their faces.

Yet, because the PCA placed tight restrictions on the visualization of violence, the film viewer does not see exactly what the crowd in Strand is witnessing. By concealing the violence while building the tension of the mob's rage, the film entices, and then frustrates, the spectator's desire to look. The PCA's concern that no explicit depictions of violence appear on film mirrored that of the popular news media. Both suggested that the sight of a lynching—the graphic rendering of violence or of lynched bodies—was far more troubling than narrative treatments of that violence. PCA regulations thus impelled filmmakers to represent violence in stylized and abstract ways, creating a poetic grammar of screen violence that included visual forms of displacement, metonym, and symbolism. *Fury*, for instance, renders the force and trauma of the violence palpable to audiences through the reactions on the faces of the on-screen spectators, reactions that in turn directed and shaped audiences' response to and judgments about the lynching. In doing so, *Fury* replicates cinematically what contemporary newspapers were doing in cropping lynching photographs and using text to direct viewers' attention away from the violence in the image and onto the faces of the white crowds.[33]

While most of the on-screen spectators watch the fire in awe or amusement, the film includes two spectators in particular whose horrified reactions audiences were meant to identify with and adopt. During the fire and spectatorship sequence, the camera cuts to an elderly woman who kneels and begins to pray, her voice resounding as other shots depict the woman with a baby, a man eating a hot dog. Her prayer, which includes a line from the Lord's Prayer—"forgive us our trespasses as we forgive them who trespass against us"—unites in sin both those who commit violence and those who watch it. It also directs the viewer to respond to the crowd's callous spectatorship with horror. In censuring the lynching spectators in this way, *Fury* asks the filmgoer to evaluate his or her own moral position

FIGURE 7.5 Katherine witnesses the burning of the jail, *Fury*, MGM, 1936.

as a viewer, to reject the passivity of the spectators on-screen and, like the praying woman, to bear witness to the ghastly reality unfolding before them.

The audience experiences the full force of what has happened to Joe, however, primarily through Katherine's eyes. Viewers learn that the mob has set the jail afire only when Katherine learns this news, and they see the scene only when Katherine herself arrives in Strand and runs into the crowd. The camera moves backward as Katherine runs toward it, through the crowd toward the jail, and then pulls back quickly the moment she spots Joe in the window, creating a sense of vertigo in the viewer. The film then cuts to her point of view—a shot of Joe in the window—as someone in the crowd yells, "There he is!" before cutting back to a close-up of Katherine's face, frozen in horror (figure 7.5).[34] She then loses her balance and faints. In her role as witness, Katherine, along with the woman praying, inverts the standard role that white women often played in spectacle lynchings. As noted in previous chapters, in cases of sexual assault, white women commonly served as the only witness of the black man's alleged crime; her testimony roused and justified the mob's violence. White women's presence at a lynching further validated the violence, as their supposed virtue lent it an aura of righteousness. But, in *Fury*, Katherine's suffering gaze testifies only to the cruelty and brutality of the scene.

The film, moreover, makes the physical effects of the lynching apparent not through Joe's body but through Katherine's, for the trauma of seeing Joe's lynching becomes fixed on Katherine's face. Katherine's role as the traumatized witness here shadows common antilynching arguments, particularly those that Jesse Daniel Ames and other southern women lynching opponents put forward, that lynching did not protect or defend women's honor but rather did irreparable harm to them. Afterward, when Joe's brothers visit Katherine to enlist her help in the prosecution of the mob, she has become an invalid, staring with the same horrified gaze. "I saw him. I saw him in that burning jail," she says. Just as Joe experiences his own death repeatedly in the movie house, Katherine has been witnessing his death in her mind's eye over and over. On the witness stand at the trial of the mob, she repeats the claim, adding that she will "always see it."

The lynching in *The Ox-Bow Incident* also happens outside the frame of action, such that, as in *Fury*, the film viewer experiences it only through the eyes of the on-screen spectators. To suggest the lynching, the camera shows only the mob lifting the condemned men toward the nooses hanging above them and whipping away the horses. In the next shot, one of the posse shoots upward at the hanging bodies hidden from view, before the camera pans to the film's only black character, the preacher Sparks (Leigh Whipper), kneeling and singing a spiritual as the mob walks away. The camera continues panning to reveal the shadows of the three hanging bodies, while Sparks can be heard singing, "You've got to stand before your maker. You got to stand there by yourself" (figure 7.6). The entire shot creates a visual metonym between the silhouettes of the three hanging forms and the Crucifixion, compounding the emotional effect of the scene.[35] Not only does Sparks's presence remind viewers that most lynching victims were African American, but he acts as the moral and spiritual conscience of the film. Although he appears to be singing the spiritual to the lynched men as a sort of prayer, the song refers also to the members of the mob, who may escape indictment on earth but will have to face final judgment, as individuals, "before [their] maker." Whereas some of the white characters act as more outspoken defenders of law and order, Sparks's actions posit him as a figure of Christian mercy, overseeing the mob's rush to judgment not with anger but with a solemn lament and warning.[36]

In this scene, Sparks becomes the film viewer's surrogate witness of the lynching. His sorrow directs moviegoers to respond likewise. What is more, the film indicates that this lynching is not the first Sparks has witnessed. Earlier in the film, he tells the protagonist, Gil (Henry Fonda), "I seed my own brother lynched. I wake up dreaming," a remarkable inclusion that points to the harrowing effects of lynching on African American families. Sparks is already a traumatized figure, continually seeing the lynching replayed before him.[37] His role stood out at the time as an exceptionally nuanced representation of a black man in film and was seen by black audiences, at least, as an indication of the film's more direct sociological comment, "the

FIGURE 7.6 The lynching scene, *The Ox-Bow Incident*, Twentieth Century–Fox, 1943.

symbol indicating the sanguinary Southern pastime of lynching," according to one author in the black magazine *Opportunity*.[38]

However, although *Ox-Bow* and *Fury* make viewers witness the physical effects of the violence through the faces of the spectators, they represent lynching in a way that no photograph could represent it and, even more significant, no spectator would really experience it. In *Fury*, the entire sequence of the mob's attack on the jail and the subsequent fire unfolds through a series of camera pans and cuts, which include both shots of the crowd and a number of point-of-view shots that depict the action from the perspectives of the crowd, Katherine, and even Joe as he looks out the window of his cell. These multiple perspectives offer a panoptic visual experience of the lynching that transcends the limitations of individual sight. Yet, although the film presents the lynching in a way that no actual spectator would see it, to moviegoers, the scene felt like an accurate reflection of reality. In reviewing the film, critics commonly praised this particular scene for its terrifying realism. For Kenneth Fearing, in the *New Masses*, the burning of the jail was "so realistic that when flames leap up . . . and encircle the caged victim, you actually smell the burning flesh." Indeed, in an interview with the *Los Angeles Times*, Lang touted realism as the hallmark of modern cinema. "Through proper use of the camera it is a comparatively simple matter to make audiences feel they actually are taking part in the action of a picture," he explained. With motion pictures, "audiences have been projected into the positions of the actors, seeing with their eyes, thinking with their brains, experiencing with their emotional reactions."[39]

For some reviewers, the sense of realism created through the camera's multiple perspectives was the source of the film's political power to horrify Americans and engage their sympathy with the antilynching movement. Critic Frank Nugent in the *New York Times* lauded Lang's "camera genius" for making it so that "we see it as the victim sees it, as the mob sees it, as the community sees it, as the law sees it, as the public sees it." The film, he continued, allowed viewers to "see a lynching, its prelude and its aftermath, in all its cold horror, its hypocrisy and its cruel stupidity," which "disgusts us and fills us with shame for what has been done, and is being done, in our constitutional republic."[40] The "us," for Nugent, were presumably fellow white Americans who, except for experiencing a lynching in this way, would not fully recognize and indict lynching as the terrible crime that it was. In this regard, the repeated use of the word "indictment" in both MGM's promotional materials and in film reviews to refer to *Fury*'s impact is telling. The term positioned the film within the realm of legal judgment, as if witnessing the film rendered the moviegoer as judge and jury, mirroring the criminal indictment of the members of the mob that happens within the film. Ideally, as Walter White hoped, viewers would leave the theater ready to support legislation against lynching.

Fury is most self-reflexive, however, in its use of mass media within the film. Characters come to understand what is happening around them through news stories and, notably, movie newsreels. Even as movie audiences were made to accept *Fury* as an accurate representation of lynching's reality, the film continually questions cinema's moral culpability in sensationalizing that reality. *Fury* reveals the kidnapping of the young woman, Joe's arrest, and Joe's supposed lynching through shots of bold newspaper headlines, which evoke a sense of documentary realism while carrying the story forward. The trial of the mob is broadcast over the radio, and the announcer summarizes events for both the public within the film and the audience in the movie theater.[41]

But in addition to these standard narrative devices of 1930s cinema, *Fury* makes unexpected use of newsreels. As the mob builds in Strand, newsreel cameramen rush to the scene to capture it all on film. Katherine learns of Joe's arrest and the attack on the jail through these newsmen. The film indicts the greed and callousness of these journalists who exploit Joe's suffering for their own profit. Filming the fire, one cameraman shouts with delight, "Oh boy, oh boy, oh boy, what a shot this is. We'll sweep the country with this!" — a line that calls attention to the double meaning of "shot" as the camera's field of vision and as an act of violence. Yet these cameramen were filming what the movie audience itself was viewing as entertainment.

By 1936, movie audiences had likely viewed actual newsreels about certain high-profile lynchings, including the lynching of John Holmes and Thomas Thurmond in San Jose and the 1934 lynching of Claude Neal in Marianna, Florida.[42] Such footage was, to be sure, rare and controversial. Although early cinematic "actualities" had covered news events, newsreels developed into a distinct cinematic category and industry only in the 1920s. Newsreel cameramen began to compete with photojournalists to capture on film the major news stories of the day, including images of the Tulsa race riot in 1921. But because they were shown in movie theaters as a sort of appetizer along with cartoons and other shorts before the main feature, newsreels egregiously blended news and entertainment. Many newsreel companies forcefully sought to establish themselves as reputable journalistic outlets, yet the Hollywood studios that owned them, as well as theater owners, concerned with alienating movie audiences, pressured them to avoid any perspective or material that they deemed controversial or propagandistic. Most newsreel companies thus avoided lynching coverage and would never have projected images of lynched corpses. *Variety* reported shortly after the San Jose lynchings that Universal was showing two corpses from a recent Colorado mining accident and noted sardonically that the newsreel company "never overlooks a gruesome subject — except lynchings."[43]

Variety was certainly referring to the fact that Universal had shot footage about the San Jose lynchings, including a statement from Governor Rolph, but had chosen not to exhibit it, a decision that was also made by Fox. Paramount, the most aggressive and respected of the newsreel companies, did produce and distribute a newsreel "résumé of the lynching situation" in the week following the lynchings.[44] Although Paramount did not include any images from the lynching itself in its U.S. version, it did release a version in London that concluded with a still image of John Holmes's naked corpse. The footage was quickly denounced by both the London press and the House of Commons, leading Paramount to withdraw the newsreel from exhibition, even though the same image had appeared in London's *Daily Mirror* without comment.[45] Newsreel cameras were also on hand for a riot that broke out in Salisbury, Maryland, just after the San Jose lynchings. Maryland governor Albert Ritchie had arrested four men implicated in the lynching of a black man, George Armwood. A large mob battled national guardsmen to free the men. Cameramen caught some of it on film despite that rioters stole the equipment from one freelancer, pushed a Paramount camera truck into the water, and attempted to destroy a sound wagon owned by Pathé—just as lynch mobs ripped cameras from photojournalists. The Maryland board of censors tried to repress the footage that remained, excising "all riot and lynching scenes from newsreels" shown in the state, most likely wanting to quell the storm.[46]

As these incidents make evident, newsreel images of lynching-related violence provoked even more discomfort and outrage than did still images. Moving images were projected larger than life before audiences soaking in an evening's entertainment—all the spectacle of lynching writ large. *Fury* recalls and comments on these controversies. After escaping the jail fire, Joe reexperiences his own lynching when he attends a movie and sees the newsreel footage of his supposed death. He is doubly outraged; not only did he suffer the mob's attack, but people are being entertained by his suffering. "[I was] watchin' a newsreel . . . of myself. Gettin' burned alive. I watched it ten times—or twenty—over and over again," he tells his brothers. "The place was packed. They liked it. They get a big kick out of seeing a man burned to death. A big kick." Like Sparks's reference to his brother's lynching in *The Ox-Bow Incident*, Joe experiences a traumatic reenvisioning of the lynching, except for Joe, the projected repeated image is not in his mind's eye but on the movie screen. Furthermore, the newsreel does not present what he himself experienced or saw; rather, it presents what the lynching crowd, or more specifically the cameramen, saw. The movie-within-the-movie audience thus stands in for the crowd at the lynching. The line "The place was packed. They liked it. They get a big kick out of seeing a man burned to death" could refer to the newsreel audience, to the spectators at the lynching, and to the viewers sitting in the movie theater watching *Fury*. The film, in this way, slyly presses audiences to evaluate their own spectatorship of lynching, impelling them not to identify with the greedy spectators within the film but rather those witnesses, like Katherine and the praying woman, who watch the lynching crowd not in sympathy or morbid curiosity but in judgmental horror.

This same newsreel footage is then used as evidence in the courtroom

FIGURE 7.7 Newsreel footage is revealed in the courtroom, *Fury*, MGM, 1936.

sequence, a scene that transforms the footage from a form of tabloid sensationalism into a political and moral tool. When witness after witness refuses to testify that any of the accused men were at the scene of the lynching, the district attorney reveals his trump witness: the newsreel projector. In the darkened courtroom, the near lynching is replayed on the movie screen, rendering the courtroom spectators movie spectators and, in turn, the movie audience moral witnesses (figure 7.7). The district attorney's use of the newsreel, in this respect, echoes the use of lynching photographs in the 1930s media. As the footage plays, he repeatedly pauses the film to create stills of the condemned men—one pouring the kerosene, another throwing the torch—in effect, holding their guilt up for view. Again the visual focus is on the perpetrators, not their victim. As with lynching photographs, the camera's gaze indicts members of the mob, and actions that in one context were seen as justified and heroic become ghastly and criminal in another. The media are thus shown to bear a factual authority that supersedes that of eyewitnesses. Indeed, after telling his brothers about the newsreels, Joe says, "I'm a dead man. I'm dead. The whole country knows about it," suggesting that the news media have claimed a truth that his own physical presence cannot deny.

But the lynching in *Fury* never really occurred. Nothing that these witnesses—Katherine, the townspeople, or the newsmen—saw is what they think they saw. The news camera has fixed "proof" while misrepresenting truth. In this sense, the film challenges the camera's ability to capture and uphold truth and sets up vision as precisely that which cannot be trusted.[47] The trial sequence underscores this point when the defense attorney (Jonathon Hale) cross-examines Katherine on the witness stand to cast doubt on her assertion that she saw Joe burn to death in the jail. The defense of the alleged members of the mob initially rests on the lack of proof that they participated in the lynching. Once the newsreel footage determines their participation, the defense moves to place doubt on the fact that Joe was killed. Although Katherine is the key witness in the film, the validity of her eyewitness account is called into question—after all, though she "saw him in that burning jail," Joe is not dead. And her spectatorship is presented as unreliable precisely because she is traumatized. On cross-examination, the defense attorney undermines Katherine's testimony by suggesting that her image of Joe in the jail could be a hallucination. "According to the fact of psychology that under great emotional stress the mind sees what it has expected to, whether the thing is actually there or not," he says, "is it not possible that you did not see Joseph Wilson, but only the image of him your imagination had created in your head?" The scene inverts the conundrum defenders of lynching faced when, as discussed in chapter 3, they justified their lynchings of presumed black rapists based on the testimony of "hysterical" white women. But Katherine's experience here also replicates that of the movie viewer, who saw only what Katherine saw and who would also have assumed that Joe was dead after the fire, before his surprise arrival in the second half of the film. The film sets up the viewer to see what he or she expected to see.

WHILE *FURY* CHALLENGES the authority of visual representation, it also asks viewers to believe the authenticity of its account of lynching. In other words, although the film critiques the ways in which the news media blur distinctions between news and entertainment, the filmmakers blurred those same distinctions in promoting *Fury* as an antilynching film with real political impact. Lang himself maintained that he wanted *Fury* to resemble newsreel footage, claiming in one interview, "I always tell my cameraman, I don't want fancy photography—nothing 'artistic'—I want newsreel photography." He did so because he believed that a serious film "should be a kind of documentary of its time. Only then, in my opinion, do you get a quality of truth into a picture." He boasted, "In this way, *Fury* is a documentary." He also maintained that motion pictures had come to supersede newspapers as "the medium for the masses" that served as "propaganda for the American way of life."[48]

Lang's comments recall Walter Benjamin's "The Work of Art in the Age of Mechanical Reproduction," published, incidentally, the same year as Fury's release, in which Benjamin theorized that motion pictures held a particular capacity to serve as political propaganda because of their mass, democratic quality. According to Benjamin, films could persuade and mobilize the masses more effectively than could other forms of art, not only because they were affordable and accessible to wide audiences but also because they did not demand thoughtful contemplation. Audiences consumed them distractedly, much like modern advertisements, and so they quickly became habituated to the messages they contained. It was precisely this understanding of film's tremendous power to influence social and political behavior that had led to PCA regulations.[49]

In this way, Fury, as well as the two antilynching films that followed, had a capacity to shape and frame popular understandings of lynching more successfully than did more overt forms of political propaganda. At the same time, they were distinctly marketed and received as realistic and hard-hitting dramas that addressed the social problem of lynching in America. Despite that these films contained only abstract and stylized depictions of mob violence and made only oblique references to regional or racial strife, publicity material and reviews regularly emphasized their stark realism, referring not only to their filmic naturalism but also to their timeliness and newsworthiness. "Fury is a vivid pictorial indictment of lawless outbursts in supposedly civilized communities in this country," pronounced MGM in the press book sent to exhibitors. "Aside from its unusual merit as screen drama, it carries a message for good citizens!" The publicity for Fury also collapsed distinctions between entertainment and serious news when the studio suggested that exhibitors deploy newspaper headlines to hawk the film and even "shoot for editorials" about the film in their local newspapers. "No other theme has given rise to more columns of newspaper space than the one so graphically exploited in the picture," read one "editorial comment" suggested by the studio. Fury exploited "a terrific lesson in public confidence in our established law and order institutions."[50]

Because lynching is sanitized and abstracted in these films, however, their realism also depended on the foreknowledge of moviegoers. That is, the films could be considered realistic only because viewers, in another act of visual displacement, understood them through the images and stories of actual lynchings they had seen and read in the press. Most newspaper advertisements for *Fury* included a blurb proclaiming that the film offered "a shocking sense of reality reminiscent of recent mob outbursts," a line that reviewers commonly included in their appraisals of the film. One paper even mislabeled the film as "a story of southern justice," a telling slip of the pen that suggests that, despite *Fury*'s western setting, some viewers received the film according to their own assumptions about where most lynchings were committed.[51]

These kinds of assessments do more than reveal how critics interpreted the films; they also suggest the ways in which ordinary moviegoers were prepared to receive the pictures, as both reviews and advertisements guided viewer responses to the films. After all, the photographs of Roosevelt Townes's and Robert McDaniels's lynched bodies had appeared in *Time* and other national news media just six months before *They Won't Forget* opened around the nation. In addition, the Scottsboro case was still making national headlines in 1937. In 1931, nine black teenagers in Scottsboro, Alabama, were charged with raping two white women, for which they were sentenced to death or long prison terms based on the women's unreliable testimony and flimsy circumstantial evidence. Their convictions were challenged in a series of sensational trials and hearings throughout the 1930s, until charges against five of the boys were finally dropped in 1937. Most reviewers understood *They Won't Forget* as a replay of the Leo Frank case, despite that, for legal reasons, Warner Brothers promoted the film as strictly fictional. But reviewers also drew parallels between the film and the Scottsboro case, praising the picture for its courage and timeliness. *They Won't Forget* "can't be dismissed as a Hollywood exaggeration of a state of affairs which once might have existed but exists no longer," wrote Frank Nugent in the *New York Times*. "Between the Frank trial at Atlanta and the more recent ones at Scottsboro is a bond closer than chronology indicates." Although there is no evidence that the filmmakers had Scottsboro in mind, these critics, and perhaps viewers too, interpreted the film in light of what they already knew about the case and the larger issue of racial injustice. As the *New Masses* noted, the courtroom scenes in which circumstantial evidence, piece by piece, condemns the accused had particular resonance in light of the Scottsboro case. *Life* magazine even printed a story about the film directly following a photo essay about the Scottsboro boys.[52]

Incidentally, during the summer that *They Won't Forget* was playing in theaters, four of the Scottsboro boys took to the stage at the Apollo Theater in Harlem. In a seven-minute skit, the boys reenacted a scene from their trial and then remained onstage for an interview, with the intent, they wrote in an open letter to the press, to "pay our way through school" and "help our mothers who are poverty stricken." The engagement, however, brought a flurry of objections, including from the Scottsboro Defense Committee, which had organized the boys' legal defense. It claimed that to commercialize the affair was "distasteful" and "exploitative." For several weeks after it reported the story, the *New York Amsterdam News* published letters from dismayed and outraged readers who agreed. The Scottsboro case had inspired several plays and one independent agitprop film without controversy. The boys' appearance on the stage, however, provoked such apprehension undoubtedly because detractors saw the boys as particularly vulnerable to exploitation, but also because it obscured the boundaries between news and entertainment more profoundly than politically pointed theatrical representations had and certainly more than *Fury* and *They Won't Forget* had.[53]

Not only did viewers receive the films through their preconceived understandings of racial violence, but the films also became the lenses through which they experienced and made sense of the actual mob violence they heard and read about or even committed. For instance, one magazine story on *The Ox-Bow Incident* asserted that anyone who "sees the film will feel more intensely about what happened in Mobile, Beaumont, Detroit," referring to a number of recent race riots around the country. The studios encouraged viewers to make these kinds of connections between the films and real events in part to bolster the social import of the films. In promoting *Fury*, MGM recommended that exhibitors hold special screenings for law enforcement officers and city officials. Such advance publicity associating the film with law and order suggested to moviegoers that the film should have an impact on their social mores and behavior. At least one exhibitor, in Buffalo, New York, used this promotional technique to much success. As an accompaniment, the *Buffalo (N.Y.) Times* wrote a "special editorial" that discussed the "mob psychology angles of the picture" in relation to the Black Legion, a notorious Klan-like group in Michigan that targeted African Americans and foreigners.[54]

In their reviews of antilynching films, some northern leftist journals as well as the black press took the opportunity to call for more direct political action against lynching. Like Walter White and the NAACP, these critics recognized cinema's potential to shape popular consciousness about both lynching and antilynching legislation. *New Theatre Magazine*, a leftist paper centered in New York, included with its review of *Fury* a collage of news headlines, reports, and photographs of lynchings that pointedly presented lynching as a southern form of terror that targeted African Americans. Pasted over this collage, the editors included the text of the Fourteenth Amendment, facts and figures on lynching, and an editorial that appropriated the title "FURY" and denounced the "hysterical outrages that [are] so unforgettably depicted in *Fury*." The editorial called for the passage of the Costigan-Wagner federal antilynching bill. Calling lynching "a national danger and a national disgrace," the editors entreated readers "to demand [of] their Congressional representatives that they support the bill."[55]

Similarly, the Commission on Human Relations, together with the Progressive Education Association, created a study guide on *Fury* for educators to use in high school and college classrooms. These liberal organizations hoped that teachers would use the film to inform students about lynching and, in addition, arouse action against it. The guide contained a synopsis of the film along with news stories, NAACP statistics on lynching, and a bibliography. The suggested questions for class discussion pertained not only to the film but also to broader issues about lynching, such as "How would you answer persons who justified lynching under certain conditions?" and "What would you do to prevent lynching?"[56]

At times, antilynching films did inspire direct action. When *They Won't Forget* played in Times Square in July 1937, proponents of federal antilynching legislation picketed in front of the theater, holding signs that called for passersby to see the film and to support federal legislation (figure 7.8). They also passed out handbills that exhorted people to wire their congressmen. According to the *New York Amsterdam News*, the demonstration "attracted a huge crowd in the 'busiest square in the world.'" Although the picketers, most of whom were black, may have frightened off some potential moviegoers, their presence made the link between the film and antilynching activism conspicuous.[57]

Black critics and exhibitors throughout the country were particularly forthright in attaching these films to their larger political battle against lynching. Advertisements and reviews in the black press did not hesitate to promote the pictures as antilynching films despite their absence of black protagonists. Advertisements for *Fury* in black newspapers invariably included an endorsement from the NAACP, and a promotional article on the film appeared in several black papers, describing *Fury* as a "challenge to every right-thinking adult in America, not as a preachment, for it is stated with complete objectivity, but as gripping real life drama that recurs constantly on the front page of the nation's newspapers."[58]

For the majority of African American critics, that these films sanitized

FIGURE 7.8 Members of the NAACP's New York City Youth Council picketing outside the Strand Theater, New York, September 1937. Prints and Photograph Division, Library of Congress, Washington, D.C. Courtesy of the National Association for the Advancement of Colored People.

lynching and marginalized black characters did not detract from their meaningfulness for black audiences. Indeed, their responses speak to the ways in which African American viewers were accustomed to interpreting Hollywood films against the grain, either by adopting a film's white point of view as their own or by inserting their social experiences into a picture dominated by white characters and perspectives. The film critic for the *New York Amsterdam News*, Roi Otley, raised his "unstinted hosannas" to *Fury* as "an accurate analysis of a phase of our social scene" because its "details are patterned after countless hundreds of typical" cases. For this reason, he noted, "the Negro . . . will have no difficulty in identifying himself with Joe Wilson and appreciate his bitter experience." Similarly, in promoting *They Won't Forget* in the black press, some exhibitors posited Clinton Rosemond, who played the janitor Tump Redwine, as the star of the film and implied that Redwine was the film's lynching victim. For example, an article in the *New York Amsterdam News* hailed *They Won't Forget* as a film that "deals with the problem of the Negro in the South," while another, in the *Washington Afro-American*, claimed it was "a story of a colored man accused of murder in the deep South." The promotion further enticed readers' interest by asking, "Will they give him a fair trial or will southern prejudice overrule justice?" Some papers, including the *Atlanta Daily World*, printed a still from the film in which a number of unidentified white hands clutch at Redwine, who, lying prone, looks terrified. The image is from a scene in which police detectives question Redwine about the death of Mary Clay, a scene that alludes to Redwine's vulnerability as a black man who has found a murdered white girl, even though Redwine is not a suspect for long. The *Atlanta Daily World* nevertheless publicized Rosemond's role in "the sensational new Deep South antilynching film" along with the image without any clarification, suggesting that Redwine was the mob's victim.[59] As noted, *They Won't Forget* had been banned in Atlanta. In printing an image of Redwine's captive body, therefore, the paper was taking an oppositional, even subversive, stance against the city's desire to keep these kinds of charged images out of motion picture theaters. The image represents precisely what made the Atlanta censors and exhibitors so anxious—a scene of racial terror and injustice. It evokes, in this sense, a lynching photograph.

Not only did most black viewers of *Fury* express little frustration that the film marginalized black suffering, but some African American critics, like Walter White, argued that *Fury*'s effectiveness as a political tool rested precisely on its displacement of race, just as antilynching activists latched onto the lynching of the two white men in San Jose as an expedient way to gain the attention and sympathy of white Americans. Roi Otley, for instance, deemed the film an "important contribution to the fight against lynching" *because* the would-be victim was white. The casting circumvented factors "which complicate the fight against lynching in its interracial aspects," he argued, and thus "the picture will have a wider and more sympathetic audience." Just as Otley understood that black audiences could assume the perspective of a white lynching victim, he also recognized the near impossibility of asking white audiences to view the world through a black character's eyes.[60]

MGM recognized the same. Although it publicized *Fury* as a film about "mob rule" with "national civic significance," it assured exhibitors that it was "without any racial angle involved." The studio was concerned that the film not alienate white audiences, a particular point of apprehension for southern exhibitors. A film's profit did not necessarily depend, however, on its box office appeal in the South, which in the 1930s lagged behind the rest of the nation in motion picture attendance. The trade papers did not even track box office receipts for most southern cities. The South was still largely rural, and poverty and geography kept most southerners from the theater. Even in the largest of southern cities, box office receipts were lower than in comparable northern cities, largely because of the lack of air-conditioning in the summer and also because most southern cities forbade theater owners from operating for profit on Sundays, a key moviegoing day in places where people worked six-day weeks. In some ways, then, the studio's assurance that *Fury* avoided "any racial angle" reflected a concern less with how well it played in the South than with appeasing white audiences more generally.[61] But although southerners attended the theater less frequently than did their northern counterparts, motion pictures were one of the most popular forms of entertainment in southern towns and cities. Except for the most rural places, most towns boasted at least two motion picture theaters with several hundred seats each. Movies were enough of a draw that they provided tough competition for traditional recreations, like circuses, and caused no end of concern for moralists.[62]

And *Fury* did play widely across the South, in part because, unlike *They Won't Forget*, it stayed clear of any indictment against racial prejudice or segregation and made no explicit mention of the South. As a major release, *Fury* undoubtedly played in all theaters that MGM/Loews owned in the South, for one or two nights at least. Theaters in small cities and towns were more likely to be independently owned, and small-town and rural newspapers tended not to advertise motion picture showings, so it is more difficult to determine what films played there. Theater owners in the small towns of Flomaton, Alabama, and Hopewell, Virginia, however, wrote to the *Motion Picture Herald* to say they ran *Fury*. Although it was not popular in Hopewell, the exhibitor in Flomaton, Alabama, praised it as a "wonderful picture." Presumably, if it played in these places, it played in other towns of comparable size throughout the South to varying degrees of success.[63]

African Americans also had access to view *Fury* in southern towns and cities, either in their own neighborhood theaters or in segregated theaters, sitting in Jim Crow balconies. And just as readers of the *Atlanta Daily World* knew about *They Won't Forget* even though they could not see it, black southerners were undoubtedly aware of *Fury* before it reached their town or city, since black newspapers were distributed widely. The advertisements in these papers would have prepared them to watch *Fury* as a film that spoke to their experiences and fears, even if white-owned papers in the South were more circumspect in advertising *Fury* as an antilynching film. The manager of a black movie theater in Atlanta, for instance, advertised the picture in the *Atlanta Daily World* with a film still of the mob ramming the door of the jail and a headline that read "A Mob Storms the Jail." Set up like a news headline and image, the ad blurred distinctions between the film and news stories these readers would have been familiar with, a blurring that audiences would have taken into the theater with them.[64]

Wanting to draw the largest audience possible, however, white theater owners in the South tailored the publicity for *Fury* to white southerners' preferences and prejudices. By 1936, few white southerners openly defended lynching, but, all the same, they did not want to see projected on-screen what had become a regional embarrassment for them. Exhibitors were clearly sensitive to the notion that white southerners would reject a film that insulted their racial or regional sensibilities or overtly preached to them about the horrors of lynching. For this reason, advertisements for *Fury* in southern papers tended to downplay the antilynching message of the film and instead marketed it as a thrilling drama. Whereas the advertisements in the northern press, and of course the black press, often highlighted *Fury* as a film about "recent mob outbursts," southern exhibitors, particularly in smaller cities, largely avoided the use of the words "mob violence" and "lynching" in publicizing the film, preferring euphemisms like "class lawlessness" and "murderous justice" instead. One theater manager in Augusta, Georgia, felt compelled to attach a personally signed notice to his ad for the film in the city paper, evidently worried that audiences would avoid the film because of either the trailer or the ad itself, which, while vague about the film's plot, did refer to "the fury of the mob." In it, he assured moviegoers that critics considered *Fury* "the most exciting, powerful entertainment ever produced" and that "from all advance reports, we heartily recommend 'fury' as outstanding entertainment," as if to convince viewers that the film was no social commentary but merely pulsating fun.[65]

Other advertisements in southern papers promoted the film as a story of thwarted romance, featuring close-ups of Sylvia Sidney, who was a bigger star than Spencer Tracy at the time, and taglines such as "Why Did It Have to Be the Man I Love?" and "On Their Wedding Night—It Happened!" with no explanatory text. Some of these ads included a smaller image of angry, fisted men surrounding Sidney's face, as if the mob were charging not the jail but the pretty starlet. The arrangement of the graphics implied that the victim of mob violence in *Fury* is not a jailed man but a helpless and pleading white woman, an image that, by evoking prolynching defenses, undermined the antilynching message of the film.[66]

In a similar way, although most reviewers in southern papers praised *Fury*, they were more likely than northern critics to disassociate the film from the South and from southern incidents of mob violence. The *Atlanta Constitution* lauded the film's "discerning comment on the ways of justice" while avoiding the term "lynching." The piece also pointedly connected the film to recent incidents of mob vigilantism far from the South, in Michigan, in calling the film "timely because of the activities of the 'Black Legion.'" Critic John Rosenfield in the *Dallas Morning News* considered *Fury* a "weighty document" and "an absorbing melodrama," though unlike the vast majority of reviewers, he dismissed the film's realism, deeming the story implausible. He did mention the film's "sensational topicality" since it "reflects even if it does not parallel the Hauptmann case," referring to the trial of the man who kidnapped Charles Lindbergh's baby, as if the film's relevance to the San Jose lynching and any other more recent episodes of mob violence escaped him.[67]

Considering the deliberate silence about lynching in the southern press, it is remarkable that a number of southern critics did use the film to comment on and condemn southern lynching practices. A review in the *Richmond (Va.) News Leader*, for instance, hailed *Fury* as a "mature and relentless X-ray into mob violence and its results" and included lynching statistics both for the nation and for Virginia to remind readers of *Fury*'s relevance. The review, however, also cautioned that "[*Fury*] may not be popular in the lynch-belt because it tells the truth about mob violence and the mentality of those who participate in the legal murders which take place in appalling totals throughout the country," with a tone that assumed that the urbane Virginians reading the review lived outside the so-called lynch belt.[68]

But even in the lynch belt of the Deep South, *Fury* captured the attention of some who bemoaned southern lynching practices. Although it avoided specific references to lynching, a review in the *Birmingham (Ala.) News* deemed the film a "very eloquent . . . message" and a "wise picture," especially "good . . . to see in view of the hysteria that had swept sections of Alabama at various times." In the small city of Rome, Georgia, one regular columnist felt compelled to tout the film on the editorial page of the local paper as one that "every man, woman, and youth in America should see." *Fury*, he wrote, "shows what can happen—and does happen—when reason becomes dethroned in consequence of mob fury, and when cowardly and designing public officials trade the virtues of honor and duty for cheap political advantages." Although his piece made no mention of race, it did recognize the social and political significance of the film. He concluded, "It will make wiser if not better citizens of all who see it." Throughout, this editorialist was careful to denounce the "lawless" elements in the nation as a whole, without impugning the South specifically, a rhetorical maneuver that the film itself made possible.[69]

Despite that promotions for *Fury* avoided direct references to lynching, southern moviegoers would have been well aware of the relevance of the film's antilynching message to their own lives and communities. Viewers could recognize themselves and their history in the film, even as the picture allowed them to distance themselves from the mob lawlessness on-screen. Just as antilynching activists had done, *Fury* impelled white southern viewers to support law and civility without directly attacking their regional pride or their notions of white supremacy. After all, moviegoers would have watched the film in segregated theaters, the racial hierarchy firmly in place both during and after the film.

With *Fury*, the images and rhetoric of the antilynching movement reached the widest audience possible. The NAACP and the black press recognized that if they could harness the power and popularity of Hollywood film, they could shape popular consciousness against lynching in far broader ways than even the mainstream press could. Ordinary southerners were more likely to encounter the kind of opposition to lynching that *Fury* presented at the movies than in any other medium, especially because most southern newspapers only sparingly reported on antilynching activism, if at all. Moreover, whereas the speeches and stories of activists appeared as political propaganda, imploring readers to take an active political stance, the films allowed viewers to adopt an antilynching position comfortably and quietly, as entertainment. As the Rome, Georgia, columnist noted, the film did not necessarily impel individuals to take political action; rather, just seeing the film would make them "wiser if not better citizens." Indeed, the film offered them the same redemption that both the mob and Joe receive. Furthermore, unlike reading a newspaper, moviegoing is largely a social act. Individual viewers would have recognized themselves as part of a crowd, a community, within the theater—albeit a segregated one—and would have adjusted or at least muted their personal feelings in response to the tenor and outlook of the group. The film's reception, in this sense, reflected the manner in which lynching itself declined in the South. Lynching occurred far more infrequently throughout the 1930s not because white southerners embraced antilynching legislation or began taking legal action against mobs but because there was a perceptible, large-scale shift in attitude.

CONCLUSION

BY WORLD WAR II, THE NAACP and other antilynching activists and sympathizers had created a national perception that lynching was a brutal and degenerate practice at odds with modern civilized ideals. The spectacles surrounding lynching—the crowds of spectators, the tortures, and the photographs—were well suited to substantiate this perception. By lingering over images of unruly and sadistic mobs in news accounts and reimagining them in Hollywood films, lynching opponents reignited lynching spectacles, bestowing on them a new kind of cultural force and authority. They, in fact, came to epitomize the antilynching position. They signified more than the excess and sensationalism of lynching; they constituted its central injustice, at least in the popular imagination, so that most Americans came to associate lynching with its most extreme and grotesque manifestations.

Lynching had been on a gradual decline since the early twentieth century, despite flare-ups just after World War I and after the start of the Depression, in 1930. By the mid-1930s, the annual number of lynchings had fallen to the single digits. Mobs could no longer kill African Americans without incurring sharp local and national disapproval and inviting state or federal investigation. African Americans were still victimized by violence and threats of violence, but lynching had fully become the province of small bands of white men who murdered blacks swiftly and secretly, far from public view.[1] This change in behavior corresponded to a perceptible shift in southern public opinion. Activists had succeeded in shifting the terms of the debate so that forward-looking white southerners were compelled to adopt the position that lynching was barbaric and disgraceful, even as they continued to defend white supremacy or rail against black criminality.

Antilynching activists, to be sure, were not the sole cause of this shift. They succeeded in transforming public opinion because other factors lent their arguments a certain amount of currency within the South. African Americans migrated out of the South in ever greater numbers after World War I, in part because of the decline of southern agriculture and the lure of northern industrial work, but also in response to lynching and the oppressiveness of Jim Crow conditions. In some places, local blacks had retaliated against lynchings, mobilized to protect lynching targets, or launched public protests. Both black migration and black resistance posed viable threats to social order and to elite and middle-class whites accustomed to cheap black labor. These elites, eager to attract northern capital and investment into their cities and towns, did not want to present their communities as out of step with national norms. At the same time, as southern cities and towns continued to modernize, older traditions of popular justice began to wane. Criminal punishment was increasingly centralized under state authority, making it more likely that the state would intervene to either prevent or punish lynchings. Finally, in the 1930s, the New Deal brought a new level of federal involvement in southern economic and social life, which opened up the prospect of federal intervention into local legal and criminal affairs.[2]

Although antilynching activists did not unilaterally cause the decline of lynching, they did provide the rhetorical and visual frameworks through which Americans, including white southerners, could turn against lynching. Lynching spectacles, which had once served to substantiate and normalize white claims to moral superiority, now served as documentary and incontrovertible evidence of just the opposite, even when encountered in Hollywood melodramas. To view a lynching spectacle was to witness—to bear witness to—a most deplorable act of moral barbarism; any other response to the sight soon became unimaginable. Once white elite and middle-class southerners began to perceive lynching in this way, the white solidarity that lynching was meant to enact showed signs of fissure. The representations of white mobs and crowds in southern newspapers began to change, for instance, from images of orderly and respectable citizens enacting punitive justice to ones of unruly, disreputable men and boys. And once lynch mobs were imagined as lawless, bloodthirsty renegades, then those whites who previously might have participated in or watched a lynching to experience a collective sense of white superiority now turned away. Indeed, to maintain their claims to racial supremacy, white southerners had to disavow lynching practices.

White southerners shifted their attitudes not because there were concrete consequences of the act of lynching—lynch mobs still largely escaped prosecution, and neither federal legislation nor intervention ever came to pass—but because it had become unfeasible not to and still maintain a sense of moral righteousness. In 1937, the results of two Gallup polls revealed that a large portion of white southerners supported federal legislation against lynching. Yet respondents also told pollsters that they opposed any specific measures against the practice, and, under the banner of states' rights, southern politicians continued to rail against any federal attempts to interfere. Although these results appear confounding, they reflect white southerners' recognition that supporting lynching publicly was untenable even as they sought to retain their sectional sovereignty and racial authority.[3]

Lynchings also declined because the moment of transition that gave rise to them shifted. Lynching spectacles emerged from the collision between old and new. The desire to reestablish a racial hierarchy was felt with particular urgency amid the social flux and instability of the urbanizing South, and that desire was offered full expression through modes of modern spectacle. But, by the 1930s, lynching spectacles had become entirely modernized. Most Americans came to witness lynching only through its media representations—photographs and, even more, motion pictures—representations that came to stand, in all their excess, as the reality of lynching. These were national, rather than local, images, projected and circulated through the commercial channels of modern media.

White supremacy, of course, persisted in the South long after lynching declined, in the forms of black disenfranchisement, segregation, and humiliating codes of racial etiquette, and it did so, in part, because the threat of violence still pervaded black southerners' daily lives. But, once white supremacy was firmly entrenched in the South, white southerners no longer needed to reenact their supremacy and unity continually through spectacles of violence. Not only did the practice of lynching decline, but white southerners began to repress its most public manifestations and representations. Communities that had previously celebrated lynching, commemorating the event in local newspapers and in photographs, stories, and songs, began to maintain a sort of embarrassed and horrified silence about it. Although many black communities preserved their own memories of racial violence, white southerners eventually came to deliberately omit stories of lynchings from local histories, museums, and other official organs of public memory.[4]

Thus, although violence against African Americans did not disappear in the postwar period by any means, until the rise of the black freedom struggles of the late 1950s and early 1960s, it did largely disappear from public view. That violence could also no longer be understood as simply a southern phenomenon. As African Americans migrated into northern cities amid the war and postwar industrial boom, they were met with antagonism and harassment from working-class whites who resented black encroachment into their labor and housing markets. Racial conflicts and riots subsequently erupted in cities like Detroit, Philadelphia, and Chicago throughout the 1940s and 1950s. These conflicts threw a wrench into the progressive claims of thinkers like Gunnar Myrdal that economic and social modernization would rid Americans of their racial prejudices and tensions; instead, experiences in northern cities only seemed to confirm that racial strife was entrenched in the American social landscape. These conflicts represented, however, what has been called the "hidden violence" of the postwar era, violence that never garnered the popular attention that lynching drew before the war.[5]

Rather, many Americans in the 1940s preferred to embrace alternative images of black mobility and achievement, images that came to challenge lynching as the dominant picture of African American experiences. During the war, the NAACP had initiated a concerted lobbying effort, spearheaded by Walter White, to compel Hollywood studios to project more positive images of African Americans on-screen. They were aided in these efforts by the governmental Office of War Information, which wanted to ensure that Hollywood movies downplayed American racial strife so as not to undermine the nation's international image as the beacon of democracy. Although, to be sure, degrading characterizations of African Americans persisted in American cinema, these efforts did result in more complex black characters, as seen in *The Ox-Bow Incident*. The postwar period also gave rise to a number of consciously liberal Hollywood films, such as *Pinky* and *Lost Boundaries*, which attempted to address not racial violence but racial prejudice, representing it as a psychological sickness damaging the American body politic. Americans at this time were introduced to stars like Lena Horne, Paul Robeson, and eventually Sydney Poitier, all of whom seemed to embody racial progress not only in the characters they played but in their very personas. Likewise, as Joe Louis and Jesse Owens had begun to do in the 1930s, Jackie Robinson provided Americans with a new image of black manly athleticism that was both inspiring and nonthreatening. These figures and images became new racial spectacles, ostensibly upending the logic of lynching images. Many Americans, white and black, eagerly embraced them as signs of racial reparation and symbols of American civic, democratic ideals. But they also allowed white Americans to overlook the racial prejudice and discrimination that persisted in southern towns and festered in northern cities.[6]

These popular representations of race in the 1940s nevertheless prepared white Americans to receive and interpret the photographs and televised images of black protest and white massive resistance that emerged from the South in the 1950s and 1960s as startling reminders that these civic ideals had yet to be realized. Images of peaceful black protestors facing angry white mobs, fending off police dogs, and withstanding blasts of water from hoses garnered widespread white northern sympathy for black freedom struggles and played a critical role in shoring up national support for civil rights legislation. These images struck emotional chords because they made manifest the ugliness and brutality of white racism and imprinted in the public mind black stoicism and innocence in the face of that brutality. Unlike images of lynching, however, civil rights images did not call attention to the dangers of frenzied mob violence as much as they encapsulated in visual form all the injustices of racism. That is, racial prejudice could not be read out of these images or displaced from them; it was central to them. The popular reception of civil rights reflected an increasing emphasis in liberal and, eventually, mainstream discourse that not only racial violence but racial prejudice itself was at odds with the nation's civic ideals, that it was simply un-American.

Arguably the most infamous lynching photograph hit the newsstands at the cusp of these struggles. In September 1955, *Jet* magazine, followed by African American newspapers, published a photograph of young Emmett Till's bruised and battered corpse in his funeral casket (figure c.1). Several weeks before, Till, a fourteen-year-old Chicago boy visiting relatives in Money, Mississippi, was accused of "wolf-whistling" at a white woman, Carolyn Bryant, in a local grocery. Bryant's husband and his half-brother, J. W. Milam, avenged this perceived racial transgression by beating and shooting Till and then dumping his body in the Tallahatchie River. The murder did not involve mob violence and was committed privately, but it resonated nevertheless within black communities as a lynching, and the NAACP and the black press deemed it one, stirring controversy within the southern white press. The murder was, after all, motivated by the same accusations that felled so many other black men, and it met with a comparable community sanction. Although Bryant and Milam were prosecuted for their crime, the all-white jury acquitted them. And although it was covered in the mainstream press as an isolated and exceptional instance of violence, the murder was not unrelated to increasing calls for black freedom and enfranchisement. In the wake of the Supreme Court's *Brown v. Board of Education* decision the previous year, civil rights groups had begun to mobilize

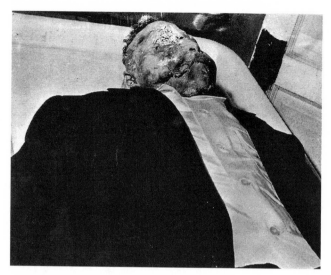

FIGURE C.1 Emmett Till in his casket, 1955.
Courtesy of the *Chicago Defender*.

throughout the South, and, in turn, white resistance groups, like the White Citizens Council and the KKK, began to organize to stop them at any cost. In the months leading up to Till's murder, two black Mississippians, George Lee of Belzoni and Lamar Smith of Brookhaven, were shot to death for their attempts to register black residents to vote. Another organizer, Gus Courts, was murdered in December of that same year. For many African Americans, Till's murder was yet another tragic strike along a long continuum of racial violence and bloodshed.[7]

It was also one that carried unprecedented symbolic value. Photographs of Till's funeral, including images not only of his open casket but also of grieving friends and family, were splashed across the pages of black newspapers around the country, making it, as civil rights activist Amzie Moore noted, "the best advertised lynching." In 1987, U.S. Representative Charles Diggs deemed it "the greatest media product in the last forty or fifty years." Few remember, however, that photographs of George Lee's funeral, including one of his corpse in his casket, were published in the *Chicago Defender* just a few months before the paper displayed the better-known images of Till's funeral. The attention Till's murder drew had everything to do with his youth and the circumstances of his death—the disproportionate penalty for an alleged act of boyish sexual insolence. If activists in the 1930s had sought to draw attention away from black lynching victims because they might stand as uncomfortable reminders of black criminality, images in the civil

FIGURE C.2 Emmett Till, undated. © Bettmann/CORBIS.

rights era assumed cultural force because they represented and placed in view black innocence. Till embodied that innocence; many papers printed a portrait of him, smiling and looking younger than his fourteen years, that made the photograph of his mutilated corpse all the more disturbing (figure c.2). Stories and images of his mother's inconsolable grief added to the public impression that Till's murder represented stolen childhood. His lynching was not just "the best advertised lynching"; it also served as the best "advertisement" for the simple injustice of white supremacy. As the *Chicago Defender* declared, Till's death had "turned the spotlight on Mississippi shame."[8]

The photograph of Till's corpse that circulated in the black press, however, was not a standard lynching photograph in any sense. It was a private funeral photograph that was made public only because Till's mother, Mamie Bradley, wanted "all the world to see" what had happened to her son. She brought Till's body back to Chicago, where it lay in state in an open casket for three days before his funeral, to which Bradley issued an open invitation. Unlike earlier lynching photographs, the image of Till's corpse stood, above all else, as an image of mourning. In this instance, as well as in, to a lesser extent, the death of George Lee, the black corpse and the grieving community—the full ripple effects of the violence—were placed at the center of antilynching discourse, at least within the black press's narrative of the event. In contrast to many earlier images of anonymous victims, Till's image was, and remains, inseparable from his larger story—from the story of his murder, the town of Money and the trial of his murderers, and his mother's grief. Moreover, the focal point of the image is Till's bloated and almost unrecognizable face, on which is imprinted the full brutality that his murderers wrought. Lee's funeral picture similarly focuses on his face, revealing the wounds from the gunshots that killed him. The visual impact of their deaths drew force not from images of the violence itself or of its perpetrators but from its physical effect on the victims' personhood.[9]

Taking and displaying a photograph of a corpse was not extraordinary at this time. As noted in chapter 6, a long tradition of memorial photography, which allowed mourners to honor the deceased and focus their grief, continued in some communities well into the twentieth century. Yet, by publicizing Till's memorial, Bradley insisted on making public her private tragedy and called on "the world" to grieve alongside her. White southern defenders of Bryant accused Bradley and her allies of exploiting her son's death by rendering his funeral a grotesque spectacle. Bryant and Milam's trial became its own media spectacle. Photographers and cameramen flocked to Money to cover it, and pictures of the Bryant family circulated in mainstream newspapers across the country, although images of Till and his mourners were markedly absent in the white-owned press.[10]

For many African Americans, the photograph of Till's corpse left a dark and lasting imprint. A number of black activists and writers have recounted that the image struck them with full force and ultimately spurred their commitment to racial equality. Some have testified that seeing Till's image as children awoke them to the reality of their own stolen innocence as black youth in America. Kareem Abdul-Jabbar, for instance, recalled seeing the image as an eight-year-old boy, and he described the "indelible image" it left that he "could never forget." "The murder shocked me," he wrote. "I began thinking of myself as a black person for the first time, not just a person. And I grew more distrustful and wary." More than any other image, the photograph of Till assumed an extraordinary power to engage and activate viewers. Julian Bond wrote that the picture gave him "an unforgettable insight into the cruelties of southern-style racism," which "moved [him] along the path to later activism." He and his peers were so affected by the image because "we all thought: it could easily be me." The photograph became a singular image that precipitated the surge of civil rights activity in the late 1950s and early 1960s, rallying young blacks in a shared sense of outrage and purpose.[11]

Even as the civil rights movement succeeded in dismantling institutionalized white supremacy, the spectacle of lynching continued to resonate. For many, it persisted, and still persists, as the most vivid and forceful symbol of racial terror and injustice. Most Americans today encounter lynching only through photographs of anonymous mobs and nameless, faceless victims, or through cinematic fictions. Even Till's image has lost some of its exceptionalism. Lynching has come to exist only as spectacle, only as an image, uprooted from its context, from the narratives and the people that surrounded them. The term is thus subject to misperception and willful distortion. To this day, the specter of lynching can be wielded with terrifying force as a rhetorical weapon or a form of racist intimidation. In detaching images of lynching from local practices and transforming them into icons of oppression, antilynching activists unwittingly succeeded in detaching them from history itself.

NOTES

ABBREVIATIONS USED IN NOTES

AC   *Atlanta Constitution*

NYT   *New York Times*

RT   *Rome (Ga.) Tribune*

SN   *Statesboro (Ga.) News*

VEP   *Vicksburg (Miss.) Evening Post*

WTH   *Waco (Tex.) Times-Herald*

INTRODUCTION

1. Wright, *Black Boy*, 84; Toomer, "Blood-Burning Moon," 67. On the ways in which lynching came to serve as a metaphor for racial terror and injustice in the early twentieth century, see Waldrep, *Many Faces of Judge Lynch*, 8–9, 151–53, and Markowitz, *Legacies of Lynching*. On the ways in which lynching existed on a continuum of racist terror and violence, see Williams, "Resolving the Paradox of Our Lynching Fixation," and Campney, "'And This Is Free Kansas.'"

2. According to Brundage (*Lynching in the New South*, 19–45), mass mob lynchings were the most common form of lynching in the late nineteenth and early twentieth centuries, accounting for 34 percent of all lynchings in Georgia and 40 percent in Virginia. Despite differences across time and place, lynch mobs of varying sizes and compositions seemed to follow an unvarying script, although Brundage (39) states that the most spectacular lynchings, what he terms "mass mob lynchings" (those that included more than fifty people in the mob), were more likely to be ritualized and standardized. On the ways in which private lynchings became public through visual and narrative practices, see Hale, *Making Whiteness*, 357 n. 7.

3. Wright, *Black Boy*, 190.

4. Brundage, *Lynching in the New South*, 8; Tolnay and Beck, *Festival of Violence*, ix. On the ways in which the definition of lynching was politically charged, see Waldrep, *Many Faces of Judge Lynch*, 127–50.

5. For studies of lynching outside the South, see Madison, *Lynching in the Heartland*; Gonzales-Day, *Lynching in the West*; Pfeifer, *Rough Justice*; and Barrow, "Lynching in the Mid-Atlantic." On the lynching of members of groups other than African American men, see Carrigan and Webb, "Lynching of Persons of Mexican Origin," and Feimster, "'Ladies and Lynching.'"

6. See, for instance, Mencken, "Death in the Afternoon," 141.

7. Theories on the act of witnessing have tended to focus on the experiences of those who have suffered, and thus witnessed, trauma, and the issues of truth, social responsibility, and social authority that arise from traumatic witnessing. The theory of witnessing I posit here, however, derives from the ways in which turn-of-the-century Americans used and understood the term in legal, religious, and popular culture contexts. On witnessing and trauma, see Felman, *Testimony*, and Douglass and Vogler, *Witness and Memory*.

8. Mencken, "Sahara of the Bozart," 151. White, in *Rope and Faggot* (9), repeated Mencken's claim, as did Myrdal in *American Dilemma* (564–656). On American liberalism and modernization, see King, *Race, Culture, and the Intellectuals*, 21–31, 123–38.

9. Ayers, *Vengeance and Justice*, 238–55; Brundage, *Lynching in the New South*, 14; Dailey, "Deference and Violence in the Postbellum Urban South."

10. Black activists from Ida B. Wells to Walter White routinely poked holes in the myth of black rape, in part by pointing out that most lynchings stemmed from crimes other than sexual assault. More recently, Tolnay and Beck (*Festival of Violence*, 48) have posited that 37.3 percent of lynchings in the South avenged an alleged murder, whereas 33.6 percent were for "sexual violations." Dorr, in *White Women, Rape and the Power of Race*, has shown that not all accusations of black rapes of white women ended in lynching. Whether white southerners chose to lynch an accused rapist or try him in court had everything to do with local context and contingencies. For the ways in which lynching stemmed from a confluence of white men's racial fears and sexual anxieties, see Hall, *Revolt against Chivalry*, 129–58, and Williamson, *Crucible of Race*. For the ways in which white men understood black citizenship as a threat to their masculine authority and an attack on their patriarchal power in the home, see Hodes, *White Women, Black Men*, 147, 166–67, and Edwards, *Gendered Strife and Confusion*.

11. Determining the makeup of particular mobs is difficult, but this conclusion is based on evidence from grand jury investigations, when alleged members of the mob were named, from certain NAACP investigations and other case histories of lynchings. McGovern (*Anatomy of a Lynching*, 4, 67–68) found, for instance, that the members of the lynch mob who tortured and killed Claude Neal in Marianna, Florida, in 1934 were "middle to lower-middle class: clerks, salesmen, mechanics, petty merchants, servicers, and farmers." He characterized these men as "in-between" types, who, "economically solvent even during the Depression," owned both their own homes and cars. Rural whites did, at times, lash out violently at African Americans who they believed were economic threats, by terrorizing black tenants and landowners to drive them off their land or by threatening white farmers who hired black workers at the expense of white workers. Many of what Brundage

(*Lynching in the New South*, 18–28) terms "terrorist" mobs performed lynchings precisely to create a black labor shortage so that planters would be more likely to hire and rent to white farmers. This type of lynching, however, was relatively uncommon, representing only 59 of the 460 total lynchings in Georgia, for instance.

12. Ayers, *Promise of the New South*, 64–66; Dollard, *Caste and Class in a Southern Town*, 77. Dollard, whose study centered on the people of Indianola, Mississippi, noted that "strainer" was the term local African Americans used for this type of white middle-class citizen. On the intricate social maneuverings of the white middle classes, see also Davis, Gardner, and Gardner, *Deep South*, 171–207. MacLean, in *Behind the Mask of Chivalry*, argues that these same "petit bourgeoisie" came to embrace the "reactionary populism" of the 1920s Ku Klux Klan.

13. Fields, in "Ideology and Race in American History" (156–58), maintains that white solidarity was a political tool or "slogan" through which southern elites deflated class conflict, ensured their own dominance over other whites, and encouraged social stability. On the construction of white supremacy as a political ideology, see Kantrowitz, *Ben Tillman and the Reconstruction of White Supremacy*, 2–3.

14. Most studies of lynching rituals and spectacle have understood them as dramatizations or expressions of an already established white supremacy. See, for example, Harris, *Exorcising Blackness*, 11–19, and Fouss, "Lynching Performances, Theatres of Violence."

15. Many scholars have focused on the narrative discourse surrounding lynching for these reasons. Indeed, our primary access to what happened at lynchings is through highly biased news accounts and prolynching pamphlets. Because of the scarcity of other kinds of written sources, any historical study of lynching is inevitably a study of its narrative representations in southern white culture. See, for example, Waldrep, *Many Faces of Judge Lynch*, 86–88; Hall, *Revolt against Chivalry*, 150; Fouss, "Lynching Performances, Theatres of Violence," 25; Baker, "North Carolina Lynching Ballads," 223; and Jean, "'Warranted' Lynchings."

16. Hale, *Making Whiteness*, 199–239; Goldsby, *Spectacular Secret*. "Sensationalism" itself was a relatively modern term, coined in the late eighteenth century to refer to commercial literature that pandered to the sensibilities of an urban public, who sought to experience the thrills and shocks of modern city life from a safe distance. See Halttunen, "Humanitarianism and the Pornography of Pain," 312.

17. Because spectators were perpetually inundated with images and captive to the spectacles before them, critics have imagined them as relatively passive and alienated from their own bodies. On this view of modern spectacle, largely associated with the Frankfurt School, see Debord, *Society of the Spectacle*; Benjamin, "Work of Art in the Age of Mechanical Reproduction"; Charney and Schwartz, *Cinema and the Invention of Modern Life*, 1–4; Friedberg, *Window Shopping*, 1–44; and Singer, *Melodrama and Modernity*, 17–35, 101–30.

18. On lynching as rooted in antebellum vigilante traditions, see Waldrep, *Many Faces of Judge Lynch*, 111–12; Ayers, *Vengeance and Justice*, 238–55; Hall, *Revolt against Chivalry*, 144–45; Pfeifer, *Rough Justice*; and Carrigan, *Making of a Lynching Culture*.

19. Halttunen, "Humanitarianism and the Pornography of Pain," 303–10; Turner,

Reckoning with the Beast, 79–82; Keane, *Reflections on Violence,* 3–31; Ariès, *Western Attitudes toward Death,* 85–103; Farrell, *Inventing the American Way of Death,* 55–57; Laderman, *Sacred Remains,* 76–77, 172–74.

20. Halttunen, "Humanitarianism and the Pornography of Pain," 312–18; Halttunen, *Murder Most Foul,* 2–3; Cohen, *Pillars of Salt,* 25–26.

21. In this respect, lynching opponents drew on humanitarian tactics forged in the antebellum period, as those who fought against cruelty and human suffering— abolitionists, for instance—relied on excessively graphic accounts and images of that cruelty and suffering. As Halttunen ("Humanitarianism and the Pornography of Pain," 304) has argued, sensationalistic literature, which created and fostered a titillating interest in the "pornography of pain," thus became "an integral aspect of the humanitarian sensibility."

22. These localities are Statesboro, Rome, and Lawrenceville, Georgia; Oxford, Vicksburg, and Wiggins, Mississippi; and Dallas, Waco, and Paris, Texas.

CHAPTER ONE

1. *SN,* 2 Aug. 1904, 1. For detailed narratives of the murder of the Hodgeses and the lynching of Reed and Cato, see Moseley and Brogdon, "Lynching at Statesboro," and Smith, "Statesboro Blues." Paul Reed's last name is spelled "Reid" in some accounts; most accounts, however, refer to him as "Reed." He appears in the 1900 census as Paul Reed, a "turpentine laborer." U.S. census records, Bulloch County, Ga., 1900.

2. *SN,* 2 Aug. 1904, 1.

3. Brannen, *Life in Old Bulloch,* 113, 207; Baker, "What Is a Lynching," 301. Farmers in the county were reasonably well-off, as the 1900 census for one militia district shows that only 8 percent of farms were mortgaged. Brannen, *Life in Old Bulloch,* 87.

4. *SN,* 2 Aug. 1904, 4; *SN,* 5 Aug. 1904, 4; Baker, "What Is a Lynching," 300–302; Smith, "Statesboro Blues," 5–7.

5. *SN,* 2 Aug. 1904, 4.

6. Ibid., 1.

7. *SN,* 12 Aug. 1904, 1; *SN,* 9 Sept. 1904, 4; *SN,* 13 Sept. 1904, 1; Baker, "What Is a Lynching," 307.

8. *SN,* 5 Aug. 1904, 4; Baker, "What Is a Lynching," 307.

9. Baker, "What Is a Lynching," 307.

10. Ibid.

11. These men were Albert Rogers, a seventy-year-old black farmer; his seventeen-year-old son; and Sebastian McBride, a nineteen-year-old sharecropper. *SN,* 26 Aug. 1904, 2; *SN,* 30 Aug. 1904, 3; Smith, "Statesboro Blues," 39–40.

12. Baker, "What Is a Lynching," 308.

13. Smith, "Statesboro Blues," 43–46.

14. Ibid., 5–6.

15. *Atlanta Journal* quoted in *SN,* 19 Aug. 1904, 1.

16. Local historian Charlton Moseley has indicated that the mob might have

planned the lynching, because a local woman remembers that women were ready to hand out buckets of kerosene to members of the mob. But according to news reports and to Baker's account—in which the mob went back into town to get chains and kerosene—the lynching does appear to have been a semispontaneous reaction to the removal of the prisoners to Savannah. Sally Pearl Thompson, interview by Charlton Moseley, 25 July 1974, 3, Genealogy Department, Statesboro Regional Library, Statesboro, Ga.; Baker, "What Is a Lynching," 307.

17. As early as 1905, Cutler (*Lynch-Law*, 269) argued that lynching stemmed from a peculiarly American sensibility that "the people consider themselves as law unto themselves." Pfeifer uses the term "rough justice" to refer to the notions of popular sovereignty and resistance to modern state authority that lynching enacted and points out that these ideas about the law and justice held powerful sway in both the South and the West. See also Waldrep, *Many Faces of Judge Lynch*, 56–61, and Vandiver, *Lethal Punishment*, 89–102.

18. Linders, "Execution Spectacle and State Legitimacy."

19. The racial bias against African American criminals has been well documented. For instance, in Mississippi between 1890 and 1930, there were 237 legal executions. In only 27 of those executions were the condemned white (1 for the murder of a black man, 26 for the murders of white men). Fifteen men, all black, were hanged for the crime of rape. Mississippi Executions File, Special Collections, University of Mississippi, Oxford. See also Vandiver, *Lethal Punishment*, 9–11, and Bedau, *Death Penalty in America*, 194–205. Banner (*Death Penalty*, 155) notes that Arkansas abolished public executions *except* in cases of rape in 1901, as did Kentucky in 1920. According to Beck, Massey, and Tolnay ("Gallows, the Mob, and the Vote," 329), although black men were executed for the crime of rape in both Georgia and North Carolina, they were more likely to be lynched than executed when accused of a sexual offense.

20. Baker, "What Is a Lynching," 305. On the ways in which legal executions differed from lynchings in their semblance of restraint and order, see Brundage, *Lynching in the New South*, 255–57.

21. Vandiver, *Lethal Punishment*, 14–17; Garner, "Crime and Judicial Inefficiency"; Cutler, *Lynch-Law*, 260–62; Cutler, "Capital Punishment and Lynching," 182. Dorr (*White Women, Rape and the Power of Race*, 5, 17) has shown how legal trials, particularly of black men accused of raping white women, were often themselves "ritualistic spectacles" and "thinly veiled substitutes for mob violence." Yet, by bringing the accused to trial and refraining from lynching, white southerners could project an image of themselves as civilized and restrained.

22. Wright, "By the Book," 251–52. See also Wright, *Racial Violence in Kentucky*, chapters 7–8; Clarke, *Lineaments of Wrath*, 167–72; Phillips, "Exploring Relations"; Pfeifer, *Rough Justice*, 139–47; and Vandiver, *Lethal Punishment*, 77–78.

23. In 1933, both Arthur F. Raper (*Tragedy of Lynching*, 35–36) and James Harmon Chadbourn (*Lynching and the Law*, 5–12) of the Southern Commission on the Study of Lynching critiqued the common and long-standing assumption that lynching occurred as a response to a weak and unresponsive legal system. On incidents when legal executions were consciously used to deter lynching, see Pfeifer, *Rough Justice*,

73, and Vandiver, *Lethal Punishment*, 87–88. Tolnay and Beck conducted the most extensive quantitative research into this topic and found no consistent, systematic relationship between lynching and executions. They found, for instance, that although legal executions did increase at the same time that lynching began to decline in the 1930s, they also sharply increased in the 1890s, when lynching rates were at their highest. See Beck, Massey, and Tolnay, "Gallows, the Mob, and the Vote," and Tolnay and Beck, *Festival of Violence*, 98–113.

24. Masur, *Rites of Execution*; Halttunen, *Murder Most Foul*, 8–14; Cohen, *Pillars of Salt*, 6–7; Banner, *Death Penalty*, 144–50; Linders, "Execution Spectacle and State Legitimacy," 607–22.

25. Masur, *Rites of Execution*, 20–21, 50–55, 95–97. On the cessation of public executions in Europe, where many of the same concerns were expressed, see Laqueur, "Crowds, Carnival, and the State"; McGowan, "Body and Punishment"; and Spierenburg, *Spectacle of Suffering*, 188–89.

26. Friedman, *Crime and Punishment*, 168–71; Largey, "Hanging"; Banner, *Death Penalty*, 159, 162; Linders, "Execution Spectacle and State Legitimacy," 615; Madow, "Forbidden Spectacle." These kinds of incidents led some states to tighten laws banning public executions, for instance by mandating, in what were known as "midnight assassination laws," that executions be conducted in the dead of night to keep the masses away. Bessler, *Legacy of Violence*, 113–40.

27. Linders, "Execution Spectacle and State Legitimacy," 637–42; Madow, "Forbidden Spectacle," 519–23; Bessler, *Legacy of Violence*, 113–40.

28. Masur, *Rites of Execution*, 95–110; Laqueur, "Crowds, Carnival, and the State," 354; McGowan, "Body and Punishment," 673–74; Spierenburg, *Spectacle of Suffering*, 305–55; Banner, *Death Penalty*, 157–58.

29. Rainey Bethea was hanged in Daviess County, Kentucky, for the rape and murder of a white woman in August 1936. By then Kentucky was using the electric chair for capital offenses, but it retained hanging for criminal assaults (that is, rape, a crime that only black men were executed for) and allowed local officials to decide whether to perform them publicly or not. According to news estimates, over 10,000 people attended Bethea's hanging. The execution engendered a vociferous public outcry in the state. *NYT*, 15 Aug. 1936, 30; *NYT*, 23 Aug. 1936, E6.

30. The Georgia state legislature in 1882 revised its code to allow judges to order public hangings, and then overturned that law in 1893. Coulter, "Hanging as a Social-Penal Institution," 21. According to Banner (*Death Penalty*, 154–55), Mississippi and Alabama similarly outlawed public hangings in the mid-nineteenth century without great effect.

31. Virginia and North Carolina were the first southern states to adopt the electric chair, effectively abolishing public hangings, in 1908 and 1909, followed by Tennessee and Arkansas in 1913. Texas and Georgia centralized executions in 1923 and 1924. The last public hanging in Texas was probably that of Roy Mitchell in Waco, Texas, in 1923. *Waco (Tex.) Daily Times*, 30 July 1923, 1. Mississippi and Louisiana did not bring executions under state control until the 1950s, when each state obtained a centralized electric chair. Both states had begun using a "portable" electric chair in 1940. As a rule, states in the South began using the electric chair some ten

or twenty years behind northern states. Bowers, *Legal Homicide*, 46–48; Vandiver, *Lethal Punishment*, 19–23; Essig, *Edison and the Electric Chair*, 277–79; Death Sentences File, 1908–1948, Mississippi Department of Archives and History, Jackson; King, *Execution of Willie Francis*, 7, 18.

32. Public executions drew such widespread attention that one clever entrepreneur in Vicksburg, Mississippi, advertised his wallpaper business in the local newspaper with a large, bold headline stating "Public Hanging." He evidently recognized that even his more upscale potential clientele would be drawn to such a message. *Vicksburg (Miss.) American*, 7 July 1903, 7.

33. *Chicago Tribune*, 31 Mar. 1879, 4.

34. *AC*, 30 June 1891, 4; *Macon County (Ga.) Citizen* reprinted in *AC*, 10 Oct. 1893, 4.

35. *Brandon (Miss.) News*, 29 July 1909, 1. In 1979, the *Jackson (Miss.) Clarion-Ledger* reported that Mack's execution was the last public hanging in Mississippi, although one reader objected that his father had witnessed an execution in 1912 or 1913, and the *Hattiesburg (Miss.) News* (22 Dec. 1916) mentioned a public execution as late as 1916. Death Sentences File, 1955–1956.

36. *Savannah (Ga.) Morning News*, 2 Dec. 1893, 1; *Hattiesburg (Miss.) News*, 7 Aug. 1915, 1; *Jackson (Miss.) Daily News*, 8 Aug. 1915, 5; *Starkville (Miss.) News*, 7 Aug. 1915, 1. "Flying jennies" was another term for flying horses, or a carousel, and "fake shows" were more than likely the games of grifters, such as shell games. These kinds of "side attractions" were apparently quite common. The *Gainesville (Ga.) Eagle*, for instance, commended the first private hanging in that city, in 1899, especially because the usual "street fakirs, patent medicine men and lemonade vendors" were absent. *Gainesville (Ga.) Eagle*, 15 Apr. 1899, quoted in Dorsey, *History of Hall County*, 294. The *Starkville (Miss.) News* printed a report of the 1915 execution that had appeared in the *Chicago Tribune*, which made much of the festive, picnic-like atmosphere. The *News* then protested that the Chicago paper had printed such "slander" about the county, insisting that the two men hanged were "convicted of the most heinous crime" (a point the *Tribune* had not questioned—evidently the *Starkville News* was defending the executioners against a potential charge of lynching), and that the crowd was reverently solemn. Other Mississippi newspapers, however, reported the execution in similar terms as the *Tribune* had, though with a bit less sensationalism. Other papers around the country picked up the story, lamenting the "Roman holiday" that had occurred in Starkville and its degrading effect on the populace. *Literary Digest*, 21 Aug. 1915, 338.

37. *Lawrenceville (Ga.) News-Herald*, 14 May 1908, 1; *Lawrenceville (Ga.) News-Herald*, 17 May 1906, 1. This was a customary practice for some time in Lawrenceville. Before Will Gordon was hanged in 1906, also behind the Baptist church, he spoke to the crowd gathered outside the jail for a full thirty minutes. Sometime later, the sheriff marched him to the gallows.

38. *Bulloch County (Ga.) Times*, 17 Dec. 1897, 1; Brannen, *Life in Old Bulloch*, 182–84; *Bulloch County (Ga.) Times*, 24 June 1897, 1; *WTH*, 27 Oct. 1916, 4.

39. *Lawrenceville (Ga.) News-Herald*, 17 May 1906, 1; *Bulloch County (Ga.) Times*, 24 June 1897, 1; *WTH*, 27 Nov. 1906, 5.

40. For critics of public hangings, the presence of women and children only testified to the perversity of the event.

41. *RT*, 2 Nov. 1901, 5; *Waco (Tex.) News-Tribune*, 31 July 1923, 1; *Lawrenceville (Ga.) News-Herald*, 19 Dec. 1907, 1. As he had done with other condemned men in Lawrenceville, the sheriff processed Howell through town on a wagon that also bore his coffin. Despite the rain, "a strong array of guards were deputized to keep the crowd orderly."

42. *Brandon (Miss.) News*, 29 July 1909, 1.

43. *SN*, 5 Aug. 1904, 4; *Gainesville (Ga.) Eagle*, 15 Apr. 1899, quoted in Dorsey, *History of Hall County*, 294.

44. *Brandon (Miss.) News*, 29 July 1909, 1.

45. *VEP*, 20 May 1891, 4; *WTH*, 20 Nov. 1906, 1. At some executions, the whole crowd took part in the singing. Such was the case at the double hanging in Starkville, Mississippi, in 1915, where "at the special request of the condemned men, the whole vast crowd joined in singing 'There is a Land of Pure Delight.'" *Hattiesburg (Miss.) News*, 7 Aug. 1915, 1. This Jesse Washington had no connection to the young man of the same name who was lynched in Waco in 1916.

46. *AC*, 26 Jan. 1889, 1.

47. *Rome (Ga.) Hustler*, 29 Mar. 1896, 4; *Savannah (Ga.) Morning News*, 2 Dec. 1893, 1.

48. Emanuel County Historic Preservation Society, *Images of America*, 117; *WTH*, 26 Oct. 1901, 5; *WTH*, 30 Nov. 1906, 1.

49. *AC*, 28 Mar. 1871, 2; Carrington, "History of Electrocution in the State of Virginia," 353.

50. *SN*, 5 Aug. 1904, 4; *Brandon (Miss.) News*, 29 July 1909, 1.

51. *Brandon (Miss.) News*, 29 July 1909, 1; *Jackson (Miss.) Daily News*, 8 Aug. 1915, 5.

52. Sharpe, "'Last Dying Speeches,'" 156–57.

53. *Lawrenceville (Ga.) News-Herald*, 17 May 1906, 1.

54. *Oxford (Miss.) Globe*, 27 June 1889, 2; *Hattiesburg (Miss.) News*, 7 Aug. 1915, 1.

55. *AC*, 26 Jan. 1889, 1.

56. In Georgia, for instance, R. G. Turner, who was the city electrician for Atlanta, began petitioning the state legislature for the use of the electric chair as early as 1911. Turner declared that "the capital sentence can be no more humanely executed than by the use of the electric chair" and stated that hangings were "barbarous," whereas the chair was "absolutely painless." *AC*, 2 Dec. 1911, 8. On the other hand, even as late as 1940, the *Jackson (Miss.) Clarion-Ledger* printed photographs of the first use of the electric chair in Mississippi and pointed out to its readers, quite straightforwardly, the suffering of Willie Mae Bragg, a black man convicted of murder: "Note Bragg's hands gripping the chair and his neck bulging in death's throes." *Jackson (Miss.) Clarion-Ledger*, 13 Oct. 1940, Death Sentences File, 1900–1948.

57. *Brandon (Miss.) News*, 29 July 1909, 1; *VEP*, 19 May 1892, 4.

58. *WTH*, 27 Nov. 1906, 5; *WTH*, 30 Nov. 1906, 1; "Lynching, 1920, cases of,"

series 2, Lynching, 1899–1966, reel 222, Tuskegee Institute News Clippings File, microfilm edition; *AC*, 26 Jan. 1889, 1.

59. Haldeman-Julius, *Story of a Lynching*, 43, 39.

60. Benjamin, *Southern Outrages*, 45; Baker, "What Is a Lynching," 305.

61. Haldeman-Julius, *Story of a Lynching*, 42; James, *Facts in the Case*, 54.

CHAPTER TWO

1. Eight of the twelve thought Tunstal guilty beyond a doubt, while the remaining four thought there might be a chance he was innocent.

2. *Memphis Commercial Appeal*, 14 July 1885, 1.

3. As Waldrep (*Many Faces of Judge Lynch*, 106–9) has pointed out, before lynching became widely understood as a white supremacist form of terror, many African Americans, including Ida B. Wells, supported it as a legitimate means to punish criminals.

4. Doyle, *Faulkner's County*, 108–20, 334; Skipwith Historical and Genealogical Society, *Heritage of Lafayette County*, 61–68.

5. *Memphis Commercial Appeal*, 9 Sept. 1908, 1; *Oxford (Miss.) Eagle*, 10 Sept. 1908, 3; *Jackson (Miss.) Clarion-Ledger*, 9 Sept. 1908, 1. Faulkner denied ever having witnessed a lynching, but he certainly would have heard all the details of this one. In a letter to Governor Noel about the lynching, county judge W. A. Roane, who had also tried to stop the mob, reported that Reverend H. S. Spraggins "of the Methodist church" had urged the crowd to desist. Judge W. A. Roane to Governor E. F. Noel, 13 Sept. 1908, E. F. Noel Papers, Mississippi Department of Archives and History, Jackson. See also Doyle, *Faulkner's County*, 321–26; Williamson, *William Faulkner and Southern History*, 156–61; and Cullen, *Old Times in Faulkner Country*, 89–96.

6. Faulkner, *Light in August*, 379, 404–5, 407.

7. Evangelical Protestantism in the South was dominated by the Baptist and Methodist faiths but also included Presbyterians and other smaller denominations. Evangelicalism was so dominant in the South that even nonevangelical Protestants, such as Episcopalians, found themselves attending revivals and taking part in other evangelical-like practices. But, as Schweiger (*Gospel Working Up*, 8–9) has pointed out, southern evangelicals were not a monolithic group. There were significant differences not only among denominations but across region, class, and, of course, race—and they certainly did not use the term "evangelical" to describe themselves. Nonetheless, these relatively diverse faiths did share common tenets—most conspicuously, an overarching trust in the personal conversion experience—that distinguished them from other forms of Protestantism. Evangelicals tended to call themselves simply "Christians," not because the distinctions from other Christians were unimportant to them but, rather, because their beliefs were so overwhelmingly dominant. Because of that dominance, the terms "evangelical" and "Protestant" will be used at times interchangeably here.

8. Harris, *Exorcising Blackness*, 103–4; Apel, *Imagery of Lynching*, 112–16; Patterson, *Rituals of Blood*, 224–32; Mathews, "Southern Rite of Human Sacrifice";

Mathews, "Lynching Is Part of the Religion." Many black writers and commentators, including Ida B. Wells and W. E. B. Du Bois, eschewed what they considered these "passive" Christian conceptualizations of black suffering. Although he pays convincing attention to the theological specifics of evangelical Christianity and to the particularities of New South racial ideologies, Mathews roots his argument in a more universal understanding of ritual sacrifice, particularly that posited by Rene Girard in *Violence and the Sacred*. According to Girard, sacrificial rites were the means through which premodern societies imposed order and control on what could be endless cycles of retaliatory and vengeful violence, playing a role that law came to perform in modern societies. When a community was beset with violence and social disorder, it could deflect that violence onto the body of the scapegoat, the surrogate victim, who came to embody all the impurity and woes that threatened that community's integrity. Through his death, the group rid the community of impurity and protected themselves from further violence.

9. Girard (*Violence and the Sacred*, 95) points out that while the sacrificial victim is an object of scorn and derision, he is also "surrounded by a quasi-religious aura of veneration" and becomes a "cult object," a conception of the sacrificial victim that makes little sense in a southern context. The term "sacrifice" itself denotes a renunciation, a giving up of something of worth and value. It was God—not the Romans or the Jews—who underwent the sacrifice when Jesus was crucified. Even in the Old Testament, when the Israelites murdered the proverbial scapegoat to atone for their sins, they were sacrificing food and sustenance in a time when they were not uncommonly beset with famine and starvation.

10. Poole ("Confederate Apocalypse," 39–40) makes a similar argument to analyze racial violence during Reconstruction, which he sees as dominated by apocalyptic thinking. Defenders of lynching did not deploy the specific language of the apocalypse, rooted in the book of Revelation, as much as they suggested a more general notion of divine fury and judgment, a notion that permeates both the Old and New Testaments. In this sense, the specifics of Christian theology, about which most laypeople did not have specific knowledge, were less important than the ways in which white southerners felt impelled to sanction and interpret their violence through a less rigorous, though still potent, eschatological view.

11. Church membership increased over 50 percent between 1890 and 1906 (from about 6.1 million to more than 9.2 million)—the same period during which lynching peaked in the South. The overall population, in comparison, increased only 39 percent in this period. This increase was felt mostly in the Southern Baptist faith, which grew at nearly twice the rate of the general population and had, by the turn of the century, overtaken Methodism as the largest religious body in the South. By 1906, Baptists composed 44 percent of all southern church members. Methodists were second at 30 percent. What is more, these figures of southern church membership represent only those people who had been converted and officially joined the church. Actual attendance numbers may have been even higher. Woodward, *Origins of the New South*, 449. See also Hill, "South's Two Cultures," 37; Finke and Stark, *Churching of America*, 146–47; Flint, "Impact of Social Factors on Southern Baptist Expansion," 23; and Mathews, "Southern Rite of Human Sacrifice."

12. Mathews, "Southern Rite of Human Sacrifice"; Edwards, *Gendered Strife and Confusion*; Kellison, "Parameters of Promiscuity."

13. White, *Rope and Faggot*, 40–43; Raper, *Tragedy of Lynching*, 22. See also Miller, "Protestant Churches and Lynchings," 118. Other commentators who placed partial blame on southern churches for encouraging or acquiescing to lynching included Reinhold Niebuhr, Frank Tannenbaum, and Gunnar Myrdal.

14. Miller, "Protestant Churches and Lynchings," 121–26; *Wesleyan Christian Advocate*, 15 Sept. 1904, 1.

15. Methodist Episcopal Church, South, *Minutes South Georgia Conference, 1929*, 88–89, library of the Statesboro First Methodist Church; *Wesleyan Christian Advocate*, 25 Aug. 1904, 3; *SN*, 6 Sept. 1904, 2; *SN*, 10 Sept. 1904, 1. Langston was assigned to serve as pastor for the Statesboro Methodist Episcopal Church from 1901 to 1904, leaving shortly after the lynching. He received commendations for his anti-lynching action from all over the United States, Canada, and Europe. Unfortunately, church records from this time no longer exist, but Langston reported the expulsions and the resignations to journalist Ray Stannard Baker. Moreover, a local white woman, Sally Pearl Thompson, who was nine years old at the time of the lynching, recalled in a 1979 interview that "many" women were "turned out of the church" for handing the lynch mob jugs of kerosene from their homes. She did not elaborate on this statement, except to say that she did not agree with the "turning out," adding, "I could have struck the match myself." Baker, "What Is a Lynching," 308; Thompson, interview, 3.

16. Miller, "Protestant Churches and Lynchings," 119; Morrow, *History of the First Presbyterian Church of Oxford*, 20, 28; church minutes, 27 Aug. 1904, Statesboro First Baptist Church Records, Special Collections, Henderson Library, Georgia Southern University, Statesboro.

17. Miller, "Protestant Churches and Lynchings," 120; Raper, *Tragedy of Lynching*, 22; *Paris (Tex.) News*, 10 July 1920, 1. The next week, the Reverend L. C. Kirkus of the First Presbyterian Church in Paris joined his colleague and devoted his Sunday sermon to "the cause and cure of mobs." *Paris (Tex.) News*, 18 July 1920, 3.

18. Haygood, "Black Shadow of the South."

19. Wells-Barnett, *Crusade for Justice*, 154. For the ways in which southern Christianity acted as a conservative force, legitimizing white supremacy, see Hill, *Southern Churches in Crisis*; Eighmy, *Churches in Cultural Captivity*, 41–71; and Brauer, "Regionalism and Religion in America." On the ways in which white evangelicals were deeply engaged in reforming secular society, in what could be called a "social gospel" or "social Christianity," see Schweiger, *Gospel Working Up*; Flint, *Alabama Baptists*; Sparks, *Religion in Mississippi*; and Harvey, *Redeeming the South*.

20. *RT*, 16 Dec. 1900, B9; "20th Century Rome: A Résumé of Her Past, Present and Future, Illustrated," special industrial issue, *RT*, 12 Oct. 1902; Aycock, *All Roads to Rome*, 159–69, 179–89, 200–209, 214–27, 255–66; Rome, Georgia, city directories, 1895–96, 1904, 1913.

21. Gardner, *First Baptist Church, Rome*, 100–106, 111–15; Aycock, *All Roads to Rome*, 190–91.

22. *RT*, 22 Apr. 1902, 2.

23. Gardner, *First Baptist Church, Rome*, 112–15; 143; Aycock, *All Roads to Rome*, 191, 266–74.

24. *RT*, 2 Apr. 1902, 1, 4. The others lynched in this period were Bud Rufus on 7 Dec. 1900 and George Reed on 3 Jan. 1901. Sermons given at the principal churches in the city after these lynchings, which were reprinted in the local paper, made no mention of the recent violence. The leader of the movement to replace the city's saloons with a centralized dispensary was Seaborn Wright, a local attorney and state legislator. After the lynching of Reed, Wright wrote two editorials for the local paper condemning the mob's actions and urging church leaders to take a stand. The following year, however, when the mob lynched Walter Allen for his purported assault on Blossom Adamson, who happened to be Wright's niece, he made no such public statements. Another uncle of Adamson, A. B. S. Moseley, a former Confederate captain and the clerk for the First Baptist Church in Rome, led the posse that captured Allen. Moseley himself shot Allen three times with his pistol. *RT*, 8 Dec. 1900, 8; *RT*, 9 Dec. 1900, B9; *RT*, 11 Dec. 1900, 8; *RT*, 4 Jan. 1901, 1; *RT*, 5 Jan. 1901, 1; *RT*, 6 Jan. 1901, 1, 5; Gardner, *First Baptist Church, Rome*, 141.

25. *RT*, 15 Apr. 1902, 5; *RT*, 25 Feb. 1902, 5. These examples were selected from sermons reprinted in the city newspaper in the weeks surrounding the lynching of Walter Allen.

26. On the role of religion in Lost Cause ideology and in white southern conceptions of Reconstruction and Redemption, see Wilson, *Baptized in Blood*; Poole, *Never Surrender*; Blum and Poole, *Vale of Tears*; and Whitley, "Precious Memories."

27. Ownby, *Subduing Satan*, 167–212; Link, *Paradox of Southern Progressivism*, 31–57; Willis, *Democratic Religion*, 9–10, 121–39. Willis indicates that this new social role, though seemingly hostile to the secular world, reflected a less troubled, exclusionary, and contentious relationship to secular society. Church disciplines became less and less demanding in the early twentieth century, especially in urban churches, and disappeared from most churches by the 1920s. Moral campaigns waged outside the church only increased, however. In the 1910s and 1920s, for instance, evangelicals railed against the threat of the automobile to traditional courtship practice and led public campaigns to regulate both the content and the exhibition of motion pictures.

28. Woodward, *Origins of the New South*, 448–50; Ayers, *Promise of the New South*, 160–62. Harvey, in *Redeeming the South* (77–78), has also shown that many urban ministers, who were becoming better educated in this period, adapted themselves and their congregations to the new dominant values of scientific management, bourgeois respectability, and social progressivism. See also Willis, *Democratic Religion*, 131–39.

29. *Paris (Tex.) News*, 15 Nov. 1921, 4; Joseph Martin Dawson, "Oral Memoirs, Religion and Culture Series," 19, Texas Collection, Baylor University, Waco, Tex.; *Rome (Ga.) Times-Herald*, 13 Aug. 1916, 4.

30. *Lawrenceville (Ga.) News-Herald*, 7 July 1904, 5; *Rome (Ga.) Times-Herald*, 26 Nov. 1916, 3.

31. *Rome (Ga.) Tribune-Herald*, 13 Aug. 1916, 4; *Rome (Ga.) Tribune-Herald*, 24 Sept. 1916, 3; *Rome (Ga.) Tribune-Herald*, 18 June, 1916, 3. In 1900, as a twenty-

one-year-old man, Cole was a farm laborer and tenant in nearby Bartow County. After the death of his first wife, Cole moved to Rome in 1902, according to one column, and boarded with the proprietor of a local furniture store, where he began working as a laborer. By 1916, he had married again, fathered children, and become a furniture salesman. *Rome (Ga.) Tribune-Herald*, 30 July 1916, 3; U.S. census records, Bartow County, Ga., 1900; U.S. census records, Floyd County, Ga., 1910, 1920.

32. *Stone County (Miss.) Enterprise*, 3 Jan. 1919, 2; *Stone County (Miss.) Enterprise*, 24 May 1919, 1; "Mississippi Governor Again Asked If Lynchers Are to Be Prosecuted," part 7, series A, reel 13, National Association for the Advancement of Colored People Papers, microfilm edition (hereafter cited as NAACP Papers); *Rome (Ga.) Tribune-Herald*, 26 Nov. 1916, 3; *Rome (Ga.) Tribune-Herald*, 11 Nov. 1916, 1; *Rome (Ga.) Tribune-Herald*, 12 Nov. 1916, 1; *Rome (Ga.) Tribune-Herald*, 25 Nov. 1916, 1; *Rome (Ga.) Tribune-Herald*, 28 Nov. 1916, 1.

33. Mathews, "Southern Rite of Human Sacrifice."

34. James, *Facts in the Case*, 3, 5, 9, 47, 62.

35. *Oxford (Miss.) Eagle*, 10 Sept. 1908, 3; *Lafayette County (Miss.) Press*, 9 Sept. 1908, 4.

36. The argument here is informed by performance and practice theory studies of ritual, which understand ritual not simply as a physical manifestation or reflection of belief but as itself, in its physical action, intrinsic to the formation of belief. Through directing the individual body in collective, routinized action, ritual shapes people's perceptions and connections to the social world and social order. See Bell, *Ritual Theory, Ritual Practice*; Kertzer, *Ritual, Politics, and Power*; Tambiah, "Performative Approach to Ritual"; and Connerton, *How Societies Remember*.

37. *Rome (Ga.) Hustler*, 27 Sept. 1897, 1; *AC*, 27 Sept. 1897, 1.

38. *AC*, 24 Apr. 1899, 1; Ginzberg, *One Hundred Years of Lynching*, 11, 145; *WTH*, 8 Aug. 1905, 1.

39. Baker, "What Is a Lynching," 307.

40. *Oxford (Miss.) Globe*, 2 Oct. 1902, 1.

41. James, *Facts in the Case*, 14; John Hamm quoted in ibid., 149.

42. *VEP*, 15 May 1919, 1; Ginzberg, *One Hundred Years of Lynching*, 145; *St. Louis Post-Dispatch* reprinted in National Association for the Advancement of Colored People, *Thirty Years of Lynching*, 22.

43. As Scarry (*Body in Pain*, 37, 56–57) has argued, torture and its infliction of pain on the body detach the victim from his personhood so that he becomes most of all a body. The pain robs him of his language and complex thought, reducing him to screams, cries, and groans as he becomes trapped in the sentience of his own body. Antilynching commentaries also focused on the victim's suffering, but for different ends. For lynching opponents, the severe tortures that mobs inflicted on black bodies were signs of utter barbarity. Activists belabored and sensationalized the suffering of the victims to agitate and horrify their readers to compel them to act against lynching.

44. James, *Facts in the Case*, 24; eyewitness report quoted in National Association for the Advancement of Colored People, *Thirty Years of Lynching*, 12.

45. James, *Facts in the Case*, 13, 18, 9; Baker, "What Is a Lynching," 307; Felton quoted in Litwack, *Trouble in Mind*, 304.

46. *WTH*, 8 Aug. 1905, 1; *San Antonio Express* editorial reprinted in James, *Facts in the Case*, 111. The mob in Waco subsequently attempted to burn Majors but could not get the fire started properly and so hanged him instead.

47. *WTH*, 15 May 1916, 1.

48. *RT*, 2 Apr. 1902, 1.

CHAPTER THREE

1. James, *Facts in the Case*, 11, 15. In her 1894 antilynching pamphlet *A Red Record* (91–98), Ida B. Wells recounted Smith's lynching and included the point of view of a local black minister who was "ridden out of Paris on a rail" for objecting to Smith's treatment.

2. James, *Facts in the Case*, 19–20.

3. Burdett, *Test of Lynch Law*, 17–19. Burdett was a veterinarian in Seattle who was involved with local Republican politics before becoming active in the antilynching movement.

4. *New York Age*, 5 Aug. 1909, 6; Everett, *Returning the Gaze*, 19–20.

5. Hale, *Making Whiteness*, 207–9; Goldsby, *Spectacular Secret*, 13–15.

6. James, *Facts in the Case*, 3, 5, 149.

7. For the ways in which photography can serve to represent war, violence, and aggression as normal and acceptable practice, rendering that violence nonthreatening to the white, middle-class domestic sphere, see Wexler, *Tender Violence*.

8. Lalvani, *Photography, Vision, and the Production of Modern Bodies*, 1–41; Slater, "Photography and Modern Vision," 219–20.

9. Hale, *Making Whiteness*, 202–5; Goldsby, *Spectacular Secret*, 5, 12–42. Benjamin, in "The Work of Art in the Age of Mechanical Reproduction," most notably theorized on the way the "mechanical reproduction" of images, through photography and film, detached images (or art) from their "aura"—their ritualized specificity in locality and time—as they became available for collective consumption.

10. These first cameras cost twenty-five dollars, a month's wages for the average American laborer. By 1900, however, Eastman had introduced the popular Brownie camera, which cost only one dollar. Exposed film could be sent off to the Kodak Company or developed by a local studio. Lynching photographs that bear the marks of local studios could thus have been taken by amateurs. Jenkins, "Technology and the Market," 12–16; Conniff, "When Fiends Pressed the Button," 114.

11. Quoted in *Crisis*, June 1915, 71.

12. James, *Facts in the Case*, 19–20; *WTH*, 15 May 1916, 1; "The Waco Horror," *Crisis*, July 1916, S6; Elizabeth Freeman, "The Waco Lynching," 21, part 7, series A, reel 19, NAACP Papers. According to Freeman's report, by arrangement with the mayor, Gildersleeve left his camera at city hall beforehand and then was "called by telephone at the proper moment."

13. Reports of photographers at work, as noted below, sometimes mention that the photographers took many pictures, from different vantage points, over the

course of the lynching, yet in these instances only a handful of images were developed or were preserved.

14. Highly descriptive news accounts of more "private" lynchings served the same purposes. *Louisville (Ky.) Courier-Journal*, 27 Sept. 1913, 1; *NYT*, 12 Feb. 1906, 4. The photographs of Joseph Richardson's and Bunk Richardson's lynchings appear in Allen, *Without Sanctuary*, plates 39, 86, 87.

15. McGovern, *Anatomy of a Lynching*, 80–85.

16. Trachtenberg, *Reading American Photographs*, 17–20; Barthes, *Camera Lucida*, 28; Lalvani, *Photography, Vision, and the Production of Modern Bodies*, 14; Zelizer, *Remembering to Forget*, 8–10.

17. On the very active roles that white women played in lynchings, including their role as accusers, despite the cultural mythology that depended on their submissive weakness, see Feimster, "'Ladies and Lynching,'" 108–63, and Hall, *Revolt against Chivalry*, 149–57.

18. White died a few days later, and the Rufus family was ordered to leave the county. *RT*, 8 Dec. 1900, 1; *RT*, 9 Dec. 1900, 1; *RT*, 11 Dec. 1900, 2; *RT*, 12 Dec. 1900, 2; U.S. census records, Floyd County, Ga., 1900.

19. For a literary examination of this problem, see William Faulkner's "Dry September." The 1919 lynching of Lloyd Clay in Vicksburg, Mississippi, exemplifies the ways in which the hysteria of the white female witness undermined the validity of the lynching. This lynching generated a public outcry in part because of the fallibility of the female witness. Those who opposed the lynching doubted the identification made by Clay's alleged victim, Hattie Hudson, because it was made "in an uncertain manner" while she was in a "hysterical condition." When Clay was brought before Hudson, a large crowd had gathered, waiting for her identification. Although she could not state with certainty that Clay was the man who raped her, he was kept in custody and brought before her a second time. At this time, "in the presence of 1000 citizens, she admitted he was the guilty one . . . [and] a thunderous shout went up." Those present were already convinced Clay was guilty and were eager to lynch him, but they knew they could not do so without Hudson's identification to protect their own sense of integrity and righteousness. But rumors persisted that Hudson was not as respectable as news accounts imagined and that she was having an affair with a white man from Jackson, an affair she covered up by crying rape. *VEP*, 14 May 1919, 1; *VEP*, 15 May 1919, 4; National Association for the Advancement of Colored People, *Burning at the Stake*, 5–6; "Lynching, 1919, cases of," series 2, Lynching, 1899–1966, reel 222, Tuskegee Institute News Clippings File, microfilm edition.

20. *AC*, 4 Jan. 1901, 2; *RT*, 4 Jan. 1901, 1, 5. Mr. Locklear rented his farm, yet the Locklears also had a black cook who lived with them. Their situation reveals the difficulty of fixing class position in southern towns and cities. U.S. census records, Floyd County, Ga., 1900.

21. *RT*, 4 Jan. 1901, 1, 5; *RT*, 5 Jan. 1901, 1. Part of the new evidence was furnished by the coerced testimony of Reed's wife. When the mob was searching for Reed, they questioned his wife, and with "a little force made her tell where he could be found." Later, at the coroner's inquest, Mrs. Reed testified that her husband had been away from home the night of the attack.

22. *RT*, 5 Jan. 1901, 1, 5.

23. Trachtenberg, *Reading American Photographs*, 21–29; Smith, *American Archives*, 11–15; Benjamin, "Work of Art in the Age of Mechanical Reproduction," 226.

24. Although taken from a distance, the image of the lynching of Jesse Washington in Waco, Texas, in figure 3.4 reveals two men who appear to be beating Washington's body. A postcard of the 1908 lynching of Ted Smith in Greenville, Texas, depicts the burning of Smith's body, though, significantly, the mob has stepped back for the photographer to take the picture. See Allen, *Without Sanctuary*, plate 22.

25. Benjamin, *Southern Outrages*, 45; *AC*, 8 Apr. 1911, 1.

26. Baker, *Following the Color Line*, 186–87. Another photograph depicts the same group of white men surrounding the charred remains of Reed and Cato. "Reed-Cato Affair," Georgia Historical Society Papers, Special Collections, Henderson Library, Georgia Southern University, Statesboro.

27. Bourdieu, *Photography*, 24.

28. Trachtenberg, *Reading American Photographs*, 27–29; Sekula, "Body and the Archive," 10–12; Tagg, *Burden of Representation*, 37–40.

29. For instance, in Lawrenceville, Georgia, three photographers were listed in the 1910 census, when the town's population was around 1,000. A traveling photographer advertised his services in the Gwinnett County paper that same year. Larger cities had local photographers much earlier. For example, Paris, Texas, with a population of around 8,000, claimed three photographers in its 1891 city directory, including both Mertins and Hudson, who took the pictures of Smith's lynching. U.S. census records, Gwinnett County, Ga., 1910; *Gwinnett County (Ga.) Journal*, 3 Aug. 1910; Paris, Texas, city directory, 1891.

30. *Rome (Ga.) Commercial Argus*, 18 Feb. 1899, 3. This observer was unaware that black southerners were posing for and purchasing their own photographic portraits at this time. For the ways in which African Americans at the turn of the last century adopted the conventions of bourgeois portrait photography to visually construct a sense of respectability for themselves that subverted the "white supremacist gaze" of scientific and institutional photographic practices in America, see Smith, *Photography on the Color Line*, 43–112.

31. Law enforcement agencies also commonly used postcards to circulate images and descriptions of criminals through the mail. Sekula, "Body and the Archive," 6–7; Tagg, *Burden of Representation*, 71–87; Morgan and Brown, *Prairie Fires and Paper Moons*, 105.

32. James, *Facts in the Case*, 3.

33. *SN*, 30 Aug. 1904, 4; photographs of the Hodges family and of the Reed and Cato lynching, Bulloch Crime folder, Genealogy Department, Statesboro Regional Library, Statesboro, Ga.; *AC*, 17 Aug. 1904, 1.

34. Baker, *Following the Color Line*, 174, 178–79.

35. Allen, *Without Sanctuary*, plate 93. Although it is mislabeled, the postcard of Stanley's lynching appears, with a written message, in Allen, *Without Sanctuary* (plates 25, 26). Stanley was accused of murdering three white children. He was burned to death in the center of town before a crowd of between 5,000 and 10,000

in July 1915. After the burning, the mob strung Stanley's corpse from a telephone pole, presumably to offer the crowd a better view and to take the picture. Postcards of Stanley's lynching were sold on the streets in nearby Waco, Texas, for ten cents each. Jesse Washington was burned to death in Waco in a similar manner the following summer. See Carrigan, *Making of a Lynching Culture*, 185–86, and *Crisis*, Jan. 1916, 145.

36. Marriott (*On Black Men*, 9) notes that, in lynching photographs, white men were accorded the right to self-presentation that black men were denied.

37. *AC*, 1 Mar. 1893, 2.

38. *Crisis*, Dec. 1911, 60; *AC*, 8 Apr. 1911, 1.

39. John Haynes Holmes quoted in *Crisis*, Jan. 1912, 109.

40. *Paris (Tex.) News*, 29 Oct. 1911, 3; Ownby, *Subduing Satan*, 21–37; Wyatt-Brown, *Southern Honor*, 195–97. Proctor (*Bathed in Blood*) argues that hunting developed as a venue for displays of white masculine power in the antebellum South, when the ownership of guns was reserved for white men.

41. *AC*, 8 Apr. 1911, 1.

42. Conniff, "When Fiends Pressed the Button," 107; *Hattiesburg (Miss.) American*, 12 Apr. 1919, 7; *WTH*, 3 Jan. 1908; Sontag, *On Photography*, 14–15.

43. Sheriff Mike Haynie quoted in Haldeman-Julius, *Story of a Lynching*, 46.

44. Harris, *Exorcising Blackness*, 22.

45. Brundage, *Lynching in the New South*, 66; McGovern, *Anatomy of a Lynching*, 80–81; Freeman, "Waco Lynching."

46. Smith, *Killers of the Dream*, 145.

47. As images that display objectified others and that create bonds between men, lynching photographs do resemble "folk pornography," as Hall, in *Revolt against Chivalry* (150), terms the lurid lynching narratives and tales that circulated throughout the South, a term that other scholars have frequently repeated. However, although they do appear obscene to contemporary eyes, the word "pornography" suggests that these narratives and images were considered illicit or obscene at the time and elides the ways ordinary people celebrated them publicly.

48. Feimster, "'Ladies and Lynching,'" 153–55; Benjamin, *Southern Outrages*, 42–43; *Chicago Defender*, 24 May 1919, 1.

49. Raper, *Tragedy of Lynching*, 421.

50. *VEP*, 15 May 1919, 1, 4; *Vicksburg (Miss.) Herald*, 22 May 1919, 4; *VEP*, 17 May 1919, 2; U.S. census records, Warren County, Miss., 1920. Keefe was home alone with her daughter and granddaughter. When the mob arrived, they called a male relative to come sit with them, and afterward retired to the home of a neighbor. Later, Keefe asked the city to cut down the tree from which Clay was hanged. *VEP*, 15 May 1919, 1.

51. There are a few exceptions, such as a photograph of an unidentified black man taken circa 1910 (Allen, *Without Sanctuary*, plate 98) and the photograph of the body of Claude Neal, lynched in Marianna, Florida, in 1934. Neal was castrated. Although apparently hundred of pictures were taken, the photograph that was most regularly circulated and printed shows Neal from the side. See McGovern, *Anatomy of a Lynching*, 83, 84.

52. Madison, *Lynching in the Heartland*, 9–11; Fanon, *Black Skin, White Masks*, 165, 170; James, *Facts in the Case*, 22.

53. Allen, *Without Sanctuary*, plate 32, shows a photograph of the lynched bodies of Abe Smith and Thomas Shipp, hanged in Marion, Indiana, in 1930, in a frame with a lock of one of the victims' hair.

54. *Newnan (Ga.) Herald and Advertiser*, 28 Apr. 1899, 7; *SN*, 30 Aug. 1904, 4; *Charlotte (N.C.) News*, 11 Aug. 1893, 4; *Crisis*, June 1915, 71. Jackson was listed as a professional photographer in the 1899 Newnan city directory. The sale of lynching photographs was not always without controversy. In August 1915, a "small riot" broke out in Columbus, Georgia, when one man exhibited a photograph of Leo Frank's lynching in the store of a local merchant. The merchant, who apparently objected to the photograph, attempted to take it away from its owner, and a fight broke out between the men. After both were arrested, however, "several hundred persons" congregated around the store, and some made an attempt to burn it down, presumably because they felt that the merchant's objection to the photograph reflected his sympathies for Frank. *Columbia (S.C.) State*, 29 Aug. 1915, 1.

55. These cards, held at the Prints and Photographs Division at the Library of Congress in Washington, D.C., were produced and copyrighted by two men, Beckenridge and Scruggs, in Tyler, Texas. Advertisement quoted in National Association for the Advancement of Colored People, *Thirty Years of Lynching*, 12. On the lynching of Hilliard, see also the *Independent*, 7 Nov. 1895, 15.

56. Hale, *Making Whiteness*, 203.

57. Taft, *Photography and the American Scene*, 446–47; *Memphis Appeal-Avalanche* reprinted in *Columbia (S.C.) State*, 4 Mar. 1892, 6. This item is also noteworthy because the reporter expressed astonishment that the men had the "audacious design" to photograph themselves with the lynched body of their victim and remarked on the "novelty" of the image, which "fairly outdoes anything ever recorded in the annals of photography." Though later commentators often noted the photographing of lynchings casually, in 1892 such images were still rare. Smaller newspapers did not have the means to print photographs until the 1920s.

58. *AC*, 12 Nov. 1895, 4; *Dawson (Ga.) News*, 1 Feb. 1916, 6; *Dawson (Ga.) News*, 9 Feb. 1916, 4.

59. Allen, *Without Sanctuary*, plate 10; *Dallas Times-Herald*, 4 Mar. 1910, 1; *AC*, 17 Aug. 1915, 1; *AC*, 18 Aug. 1915, 1; *Columbia (S.C.) State*, 1 Sept. 1915, 4. A copy of a Leo Frank lynching photograph exists in the Kenneth Rogers Papers at the Atlanta History Center. Rogers was head of the photography department at the *Atlanta Constitution* and the *Atlanta Journal-Constitution* between 1924 and 1972. Although he could have obtained the photograph privately, it is reasonable to assume that he obtained it from the newspaper's files.

60. *St. Joseph (Mo.) News-Press*, 12 Jan. 1931, 1–2; Raper, *Tragedy of Lynching*, 419–20.

61. Morgan and Brown, *Prairie Fires and Paper Moons*, xiv–xv.

62. Ibid., xiii–xiv.

63. Allen, *Without Sanctuary*, plates 26, 10, 11, 54, 55.

64. Ibid., plates 74, 75; *AC*, 18 Aug. 1908, 2.

65. Massachusetts was one of four states that had no recorded lynchings between 1889 and 1968; the other three were its neighbors, Rhode Island, New Hampshire, and Connecticut. William Otis Sweet was a horticulturalist; his son, the photographer, Frank R. Sweet, age eighteen at the time, later became a jewelry manufacturer. In other photos, Frank Sweet re-created scenes of a "bicycle smash-up," yet another common "spectacle" for visual consumption. I owe enormous thanks to John Wood Sweet for sharing these images of his grandfather and great-grandfather from his family's personal collection.

CHAPTER FOUR

1. News accounts of the fight and the subsequent lynching differ. This account of the fight, which presents Mitchell as the instigator, is from the *Owensboro (Ky.) Daily Inquirer*, 21 Apr. 1911, 1. Owensboro is a small city located near Livermore, in the western region of the state. A border state, Kentucky had relatively high rates of racial violence, especially in western and central Kentucky, where African Americans were more highly concentrated than in the eastern counties, and where white Kentuckians were more likely to identify themselves as southern. See Wright, *Racial Violence in Kentucky*, 5, 70–72, 118–19.

2. *Louisville (Ky.) Courier-Journal*, 21 Apr. 1911, 1. According to the *Owensboro (Ky.) Daily Inquirer*, Potter was lynched on stage by the light of lanterns, not footlights.

3. *Louisville (Ky.) Courier-Journal*, 21 Apr. 1911, 1.

4. Wright, *Racial Violence in Kentucky*, 118, 165; *NYT*, 22 Apr. 1911, 12; *Louisville (Ky.) Courier-Journal*, 13 May 1911, 1. The NAACP wrote to both President Taft and Kentucky governor Augustus Wilson in protest. This national attention compelled Governor Wilson to write to the NAACP to express his opposition to injustice and mob action but also to clarify that the lynching, "while it was bad enough," was not as bad or as sensationalistic as reported. Although indictments were made, no one was ever convicted for the lynching. *Crisis*, June 1911, 61.

5. *Owensboro (Ky.) Daily Inquirer*, 21 Apr. 1911, 1; *Louisville (Ky.) Courier-Journal*, 13 May 1911, 1. The *Owensboro (Ky.) Daily Inquirer* initially reported that Mitchell was a troublemaker and a "Negro-hater" and that the mob was "composed of young hot-headed fellows, and not of the older and very best citizens of the town." But it also made note that Mitchell's father was "well-respected by those who knew him." *Owensboro (Ky.) Daily Inquirer*, 21 Apr. 1911, 1.

6. Although some of these films are available at the Motion Picture Reading Room of the Library of Congress, many, including those that show live hangings, no longer exist. Our knowledge of them for the most part derives from production companies' catalogs. Other films that could be placed within this genre include those showing executions in international contexts, such as *Execution of the Spanish Spy* (Lubin, 1898) and *Beheading of a Chinese Prisoner* (Lubin, 1900); films showing the corporal punishment of prisoners, such as *The Whipping Post* (Biograph, 1902)

and *The Convict's Punishment* (Biograph, 1902); and films showing scenes of white-capping or nonlethal vigilante violence, such as *Indiana Whitecaps* (Biograph, 1900) and *The White Caps* (Edison, 1905).

7. *American Mutoscope and Biograph Company Picture Catalog*, Nov. 1902, 240, 244, Motion Picture, Broadcasting, and Recorded Sound Division, Library of Congress, Washington, D.C. (hereafter cited as MPD); *Edison Films Catalog*, Sept. 1902, 91, MPD; *New York Clipper*, 16 Nov. 1901, 832.

8. The model for the early cinema spectator in contemporary exhibition catalogs and in much academic film scholarship has been white, male, urban, and northern. More recent reception studies have challenged this model of cinema spectatorship, which tends to assume a monolithic and historically and regionally static reception of film. Staiger, in *Interpreting Films* (79–81), for instance, calls for a "historical materialist approach" to film reception studies, in which film interpretation involves "an interaction among context, text and individual." See also Staiger, *Perverse Spectators*, 1–57; Hansen, *Babel and Babylon*, 7; and Gunning, "Whole Town's Gawking," 192.

9. Gunning, "Cinema of Attractions"; Gunning, "'Now You See It, Now You Don't.'"

10. Musser, "Rethinking Early Cinema," 213; Musser, *Emergence of Cinema*, 79–81; Staiger, *Interpreting Films*, 102–3.

11. For a clear, historically contextualized definition of melodrama, see Singer, *Melodrama and Modernity*, 7, 37–58. Williams, in *Playing the Race Card* (xiv, 11–18), argues that melodrama was central to American theater and cinema and that it has been a primary means by which Americans have formulated and interpreted racial dramas.

12. Lewisohn, "Cult of Violence," 118.

13. Fuller, *At the Picture Show*; Waller, *Main Street Amusements*; Goodson, *Highbrows, Hillbillies, and Hellfire*, 78–107.

14. *Lawrenceville (Ga.) News-Herald*, 4 Aug. 1899, 1; *Lawrenceville (Ga.) News-Herald*, 27 Sept. 1900, 3; *Lawrenceville (Ga.) News-Herald*, 18 Oct. 1900, 1; *SN*, 19 Apr. 1901, 4. The first movie exhibition in Atlanta, population 100,000, took place at the World Exposition in 1895, and the first Vitascope showing at a theater took place in November 1896. Dallas, the largest city in Texas, with a population of around 42,000 in 1900, saw moving pictures for the first time at the opera house in February 1897. The Vitascope arrived in Vicksburg, Mississippi, with a population around 15,000, even earlier, in December 1896. It also appeared in Jackson, Mississippi, that month. By 1899, motion pictures were being exhibited in Rome, Georgia, with a population of 14,035 in 1900, regularly as parts of theatrical programs in the opera house and in the outdoor theater at Mobley Park. The first movies were shown in Statesboro, Georgia, in April 1901, when the city had a population of around 1,150. Most nickelodeon theaters opened in southern cities around 1907–8, though small cities like Statesboro lagged by a few years. (Statesboro saw its first motion picture theater in 1911.) Goodson, *Highbrows, Hillbillies, and Hellfire*, 78–80; *Atlanta Journal*, 17 Nov. 1896, 12; *Dallas Morning News*, 1 Feb. 1897, 5; *VEP*, 7 Dec. 1896, 4; *Jackson*

(Miss.) Clarion-Ledger, 15 Dec. 1896, 1; Rome (Ga.) Commercial Argus, 23 Jan. 1899, 1; Billy Holcomb, "The Great Movie Palaces of Paris," Aiken Archives, Paris Junior College, Paris, Tex.; Doyle, Faulkner's County, 334; Coleman, Statesboro, 255, 296.

15. Dallas Morning News, 2 Feb. 1897, 8; Maguire and Baucus Ltd. Catalog, Fall 1897, Mar. 1898, MPD; Musser, Edison Motion Pictures, 191–92; VEP, 11 Dec. 1896, 4; Jackson (Miss.) Clarion-Ledger, 15 Dec. 1896, 1; WTH, 24 Oct. 1904, 5; WTH, 27 Oct. 1904, 5. Although both these lynching films first appeared in 1897 catalogs, they were presumably made in 1896, as they were shown in Vicksburg in late 1896 and Dallas in early 1897. Unless there was another hanging scene produced that was not listed in any catalog, these two films are the only possibilities.

16. On class fragmentation and hierarchies in entertainments and cinema in the North, see Levine, High Brow/Low Brow; Nasaw, Going Out; Sklar, Movie-Made America; and Gomery, Shared Pleasures. For the ways in which southern audiences often crossed class lines, see Goodson, Highbrows, Hillbillies, and Hellfire, 6; Renoff, Big Tent; and Aycock, All Roads to Rome, 404.

17. VEP, 4 Jan. 1897, 4; WTH, 29 Oct. 1904, 7.

18. Hansen, Babel and Babylon, 25; Musser, Emergence of Cinema, 19.

19. Rome (Ga.) Commercial Argus, 11 Sept. 1899, 3; Rome (Ga.) Commercial Argus, 17 Dec. 1899, 4; Fuller, At the Picture Show, 31. Much more needs to be known about black spectatorship in small towns and cities. Stewart, in Migrating to the Movies, argues that African Americans began to see themselves as spectators once they came to see themselves, through migration, as urban subjects. Early cinema became the site through which white Americans expressed their anxieties over the new heightened visibility of black Americans, but it also became the "imaginary" through which African Americans acted out and negotiated their own presence as urban spectators and subjects.

20. Dallas Morning News, 2 Feb. 1897, 8. For a fuller discussion of African American caricatures in early film, see Cripps, Slow Fade to Black, 8–23, and Stewart, Migrating to the Movies, 23–90. Other films of this subgenre include A Watermelon Feast (American Mutoscope, 1896), Who Said Watermelon? (Lubin, 1902), and The Watermelon Patch (Edison, 1905).

21. VEP, 11 Dec. 1896, 4; Jackson (Miss.) Clarion-Ledger, 15 Dec. 1896, 1. American Mutoscope produced a similar film, also in 1896, called A Hard Wash.

22. These included Execution of a Spy (American Mutoscope and Biograph, 1902), Execution of the Spanish Spy (Lubin, 1898), An Execution in Peking (Pathé Frères, 1903), Beheading Chinese (Selig Polyscope, 1903), and Tortured by Boxers (American Mutoscope and Biograph, 1902). Pathé Frères, the French film distribution company that dominated American film distribution in this period, even compiled six execution films from six countries in its 1903 catalog, on a page titled "Capital Executions." Musser, Emergence of Cinema, 365, 488–89; American Film Institute Catalog, A:320; Pathé Frères Catalog, May 1903, 63, 83, MPD; American Mutoscope and Biograph Company Picture Catalog, 1902, 245, MPD.

23. These included The Story of a Crime (Pathé Frères, 1903) and The Gambler's Life and End (Lubin, 1904). The latter was advertised as a film with "a very strong moral."

Another Lubin film made in 1906, *The Gambler's Nightmare*, shows a dissolute man who finds redemption and reforms his sinful ways. *Pathé Frères Catalog*, 1903, 80, MPD; *Lubin Catalog*, 1905, 31, MPD; *American Film Institute Catalog*, A:395.

24. *Atlanta Journal*, 8 Dec. 1897, 10; *VEP*, 11 Dec. 1896, 4; *Jackson (Miss.) Clarion-Ledger*, 15 Dec. 1896, 1; *Dallas Morning News*, 28 Oct. 1897, 3; *Atlanta Journal*, 22 Jan. 1901, 10.

25. Slater, "Photography and Modern Vision," 219–31; *Jackson (Miss.) Clarion-Ledger*, 15 Dec. 1896, 1; *VEP*, 8 Dec. 1896, 4; *WTH*, 14 Apr. 1900, 4.

26. *American Mutoscope and Biograph Company Picture Catalog*, 1902, MPD; *American Film Institute Catalog*, A:320.

27. *Florida Times Union and Citizen*, 7 July 1898, 6. My research indicates that Heinson was the only black man who was executed in Jacksonville in the spring or summer of 1898. He was hanged on 6 July, which coincided with the film's release.

28. *Florida Times Union and Citizen*, 7 July 1898, 6.

29. Musser, "Passions and the Passion Play," 419, 438, 448, 450; Benjamin, "Work of Art in the Age of Mechanical Reproduction." Protestant leaders who protested theatrical reproductions of the Passion claimed not only that having a human actor play Christ was sacrilegious but that theaters themselves were profane places that corrupted audiences. They also maintained that Christ's story should not be sensationalized or commercialized.

30. *Dallas Morning News*, 2 Dec. 1897, 10; *Dallas Morning News*, 28 Nov. 1897; Musser, "Passions and the Passion Play," 448.

31. Advertisements for *The Hanging of William Carr* and *An Execution by Hanging* claimed that each was the only motion picture depicting an actual execution. *American Mutoscope and Biograph Company Picture Catalog*, 1902, MPD; *New York Clipper*, 29 Jan. 1898, 799.

32. *St. Louis Post-Dispatch*, 17 Dec. 1897, 5; *Kansas City (Mo.) Star*, 26 Oct. 1897, 1; *Kansas City (Mo.) Star*, 16 Nov. 1897, 1; *Kansas City (Mo.) Star*, 16 Dec. 1897, 1; *St. Louis Globe-Democrat*, 18 Dec. 1897, 5.

33. The estimated number of people at the hanging ranged from 400 to 800. *Topeka (Kans.) Weekly Capital*, 21 Dec. 1897, 6; *St. Louis Globe-Democrat*, 18 Dec. 1897, 5; *St. Louis Post-Dispatch*, 18 Dec. 1897, 4.

34. *St. Louis Post-Dispatch*, 18 Dec. 1897, 4.

35. *Kansas City (Mo.) Star*, 26 Oct. 1897, 1; *St. Louis Post-Dispatch*, 17 Dec. 1897, 1; *Topeka (Kans.) Weekly Capital*, 21 Dec. 1897, 6; *Kansas City (Mo.) Star*, 25 Dec. 1897, 5.

36. *Topeka (Kans.) Weekly Capital*, 21 Dec. 1897, 6; *Kansas City (Mo.) Star*, 17 Dec. 1897, 1; *Phonoscope*, Jan. 1898, 11.

37. *Phonoscope*, Jan. 1898, 11. Although Guth said he left as soon as Carr dropped, advertisements for the film noted that the film continued until "the murderer was pronounced dead," some ten minutes later. *Kansas City (Mo.) Star*, 25 Dec. 1897, 5.

38. *Kansas City (Mo.) Star*, 25 Dec. 1897, 5; *Kansas City (Mo.) Star*, 26 Dec. 1897, 1. It is unclear why the film never played at the Academy of Music. A showing on Christmas Day was cancelled because the film did not arrive in time, but it appears that the showing was never rescheduled.

39. *Kansas City (Mo.) Star*, 27 Dec. 1897, 4; *New York Clipper*, 29 Jan. 1898, 799; *Kansas City (Mo.) Star*, 7 Jan. 1898, 2; *Kansas City (Mo.) Star*, 8 Jan. 1898, 4; *Phonoscope*, Jan. 1898, 11.

40. Niver, *Early Motion Pictures*, 94; Fielding, *American Newsreel*, 62–63; *NYT*, 28 Nov. 1905, 6; *NYT*, 8 Dec. 1905, 4; *NYT*, 9 Dec. 1905, 7. *An Execution by Hanging* was also referred to as *Execution of a Murderess*. Although both Niver and Fielding assert that Rogers received a reprieve, she was in fact executed.

41. *New York Clipper*, 16 Nov. 1901, 852. The film was popular enough that it continued to be listed in Edison's 1904 and 1907 catalogs.

42. *SN*, 27 Sept. 1901, 8; *NYT*, 28 Sept. 1901, 2; *NYT*, 30 Oct. 1901, 4; *RT*, 30 Oct. 1901, 1.

43. *Edison Films Catalog*, Sept. 1902, 91, MPD; *New York Clipper*, 16 Nov. 1901, 852. As Friedberg (*Window Shopping*, 86–87) argues, cinematic panoramas encapsulated the ideal of modern visuality, a gaze that was mobile and omniscient.

44. *New York Clipper*, 16 Nov. 1901, 852; *Edison Films Catalog*, Sept. 1902, 91, MPD. For the ways in which electrocution was promoted as both a progressive and awe-inspiring method of execution, despite that early attempts produced gruesome results, see Essig, *Edison and the Electric Chair*, and Martschukat, "'Art of Killing by Electricity.'"

45. *NYT*, 30 Oct. 1901, 4; *RT*, 30 Oct. 1901, 1.

46. *VEP*, 29 Oct. 1901, 1; *SN*, 1 Nov. 1901, 3; *SN*, 27 Sept. 1901, 4. Although this statement implied a degree of sectional discord, the southern response to Czolgosz's crime and punishment revealed a sense of commonality and even reconciliation between the North and the South. This sense of national unity worked both ways, of course. As the *Statesboro (Ga.) News* editorial anticipated, American imperialism in the Philippines and the large influx of immigrants from southern and eastern Europe at the turn of the century led many white northerners to express a new understanding for white southerners, as suddenly they themselves were grappling with a racially different and seemingly undisciplined labor force. Just as white northerners consumed lynching photographs and narratives out of morbid fascination and sympathy with southern racial violence, white southerners took interest in Czolgosz's trial, and most probably watched Edison's reproduction of his execution in a similar sort of sympathetic voyeurism. On the other hand, Samuel Burdett questioned in his 1901 antilynching tract *A Test of Lynch Law* (83) why Americans were so horrified by Czolgosz's act of anarchism, "while at the same time overlooking, or rather paying but a casual glance at other acts of anarchy in the land being committed by anarchists no less culpable than Czolgosz, only ours are every-day anarchists belonging to the gang which Judge Lynch presides over."

47. *Lubin Catalog*, 1907, 114, MPD; *Maguire and Company Catalog*, 1898, 29, MPD; Musser, *Edison Motion Pictures*, 191–92.

48. *International Photographic Film Company Catalog*, Winter 1897–98, 18, MPD. I can only assume that the lynching took place in Texas because the code word for exhibitors to use in ordering the film was "Texas."

49. *VEP*, 7 Dec. 1896, 4; *VEP*, 11 Dec. 1896, 4; *VEP*, 12 Dec. 1896, 4; Mississippi Lynchings File, Special Collections, University of Mississippi, Oxford.

50. *VEP*, 11 Dec 1896, 4.

51. Selig, "Cutting Back," 45; *WTH*, 29 Oct. 1904, 5.

52. *Lubin Catalog*, 1907, 114, MPD; *American Film Institute Catalog*, A:57–58. Only a few scenes of this film survive; I have pieced together the plot from my own viewing at the Library of Congress and from the catalog description, which is quite detailed.

53. On the increasing use of blackface in early narrative film, see Stewart, *Migrating to the Movies*, 57–58. On the cinematic "kinship" between minstrelsy and lynching, see Taylor, "Re-birth of the Aesthetic," 28. On minstrelsy and cross-racial desire, see Roediger, *Wages of Whiteness*, and Lott, *Love and Theft*.

54. *Lubin Catalog*, 1907, 115, MPD. The only existing copy of the film breaks off just as the men are setting up the stake.

55. *American Film Institute Catalog*, A:108.

56. The Edison catalog indicated that exhibitors could choose to end or begin the film with this shot. It appears at the end of most existing prints of the film.

57. Although William Selig produced *Tracked by Bloodhounds*, both films were distributed by Edison's Vitagraph Company.

58. Benjamin, "Work of Art in the Age of Mechanical Reproduction"; Kracauer, "Cult of Distraction"; Gunning, "Whole Town's Gawking"; Singer, *Melodrama and Modernity*, 8–9, 59–130; Charney and Schwartz, *Cinema and the Invention of Modern Life*; Doane, "Technology's Body." For a critique of this "modernity thesis," see Bordwell, *On the History of Film Style*, 141–46.

59. Singer, *Melodrama and Modernity*, 59–99; Essig, *Edison and the Electric Chair*, 75; Martschukat, "Art of Killing by Electricity."

60. For the ways in which modernization triggered anxieties over the value and meanings of popular conceptions of manliness, see Bederman, *Manliness and Civilization*, and Kasson, *Houdini, Tarzan, and the Perfect Man*. On the ways in which early cinema represented and eased these white male anxieties over their sense of diminished power, see Doane, "Technology's Body," and Courtney, *Hollywood Fantasies of Miscegenation*, 22.

CHAPTER FIVE

1. *AC*, 7 Dec. 1915, 7; *AC*, 10 Dec. 1915, 14; *AC*, 22 Dec. 1915, 14; *Atlanta Journal*, 7 Dec. 1915, reprinted in Lang, *Birth of a Nation*, 179.

2. Ward Greene also covered Frank's trial for the *Atlanta Journal* and later, in 1936, wrote a fictionalized account of both the trial and the lynching in *Death in the Deep South*, which was made into the antilynching film *They Won't Forget* (Warner Brothers, 1937).

3. Reid also produced a fictional film, *Thou Shall Not Kill*, which was loosely based on Frank's case. On these films, see *American Film Institute Catalog*, F1:925–26; Oney, *And the Dead Shall Rise*, 534–37, 557–58. For brief accounts of the newsweekly and its suppression in various places, including Boston, Denver, and Kansas, see *Motion Picture News*, 11 Sept. 1915, 69; *Motion Picture News*, 18 Sept. 1915, 73; and *Motion Picture News*, 25 Sept. 1915, 80.

4. *AC*, 14 Dec. 1915, 14.

5. *Atlanta Journal*, 28 Nov. 1915, 8; *AC*, 9 Dec. 1915, 2; Stern, "Griffith," 80; Simcovitch, "Impact of Griffith's *Birth of a Nation*," 46. See also Wade, *Fiery Cross*, 140–46.

6. Dixon wrote his play by cobbling together elements from two of his novels, *The Clansman* (1905) and *The Leopard's Spots* (1903). He helped Griffith write and promote the film, which was originally titled *The Clansman*.

7. *Dallas Morning News* quoted in *Atlanta Journal*, 28 Nov. 1915, 6–7.

8. Again, as with lynching itself, most of the evidence of how audiences responded to the film comes from subjective and biased accounts. However, the ways in which these commentators chose to present audiences are in themselves significant. These commentaries created a public image of the audience and, furthermore, guided audiences to understand how they felt or should feel.

9. When the Klansmen save Elsie from the clutches of Silas Lynch, they simply lead him out of his office. Although viewers may have surmised what happened, the film leaves his fate undetermined.

10. Seymour Stern claimed to have seen the deleted footage at a special screening in 1933. He contended audiences saw it in Los Angeles and New York and, for the first half decade after *Birth*'s release, in the South. According to Stern, in the original footage, a Klansman kills Gus by "castration" with a small sword just after the intertitle reading "Guilty"—footage that Stern recalled with exacting detail. This scene was reportedly cut when NAACP pressure induced New York mayor John Purroy Mitchel to convince Griffith to cut a number of scenes, including both the lynching and Gus's raping of Flora. However, although it is puzzling that Stern would fabricate such a detailed description of the lynching, neither the transcript of the mayor's hearing nor NAACP reports on the initial screening of the film make any reference to either of these scenes, and Karl Brown, the assistant cameraman for the film, denied in a 1975 interview that they ever existed. Stern, "Griffith," 122–24; part 2, series A, reel 32, NAACP Papers; Cuniberti, *Birth of a Nation*, 125, 132; Lang, *Birth of a Nation*, 277.

11. Quoted in Jowett, "'Capacity for Evil,'" 22.

12. Cuniberti, *Birth of a Nation*, 132; Stern, "Griffith," 41.

13. Thomas Dixon, in *The Clansman*, was apparently the first to associate the Klan with burning crosses; the original (Reconstruction) Klan never actually did so. Griffith appropriated the idea from Dixon. In a further conflation of reality and entertainment, Simmons borrowed this symbolism for his resurrection of the Klan.

14. Griffith even managed to insert a moral, pro-Prohibition message into the story by having Gus initially hide from the Klan in a saloon populated by African American men. See Silverman, "*Birth of a Nation*: Prohibition Propaganda."

15. On the ways Griffith deployed the "trope of melodrama," see Lang, "*Birth of a Nation*: History, Ideology and Narrative Form," and Williams, *Playing the Race Card*, 96–135.

16. On the ways in which the suffering white woman's body becomes the visual center of the film, see Williams, *Playing the Race Card*, 107. Courtney (*Hollywood Fantasies of Miscegenation*, 65, 76) argues that the violated female body in *Birth* acts

as a stand-in not for the suffering black body but for the frailty of white masculinity and white men's sense of diminished power and authority.

17. In Dixon's novel, Gus rapes Ben Cameron's young sweetheart, Marion Lenoir, and her mother in their home. The women then decide that to ensure that Marion's "name is always sweet and clean," they must take their own lives by jumping off the cliff at Lover's Leap. Both Dixon's play and Griffith's film revise this scenario so that Flora is represented as even more chaste than Dixon's heroine. Changing Marion's name to Flora and making her Ben's younger sister, untainted yet by romance, only enhances her iconic status as that pure "flower" of white womanhood. Moreover, unlike Marion, Flora does not endure the black man's assault but rather flings herself over the cliff, still "clean," before Gus can reach her. Dixon, *Clansman*, 305.

18. E. E. Slosson quoted in David Wark Griffith, "Witch Burners and Motion Pictures," *Chicago Tribune*, 26 May 1915, 14.

19. For discussions of the ways in which Griffith's cinematic technique cannot be studied independently from his white supremacist perspective, see Taylor, "Re-birth of the Aesthetic," 15–37, and Dyer, "Into the Light," 165–76.

20. Dyer, "Into the Light," 172–73.

21. In *The Greaser's Gauntlet*, a mob of cowboys almost lynches the story's hero after he is framed for a theft in a western barroom, but he is saved at the last minute by his sweetheart. This storyline was repeated often in later B westerns. Gunning, *D. W. Griffith and the Origins of American Narrative Film*, 75–78, 95–96; Gaines, "Fire and Desire," 54–59.

22. According to Stern ("Griffith," 14), Griffith did not use black actors for leading parts because he believed there were no qualified black actors at the time.

23. Stern, "Griffith," 41.

24. *Richmond (Va.) News Leader* quoted in Slide, *American Racist*, 61. On the critical and popular response to *The Clansman*, see also Williams, *Playing the Race Card*, 108–11.

25. *Richmond (Va.) News Leader*, 26 Oct. 1915, 11.

26. Williams, *Playing the Race Card*, 123.

27. As Williams (ibid., 111) argues, *Birth* "swayed national sentiment toward white southerners as victims of black 'misrule,' not because it was more vehement than Dixon, but because it drew more effectively on the pathos, action, and melos" of Old South nostalgia.

28. *Dallas Times Herald*, 3 Oct. 1915, 11; *WTH*, 11 Nov. 1915, 7; *Rome (Ga.) Tribune-Herald*, 8 Feb. 1916, 6; *Charlotte (N.C.) Observer*, 16 Nov. 1915, 7; *Gwinnet County (Ga.) Journal*, 13 Dec. 1915, 1.

29. Griffith, "Witch Burners and Motion Pictures," 14.

30. *Dallas Morning News*, 10 Oct. 1915, B4; *Rome (Ga.) Tribune-Herald*, 21 Feb. 1916, 7.

31. Goodson, *Highbrows, Hillbillies, and Hellfire*, 78–107; Waller, *Main Street Amusements*, 96–113, 125–50.

32. Gomery, *Shared Pleasures*, 18–56; Ross, *Working-Class Hollywood*, 11–33; Dixon quoted in Gilmore, "'One of the Meanest Books,'" 99.

33. Merritt ("Dixon, Griffith, and the Southern Legend," 33) argues that Griffith self-consciously revised Dixon's more aristocratic image of southern society so that, in the film, southern society is made conspicuously an "informal folk society."

34. Rogin, "Sword Became a Flashing Vision," 252–58; Blight, *Beyond the Battle-field*, 170–90; Blight, *Race and Reunion*, 394–97; Silber, *Romance of Reunion*.

35. *Chicago Tribune*, 13 June 1915, E1; *Moving Picture World*, 13 Mar. 1915, 1587; *Dallas Times-Herald*, 1 Oct. 1915, 12; *WTH*, 12 Nov. 1915, 4.

36. *Chicago Tribune*, 26 Apr. 1915, 1; *Chicago Tribune*, 15 May 1915, 17. Thompson's ban of the film was eventually overturned in the courts, and the film played with great success in Chicago in June 1915. *Chicago Tribune*, 6 June 1915, A1; *Chicago Tribune*, 13 June 1915, E1.

37. *Boston Herald*, 5 May 1915, part 2, series A, reel 32, NAACP Papers. The NAACP also appealed to sectional accord in its protests against the film. For instance, in a letter to the Los Angeles City Council asking council members to ban the film in that city, the NAACP outlined its objections to the film, beginning with the concern that the film "serves to revive the differences . . . between the North and the South which led to Civil War" and "opens afresh the wounds long healed by time, patience, and forbearance." Los Angeles NAACP to City Council of Los Angeles, 2 Feb. 1915, part 2, series A, reel 32, NAACP Papers.

38. *AC*, 7 Oct. 1915, 9; *Motion Picture News*, 13 Nov. 1915, 69; Goodson, *Highbrows, Hillbillies, and Hellfire*, 103; *Elizabeth City (N.C.) Independent* quoted in *Crisis*, 15 Dec. 1915, 76.

39. Stern, "Griffith," 69; *Columbia (S.C.) State*, 22 Nov. 1915, 5; *Charlotte (N.C.) Observer*, 11 Nov. 1915, 8; *Charlotte (N.C.) Observer*, 13 Nov. 1915, 8; *Columbia (S.C.) State*, 14 Nov. 1915, 26; *Macon (Ga.) Weekly Telegraph*, 29 Sept. 1915, 9.

40. *Rome (Ga.) Tribune-Herald*, 13 Jan. 1916, 6; *Rome (Ga.) Tribune-Herald*, 30 Jan. 1916, 5; *Rome (Ga.) Tribune-Herald*, 6 Feb. 1916, 6; *Rome (Ga.) Tribune-Herald*, 9 Feb. 1916, 3; Aycock, *All Roads to Rome*, 205.

41. *Charlotte (N.C.) Observer*, 11 Nov. 1915, 3; *Charlotte (N.C.) Observer*, 29 Feb. 1916, 8; *SN*, 29 Nov. 1915, 1; *Stone County (Miss.) Enterprise*, 20 Jan. 1917, 1; Moore, "South Carolina's Reaction to the Photoplay," 30; Stern, "Griffith," 68, 70, 76. An ad in the *Rome (Ga.) Tribune-Herald* (8 Feb. 1916, 6) announced that "hundreds [were] coming from" the small towns of "Cedartown, Dalton and Cartersville, etc" to the production.

42. *Dallas Times Herald*, 15 Oct. 1916, 6; *Asheville (N.C.) Citizen* quoted in *Columbia (S.C.) State*, 7 Nov. 1915, 27. On the ways most audiences transitioned into more quiet and disciplined spectators as bourgeois norms came to dominate movie spectatorship, see Doherty, "This Is Where We Came In," and Staiger, *Perverse Spectators*, 44–57.

43. Lindsay, *Art of the Moving Picture*, 40; Stern, "Griffith," 69.

44. *Rome (Ga.) Tribune-Herald*, 9 Feb. 1916, 3; *Charlotte (N.C.) Observer*, 16 Nov. 1915, 7. On rebel yells, see also *WTH*, 12 Nov. 1915, 4, and reviews reprinted in Stern, "Griffith," 107.

45. Lindsay, *Art of the Moving Picture*, 47; *Asheville (N.C.) Citizen* reprinted in

Columbia (S.C.) State, 7 Nov. 1915, 27. Theater owners often reprinted reviews of a film and reports of audience enthusiasm for it in their local papers to advertise the film.

46. *Charlotte (N.C.) Observer*, 16 Nov. 1915, 7; *WTH*, 12 Nov. 1915, 4; *Richmond (Va.) News Leader*, 30 Oct. 1915, quoted in *Atlanta Journal*, 28 Nov. 1915, 6.

47. Moore, "South Carolina's Reaction to the Photoplay," 30; *Crisis*, June 1916, 87. The incident took place in Lafayette, Indiana, but the story, apparently taken from the local paper, made special mention that the perpetrator had recently moved there from Kentucky.

48. Stern, "Griffith," 74, 206; Simcovitch, "Impact of Griffith's *Birth of a Nation*," 48, 51.

49. Simmons and Ramsaye quoted in Simcovitch, "Impact of Griffith's *Birth of a Nation*," 46. It should be noted that the 1920s Klan publicly disavowed lynching and violence of any sort, although individual members were regularly implicated in nonlethal terrorist acts against not only African Americans but also immigrants, Catholics, and Jews, as well as white Protestants who they believed had flouted moral decency. On the second Klan in the South, see MacLean, *Behind the Mask of Chivalry*; Feldman, *Politics, Society and the Klan in Alabama*; and Newton, *Invisible Empire*.

50. On black-led protests against *Birth*, see Cripps, *Slow Fade to Black*, 41–69; Staiger, "*Birth of a Nation*: Reconsidering Its Reception"; and Gaines, *Fire and Desire*, 219–41.

51. James Weldon Johnson, "*Uncle Tom's Cabin* and *The Clansman*," quoted in Everett, *Returning the Gaze*, 69.

52. On the range of black opinion on the film, see Cripps, *Slow Fade to Black*, 56–63, and Everett, *Returning the Gaze*, 81–82. Cities that prohibited the film included Des Moines, Iowa; Gary, Indiana; Las Cruces, New Mexico; and Tacoma, Washington. In 1918, on a second tour of the production, West Virginia banned all exhibitions. Miscellaneous correspondence, part 2, series A, reel 33, NAACP Papers; *Crisis*, Dec. 1915, 85–86; *Crisis*, June 1916, 87.

53. Los Angeles NAACP to City Council of Los Angeles, 2 Feb. 1915; Ovington, *Walls Came Tumbling Down*, 128. The beginning and end of the Gus and Flora rape scene were subsequently edited out of versions shown in Boston, and, Ovington wrote, "the audience wondered why the girl was found dead." The scene was simply shortened in New York. No doubt for strategic purposes, the NAACP placed white officers and members, like Ovington, at the forefront of their campaign against the film. In its letters to public officials and to the press, it commonly included testimony against the film from prominent white progressives, like Jane Addams, and from white critics' reviews in leading journals, such as Francis Hackett's indictment of the film in the *New Republic*.

54. NAACP to John Purroy Mitchel, 19 Mar. 1915, part 2, series A, reel 32, NAACP Papers; Kellogg, *NAACP*, 121; Everett, *Returning the Gaze*, 103; *Crisis*, June 1916, 87.

55. The board had initially advised the Epoch Corporation, the film's production company and distributor, to delete certain objectionable scenes, but it reversed its

decision soon after, much to the dismay of the NAACP. See National Board of Censorship to the NAACP, 15 Mar. 1915; NAACP to John Purroy Mitchel, 19 Mar. 1915; 1 Apr. 1915; and NAACP to local branches, memorandum, 7 Apr. 1915, all in part 2, series A, reel 32, NAACP Papers.

56. Quoted in Rosenbloom, "Between Reform and Regulation," 311.

57. *Mutual Film Corp. v. Industrial Commission of Ohio*, 236 U.S. 230 (1915). On the significance of *Mutual v. Ohio*, see Jowett, "'Capacity for Evil,'" and Rosenbloom, "Between Reform and Regulation," 316–17.

58. *Dallas Times-Herald*, 8 July 1910, 2. After the fight, race riots and fighting broke out in a number of cities, and white mobs killed at least eighteen African Americans in fits of racial vengeance for Johnson's victory. In Dallas, for instance, a white man stabbed a black man, Charlie Blankenship, who had "hurrahed for Johnson" after the match. See *Dallas Times-Herald*, 6 July 1910, 3. Many public authorities feared that the film of the prizefight would cause more public harm than the fight itself. Although many simply expressed alarm that the pictures could incite more violence against blacks, the thought that moving pictures of the imposing figure of Johnson pummeling a white man would be projected repeatedly on theater screens caused particular discomfort to many whites and, indeed, led to a congressional ban on all interstate transport of films of prizefights. See Streible, "Race and the Reception of Jack Johnson Fight Films," and Courtney, *Hollywood Fantasies of Miscegenation*, 50–61.

59. As Waller (*Main Street Amusements*, 154) shows, the editor of a black newsweekly in Lexington, Kentucky, challenged city authorities on just these grounds.

60. Griffith, "Witch Burners and Motion Pictures," 14. Griffith in this piece phrases Wilson's quote as "like teaching history with lightning," a significant revision. Dixon claimed that Wilson made this remark after a screening at the White House in February 1915, though it is more likely apocryphal. Griffith also acted completely incredulous that his film might incite race hatred or violence. "That is like saying I am against children, as they were our children, whom we loved and cared for all our lives," he once said. Rather, he claimed that "more race prejudice would be aroused by the suppression of the *Birth of a Nation* than by its exhibition." Griffith also insinuated that the NAACP lacked legitimacy because it, as an organization, was, above all else, concerned with permitting and encouraging marriage between blacks and whites. See Cripps, *Slow Fade to Black*, 52, 64; Williams, *Playing the Race Card*, 98; *Chicago Tribune*, 6 June 1915, 1; and *New York Globe*, 10 Apr. 1915, reprinted in Lang, *Birth of a Nation*, 169.

61. *Crisis*, June 1915, 69–71; Los Angeles NAACP to City Council of Los Angeles, 2 Feb. 1915. *Birth* also energized the black historical profession, as it made conspicuous the need for credible and objective histories of slavery and Reconstruction to counter the film's spurious and distorted historical claims. The film, for instance, spurred Carter Woodson to establish the Association for the Study of Negro Life and History in 1915 and precipitated the founding of the *Journal of Negro History* the following year. See Brundage, *Southern Past*, 154–57.

62. Merritt, "Dixon, Griffith, and the Southern Legend," 26–27; Staiger, "*Birth*

of a Nation: Reconsidering Its Reception," 198; Gaines, *Fire and Desire*, 219–20; Stewart, *Migrating to the Movies*, 93–154.

63. *Biloxi (Miss.) Daily Herald*, 7 June 1916, 3. Black citizens took their case to city authorities in, for instance, Richmond and Norfolk, Virginia; Asheville, North Carolina; and Lexington, Kentucky. See *Richmond (Va.) Planet*, 30 Oct. 1915, 8; *Richmond (Va.) News Leader*, 23 Oct. 1915, 1–2; *Motion Picture World*, 9 Oct. 1915, 296; *Charlotte (N.C.) Observer*, 10 Oct. 1915, 5; and Waller, *Main Street Amusements*, 151–60.

64. *Richmond (Va.) Planet*, 30 Oct. 1915, 8; *Charlotte (N.C.) Observer*, 18 Nov. 1915, 4.

65. Quigless quoted in Gilmore, "'One of the Meanest Books,'" 99.

66. *Chicago Defender*, 31 Jan. 1931, 5.

67. *Chicago Defender*, 21 Mar. 1931, 3. For the complex ways in which African American viewers have adopted an "oppositional" or "reconstructive" gaze in the face of white-dominated cinema, see Stewart, *Migrating to the Movies*, 100; Diawara, "Black Spectatorship"; and hooks, "Oppositional Gaze."

68. National Association for the Advancement of Colored People, "The Branch Bulletin," Nov. 1918, 50, part 7, series A, reel 1, NAACP Papers; *Columbia (S.C.) State*, 25 May 1918, 2.

69. *Chicago Defender*, 14 Feb. 1931, 1; *Chicago Defender*, 21 Mar. 1931, 3. On the addition of sound to the film, see *Los Angeles Times*, 8 June 1930, B12. Southern white groups wrote to Will Hays, the head of the Motion Picture Producers and Distributors of America, Hollywood's self-regulatory agency that oversaw the moral content of all films, to ask him to suppress the film. The inclusion of sound was a particular worry for some. Although the new version included no dialogue, one spokesperson for the Woman's Missionary Council wrote, "We fear its effect with added emotional appeal of the human voice." Quoted in *Chicago Defender*, 22 Nov. 1930, 5.

70. Du Bois quoted in Archer, *Black Images in the American Theatre*, 197. On the impact of the NAACP campaign, see also Gaines, *Fire and Desire*, 230.

71. There is an extensive literature on the ways in which *Within Our Gates*, particularly in its graphic representations of lynchings and its depictions of white male exploitation of black women, counteracted the images of black sexual assault and white righteousness projected in *Birth*. See, for instance, Gaines, *Fire and Desire*, 161–95; Stewart, *Migrating to the Movies*, 226–44; and Markowitz, *Legacies of Lynching*, 36–41. Micheaux remade *The Gunsaulus Mystery*, with sound, in 1935, as *Murder in Harlem*. On these films, see Bernstein, "Oscar Micheaux and Leo Frank." African American support for censorship came to haunt Micheaux when he found that his films, especially *Within Our Gates*, became the object of censorship in cities and states around the country. In Chicago, for instance, still reeling from the 1919 riots, both black and white citizens feared that exhibition of the film would precipitate further rioting. Micheaux's films were banned in Virginia and, most likely, other southern states, although *Within Our Gates* did play in New Orleans. See Gaines, *Fire and Desire*, 161–62, and Smith, "Patrolling the Boundaries of Race."

CHAPTER SIX

1. Studies of this lynching include Hale, *Making Whiteness*, 215–22; Carrigan, *Making of a Lynching Culture*, 1–3, 189–206; SoRelle, "'Waco Horror'"; and Bernstein, *First Waco Horror*. See also *WTH*, 15 May 1916, 1; "Waco Horror," *Crisis*, S1–S8; and Freeman, "Waco Lynching." Estimates of the size of the crowd vary between 10,000 and 15,000 people. Although the evidence does suggest that Washington committed the murder, the police probably coerced him into confessing sexual assault, of which no apparent physical evidence existed and no mention was made in the trial.

2. *NYT*, 17 May 1916, 10; Bernstein, *First Waco Horror*, 54–62, 76–77.

3. On Waco's history, see "Waco Horror," *Crisis*, S1; SoRelle, "'Waco Horror,'" 518–19; Texas State Historical Association, *New Handbook of Texas*; McSwain, *Bench and Bar of Waco*; Conger, *Highlights of Waco History*; and Bernstein, *First Waco Horror*, 7–13, 21–28, 58. On the Sunday showing controversy and on fears of black crime, see *Waco (Tex.) News-Tribune*, 3 Jan. 1916, 1; *Waco (Tex.) News-Tribune*, 19 Feb. 1916, 9; *Waco (Tex.) News-Tribune*, 8 Mar. 1916, 1; and *Waco (Tex.) News-Tribune*, 1 Apr. 1916, 8. On Sank Majors's lynching, see *WTH*, 8 Aug. 1905, 1. On the Temple, Texas, lynching, see Carrigan, *Making of a Lynching Culture*, 185–87, and *Crisis*, Jan. 1916, 145.

4. Just after Washington's confession on 9 May, a mob from Robinson arrived in Waco with the express purpose of abducting Washington from the jail and exacting personal vengeance, claiming that their womenfolk had directed them to do their "duty" as "citizens." They desisted when the sheriff told them that he had removed Washington to Dallas for safekeeping and when, according to Freeman, they were promised that Washington would waive his legal rights and be executed immediately after the trial. *WTH*, 10 May 1916, 7.

5. Freeman, "Waco Lynching," 4–5, 9, 13, 15; Bernstein, *First Waco Horror*, 148–58. According to Freeman ("Waco Lynching," 21), another man, W. B. Steele of the Mallory Steamship Company, was with Gildersleeve when he took the pictures.

6. "Waco Horror," *Crisis*, S7–S8; *Waco (Tex.) News-Tribune*, 31 May 1916, 5; *WTH*, 15 May 1916, 1; Sorelle, "'Waco Horror,'" 528; Bernstein, *First Waco Horror*, 145. The *Waco (Tex.) News-Tribune* (17 May 1916, 6) did condemn the lynching but added that the "negro deserved death and by every consideration" and reminded readers that "the sacredness of our womanhood is a consideration that overshadows all others." On the ways in which the language southern newspapers used to describe lynch mobs changed according to their support or condemnation of mob violence, see Jean, "'Warranted' Lynchings."

7. Freeman, "Waco Lynching," 15, 21; "Waco Horror," *Crisis*, S6.

8. Bernstein, *First Waco Horror*, 161–72; *Nation*, 3 Aug. 1916, 101–2.

9. *AC*, 14 July 1916, 8; *Nation*, 3 Aug. 1916, 101.

10. Carrigan (*Making of a Lynching Culture*, 189–98) argues that the Waco lynching was a turning point in lynching's history in Texas. After Waco, state leaders no longer publicly supported or encouraged lynching, and Texans increasingly attempted to repress public memories of lynching. Waldrep (*Many Faces of Judge Lynch*, 155), on

the other hand, downplays the impact of the Waco lynching, noting that in most major papers, it was relegated to back pages as a small story and was treated as largely a local problem. Yet, as Carrigan points out, since most lynchings were not reported beyond their localities, that so many papers across the country covered it all, and that denunciations of the lynching were prominent in the liberal media, is itself notable.

11. On antilynching activism, see Brown, *Eradicating This Evil*; Grant, *Antilynching Movement*; Zangrando, *NAACP Crusade against Lynching*; Ferrell, *Nightmare and Dream*; and Jonas, *Freedom's Sword*, 1–66.

12. See part 7, series A, reels 2, 4, 5, 7, and 9, NAACP Papers. The NAACP frequently received correspondence from people wanting copies of the images they had seen in the *Crisis* or in publicity materials either to reprint in their own publications or to show in lectures.

13. Most historians see this form of racial liberalism and its emphasis on human rights as emerging in the post–World War II era, especially as it came to dominate both intellectual thinking on race and civil rights activism in the 1940s and 1950s. The work of antilynching activists in the 1930s, however, in many ways anticipated this broader intellectual and political shift. These activists also found important allies in organizations and media associated with the Popular Front in this period, although their popular rhetoric tended to downplay any Marxist or socialist interpretations of racism and lynching. On racial liberalism in the post–World War II period, see King, *Race, Culture, and the Intellectuals*, and Feldstein, *Motherhood in Black and White*.

14. For the ways in which photography "indexes" the past, particularly when that past is too terrible to comprehend, see Barthes, *Camera Lucida*, 28; Zelizer, *Remembering to Forget*, 10, 84–85; and Taylor, *Body Horror*.

15. Wells-Barnett, *Red Record*, 118–19; Raiford, "'Imprisoned in a Luminous Glare,'" 85–94. There is substantial literature on Wells's antilynching campaigns. See, for instance, Bederman, *Manliness and Civilization*, 45–76; Royster, introduction to Wells-Barnett, *Southern Horrors and Other Writings*, 1–41; Waldrep, *Many Faces of Judge Lynch*, 103–26; and Goldsby, *Spectacular Secret*, 43–104. Because reproducing photographs was an expensive process in the late nineteenth century, Wells and other black journalists more commonly printed etchings or drawings of lynchings to illustrate their antilynching narratives and editorials in newsprint and pamphlets. See, for example, Benjamin, *Southern Outrages*, 45, and Burdett, *Test of Lynch Law*, 17–19. In the 1880s, editor John Mitchell, an outspoken opponent of lynching, began including weekly lynching statistics in his paper, the *Richmond (Va.) Planet*, accompanied with an illustration of a lynched black man hanging from a tree. Alexander, *Race Man*, 41.

16. *AC*, 29 July 1894, 8.

17. *Crisis*, Jan. 1912, 109–10. For other references to the taking of lynching photographs, see *Crisis*, Dec. 1911, 60–61, and *Crisis*, June 1915, 71. Similarly, Wells reproduced the back side of the Clanton lynching postcard in *A Red Record*. The postcard had been sent to novelist and civil rights advocate Albion Tourgée with an inscription signed only by "The Committee." The message, which mocked Tourgée's own

words, noted that the "S.O.B." in the photograph was a "good specimen of your 'Black Christians hung by White Heathens.'" Wells did not provide any details about the lynching, even the victim's name. She noted only that the card was sent to Tourgée and that it was "the exact reproduction" of a photograph "taken at the scene."

18. *Crisis*, Mar. 1912, 209.

19. *Crisis*, Dec. 1911, 70–74.

20. *Crisis*, Jan. 1912, 122; National Association for the Advancement of Colored People, *Some of the 51 Lynchings Which We Have Recorded during the Past Six Months — and There Are Others* (1911), part 7, series A, reel 1, NAACP Papers.

21. Similarly, as Waldrep (*Many Faces of Judge Lynch*, 151–83) and Markowitz (*Legacies of Lynching*, xvii–xix, 1–31) have pointed out, by the 1930s, antilynching activists had successfully transformed the term "lynching" into a metaphor, a discursive touchstone for terror and injustice detached from any particular physical action or locality.

22. The caption indicates that Hughes was lynched on 17 May 1930, though the lynching actually took place on 9 May.

23. *Baltimore Afro-American*, 28 Dec. 1934, 3. The full photograph also appeared in the *Chicago Defender* (17 May 1930, 1), with the headline "Godless America!" — inverting the semblance of a crucified Christ that the image evokes. The NAACP originally wanted to include photography in its 1935 antilynching art exhibit and even offered a prize for the best photograph of a lynching or lynch mob. For unspecified reasons, photographs were not included in the final exhibition, although a news agency did send in a lynching photograph from San Jose, California, that had been widely published throughout the country. Although the black press was able to recontextualize photographs in its pages, exhibition organizers presumably recognized the difficulties in assessing a photograph's artistic worth when so many were created from the perpetrator's point of view. See "Art Exhibit, 1934–36, correspondence," and "Exhibit Catalogue: An Art Commentary on Lynching," both in part 7, series B, reel 2, NAACP Papers. See also "An Art Exhibit against Lynching," *Crisis*, Apr. 1935, 106; Apel, *Imagery of Lynching*, 83–131; Vendryes, "Hanging on Their Walls"; and Park, "Lynching and Anti-lynching."

24. *Chicago Defender*, 21 May 1927, 3.

25. *Chicago Defender*, 4 June 1927, 2; *Chicago Defender*, 9 May 1936, 1. The image of John Carter's lynching was also reproduced in Haldeman-Julius's *Story of a Lynching*, a 1927 antilynching book.

26. Carlebach, *American Photojournalism Comes of Age*, 5–12, 184–89; Brennen and Hardt, *Picturing the Past*, 2–3, 18–19.

27. In one of the first professional guidebooks of modern advertising, Scott (*Psychology of Advertising*, 82–83) argued that consumers acted not as individuals but as members of a crowd. In fact, he likened the hypnotic or suggestive effect of advertising to that of mob psychology, in which "the crowd is a 'lynching party'" whose influence the individual can hardly resist. On the rise of modern advertising, see also Craig, "Fact, Public Opinion, and Persuasion"; Ohmann, *Selling Culture*, 81–117; and Lears, *Fables of Abundance*.

28. Raiford, "'Imprisoned in a Luminous Glare,'" 95–97; John Ross to W. E. B. Du

Bois, 18 Apr. 1916, part 7, series A, reel 1, NAACP Papers; Roy Nash to John Ross, 20 Apr. 1916, part 7, series A, reel 1, NAACP Papers.

29. "NAACP Publishes Photograph of Florida Lynching," part 7, series A, reel 8, NAACP Papers; antilynching pamphlet (1935), part 7, series A, reel 9, NAACP Papers; Walter White to the *Chicago Defender*, telegram, 18 May 1936, part 7, series A, reel 11, NAACP Papers; Charlie [last name not given] to Walter White, 7 May 1936, part 7, series A, reel 11, NAACP Papers. For correspondence regarding antilynching stories in *Look* (in 1938) and *Life* (in 1937), including, in the latter case, an inventory of lynching photographs that the NAACP could provide, see part 7, series A, reel 5, NAACP Papers.

30. *New York Amsterdam News*, 3 Nov. 1934, 1. Although over sixteen antilynching bills were written in the early 1920s, only the Dyer bill reached a vote; it passed in the House but was blocked in the Senate. Lynching opponents were more successful in the mid-1930s, however, as a number of bills came to votes and two passed the House. Again, these bills failed to overcome Senate filibustering.

31. *NYT*, 14 Apr. 1937, 52; Howard Kester, "Lynching by Blow Torch," part 7, series A, reel 13, NAACP Papers; *Time*, 26 Apr. 1937, 17; Zangrando, *NAACP Crusade against Lynching*, 147; *Chicago Tribune*, 5 Dec. 1937, H2. Like others before it, the Wagner–Van Nuys bill was eventually stymied by southern filibustering.

32. Arthur Raper, the North Carolina sociologist who wrote the 1933 study *The Tragedy of Lynching*, for instance, believed, contrary to most other white southern liberals, that prolynching sentiment was so widespread in the South that only such a dramatic and symbolic intervention as federal antilynching legislation could uproot it. See Sosna, *In Search of the Silent South*, 32–33.

33. *Crisis*, June 1936, 172–73.

34. *Atlanta Daily World*, 30 Nov. 1933, 1. The pictures not only appear like drawings but were altered to conceal Thurmond's nudity.

35. These concerns arose when photographs in James Allen's *Without Sanctuary* collection toured the country in a series of exhibitions, were reproduced in book form, and were exhibited on the Internet between 2000 and 2005. See, for example, Wypijewski, "Executioner's Song"; Hale, "Exhibition Review"; and Sontag, *Regarding the Pain of Others*, 91–92. For an excellent discussion of the ways in which public exhibitions of *Without Sanctuary* addressed these difficulties as well as the critical response to them, see Apel, "On Looking."

36. *Crisis*, Feb. 1937, 61; *Crisis*, Mar. 1937, 93. Goldsby (*Spectacular Secret*, 250–51) asserts that both James Weldon Johnson and W. E. B. Du Bois were faced with moral doubts that reprinting photographs in NAACP pamphlets and in the *Crisis* would risk reengaging in the violence, but there is no solid evidence for this claim.

37. As Bederman (*Manliness and Civilization*, 45–60) has shown, Ida B. Wells engaged in this rhetorical inversion, trumping white southerners' claims to civilized superiority by highlighting the brutality of lynching violence.

38. *New York Amsterdam News*, 22 Oct. 1938, 1; *Chicago Defender*, 25 Nov. 1933, 24; *Pittsburgh Courier*, 17 May 1930, 1.

39. *Chicago Defender*, 10 June 1916, 8; *Chicago Defender*, 17 May 1930, 1; *Crisis*,

Sept. 1934, 277. The *Crisis* reprinted this advertisement repeatedly in its pages through the 1930s.

40. "Mexican Daily Features Neal Lynching Report," part 7, series A, reel 9, NAACP Papers; *Chicago Tribune*, 15 Apr. 1937, 2; *New Republic*, 13 Dec. 1933, 117. For Nazi attitudes on the U.S. South, see Apel, *Imagery of Lynching*, 56–57, and Grill and Jenkins, "Nazis and the American South in the 1930s."

41. *Chicago Defender*, 10 June 1916, 8; *Chicago Defender*, 7 Feb. 1942, 14.

42. This tactic had a longer history, of course. Abolitionists, for instance, regularly insisted not only that slavery was cruel and unjust to slaves but that it corroded and debased slaveholders.

43. Antilynching pamphlet (1935), part 7, series A, reel 9, NAACP Papers.

44. *Crisis*, Jan. 1935, 7, 18. On turn-of-the-century notions of civilization, see Bederman, *Manliness and Civilization*, 21–31. On the use of psychology to conceptualize race hatred, see Garcia, "Psychology Comes to Harlem."

45. Apel (*Imagery of Lynching*, 42) also discusses the incongruity of this woman's presence in the photograph. Raiford ("'Imprisoned in a Luminous Glare,'" 54–55) addresses African Americans' appearance in select lynching photographs as evidence of a visible but unspoken attention to the effects of lynchings on black communities.

46. NAACP to Governor Tom Rye, telegram, 24 May 1918, part 7, series A, reel 1, NAACP Papers; *Chicago Defender*, 8 Sept. 1917, 1.

47. Williams, Diary of a Mad Law Professor, 9; Baker, "Under the Rope," 322, 331. On memorial photography, see Ruby, *Secure the Shadow*, 51–99. For the popularity of memorial photography in black communities as a site of mourning, see McDowell, "Viewing the Remains," 153–77.

48. Ruby, *Secure the Shadow*, 63–65; Farrell, *Inventing the American Way of Death*, 57.

49. Madison, *Lynching in the Heartland*, 113, 115–17.

50. *Atlanta Daily World*, 30 Nov. 1933, 1; *Atlanta Daily World*, 29 Apr. 1936, 1; *Atlanta Daily World*, 30 Apr. 1936, 1. The *Richmond (Va.) Planet* did reproduce the NAACP pamphlet "The Waco Horror" (15 July 1916, 1), which included photos of the lynching, but did not reproduce some of the most circulated lynching photographs throughout the 1930s. As noted above, the paper regularly printed, as an antilynching advertisement, a drawing based on a lynching photograph with the caption, "Many of these gastly sights last week. Where are the G-Men?" See, for example, *Richmond (Va.) Planet*, 3 Aug. 1935, 1. On the other hand, the *Norfolk (Va.) Journal and Guide* published the Acme photograph of Claude Neal's lynched body in 1934, as well as an image of the Sherman, Texas, courthouse that was burned during the lynching of George Hughes in 1930. More significant, the *Norfolk (Va.) Journal and Guide* published four photographs from the lynching of Govan Ward in Louisburg, North Carolina, a lynching that would have directly affected the paper's local readership. *Norfolk (Va.) Journal and Guide*, 3 Nov. 1934, 1; *Norfolk (Va.) Journal and Guide*, 17 May 1930, 1; *Norfolk (Va.) Journal and Guide*, 3 Aug. 1935, 1.

51. An image of George Hughes, lynched in Sherman, Texas, in 1930, handcuffed

between two law officers appeared in the *Chicago Defender* (17 May 1930, 8), and another image of the local sheriff restraining Hughes with a chain, like a leash, appeared in the *Pittsburgh Courier* (17 May 1938, 1). The *Chicago Defender* (17 Jan. 1931, 2) also printed an image of Raymond Gunn, lynched in Marysville, Missouri, in 1931, in police custody. The *Atlanta Daily World* (20 Apr. 1937, 1) reproduced the mug shot of Roosevelt Townes, lynched in Duck Hill, Mississippi, in 1937, with the title "His Death Spurs Anti-lynch Law"—when most papers were publishing images of Townes's body chained to a tree in the process of being tortured. In a rare instance, the *St. Joseph (Mo.) News-Press* (12 Jan. 1931, 1) included a portrait photograph of Gunn, inset into an image of the mob preparing to burn the schoolhouse, in its coverage of the lynching.

52. *Atlanta Daily World*, 29 Apr. 1936, 1; *Atlanta Daily World*, 30 Apr. 1936, 1. The *Chicago Defender* (31 Jan. 1942, 1, 14) did include a picture of Cleo Wright's widow, Ardella Wright, in a series of photos of "scenes and principals" relating to Wright's lynching in Sikeston, Missouri, in 1942. It also included a crude pen and ink headshot of Wright.

53. Madison, *Lynching in the Heartland*, 113. Some nearby towns' newspapers did print the photograph, as did Indianapolis's black paper, the *Recorder*.

54. *Memphis News-Scimitar*, 21 Sept. 1925, 1, 5; *Washington Post*, 13 Aug. 1930, 2; *Chicago Tribune*, 30 Oct. 1934, 10. The *Chicago Tribune* (27 July 1903, 3) printed a photographic collage of the lynching of John Metcalf and the ensuing riot in Danville, Illinois, that included pictures of Metcalf's jail cell and the telegraphic pole from which he was hanged, but no pictures of the lynching itself. Although the *St. Louis Post-Dispatch* (13 Jan. 1931, 1, 10) did print photographs of the burning schoolhouse that incinerated alleged murderer Raymond Gunn, it did not include any pictures of Gunn himself. The *Kansas City (Mo.) Star* (12 Jan. 1931, 3) chose to print only images of the schoolhouse before it was burned, as well as a photograph of Velma Colter, the white schoolteacher whom Gunn allegedly murdered.

55. *Chicago Tribune*, 1 Oct. 1919, 3; *New York World*, clipping, part 7, series A, reel 11, NAACP Papers.

56. *Time*, 26 Apr. 1937, 16–17; *Life*, 26 Apr. 1937, 26; *Chicago Tribune*, 5 Dec. 1937, H2. The *Memphis Press-Scimitar* (14 Apr. 1937, 2) also printed the image, "only in hope that it will cause such a feeling of revulsion that there will never be another like it."

57. Farrell, *Swift Justice*; *San Francisco Chronicle*, 27 Nov. 1933, 1; *Los Angeles Times*, 28 Nov. 1933, 1; *NYT*, 27 Nov. 1933, 1. Estimates of the size of the crowd differed; according to news reports, the crowd numbered between 6,000 and 10,000 people, but according to FBI reports, it numbered about 3,000. The lynching of Holmes and Thurmond coincided with two other events in late 1933 that also focused national attention on lynching. Just days after the San Jose lynching, a white mob in St. Joseph, Missouri, lynched Lloyd Warner, a black man arrested for the rape of a white woman, by hanging him before a crowd of thousands and then soaking him in gasoline and lighting him on fire. Warner's lynching drew special notice in the national press because of its sensational brutality, but also because it followed so closely on the heels of the San Jose lynching and replayed some of the events. As in San Jose,

the mob used a battering ram to storm the jail and abduct Warner, battling local police, who, like their counterparts in San Jose, attempted to control the crowd with tear gas. Meanwhile, in Maryland, a riot broke out at a state armory where national guardsmen were holding four suspects in the lynching of George Armwood, a black man accused of raping a white woman. Witnesses had come forward and identified nine men who had taken part in Armwood's lynching, perpetrated five weeks earlier in Princess Anne, Maryland, without much national coverage. When the local district attorney refused to arrest those implicated, Governor Albert Ritchie intervened by arresting four of the men. Nearly a thousand white citizens charged the armory, battling national guardsmen, until a local judge freed the men—an unusual occurrence that drew flocks of reporters and photographers from major presses to the scene. There was also a lynching in Kountze, Texas, the following week, on 8 December. A white mob dragged the body of a black man, David Gregory, accused of raping and killing a white woman, through the streets of the town before setting him on fire. Perhaps because the furor over the San Jose lynching had died down, this story, though covered in the black press and local papers, did not make national news. *Chicago Tribune*, 28 Nov. 1933, 1; *Chicago Tribune*, 29 Nov. 1933, 1; *NYT*, 28 Nov. 1933, 1; *NYT*, 29 Nov. 1933, 1; *Chicago Defender*, 9 Dec. 1933, 1; *Houston Post*, 8 Dec. 1933, 1.

58. Newspapers that printed photographs of the mob in action included the *San Francisco Chronicle*, 27 Nov. 1933, 1; *Los Angeles Times*, 28 Nov. 1933, 1–3; *Los Angeles Herald*, 27 Nov. 1933, 1–3; *San Francisco Examiner*, 28 Nov. 1933, 1, 13; and *New York American*, 28 Nov. 1933, 1, 5. For images of the postcard and souvenir booklet, see Allen, *Without Sanctuary*, plates 81–84, and *New York Journal*, 27 Nov. 1933, 1, 3.

59. Farrell, *Swift Justice*, 249–50. Surprisingly, *Time*, which began printing more photographs in its pages at just this time to compete with other tabloid-style magazines, received no complaints from readers over its decision, although it had received complaints the previous week, when it published discreet photographs from a nudist wedding. *Time*, 4 Dec. 1933, 21; *Time*, 11 Dec. 1933, 15, 45; *Time*, 18 Dec. 1933, 3–4. *Time* also made note of a number of newspapers nationwide that had published nude photographs from the lynching, an indication that such publications were unusual and noteworthy. For examples, see *New York American*, 28 Nov. 1933, 8, and *Knoxville (Tenn.) Journal*, 28 Nov. 1933, 1. The *Newark Star-Eagle* (28 Nov. 1933, 4) painted underwear on Thurmond's body, but it noted in the caption that the mob had stripped Thurmond's trousers off.

Some papers, including several southern papers, did choose to publish a photograph from Lloyd Warner's lynching that shows the white mob, their backs to the camera, surrounding the tree from which Warner was hanged. Although Warner's burned body lay at the bottom of the tree, it is not visible in the image. That the image was printed at all was due, no doubt, to the fact that it followed so closely on the heels of the San Jose lynching, as these same papers did not print photographs from any other high-profile lynchings in the 1930s. See *Kansas City (Mo.) Star*, 29 Nov. 1933, 3; *Knoxville (Tenn.) Journal*, 1 Dec. 1933, 1; *Meridian (Miss.) Star*, 2 Dec. 1933, 1; and *Washington Afro-American*, 9 Dec. 1933, 2.

60. Farrell, *Swift Justice*, 250–51; *San Jose News* quoted in ibid., 251.

61. Senator Costigan, a Democrat from Colorado, introduced his bill to make lynching a federal crime in January 1934, the first of a string of such proposed legislation throughout the 1930s. On the link between the San Jose lynching and renewed calls for antilynching legislation, see, for example, *Chicago Defender*, 2 Dec. 1933, 1, 4; *New York Amsterdam News*, 29 Nov. 1933, 1; and *Atlanta Daily World*, 29 Nov. 1933, 6.

62. *Gavagan Anti-lynching Bill*, HR 1507, 75th Cong., 1st sess., *Congressional Record*, Apr. 1937, 4543–44, series 1.1.2, folder 17, Jesse Daniel Ames Papers, Southern Historical Collection, University of North Carolina at Chapel Hill.

63. Pronouncement from the Georgia Association of Women for the Prevention of Lynching, 14. Jan. 1931, series 1.1.1, folder 2, Ames Papers; Southern Commission on the Study of Lynching, *Lynchings and What They Mean*, 61. On southern liberal positions against lynching, see also Sosna, *In Search of the Silent South*, 30–31.

64. Ultimately its identification with the South led the ASWPL, in particular, to diverge bitterly from the NAACP over federal antilynching legislation. See Hall, *Revolt against Chivalry*, 193–253, and Waldrep, *Many Faces of Judge Lynch*, 127–50.

65. Odum, "Lynchings, Fears, and Folkways," 720; Sosna, *In Search of the Silent South*, 31. For a thorough analysis of white southern opposition to antilynching legislation, see Rable, "South and the Politics of Anti-Lynching Legislation."

66. ASWPL meeting minutes, 1 Nov. 1930, series 1.1.1, folder 1, Ames Papers; Waldrep, *Many Faces of Judge Lynch*, 103–26.

67. Both the *Meridian (Miss.) Star* (29 Nov. 1933, 1) and the *Vicksburg (Miss.) Herald* (30 Nov. 1933, 8), for example, printed the composite image of Holmes's and Thurmond's hanged bodies, with their nudity concealed.

68. *Jackson (Miss.) Clarion-Ledger*, 28 Nov. 1933, 6; *Birmingham (Ala.) News*, 28 Nov. 1933, 8; *Meridian (Miss.) Star*, 28 Nov. 1933, 4.

69. Rable, "South and the Politics of Anti-lynching Legislation," 209–13; Jean, "'Warranted' Lynchings," 364–66.

70. *Chicago Defender*, 8 Sept. 1917, 1. According to Farrell (*Swift Justice*, 231), photographer Howard Robbins recounted that members of the mob in San Jose threatened him with a gun to his neck, but as a scuffle broke out between people in the crowd and other newsmen, Robbins was able to take his pictures. Similarly, the mob that lynched Lloyd Warner in St. Joseph, Missouri, threw bricks and fired shots at reporters trying to telephone their reports to their papers, and reporters and photographers battled Maryland rioters who attempted to destroy their cameras. *Washington Post*, 2 Dec. 1933, 5; *Raleigh (N.C.) News and Observer*, 29 Nov. 1933, 1.

71. "Photographs of Lynching," part 7, series A, reel 4, NAACP Papers. In 1921, James Weldon Johnson telegrammed Robert R. Church of the Memphis branch of the NAACP to "forward immediately photographs . . . if obtainable" of the lynching of Henry Lowry in Nodena, Arkansas. In 1934, Howard Kester, who investigated the Claude Neal lynching, was instructed to gather "any photographs of the body, crowd, etc.," as well as "some views of the town." Both the image of Neal's hanging corpse, which also appeared in some black newspapers, and an image of a cabin similar to the one Neal lived in (his was burned to the ground) appeared in the NAACP's report. James Weldon Johnson to Robert R. Church, telegram, 29 Jan.

1929, part 7, series A, reel 8, NAACP Papers; NAACP to Howard Kester, 31 Oct. 1934, part 7, series A, reel 9, NAACP Papers; "The Lynching of Claude Neal," part 7, series A, reel 4, NAACP Papers.

72. A. E. MacNeal to H. S. Willoughby, 20 Nov. 1935, part 7, series A, reel 8, NAACP Papers; Walter White, memorandum, 24 Sept. 1935, part 7, series A, reel 8, NAACP Papers; Roy Wilkins to Earl Brown, 26 Jan. 1937, part 7, series A, reel 5, NAACP Papers; NAACP to the *Carolina Times*, 27 Apr. 1937, part 7, series A, reel 13, NAACP Papers; *Life* magazine to the NAACP, 4 May 1937, part 7, series A, reel 13, NAACP Papers. The *Pittsburgh Courier* (24 Apr. 1937, 1) printed a photograph of the lynching site at Duck Hill, taken after the lynching, whereas, as noted above, the *Atlanta Daily World* (20 Apr. 1937, 1) illustrated its story of the lynching with Townes's mug shot. These concerns make it all the more surprising that participants and spectators are gathered around the victim in quite a few photographs from the 1930s, allowing themselves to be clearly visible. For these white southerners, there seemed to be no great concern that the very assumptions about photography that motivated them to take the pictures—the authenticity and material proof of a moment they constituted—could be used against them as legal proof or even as evidence for moral judgment against them.

CHAPTER SEVEN

1. Walter White to MGM Studios, 28 May 1936, box 1, Fritz Lang Collection, Louis B. Mayer Library, American Film Institute, Los Angeles; Walter White to Eleanor Roosevelt, telegram, 29 May 1936, part 1, reel 26, NAACP Papers; Walter White to Eleanor Roosevelt, 1 June 1936, part 1, reel 26, NAACP Papers; Walter White to Roy Wilkins, telegraph, 19 May 1936, part 1, reel 26, NAACP Papers; Walter White to Eleanor Roosevelt, 11 June 1936, part 1, reel 26, NAACP Papers; memorandum of telephone conversation from Walter White to Roy Wilkins, 5 June 1936, part 1, reel 26, NAACP Papers. The film premiered in New York and Los Angeles on 1 June, though White previewed the film earlier through MGM's New York offices. It is not apparent whether he requested the preview or MGM arranged it to garner NAACP support. The NAACP worked closely with Eleanor Roosevelt throughout the 1930s to secure FDR's public endorsement for antilynching legislation. Despite the first lady's support and his private sympathies, however, the president offered only mild condemnations of lynching for fear of alienating southern Democrats whose cooperation he needed to enact his New Deal legislation. See Zangrando, *NAACP Crusade against Lynching*, 112–13, and Rable, "South and the Politics of Antilynching Legislation," 208–9.

2. White to MGM Studios, 28 May 1936; *Washington Afro-American*, 1 Aug. 1936, 10.

3. White to Roosevelt, 1 June 1936.

4. *Fury* was one of the top-grossing films for July 1936. *Motion Picture Herald*, 18 July 1936, 40; Black, *Hollywood Censored*, 266.

5. *New Republic*, 10 June 1936, 130–31. Modern scholars have also criticized *Fury*'s disavowal of the reality of lynching, to the point that some do not consider it

a film about lynching at all. See Mennel, "White Law and the Missing Black Body," and Humphries, *Fritz Lang*, 14.

6. The film was based on Ward Greene's 1936 novel, a fictionalized account of the Leo Frank case, *Death in the Deep South*. The title and other details were changed to stave off libel suits and to appease southern censors.

7. *Ox-Bow* was a labor of love for director William Wellman and star Henry Fonda, who used their standing with the studio to get the film made. Hollywood writer Julian Johnson, in a letter to producer Darryl Zanuck, called it a "bitter and sunless" picture that was "about as entertaining as watching the Nips round up our captured countrymen on Corregidor." Julian Johnson to Darryl Zanuck, 7 May 1942, *Ox-Bow Incident* correspondence, collection 10, box FX-PRS-192, Produced Scripts, Twentieth Century–Fox, Performing Arts Special Collections, University of California at Los Angeles; *The Ox-Bow Incident*, production notes, Production Files, Core Collection, Margaret Herrick Library, Academy of Motion Picture Arts and Sciences, Beverly Hills, Calif. (hereafter cited as MHL).

8. Bordwell, Staiger, and Thompson, *Classical Hollywood Style*. The authors mark 1917 and 1960 as the beginning and ending points for this style, which wed particular aesthetic norms with an economically integrated mode of production. This view of classical Hollywood style has shaped theories of modern spectacle that imagine the spectator to be disembodied, atomized, and passive.

9. For histories of the formation of the PCA, see Black, *Hollywood Censored*; Rosenbloom, "Between Reform and Regulation"; and Bernstein, *Controlling Hollywood*.

10. Production Code reprinted in Alicoate, *Film Daily Production Guide*, 41, 143; Vasey, "Beyond Sex and Violence," 72; Vasey, *World According to Hollywood*; PCA to Jason Joy (Fox public relations representative), 12 May 1942, *The Ox-Bow Incident*, Motion Picture Association of America Production Code Administration Records, MHL (hereafter cited as MPAA-PCA Records).

11. *The Oklahoma Kid* (Warner Brothers, 1939) was one of the few A-list westerns to feature a lynching. The Kid's (James Cagney) law-abiding father (Hugh Sothern) is framed and hanged by a group of thugs led by Humphrey Bogart. The scene, which is depicted with frightening detail—a series of staccato shots of the lynching is intercut with shots of the roaring crowd—seems out of place in an otherwise lighthearted western romp.

12. No prints of *Laughter in Hell* exist, so any understanding of what it depicted comes from reviews and plot synopses. The film was panned for its "amateurish" and cheap production value. *NYT*, 2 Jan. 1933, 29; *Motion Picture Herald*, 7 Jan. 1933, 26; *Variety*, 17 Jan. 1933, 15. Racialized near-lynching scenes were excised from *Imitation of Life* (Universal, 1934) and *Judge Priest* (Fox, 1934)—not because they depicted lynching per se but rather because of a suggestion of miscegenation in the former case and a legal imbroglio in the latter. On *Imitation of Life*, see Courtney, *Hollywood Fantasies of Miscegenation*, 144. In the case of *Judge Priest*, both director John Ford and actor Stepin Fetchit (who played the intended lynching victim) explained that the studio cut the scene because it was deemed too threatening. But there is evidence that the scene was intact when the film was released. The scene was most

likely cut because Fox had become embroiled in a lawsuit over the rights to the stories by writer Irvin S. Cobb on which the film was based. In particular, Fox had not obtained the rights to the story "The Mob from Massac," from which the lynching scene was adapted, a discovery that was not made until after the film's release. Ford revisited the scene (this time with white victims of the near lynching) in *Young Mr. Lincoln* (Fox, 1939) and then again with another film of Cobb's Judge Priest stories, including "The Mob from Massac," in *Sun Shines Bright* (Republic, 1953). See McBride, *Searching for John Ford*, 212, 305, and Gallagher, *John Ford*, 103. The report written by Lawrence Arnold on the film's lynching sequence and its connection to "The Mob from Massac" is dated 7 July 1936, almost two years after the film's release. Collection 095, box FX-LR-84, folder 2332, *Judge Priest*, Legal Department Records, Twentieth–Century Fox, Performing Arts Special Collections, University of California at Los Angeles. Unfortunately, PCA records for *Judge Priest* no longer exist.

13. Lamar Trotti to Darryl Zanuck, 23 Apr. 1932, MPAA-PCA Records; *The Cabin in the Cotton*, story files, Warner Bros. Archives, University of Southern California, Los Angeles. Ironically, considering this objection on behalf of the PCA, Trotti also cowrote the adapted screenplay for *Judge Priest*, including the excised near-lynching episode, and later adapted the screenplay for *The Ox-Bow Incident*.

14. Joseph Breen to Jack Warner, 30 Jan. 1937, MPAA-PCA Records; Mrs. Alonzo Richardson to Joseph Breen, 31 Aug. 1937, MPAA-PCA Records; *Southern Israelite*, 27 Aug. 1937, publicity file 690, Warner Bros. Archives. For an overview of Warner Brothers' struggles with the PCA on this film, see Bernstein, *Screening a Lynching*.

15. *Variety*, 3 Nov. 1937, 8; *Louisville (Ky.) Courier-Journal*, 28 Oct. 1937, 12. Warner Brothers included *They Won't Forget* in a series of previews of its new films in thirty-one cities around the county, including Atlanta, Dallas, and Charlotte, North Carolina. Yet, as noted, it was never distributed in Atlanta, and neither the Dallas nor the Charlotte papers mentioned its appearance in those cities. The film also did not appear in any movie pages in a cross-section of papers consulted in Virginia, North Carolina, Mississippi, and Texas. *Washington Post*, 12 July 1937, 9.

16. *New Masses*, 16 June 1936, 28.

17. Manckiewicz initially wanted to direct, but MGM hired Fritz Lang, recently arrived from Germany. Once Lang came on board, he set about educating himself on lynching, charging numerous copies of newspaper and magazine stories about the San Jose lynching and other lynchings to his account at MGM. According to one story conference, Lang sought the exact transcripts of Rolph's statement and Roosevelt's speech. Interestingly, next to the story of the San Jose lynching in the *Los Angeles Times*, which Lang ordered, appeared a small story about a prisoner who accidentally burned to death in an Illinois jail when the jail caught fire and the keys could not be found in time to save him. Fritz Lang charges to MGM in relation to the production of *Fury*, undated note, box 1, Lang Collection; Bogdanovich, *Who the Devil Made It*, 182; original "Mob Rule" treatment and story conference, 4 Sept. 1935, file 2148, box 223, *Fury* Files, MGM Collection, Cinematic Arts Library, University of Southern California, Los Angeles; *Los Angeles Times*, 27 Nov. 1933, 1.

18. G.S. [?], memorandum re: "Mob Rule," 21 Aug. 1935, MPAA-PCA Records;

Joseph Breen to L. B. Mayer, 24 Aug. 1936, 27 Jan. 1936, 14 Feb. 1936, 4 Apr. 1936, 4 May 1936, MPAA-PCA Records. Breen's office also requested that the word "lynching" be removed, presumably because the term itself had become too inflammatory and associated with racial violence. The producers ultimately ignored this objection, and the word is used throughout the film. Breen read two versions of the script before approving final changes in April 1936. In this context, "political censorship" may have referred to the southern censors, but it more likely referred to foreign censors who were wary of depictions of unruly mobs. The censorship boards of Italy, Hungary, Java, Singapore, Palestine, Latvia, Finland, Jamaica, and Iran rejected the film entirely, whereas boards in Japan, Hong Kong, and, interestingly, Sweden cut out scenes of the mob. Joseph Breen to L. B. Mayer, 10 June 1936, MPAA-PCA Records; *Motion Picture Herald*, 16 Jan. 1937, 69.

19. Breen to Mayer, 27 Jan. 1936; "Mob Rule," box 427, Motion Picture Film Scripts, Performing Arts Special Collections, University of California at Los Angeles. In the original script, Vickery advocates vigilantism in newsreel footage that Joe and Katherine watch at the beginning of the film, and Joe, before his own encounter with a mob, applauds. Similarly, the initial screenplays of both *They Won't Forget* and *The Ox-Bow Incident* represent legal authorities as complicit in the lynching in some way, representations that were altered under pressure from Breen's office.

20. *New Yorker*, 8 Sept. 1934, 27; *Crisis*, Jan. 1935, 13.

21. The photo appeared in *Time*, 11 Dec. 1933, 15. Fritz Lang ordered a copy of this issue. Lang charges to MGM, undated note. It also appeared in the *New York World-Telegram* (28 Nov. 1933) and was preserved by the NAACP (part 7, series A, reel 8, NAACP Papers).

22. *New Theatre Magazine*, July 1936, 10; *Nation*, 24 June 1936, 821. Stebbins conceded that "these weaknesses" were "in all probability compromises demanded by the box-office experts and not of Lang's making." See also Black, *Hollywood Censored*, 267.

23. Bernstein, *Screening a Lynching*; *NYT*, 7 June 1936, 142.

24. Gunning, *Films of Fritz Lang*, 230.

25. Story notes, 30, 31 Aug. 1935, box 223, *Fury* Files, MGM Collection. On Lang's interest in mob psychology, see Barbara Miller, "Fritz Lang's Study of Mob Inspires Film," *Los Angeles Times*, 14 June 1936, C1. Lang liked to say that he was told that, in America, if you wanted your character to be an everyman, a "John Doe," you made him a worker, a "man of the people." Lang saw this as a powerful lesson about American democracy: "The hero in Germany was always a superman . . . whereas in a democracy he had to be Joe Doe." Lang quoted in Bogdanovich, *Who the Devil Made It*, 184–85.

26. *Fury* press book, Press Books Collection, Cinematic Arts Library, University of Southern California, Los Angeles. This line also appeared in the film's trailer.

27. Miller, "Fritz Lang's Study of Mob"; "Notes at Random," story conference, 31 Aug. 1935, box 223, *Fury* Files, MGM Collection; "Fritz Lang Bows to Mammon," *NYT*, 14 June 1936, X2.

28. Story notes, 31 Aug. 1935, *Fury* Files, MGM Collection; "Fritz Lang Bows to Mammon," X2. In this context, "Fury" became a more apt title than the original

title, "Mob Rule," since the film was not about the mob but about the rage that could turn Americans into vengeful vigilantes.

29. The script reads, "The slap of the negro's polishing rag puts an exclamation mark to the speech," but in the final cut of the film, the slap is relatively subdued and happens almost outside the frame. Lang claimed that the studio cut this scene, as well as a scene showing a group of black men listening to the district attorney's courtroom antilynching speech over the radio. Bogdanovich, *Who the Devil Made It*, 190.

30. Mennel ("White Law and the Missing Black Body," 217–18) critiques the film on these grounds.

31. These lines, which connote the western setting of the lynching, disrupt assumptions about lynching as a peculiarly southern form of violence. They take on added meaning within the context of Lang's own early encounters with American culture. In interviews, Lang liked to talk about his interest and travels in the American Southwest, claiming to one interviewer that he spent six to eight weeks living on a Navajo reservation. McGilligan, *Fritz Lang*, 219.

32. Gunning, *Films of Fritz Lang*, 226. One of the first motion picture palaces to open in the nation was the Strand in New York City, built in 1914.

33. Prince (*Classical Film Violence*) argues that the PCA's restrictions on the depiction of violence enhanced artistic creativity by impelling directors to represent violence abstractly and imaginatively. For example, the initial screenplay for *They Won't Forget* describes a posse of masked men taking its victim by force from the train, with slaps, kicks to the groin, and shouting. After meeting PCA objections, the filmmakers excised the scene. The final version of the film shows the mob only in silhouette, and, in what critics hailed as a stroke of creative brilliance, the lynching is connoted through the shot of a railroad arm jutting out with a mail bag swinging from it, the shadows resembling a man hanging from the gallows. The visual displacement of the violence is in a sense more haunting. Reviews that made mention of the scene include *Screen and Radio Weekly* (n.d.) and *Omaha (Neb.) Evening World-Herald*, 11 Apr. 1938, 15, clippings in publicity file 690, *They Won't Forget*, Warner Bros. Archives.

34. This shot was replicated three years later in *The Oklahoma Kid* (1939), in a jarring scene in which a gang of renegades lynches the Kid's father, John Kincaid (Hugh Sothern), from the jailhouse's second-story porch. The camera tracks the female protagonist (Rosemary Lane) as she runs through the crowd, zooming in on her horror-struck gaze the moment she sees Kincaid hang.

35. Many viewers did not see even this displaced rendering of the violence. Censors in Chicago, Pennsylvania, and Ohio excised the shot of the shadows. Ohio also eliminated all the dialogue and visuals surrounding the lynching, including the hanging of the rope, the positioning of the prisoners, and the shots of the witnesses. It is quite possible that some municipal censorship boards made the same decisions. Local censorship board reviews, *The Ox-Bow Incident*, MPAA-PCA Records.

36. The viewer is also made to experience the lynching through the character of Gil (Henry Fonda), who moves from indifferent bystander in the beginning of the film to outspoken and horrified critic of the lynch mob by the end. The film operates

most successfully as a political force if viewers identify with Gil and follow his moral trajectory from spectator to active witness.

37. *They Won't Forget* also posits the only black character, the janitor Tump Redwine (Clinton Rosemond), in this role of surrogate witness, making him crucial to the film's moral purpose. Redwine witnesses what the movie audience cannot see when he finds Mary Clay's body in the school building; in fact, the viewer knows for sure that the murder has occurred only when Redwine appears in close-up on the phone with the police, crying in terror, "I didn't do it! I didn't do it!" His fear in this moment also reminds viewers of the vulnerability of a black man who has found a white woman murdered. For a detailed examination of Redwine's character, see Bernstein, *Screening a Lynching*.

38. Norford, "Future in Films," 108. In an article on Hollywood's treatment of African Americans in film, Walter White praised *The Ox-Bow Incident* as a "superb indictment of lynching" and noted Leigh Whipper's role in particular. *Chicago Defender*, 8 May 1943, 15.

39. *New Masses*, 16 June 1936, 28; *Los Angeles Times*, 16 Nov. 1936, 12.

40. *NYT*, 6 June 1936, 21.

41. *They Won't Forget* similarly uses news headlines and radio broadcasts and reproaches those sensational newsmen who treat news as entertainment and profit from the lynching.

42. *NYT*, 4 Dec. 1933, 22; *NYT*, 5 Nov. 1934, 23.

43. Fielding, *American Newsreel*; *Variety*, 12 Dec. 1933, 16. On footage of the Tulsa race riot, see Moore, "Lights, Camera, Action," 304.

44. *Variety*, 5 Dec. 1933, 15; *NYT*, 4 Dec. 1933, 22. The week before, Paramount had produced a newsreel covering Hart's kidnapping, which was playing in theaters—including, possibly, in San Jose—the night of the lynching. *Variety*, 28 Nov. 1933, 22.

45. *NYT*, 1 Dec. 1933, 23; *NYT*, 2 Dec. 1933, 9; *Times* (London), 2 Dec. 1933, 2; *Times* (London), 5 Dec. 1933, 7. In its rebuke of the newsreel, the *Times* (London, 1 Dec. 1933, 14) castigated "the growing tendency to sacrifice all decency to sensationalism" in news programming and hoped, vaguely, that "steps will be taken to safeguard the public from the exhibition of such scenes." One member of Parliament accordingly asked that Parliament take action to prevent the showing of the San Jose newsreel, since the British Board of Film Censors had no jurisdiction over news. Paramount quickly withdrew the newsreel from exhibition as a "gesture" to mollify public opinion but also, presumably, to stave off any legal censorship.

46. Fielding, *American Newsreel*, 182, 205–6. Newsreel companies protested the board's decision as an attack on their "freedom of expression" as news outlets, and Governor Ritchie duly asserted that the board's decision would be overturned. *Variety*, 5 Dec. 1933, 4.

47. As Gunning (*Films of Fritz Lang*, 225) points out, the film sets up the newsreel footage, the modern force of the camera, as a replacement for traditional circuits of communication, namely rumor and gossip, which the film mocks for their hasty indictment of Joe earlier in the film. Rumor and gossip are challenged by the supposed

veracity of the newsmen, when the news camera is revealed to be nothing more than
a modern form of rumor and gossip. See also Humphries, *Fritz Lang*, 54–55.

48. Lang quoted in Bogdanovich, *Who the Devil Made It*, 183.

49. Benjamin, "Work of Art in the Age of Mechanical Reproduction," 678–81.

50. *Fury* press book.

51. *Variety*, 19 May 1936, in *Fury* reviews, Production Files, Core Collection, MHL; *Variety*, 24 June 1936, 38.

52. *NYT*, 15 July 1937, 16; *New Masses*, 20 July 1937, 28; *Life*, 19 July 1937, 32–35. For a sampling of newspaper reviews of *They Won't Forget*, see *They Won't Forget*, box 2, Mervyn LeRoy Papers, Special Collections, MHL.

53. *New York Amsterdam News*, 21 Aug. 1937, 1, 5; *New York Amsterdam News*, 28 Aug. 1937, 1, 20; *New York Amsterdam News*, 4 Sept. 1937, 14; *New York Amsterdam News*, 11 Sept. 1937, 5. The paper reported that the Harlem show was the beginning of a "tour in several parts of the country." Plays about the Scottsboro case include John Wexley's *Thou Shall Not Die*, performed in New York in 1934; Paul Peters and George Sklar's *Stevedore*, which premiered in New York the same year; and Langston Hughes's *Scottsboro Limited* (1931) and *Angelo Herndon Jones* (1935). The Workers Film and Photo League produced a film, *Scottsboro*, copies of which no longer exist. See Archer, *Black Images in the American Theatre*, 73–76, and Denning, *Cultural Front*, 262–63.

54. Magazine clipping, July 1943, *The Ox-Bow Incident*, 1943 reviews, Production Files, Core Collection, MHL; *Variety*, 17 June 1936, 7. The Black Legion was the subject of its own "social problem film," *Black Legion* (Warner Brothers, 1936), starring Humphrey Bogart.

55. *New Theatre Magazine*, July 1936, 10.

56. Commission on Human Relations and Progressive Education Association, "Study Guide to *Fury*" (1939), Production Files, Core Collection, MHL.

57. *New York Amsterdam News*, 7 Aug. 1937, 2; *Pittsburgh Courier*, 14 Aug. 1934, 12.

58. See, for example, *Washington Afro-American*, 31 Aug. 1936, 10. It is unclear who wrote this text, but it is unlikely that MGM wrote a separate version of its promotional materials for black theaters. Considering that the language echoes Walter White's praise of the film, it is possible that the NAACP wrote the text and sent it to black papers around the country.

59. *New York Amsterdam News*, 17 July 1937, 20; *Washington Afro-American*, 23 Oct. 1937, 10; *Atlanta Daily World*, 23 Aug. 1937, 1.

60. *New York Amsterdam News*, 13 July 1936, 8.

61. Cripps, "Myth of the Southern Box Office," 118–27. *Variety* included receipts from only two southern cities—Birmingham, Alabama, and Louisville, Kentucky—while *Motion Picture Herald* ignored the South altogether. For a summary of Sunday showings in southern states, see Alicoate, *1940 Film Daily Yearbook*, 745–47.

62. Most small towns with populations of around 2,000, like Oxford, Mississippi, and Lawrenceville, Georgia, had only one theater, whereas most midsize cities with about 20,000 people, like Paris, Texas, Rome, Georgia, and Vicksburg, Mis-

sissippi, boasted three or four theaters, with a total of 2,000 seats. See Alicoate, *1935 Film Daily Yearbook*, 776–77, and Alicoate, *1940 Film Daily Yearbook*, 47, 847–48, 877–78.

63. *Motion Picture Herald*, 27 Mar. 1937, 68; *Motion Picture Herald*, 29 Aug. 1936, 69. Even independent theater owners were very likely compelled to show *Fury* because of studio distribution practices. In "block booking," studios required theater owners to buy their entire output as a block, rather than choosing particular films to show in their theaters. A theater owner could choose not to show a particular movie from the block, but he would lose the money he paid for it. Some larger city newspapers published the movie showings in surrounding towns, and they reveal that *Fury* played in smaller cities. For examples, see *Raleigh (N.C.) News and Observer*, 7 June 1936, 07; *Raleigh (N.C.) News and Observer*, 14 June 1936, 07; *Raleigh (N.C.) News and Observer*, 28 June 1936, 05; *Charlotte (N.C.) Observer*, 7 June 1936, 5; and *Charlotte (N.C.) Observer*, 21 June 1936, 5.

64. *Atlanta Daily World*, 19 July 1936, 7.

65. *Augusta (Ga.) Chronicle*, 30 June 1936, 10. For other examples of advertisements in southern papers, see *Charlotte (N.C.) Observer*, 28 June 1936, D4; *Raleigh (N.C.) News and Observer*, 6 Feb. 1938, D6; and *Vicksburg (Miss.) Post-Herald*, 21 June 1936, 8.

66. See, for example, *Savannah (Ga.) Evening Press*, 25 June 1936, 2; *AC*, 19 June 1936, 10; *New Orleans Times-Picayune*, 12 June 1936, 20; *Dallas Morning News*, 7 June 1936, 3; *Louisville (Ky.) Courier-Journal*, 12 June 1936, 5; and *Richmond (Va.) News Leader*, 20 June 1936, 6.

67. *AC*, 18 June 1936, 10; *Dallas Morning News*, 7 June 1936, M3.

68. *Richmond (Va.) News Leader*, 20 June 1936, 6. The *Richmond (Va.) Times-Dispatch* (19 June 1936, 19) also denoted *Fury* as a "sharp indictment of lynch mobs" in its review headline.

69. *Birmingham (Ala.) News*, 19 July 1936, 14; *Rome (Ga.) News-Tribune*, 21 July 1936, 4. Notably, two months earlier, this columnist, the "Roaming Roman," devoted his column to Margaret Mitchell's novel *Gone with the Wind*, which he extolled as a "real portrayal of incidents and impulses that stirred men and woman of flesh and blood" during the Civil War and Reconstruction era. The juxtaposition of columns indicates that antilynching sentiment in the South was fully detached from any larger antiracist critique of the South. *Rome (Ga.) News-Tribune*, 5 May 1936, 4.

CONCLUSION

1. Brundage, *Lynching in the New South*, 252. The last "spectacle" lynching occurred in Sikeston, Missouri, on 25 January 1942, when a white mob abducted Cleo Wright, a black oil mill worker accused of assaulting a white woman, from jail and burned him alive before a crowd of nearly 1,000 citizens. The lynching was condemned throughout the country and spurred a state grand jury investigation, as well as FBI and Department of Justice investigations. See Capeci, *Lynching of Cleo Wright*.

2. Brundage, *Lynching in the New South*, 209–12; Tolnay and Beck, *Festival of*

Violence, 219–33. On local black resistance to lynching, see Brundage, "Darien 'Insurrection' of 1899"; Brundage, "Black Resistance and White Violence"; Williams, "Resolving the Paradox of Our Lynching Fixation"; Smith, "Southern Violence Reconsidered"; Cha-Jua, "'Warlike Demonstration'"; and Hahn, *Nation under Our Feet*, 427–31.

3. Rable, "South and the Politics of Anti-lynching Legislation," 209–10, 213; Jean, "'Warranted' Lynchings," 364–66; Zangrando, *NAACP Crusade against Lynching*, 148.

4. For the ways in which white communities have been able to control the public memory of lynching over the past century and the alternative ways in which black communities have maintained memories of lynching in private discourse, see Carrigan, *Making of a Lynching Culture*, 198–206, and Baker, "Under the Rope."

5. See Gerstle, *American Crucible*, 216, 235–36; Hirsch, *Making the Second Ghetto*, xv, xviii, 53–54; and Sugrue, "Crabgrass-Roots Politics."

6. Koppes and Black, "Blacks, Loyalty, and Motion Picture Propaganda"; Cripps, *Making Movies Black*.

7. *Jet*, 22 Sept. 1955, 8; Ginzberg, *One Hundred Years of Lynching*, 112; Metress, *Lynching of Emmett Till*, 1, 14–43; Waldrep, *Many Faces of Judge Lynch*, 185–86; Whitfield, *Death in the Delta*, 60.

8. *Chicago Defender*, 28 May 1955, 5; Moore quoted in Whitfield, *Death in the Delta*, 145; Diggs quoted in Bond, "Media and the Movement," 27; *Chicago Defender*, 17 Sept. 1955, 4.

9. *Chicago Defender*, 10 Sept. 1955, 5; *Chicago Defender*, 17 Sept. 1955, 4; Metress, *Lynching of Emmett Till*, 226.

10. Feldstein, *Motherhood in Black and White*, 86–110.

11. Abdul-Jabbar quoted in Metress, *Lynching of Emmett Till*, 277; Bond, "Media and the Movement," 26–27; Whitfield, *Death in the Delta*, 91.

BIBLIOGRAPHY

MANUSCRIPT COLLECTIONS

Atlanta, Ga.
  Atlanta History Center
    Kenneth Rogers Papers
  Georgia Department of Archives and History
    Vanishing Georgia Collection
Austin, Tex.
  Center for American History, University of Texas
    Lynching, Texas, File
Beverly Hills, Calif.
  Margaret Herrick Library, Academy of Motion Picture Arts and Sciences
    Core Collection
      Clippings Files
      Production Files
    Special Collections
      Mervyn LeRoy Papers
      Motion Picture Association of America Production Code Administration
        Records
Chapel Hill, N.C.
  Southern Historical Collection, University of North Carolina
    Jesse Daniel Ames Papers
Jackson, Miss.
  Mississippi Department of Archives and History
    Death Sentences Files
    E. F. Noel Papers
Los Angeles, Calif.
  Cinematic Arts Library, University of Southern California
    MGM Collection
      Fury Files
    Press Books Collection

Louis B. Mayer Library, American Film Institute
  Fritz Lang Collection
Performing Arts Special Collections, University of California at Los Angeles
  Motion Picture Film Scripts
  Twentieth Century–Fox
    Legal Department Records
    Produced Scripts
  William Wellman Files
Warner Bros. Archive, University of Southern California
  The Cabin in the Cotton Files
  They Won't Forget Files
Oxford, Miss.
  Special Collections, University of Mississippi
    Mississippi Executions File
    Mississippi Lynchings File
Statesboro, Ga.
  Special Collections, Georgia Southern University
    Georgia Historical Society Papers
    Statesboro First Baptist Church Records
Waco, Tex.
  Texas Collection, Baylor University
Washington, D.C.
  Library of Congress
    Prints and Photographs Division
      Miscellaneous Files
      National Association for the Advancement of Colored People Files
    Motion Picture, Broadcasting, and Recorded Sound Division
      Motion Picture Catalogs (microfilm)
      Moving Image Collections

COUNTY AND CITY RECORDS

This study made extensive use of local records held in the following public libraries. County and city sources in these libraries included the federal manuscript censuses for 1900, 1910, and 1920; city directories; church minutes and records; city and county histories; cemetery files; histories of local and civic organizations; photographs; WPA histories; and miscellaneous files and folders.

Dallas, Tex.
  Texas/Dallas History and Archives, J. Erik Jonsson Central Library
Lawrenceville, Ga.
  Gwinnett County Public Library
Oxford, Miss.
  Special Collections, Lafayette County and Oxford Public Library
Paris, Tex.
  Aiken Archives, Paris Junior College

Rome, Ga.
Special Collections, Rome–Floyd County Public Library
Statesboro, Ga.
Genealogy Department, Statesboro Regional Library
Vicksburg, Miss.
Special Collections, Warren County–Vicksburg Public Library
Waco, Tex.
Waco–McLennan County Library
Wiggins, Miss.
Stone County Public Library

NEWSPAPERS AND MAGAZINES

Atlanta Constitution
Atlanta Daily World
Atlanta Journal
Augusta (Ga.) Chronicle
Baltimore Afro-American
Biloxi (Miss.) Daily Herald
Birmingham (Ala.) News
Brandon (Miss.) News
Bulloch County (Ga.) Times
Charlotte (N.C.) News
Charlotte (N.C.) Observer
Chicago Defender
Chicago Tribune
Columbia (S.C.) State
Crisis
Dallas Morning News
Dallas Times-Herald
Dawson (Ga.) News
Florida Times Union and Citizen
Gwinnet County (Ga.) Journal
Hattiesburg (Miss.) American
Hattiesburg (Miss.) News
Houston Post
Jackson (Miss.) Clarion-Ledger
Jackson (Miss.) Daily News
Jet
Kansas City (Mo.) Star
Knoxville (Tenn.) Journal
Lafayette County (Miss.) Press
Lawrenceville (Ga.) News-Herald
Life
Los Angeles Herald

Los Angeles Times
Louisville (Ky.) Courier-Journal
Macon (Ga.) Weekly Telegraph
Memphis Commercial Appeal
Memphis News-Scimitar
Memphis Press-Scimitar
Meridian (Miss.) Star
Motion Picture Herald
Motion Picture News
Moving Picture World
Nation
Newark Star-Eagle
New Masses
Newnan (Ga.) Herald and Advertiser
New Orleans Times-Picayune
New Republic
New Theatre Magazine
New York American
New York Amsterdam News
New York Clipper
New York Journal
New York Times
New York World
New York World-Telegram
Norfolk (Va.) Journal and Guide
Owensboro (Ky.) Daily Inquirer
Oxford (Miss.) Eagle
Oxford (Miss.) Globe
Paris (Tex.) News
Phonoscope
Pittsburgh Courier
Raleigh (N.C.) News and Observer

Richmond (Va.) News Leader

Richmond (Va.) Planet

Richmond (Va.) Times-Dispatch

Rome (Ga.) Commercial Argus

Rome (Ga.) Hustler

Rome (Ga.) News-Tribune

Rome (Ga.) Tribune

Rome (Ga.) Tribune-Herald

San Francisco Chronicle

San Francisco Examiner

Savannah (Ga.) Evening Press

Starkville (Miss.) News

Statesboro (Ga.) News

St. Joseph (Mo.) News-Press

St. Louis Globe-Democrat

St. Louis Post-Dispatch

Stone County (Miss.) Enterprise

Time

Times (London)

Topeka (Kans.) Weekly Capital

Variety

Vicksburg (Miss.) American

Vicksburg (Miss.) Evening Post

Vicksburg (Miss.) Evening Post

Vicksburg (Miss.) Post-Herald

Waco (Tex.) News-Tribune

Waco (Tex.) Times-Herald

Washington Afro-American

Washington Post

Wesleyan Christian Advocate

PUBLISHED PRIMARY SOURCES

Alicoate, Jack, ed. *Film Daily Production Guide, Director's Annual.* New York: Film Daily, 1935.

———, ed. *The 1935 Film Daily Yearbook of Motion Pictures.* New York: Film Daily, 1935.

———, ed. *The 1940 Film Daily Yearbook of Motion Pictures.* New York: Film Daily, 1940.

Baker, Ray Stannard. *Following the Color Line.* New York: Harper and Row, 1908.

———. "What Is a Lynching? A Study of Mob Justice, South and North." *McClure's,* Jan. 1905, 299–314.

Benjamin, R. C. O. *Southern Outrages: A Statistical Record of Lawless Doings.* Los Angeles, 1894.

Benjamin, Walter. "The Work of Art in the Age of Mechanical Reproduction" (1936). In *Film Theory and Criticism,* edited by Gerald Mast, Marshall Cohen, and Leo Braudy, 665–81. New York: Oxford University Press, 1992.

Burdett, Samuel. *A Test of Lynch Law: An Expose of Mob Violence and the Courts of Hell.* Seattle, Wash., 1901.

Carrington, Charles V. "The History of Electrocution in the State of Virginia." *Virginia Medical Semi-Monthly,* 11 Nov. 1910, 353.

Chadbourn, James Harmon. *Lynching and the Law.* Chapel Hill: University of North Carolina Press, 1933.

Cutler, J. E. "Capital Punishment and Lynching." *Annals of the American Academy of Political and Social Science* 29 (May 1907): 182–85.

———. *Lynch-Law: An Investigation into the History of Lynching in the United States.* New York: Longmans, Green, 1905.

Davis, Allison, Burleigh B. Gardner, and Mary R. Gardner. *Deep South: A Social Anthropological Study of Caste and Class.* 1941. Reprint, Los Angeles: Center for Afro-American Studies, University of California, 1988.

Dixon, Thomas, Jr. *The Clansman*. 1905. Reprint, Lexington: University Press of Kentucky, 1970.

————. *The Leopard's Spots: A Romance of the White Man's Burden*. New York: Doubleday, Page, 1903.

Dollard, John. *Caste and Class in a Southern Town*. New Haven: Yale University Press, 1937.

Faulkner, William. "Dry September"(1931). In *Collected Stories of William Faulkner*. New York: Random House, 1977.

————. *Light in August*. 1932. Reprint, New York: Random House, 1950.

Garner, James W. "Crime and Judicial Inefficiency." *Annals of the American Academy of Political and Social Science* 29 (May 1907): 161–78.

Haldeman-Julius, Marcet. *The Story of a Lynching: An Exploration in Southern Psychology*. Girard, Kans.: Haldeman-Julius, 1927.

Haygood, Atticus. "The Black Shadow of the South." *Forum*, Oct. 1893, 167–75.

James, P. L. *The Facts in the Case of the Horrible Murder of Little Myrtle Vance and Its Fearful Expiation at Paris, Texas, February 1st, 1893*. Paris, Tex., 1893.

Kracauer, Siegfried. "Cult of Distraction: On Berlin's Picture Palaces" (1926). Translated by Thomas Y. Levin. *New German Critique* 40 (Winter 1987): 91–96.

Lewisohn, Ludwig. "The Cult of Violence." *Nation*, 24 Jan. 1920, 118.

Lindsay, Vachel. *The Art of the Moving Picture*. 1915. Reprint, New York: Macmillan, 1922.

Mencken, H. L. "Death in the Afternoon" (1932). In *H. L. Mencken on American Literature*, edited by S. J. Joshi, 140–42. Athens: Ohio University Press, 2002.

————. "Sahara of the Bozart." In *Prejudices, Second Series*, 136–54. New York: Knopf, 1920.

Myrdal, Gunnar. *An American Dilemma: The Negro Problem in Modern Democracy*. New York: Harper and Row, 1944.

National Association for the Advancement of Colored People. *Burning at the Stake in the United States*. New York: NAACP, 1919.

————. *Thirty Years of Lynching in the United States, 1889–1918*. 1918. Reprint, New York: Arno Press, 1969.

Norford, George. "The Future in Films." *Opportunity*, Summer 1948, 108.

Odum, Howard. "Lynchings, Fears, and Folkways." *Nation*, 30 Dec. 1931, 720.

Ovington, Mary. *The Walls Came Tumbling Down*. 1946. Reprint, New York: Arno Press, 1969.

Raper, Arthur F. *The Tragedy of Lynching*. Chapel Hill: University of North Carolina Press, 1933.

Scott, Walter Dill. *The Psychology of Advertising*. 1913. Reprint, New York: Arno Press, 1978.

Selig, William. "Cutting Back." *Photoplay*, Feb. 1920, 43–47.

Smith, Lillian. *The Killers of the Dream*. 1949. Reprint, New York: Norton, 1978.

Southern Commission on the Study of Lynching. *Lynchings and What They Mean*. Atlanta: The Commission, 1931.

Tannenbaum, Frank. *Darker Phases of the South*. New York: G. P. Putnam's Sons, 1924.

Toomer, Jean. "Blood-Burning Moon." In *Cane*. 1923. Reprint, New York: Harper and Row, 1969.

Wells-Barnett, Ida B. *Crusade for Justice: The Autobiography of Ida B. Wells*. 1928. Edited by Alfreda M. Duster. Reprint, Chicago: University of Chicago Press, 1970.

————. *A Red Record*. In Wells-Barnett, *Southern Horrors and Other Writings*, 73–157.

————. *Southern Horrors: Lynch Law in All Its Phases*. In Wells-Barnett, *Southern Horrors and Other Writings*, 49–72.

————. *Southern Horrors and Other Writings: The Anti-Lynching Campaign of Ida B. Wells, 1892–1900*. Edited by Jacqueline Jones Royster. Boston: Bedford, 1997.

White, Walter. *Rope and Faggot*. 1929. Reprint, New York: Arno Press, 1969.

Wright, Richard. *Black Boy: A Record of Childhood and Youth*. 1937. Reprint, New York: Harper and Row, 1989.

SECONDARY SOURCES

Alexander, Ann Field. *Race Man: The Rise and Fall of the "Fighting Editor," John Mitchell, Jr.* Charlottesville: University of Virginia Press, 2002.

Allen, James. *Without Sanctuary: Lynching Photography in America*. Santa Fe, N.M.: Twin Palms, 2000.

Allen, Robert, and Douglas Gomery. *Film History: Theory and Practice*. New York: Knopf, 1985.

American Film Institute. *The American Film Institute Catalog of Motion Pictures Produced in the United States*. Vol. A, *Film Beginnings*; vol. F1, *Feature Films, 1911–1920*. Berkeley: University of California Press, 1993.

Anderson, Benedict. *Imagined Communities: Reflections on the Origins and Spread of Nationalism*. London: Verso, 1983.

Apel, Dora. *Imagery of Lynching: Black Men, White Women, and the Mob*. New Brunswick, N.J.: Rutgers University Press, 2004.

————. "On Looking: Lynching Photographs and the Legacies of Lynching after 9/11." *American Quarterly* 55 (Sept. 2003): 457–78.

Archer, Leonard C. *Black Images in the American Theatre: NAACP Protest Campaigns—Stage, Screen, Radio, and Television*. Brooklyn, N.Y.: Pageant-Poseidon, 1973.

Ariès, Phillippe. *Western Attitudes toward Death from the Middle Ages to the Present*. Translated by Patricia M. Ranum. Baltimore: Johns Hopkins University Press, 1974.

Aycock, Roger. *All Roads to Rome*. Roswell, Ga.: Wolfe Associates, 1981.

Ayers, Edward L. *The Promise of the New South: Life after Reconstruction*. New York: Oxford University Press, 1992.

————. *Vengeance and Justice: Crime and Punishment in the 19th-Century American South*. New York: Oxford University Press, 1984.

Baker, Bruce E. "North Carolina Lynching Ballads." In Brundage, *Under Sentence of Death*, 219–45.

─────. "Under the Rope: Lynching and Memory in Laurens County, South Carolina." In *Where These Memories Grow: History, Memory, and Southern Identity*, edited by W. Fitzhugh Brundage, 319–45. Chapel Hill: University of North Carolina Press, 2000.

Banner, Stuart. *The Death Penalty: An American History*. Cambridge, Mass.: Harvard University Press, 2002.

Barrow, Janice. "Lynching in the Mid-Atlantic, 1882–1940." *American Nineteenth Century History* 6 (Sept. 2005): 241–72.

Barthes, Roland. *Camera Lucida: Reflections on Photography*. Translated by Richard Howard. New York: Hill and Wang, 1981.

Beck, E. M., James L. Massey, and Stewart E. Tolnay. "The Gallows, the Mob, and the Vote: Lethal Sanctioning of Blacks in North Carolina and Georgia, 1882 to 1930." *Law and Society Review* 23 (1989): 317–31.

Bedau, Hugo Adam. *The Death Penalty in America*. New York: Oxford University Press, 1982.

Bederman, Gail. *Manliness and Civilization: A Cultural History of Gender and Race in the United States, 1880–1917*. Chicago: University of Chicago Press, 1995.

Bell, Catherine. *Ritual: Perspectives and Dimensions*. New York: Oxford University Press, 1997.

─────. *Ritual Theory, Ritual Practice*. New York: Oxford University Press, 1992.

Bernardi, Daniel, ed. *The Birth of Whiteness: Race and the Emergence of U.S. Cinema*. New Brunswick, N.J.: Rutgers University Press, 1996.

Bernstein, Matthew. "Oscar Micheaux and Leo Frank: Cinematic Justice across the Color Line." *Film Quarterly* 57 (Summer 2004): 8–21.

─────. *Screening a Lynching: The Leo Frank Case on Film and Television*. Athens: University of Georgia Press, 2009.

─────, ed. *Controlling Hollywood: Censorship and Regulation in the Studio Era*. New Brunswick, N.J.: Rutgers University Press, 1999.

Bernstein, Patricia. *The First Waco Horror: The Lynching of Jesse Washington and the Rise of the NAACP*. College Station: Texas A&M University Press, 2005.

Bessler, John D. *Legacy of Violence: Lynch Mobs and Executions in Minnesota*. Minneapolis: University of Minnesota Press, 2003.

Black, Gregory D. *Hollywood Censored: Morality Codes, Catholics, and the Movies*. New York: Cambridge University Press, 1994.

Blight, David W. *Beyond the Battlefield: Race, Memory, and the Civil War*. Amherst: University of Massachusetts Press, 2002.

─────. *Race and Reunion: The Civil War in American Memory*. Cambridge, Mass.: Harvard University Press, 2001.

Blum, Edward J., and W. Scott Poole, eds. *Vale of Tears: New Essays on Religion and Reconstruction*. Macon: University of Georgia Press, 2005.

Bogdanovich, Peter. *Who the Devil Made It*. New York: Knopf, 1997.

Bond, Julian. "The Media and the Movement: Looking Back from the Southern Front." In *Media, Culture, and the Modern African American Freedom Struggle*, edited by Brian Ward, 16–40. Gainesville: University Press of Florida, 2001.

Bordwell, David. *On the History of Film Style*. Cambridge, Mass.: Harvard University Press, 1997.

Bordwell, David, Janet Staiger, and Kristen Thompson. *Classical Hollywood Style: Film Style and Mode of Production to 1960*. New York: Columbia University Press, 1985.

Bourdieu, Pierre. *Photography*. Stanford, Calif.: Stanford University Press, 1990.

Bowers, William J. *Legal Homicide: Death as Punishment in America, 1864–1982*. Boston: Northeastern University Press, 1984.

Bowser, Eileen. *The Transformation of Cinema: 1907–1915*. Berkeley: University of California Press, 1990.

Brannen, Dorothy. *Life in Old Bulloch: The Story of a Wiregrass County in Georgia*. Gainesville, Ga.: Magnolia Press, 1987.

Brauer, Jerald. "Regionalism and Religion in America." *Church History* 54 (Sept. 1985): 366–78.

Brennen, Bonnie, and Hanno Hardt, eds. *Picturing the Past: Media, History, and Photography*. Urbana: University of Illinois Press, 1999.

Brown, Mary Jane. *Eradicating This Evil: Women in the Anti-Lynching Movement, 1892–1940*. New York: Garland, 2000.

Brundage, W. Fitzhugh. "Black Resistance and White Violence in the American South, 1880–1940." In Brundage, *Under Sentence of Death*, 271–91.

———. "The Darien 'Insurrection' of 1899: Black Protest during the Nadir of Race Relations." *Georgia Historical Quarterly* 74 (1990): 234–53.

———. *Lynching in the New South: Georgia and Virginia, 1880–1930*. Urbana: University of Illinois Press, 1993.

———. *The Southern Past: A Clash of Race and Memory*. Cambridge, Mass.: Harvard University Press, 2005.

———, ed. *Under Sentence of Death: Lynching in the New South*. Chapel Hill: University of North Carolina Press, 1997.

Campney, Brent. "'And This Is Free Kansas': Racist Violence, Black and White Resistance, Geographical Particularity, and the 'Free State' Narrative in Kansas, 1865–1914." Ph.D. diss., Emory University, 2007.

Capeci, Dominic J., Jr. *The Lynching of Cleo Wright*. Lexington: University Press of Kentucky, 1998.

Carlebach, Michael L. *American Photojournalism Comes of Age*. Washington, D.C.: Smithsonian Institution Press, 1997.

Carrigan, William D. *The Making of a Lynching Culture: Violence and Vigilantism in Central Texas, 1836–1916*. Urbana: University of Illinois Press, 2004.

Carrigan, William D., and Clive Webb. "The Lynching of Persons of Mexican Origin or Descent in the United States, 1848–1928." *Journal of Social History* 37 (2003): 411–38.

Carter, Dan T. *Scottsboro: A Tragedy of the American South*. Baton Rouge: Louisiana State University Press, 1969.

Cha-Jua, Sundiata Keita. "'A Warlike Demonstration': Legalism, Violent Self-Help, and Electoral Politics in Decatur, Illinois, 1894–1898." *Journal of Urban History* 26 (July 2000): 591–629.

Charney, Leo, and Vanessa Schwartz, eds. *Cinema and the Invention of Modern Life.* Berkeley: University of California Press, 1995.

Clark, Thomas D. *The Southern Country Editor.* 1948. Reprint, Columbia: University of South Carolina Press, 1991.

Clarke, James. *The Lineaments of Wrath: Race, Violent Crime, and American Culture.* New Brunswick, N.J.: Transaction, 1998.

Click, Patricia C. *The Spirit of the Times: Amusements in Nineteenth-Century Baltimore, Norfolk, and Richmond.* Charlottesville: University Press of Virginia, 1989.

Cohen, Daniel A. *Pillars of Salt, Monuments of Grace: New England Crime Literature and the Origins of American Popular Culture, 1674–1860.* New York: Oxford University Press, 1993.

Coleman, Leodel, ed. *Statesboro: 1866–1966; A Century of Progress.* Statesboro, Ga.: Bulloch Herald Publishing, 1969.

Conger, Roger Norman. *Highlights of Waco History.* Waco, Tex.: Hill Printing and Stationery, 1976.

Connerton, Paul. *How Societies Remember.* Cambridge: Cambridge University Press, 1989.

Conniff, Richard. "When Fiends Pressed the Button, There Was Nowhere to Hide." *Smithsonian* 19 (1988): 106–17.

Coulter, E. Merton. "Hanging as a Social-Penal Institution in Georgia and Elsewhere." *Georgia Historical Quarterly* 57 (1973): 17–55.

Courtney, Susan. *Hollywood Fantasies of Miscegenation: Spectacular Narratives of Gender and Race, 1903–1967.* Princeton, N.J.: Princeton University Press, 2005.

Craig, Robert L. "Fact, Public Opinion, and Persuasion: The Rise of the Visual in Journalism and Advertising." In Brennen and Hardt, *Picturing the Past,* 36–59.

Crary, Johnathon. *Techniques of the Observer: On Vision and Modernity in the Nineteenth Century.* Cambridge, Mass.: MIT Press, 1990.

Cripps, Thomas. *Making Movies Black: The Hollywood Message Movie from World War II to the Civil Rights Era.* New York: Oxford University Press, 1993.

———. "The Myth of the Southern Box Office: A Factor in Racial Stereotyping in American Movies, 1920–1940." In *The Black Experience in America,* edited by James C. Curtis and Lewis Gould, 116–44. Austin: University of Texas Press, 1970.

———. *Slow Fade to Black: The Negro in American Film, 1900–1942.* New York: Oxford University Press, 1993.

Cullen, John B. *Old Times in Faulkner Country.* Baton Rouge: Louisiana State University Press, 1961.

Cuniberti, John. *The Birth of a Nation: A Formal Shot-by-Shot Analysis Together with Microfiche.* New York: Research Publications, 1979.

Dailey, Jane. "Deference and Violence in the Postbellum Urban South: Manners and Massacres in Danville, VA." *Journal of Southern History* 63 (Aug. 1997): 553–90.

Daniel, Pete. *Standing at the Crossroads: Southern Life since 1900.* New York: Hill and Wang, 1986.

Debord, Guy. *Society of the Spectacle*. New York: Zone Books, 1994.

Denning, Michael. *The Cultural Front*. New York: Verso, 1997.

Diawara, Manthia. "Black Spectatorship: Problems of Identification and Resistance." In Diawara, *Black American Cinema*, 211–20.

———, ed. *Black American Cinema*. New York: Routledge, 1993.

Doane, Mary Ann. "Technology's Body: Cinematic Vision in Modernity." *Differences* 5 (1993): 1–23.

Doherty, Thomas. "This Is Where We Came In: The Audible Screen and the Voluble Audience of Early Sound Cinema." In *American Movie Audiences: From the Turn of the Century to the Early Sound Era*, edited by Melvyn Stokes and Richard Maltby, 143–63. London: British Film Institute, 1999.

Dorr, Lisa Lindquist. *White Women, Rape and the Power of Race in Virginia, 1900–1960*. Chapel Hill: University of North Carolina Press, 2004.

Dorsey, James E. *The History of Hall County, Georgia*. Vol. 1, *1818–1900*. Gainesville, Ga.: Magnolia Press, 1991.

Douglass, Ana, and Thomas A. Vogler, eds. *Witness and Memory: The Discourse of Trauma*. New York: Routledge, 2003.

Doyle, Don. *Faulkner's County: The Historical Roots of Yoknapatawpha*. Chapel Hill: University of North Carolina Press, 2001.

Dray, Philip. *At the Hands of Persons Unknown: The Lynching of Black America*. New York: Random House, 2002.

Dyer, Richard. "Into the Light: The Whiteness of the South in *The Birth of a Nation*." In *Dixie Debates: Perspectives in Southern Cultures*, edited by Richard H. King and Helen Taylor, 165–76. London: Pluto Press, 1996.

———. *White*. New York: Routledge, 1997.

Edwards, Laura F. *Gendered Strife and Confusion: The Political Culture of Reconstruction*. Urbana: University of Illinois Press, 1997.

Eighmy, John. *Churches in Cultural Captivity: A History of the Social Attitudes of the Southern Baptists*. Knoxville: University of Tennessee Press, 1987.

Emanuel County Historic Preservation Society. *Images of America: Emanuel County, Georgia*. Charleston, S.C.: Arcadia, 1998.

Essig, Mark. *Edison and the Electric Chair*. New York: Walker, 2003.

Everett, Anna. *Returning the Gaze: A Genealogy of Black Film Criticism, 1909–1949*. Durham, N.C.: Duke University Press, 2001.

Fanon, Franz. *Black Skin, White Masks*. New York: Grove Weidenfeld, 1991.

Farrell, Harry. *Swift Justice: Murder and Vengeance in a California Town*. New York: St. Martin's Press, 1992.

Farrell, James. *Inventing the American Way of Death, 1830–1920*. Philadelphia: Temple University Press, 1990.

Feimster, Crystal Nicole. "'Ladies and Lynching': The Gendered Discourse of Mob Violence in the New South, 1880–1930." Ph.D. diss., Princeton University, 2000.

Feldman, Glenn. *Politics, Society and the Klan in Alabama, 1915–1949*. Tuscaloosa: University of Alabama Press, 1999.

Feldstein, Ruth. *Motherhood in Black and White: Race and Sex in American Liberalism, 1930–1965*. Ithaca, N.Y.: Cornell University Press, 2000.

Felman, Shoshona. *Testimony: Crises of Witnessing in Literature, Psychoanalysis, and History*. New York: Routledge, 1991.

Ferrell, Claudine L. *Nightmare and Dream: Anti-lynching in Congress, 1917–1922*. New York: Garland, 1986.

Fielding, Raymond. *The American Newsreel, 1911–1967*. Norman: University of Oklahoma Press, 1972.

Fields, Barbara. "Ideology and Race in American History." In *Region, Race and Reconstruction*, edited by J. Morgan Kousser and James M. McPherson, 143–77. New York: Oxford University Press, 1982.

Finke, Roger, and Rodney Stark. *The Churching of America, 1776–1990*. New Brunswick, N.J.: Rutgers University Press, 1992.

Flint, Wayne. *Alabama Baptists: Southern Baptists in the Heart of Dixie*. Tuscaloosa: University of Alabama Press, 1998.

———. "The Impact of Social Factors on Southern Baptist Expansion, 1800–1914." *Baptist History and Heritage* 17 (1982): 20–31.

Foucault, Michel. *Discipline and Punish: The Birth of the Prison*. New York: Pantheon, 1977.

Fouss, Kirk W. "Lynching Performances, Theatres of Violence." *Text and Performance Quarterly* 19 (Jan. 1999): 1–37.

Franklin, John Hope. "'Birth of a Nation' Propaganda as History." *Massachusetts Review* 20 (Autumn 1979): 417–39.

———. *Race and History: Selected Essays, 1938–1988*. Baton Rouge: Louisiana State University Press, 1989.

Frederickson, George. *The Black Image in the White Mind: The Debate on Afro-American Character and Destiny, 1817–1914*. Middletown, Conn.: Wesleyan University Press, 1987.

———. *White Supremacy: A Comparative Study between the United States and South Africa*. New York: Oxford University Press, 1981.

Friedberg, Anne. *Window Shopping: Cinema and the Postmodern*. Berkeley: University of California Press, 1993.

Friedman, Lawrence. *Crime and Punishment in American History*. New York: Basic Books, 1993.

Fuller, Kathryn H. *At the Picture Show: Small-Town Audiences and the Creation of Movie-Fan Culture*. Washington, D.C.: Smithsonian Institution Press, 1996.

Gaines, Jane M. *Fire and Desire: Mixed-Race Movies in the Silent Era*. Chicago: University of Chicago Press, 2001.

———. "Fire and Desire: Race, Melodrama, and Oscar Micheaux." In Diawara, *Black American Cinema*, 49–70.

Gallagher, Tag. *John Ford: The Man and His Films*. Berkeley: University of California Press, 1986.

Garcia, Jay. "Psychology Comes to Harlem: Race, Intellectuals, and Culture in the Mid-Twentieth Century U.S." Ph.D. diss., Yale University, 2004.

Gardner, Robert G. *The First Baptist Church, Rome, Georgia, 1865–1913*. Rome, Ga.: Brazelton-Walls, 1980.

Geary, Christaud M., and Virginia Lee-Webb, eds. *Delivering Views: Distant Cultures in Early Postcards*. Washington, D.C.: Smithsonian Institute Press, 1998.

Gerstle, Gary. *American Crucible: Race and Nation in the Twentieth Century*. Princeton, N.J.: Princeton University Press, 2001.

Gilmore, Glenda Elizabeth. *Gender and Jim Crow: Women and the Politics of White Supremacy in North Carolina, 1896–1920*. Chapel Hill: University of North Carolina Press, 1996.

———. "'One of the Meanest Books': Thomas Dixon, Jr., and *The Leopard's Spots*." *North Carolina Literary Review* 2 (Spring 1994): 87–101.

Ginzberg, Ralph. *One Hundred Years of Lynching*. Baltimore: Black Classic Press, 1988.

Girard, Rene. *Violence and the Sacred*. Translated by Patrick Gregory. Baltimore: Johns Hopkins University Press, 1977.

Goldsby, Jacqueline. *A Spectacular Secret: Lynching in American Life and Literature*. Chicago: University of Chicago Press, 2006.

Gomery, Douglas. *Shared Pleasures: A History of Movie Presentation in the United States*. Madison: University of Wisconsin Press, 1992.

Gonzales-Day, Ken. *Lynching in the West, 1850–1935*. Durham, N.C.: Duke University Press, 2006.

Goodson, Steve. *Highbrows, Hillbillies, and Hellfire: Public Entertainment in Atlanta, 1880–1930*. Athens: University of Georgia Press, 2002.

Grant, Donald L. *The Anti-lynching Movement, 1883–1932*. San Francisco: R and E Research Associates, 1975.

Grill, Johnpeter Horst, and Robert L. Jenkins. "The Nazis and the American South in the 1930s: A Mirror Image?" *Journal of Southern History* 58 (Nov. 1992): 667–94.

Gunning, Sandra. *Race, Rape, and Lynching: The Red Record of American Literature, 1890–1912*. New York: Oxford University Press, 1996.

Gunning, Tom. "The Cinema of Attractions: Early Film, Its Spectator and the Avant-Garde." *Wide Angle* 8 (1986): 63–70.

———. *D. W. Griffith and the Origins of American Narrative Film: The Early Years at Biograph*. Chicago: University of Illinois Press, 1994.

———. *The Films of Fritz Lang: Allegories of Vision and Modernity*. British Film Institute, 2000.

———. "'Now You See It, Now You Don't': The Temporality of the Cinema of Attractions." In *Silent Film*, edited by Richard Abel, 71–84. New Brunswick, N.J.: Rutgers University Press, 1996.

———. "The Whole Town's Gawking: Early Cinema and the Visual Experience of Modernity." *Yale Journal of Criticism* 7 (1994): 189–201.

Hahn, Steven. *A Nation under Our Feet: Black Political Struggles in the Rural South from Slavery to the Great Migration*. Cambridge, Mass.: Harvard University Press, 2003.

Hale, Grace Elizabeth. "Exhibition Review: *Without Sanctuary: Lynching Photography in America.*" *Journal of American History* 89 (2002): 989–94.

———. *Making Whiteness: The Culture of Segregation in the South, 1890–1940.* New York: Pantheon Books, 1998.

Hall, Jacquelyn Dowd. "'The Mind That Burns in Each Body': Women, Rape and Racial Violence." *Southern Exposure* 12 (Nov.–Dec. 1984): 61–71.

———. *Revolt against Chivalry.* 1974. Reprint, New York: Columbia University Press, 1993.

Halttunen, Karen. "Humanitarianism and the Pornography of Pain in Anglo-American Culture." *American Historical Review* 100 (Apr. 1995): 303–34.

———. *Murder Most Foul: The Killer and the American Gothic Imagination.* Cambridge, Mass.: Harvard University Press, 1998.

Hansen, Miriam. *Babel and Babylon: Spectatorship in American Silent Film.* Cambridge, Mass.: Harvard University Press, 1991.

Harris, Trudier. *Exorcising Blackness: Historical and Literary Lynching and Burning Rituals.* Bloomington: University of Indiana Press, 1984.

Harvey, Paul. *Redeeming the South: Religious Cultures and Racial Identities among Southern Baptists, 1865–1925.* Chapel Hill: University of North Carolina Press, 1997.

Hill, Samuel S., Jr. *Southern Churches in Crisis.* New York: Holt, Rinehart and Winston, 1967.

———. "The South's Two Cultures." In *Religion and the Solid South*, edited by Samuel S. Hill Jr., 24–56. Nashville: Abingdon Press, 1972.

Hirsch, Arnold R. *Making the Second Ghetto: Race and Housing in Chicago, 1940–1960.* Chicago: University of Chicago Press, 1998.

Hodes, Martha. *White Women, Black Men: Illicit Sex in the Nineteenth Century South.* New Haven, Conn.: Yale University Press, 1997.

hooks, bell. "The Oppositional Gaze: Black Female Spectators." In Diawara, *Black American Cinema*, 288–302.

Howard, Walter T. *Lynchings: Extralegal Violence in Florida during the 1930s.* Selinsgrove, Pa.: Susquehanna University Press, 1995.

Humphries, Reynold. *Fritz Lang: Genre and Representation in His American Films.* Baltimore: Johns Hopkins University Press, 1989.

Inscoe, John C. "*The Clansman* on Stage and Screen: North Carolina Reacts." *North Carolina Historical Review* 64 (Apr. 1987): 139–61.

Jean, Susan. "'Warranted' Lynchings: Narratives of Mob Violence in White Southern Newspapers, 1880–1940." *American Nineteenth Century History* 6 (Sept. 2005): 351–72.

Jean, Susan, and W. Fitzhugh Brundage. "Legitimizing 'Justice': Lynching and the Boundaries of Informal Justice in the American South." In *Informal Criminal Justice*, edited by Dermot Freeman, 157–77. Burlington, Vt.: Ashgate, 2002.

Jenkins, Reese V. "Technology and the Market: George Eastman and the Origins of Mass Amateur Photography." *Technology and Culture* 16 (Jan. 1975): 1–19.

Jonas, Gilbert. *Freedom's Sword: The NAACP and the Struggle against Racism in America, 1909–1969.* New York: Routledge, 2005.

Jowett, Garth S. "'A Capacity for Evil': The 1915 Supreme Court *Mutual* Decision." In Bernstein, *Controlling Hollywood*, 16–40.

Kantrowitz, Stephen. *Ben Tillman and the Reconstruction of White Supremacy.* Chapel Hill: University of North Carolina Press, 2000.

Kasson, John F. *Houdini, Tarzan, and the Perfect Man: The White Male Body and the Challenge of Modernity in America.* New York: Hill and Wang, 2002.

Keane, John. *Reflections on Violence.* London: Verso, 1996.

Kellison, Kimberly R. "Parameters of Promiscuity: Sexuality, Violence, and Religion in Upcountry South Carolina." In Blum and Poole, *Vale of Tears*, 15–35.

Kellogg, Charles Flint. *NAACP: A History of the National Association for the Advancement of Colored People.* Vol. 1, 1909–1920. Baltimore: Johns Hopkins University Press, 1967.

Kertzer, David I. *Ritual, Politics, and Power.* New Haven, Conn.: Yale University Press, 1988.

King, Gilbert. *The Execution of Willie Francis: Race, Murder, and the Search for Justice in the American South.* New York: Basic Civitas, 2008.

King, Richard H. *Race, Culture, and the Intellectuals, 1940–1970.* Baltimore: Johns Hopkins University Press, 2004.

Koppes, Clayton R., and Gregory D. Black. "Blacks, Loyalty, and Motion Picture Propaganda in World War II." In Bernstein, *Controlling Hollywood*, 130–56.

Laderman, Gary. *The Sacred Remains: American Attitudes toward Death, 1799–1883.* New Haven, Conn.: Yale University Press, 1996.

Lalvani, Suren. *Photography, Vision, and the Production of Modern Bodies.* Albany: State University of New York Press, 1996.

Lang, Robert. "*The Birth of a Nation*: History, Ideology, Narrative Form." In Lang, *Birth of a Nation*, 3–24.

——, ed. *The Birth of a Nation.* New Brunswick, N.J.: Rutgers University Press, 1994.

Laqueur, Thomas W. "Crowds, Carnival, and the State in English Executions, 1604–1868." In *The First Modern Society: Essays in English History in Honour of Lawrence Stone*, edited by A. L. Beier, David Cannadine, and James H. Rosenheim, 305–55. Cambridge: Cambridge University Press, 1989.

Largey, Gale. "The Hanging." *Society* 18 (1981): 73–75.

Lears, T. Jackson. "The Concept of Cultural Hegemony." *American Historical Review* (June 1985): 567–93.

——. *Fables of Abundance: A Cultural History of Advertising in America.* New York: Basic Books, 1994.

Levine, Lawrence. *High Brow/Low Brow: The Emergence of Cultural Hierarchy in America.* Cambridge, Mass.: Harvard University Press, 1988.

Linders, Annulla. "The Execution Spectacle and State Legitimacy: The Changing Nature of the American Execution Audience, 1833–1937." *Law and Society Review* 36 (2002): 607–55.

Link, William A. *The Paradox of Southern Progressivism, 1880–1930.* Chapel Hill: University of North Carolina Press, 1992.

Litwack, Leon. *Trouble in Mind: Black Southerners in the Age of Jim Crow.* New York: Knopf, 1998.

Lott, Eric. *Love and Theft: Blackface Minstrelsy and the American Working Class.* New York: Oxford University Press, 1995.

MacLean, Nancy. *Behind the Mask of Chivalry: The Making of the Second Ku Klux Klan.* New York: Oxford University Press, 1994.

Madison, James H. *A Lynching in the Heartland: Race and Memory in America.* New York: Palgrave, 2001.

Madow, Michael. "Forbidden Spectacle: Executions, the Public and the Press in Nineteenth Century New York." *Buffalo Law Review* 43 (1995): 461–562.

Markowitz, Jonathan. *Legacies of Lynching: Racial Violence and Memory.* Minneapolis: University of Minnesota Press, 2004.

Marriott, David. *On Black Men.* Edinburgh: Edinburgh University Press, 2000.

Martschukat, Jurgen. "'The Art of Killing by Electricity': The Sublime and the Electric Chair." *Journal of American History* 89 (2002): 900–921.

Masur, Louis P. *Rites of Execution: Capital Punishment and the Transformation of American Culture, 1776–1865.* New York: Oxford University Press, 1989.

Mathews, Donald G. "Lynching Is Part of the Religion of Our People: Faith in the Christian South." In *Religion in the American South: Protestants and Others in History and Culture,* edited by Beth Barton Schweiger and Donald G. Mathews, 153–94. Chapel Hill: University of North Carolina Press, 2004.

———. "The Southern Rite of Human Sacrifice." *Journal of Southern Religion* 3 (2000), ⟨http://jsr.fsu.edu/mathews.htm⟩.

May, Lary. *Screening Out the Past: The Birth of Mass Culture and the Motion Picture Industry.* New York: Oxford University Press, 1980.

McBride, Joseph. *Searching for John Ford: A Life.* New York: St. Martin's Press, 2001.

McDowell, Deborah E. "Viewing the Remains: A Polemic on Death, Spectacle, and the Black Family." In *The Familial Gaze,* edited by Marianne Hirsch, 153–77. Hanover, N.H.: University Press of New England, 1999.

McGilligan, Patrick. *Fritz Lang: The Nature of the Beast.* New York: St. Martin's Press, 1997.

McGovern, James R. *Anatomy of a Lynching: The Killing of Claude Neal.* Baton Rouge: Louisiana State University Press, 1982.

McGowan, Randall. "The Body and Punishment in Eighteenth-Century England." *Journal of Modern History* 59 (Dec. 1987): 651–79.

McMillan, Neil. *Dark Journey: Black Mississippians in the Age of Jim Crow.* Urbana: University of Illinois Press, 1989.

McSwain, Betty Ann McCartney, ed. *The Bench and Bar of Waco and McLennan County, 1849–1976.* Waco, Tex.: Texian Press, 1976.

Mennel, Barbara. "White Law and the Missing Black Body in Fritz Lang's *Fury* (1936)." *Quarterly Review of Film and Video* 20 (2003): 203–23.

Merritt, Russell. "Dixon, Griffith, and the Southern Legend." *Cinema Journal* 12 (Fall 1972): 24–45.

Metress, Christopher, ed. *The Lynching of Emmett Till: A Documentary Narrative*. Charlottesville: University of Virginia Press, 2002.

Miller, Robert Moats. "The Protestant Churches and Lynchings, 1919–1939." *Journal of Negro History* 42 (Apr. 1957): 118–31.

Moore, Bill. "Lights, Camera, Action! Newsreel Cameramen of Oklahoma, 1910–1940." *Chronicles of Oklahoma* 71 (Fall 1993): 302–21.

Moore, John Hammond. "South Carolina's Reaction to the Photoplay, *The Birth of a Nation*." *Proceedings of the South Carolina Historical Association*, 1963, 30–40.

Morgan, Hal, and Andreas Brown. *Prairie Fires and Paper Moons: The American Photographic Postcard, 1900–1920*. Boston: Godine, 1981.

Morrow, Maud. *History of the First Presbyterian Church of Oxford, Mississippi*. Oxford, Miss., 1952.

Moseley, Charlton, and Frederick Brogden. "A Lynching at Statesboro: The Story of Paul Reed and Will Cato." *Georgia Historical Quarterly* 65 (1981): 104–18.

Musser, Charles. *Edison Motion Pictures, 1890–1900: An Annotated Filmography*. Washington, D.C.: Smithsonian Institution Press, 1997.

———. *The Emergence of Cinema: The American Screen to 1907*. Berkeley: University of California Press, 1990.

———. "Passions and the Passion Play: Theater, Film and Religion, 1880–1900." *Film History* 5 (1993): 419–56.

———. "Rethinking Early Cinema: Cinema of Attractions and Narrativity." *Yale Journal of Criticism* 7 (1994): 203–32.

Nasaw, David. *Going Out: The Rise and Fall of Public Amusements*. New York: Basic Books, 1993.

Newton, Michael. *The Invisible Empire: The Ku Klux Klan in Florida*. Gainesville: University Press of Florida, 2001.

Niver, Kemp R. *Early Motion Pictures: The Paper Print Collection in the Library of Congress*. Edited by Bebe Bergsten. Washington, D.C.: Motion Picture, Broadcasting, and Recorded Sound Division, Library of Congress, 1985.

Ohmann, Richard. *Selling Culture: Magazines, Markets, and Class at the Turn of the Century*. New York: Verso, 1996.

Oney, Steven. *And the Dead Shall Rise*. New York: Pantheon Books, 2003.

Ownby, Ted. *Subduing Satan: Religion, Recreation, and Manhood in the Rural South, 1865–1920*. Chapel Hill: University of North Carolina Press, 1990.

Park, Marlene. "Lynching and Anti-lynching: Art and Politics in the 1930's." *Prospects* 18 (1993): 311–65.

Patterson, Orlando. *Rituals of Blood: Consequences of Slavery in Two American Centuries*. Washington, D.C.: Civitas/Counterpoint, 1998.

Pfeifer, Michael J. *Rough Justice: Lynching and American Society, 1874–1947*. Urbana: University of Illinois Press, 2004.

Phillips, Charles David. "Exploring Relations among Forms of Social Control: The Lynching and Execution of Blacks in North Carolina, 1889–1918." *Law and Society Review* 21 (1987): 361–73.

Poole, W. Scott. "Confederate Apocalypse: Theology and Violence in the White Reconstruction South." In Blum and Poole, *Vale of Tears*, 36–52.

————. *Never Surrender: Confederate Memory and Conservatism in the South Carolina Upcountry*. Athens: University of Georgia Press, 2004.

Prince, Stephen. *Classical Film Violence: Designing and Regulating Brutality in Hollywood Cinema, 1930–1968*. New Brunswick, N.J.: Rutgers University Press, 2003.

Proctor, Nicolas W. *Bathed in Blood: Hunting and Mastery in the Old South*. Charlottesville: University Press of Virginia, 2002.

Rable, George C. "The South and the Politics of Anti-lynching Legislation, 1920–1940." *Journal of Southern History* 51 (May 1985): 201–20.

Raiford, Leigh Renee. "'Imprisoned in a Luminous Glare': Social Movement Photography." Ph.D. diss., Yale University, 2003.

Renoff, Gregory J. *The Big Tent: The Traveling Circus in Georgia, 1820–1930*. Athens: University of Georgia Press, 2008.

Roddick, Nick. *A New Deal in Entertainment: Warner Brothers in the 1930s*. London: British Film Institute, 1983.

Roediger, David. *The Wages of Whiteness: Race and the Making of the American Working Class*. New York: Verso, 1991.

Roffman, Peter, and Jim Purdy. *The Hollywood Social Problem Film*. Bloomington: Indiana University Press, 1981.

Rogin, Michael. "'The Sword Became a Flashing Vision': D. W. Griffith's *The Birth of a Nation*." In Lang, *Birth of a Nation*, 250–93.

Rosenbloom, Nancy J. "Between Reform and Regulation: The Struggle over Film Censorship in Progressive America, 1909–1922." *Film History* 1 (1987): 307–22.

Ross, Steven J. *Working-Class Hollywood: Silent Film and the Shaping of Class in America*. Princeton, N.J.: Princeton University Press, 1998.

Ruby, Jay. *Secure the Shadow: Death and Photography in America*. Cambridge, Mass.: MIT Press, 1995.

Scarry, Elaine. *The Body in Pain: The Making and Unmaking of the World*. New York: Oxford University Press, 1985.

Schindler, Colin. *Hollywood in Crisis: Cinema and American Society, 1929–1939*. New York: Routledge, 1996.

Schwartz, Vanessa. *Spectacular Realities: Early Mass Culture in Fin-de-Siecle Paris*. Berkeley: University of California Press, 1998.

Schweiger, Beth Barton. *The Gospel Working Up: Progress and Pulpit in Nineteenth Century Virginia*. New York: Oxford University Press, 2000.

Sekula, Allan. "The Body and the Archive." *October* 39 (Winter 1986): 3–64.

Sharpe, J. A. "'Last Dying Speeches': Religion, Ideology and Public Executions in 17th Century England." *Past and Present* 107 (May 1985): 144–57.

Silber, Nina. *The Romance of Reunion: Northerners and the South, 1865–1900*. Chapel Hill: University of North Carolina Press, 1993.

Silverman, Joan L. "*The Birth of a Nation*: Prohibition Propaganda." *Southern Quarterly* 19 (Spring–Summer 1981): 14–21.

Simcovitch, Maxim. "The Impact of Griffith's *Birth of a Nation* on the Modern Ku Klux Klan." *Journal of Popular Film* 1 (Winter 1972): 45–64.

Singer, Ben. *Melodrama and Modernity: Early Sensational Cinema and Its Contexts.* New York: Columbia University Press, 2001.

Sklar, Robert. *Movie-Made America: A Cultural History of American Movies.* New York: Vintage Books, 1995.

Slater, Don. "Photography and Modern Vision: The Spectacle of 'Natural Magic.'" In *Visual Culture,* edited by Chris Jenks, 218–37. New York: Routledge, 1995.

Slide, Anthony. *American Racist: The Life and Films of Thomas Dixon.* Lexington: University Press of Kentucky, 2004.

Smith, Albert C. "Southern Violence Reconsidered: Arson as Protest in Black Belt Georgia, 1865–1910." *Journal of Southern History* 51 (1985): 527–64.

Smith, J. Douglas. *Managing White Supremacy: Race, Politics, and Citizenship in Jim Crow Virginia.* Chapel Hill: University of North Carolina Press, 2002.

———. "Patrolling the Boundaries of Race: Motion Picture Censorship and Jim Crow in Virginia, 1922–1932." *Historical Journal of Film, Radio and Television* 21 (2001): 273–91.

———. "Statesboro Blues." M.A. thesis, University of Virginia, 1993.

Smith, Shawn Michelle. *American Archives: Gender, Race and Class in Visual Culture.* Princeton, N.J.: Princeton University Press, 1999.

———. *Photography on the Color Line: W. E. B. Du Bois, Race, and Visual Culture.* Durham, N.C.: Duke University Press, 2004.

Sontag, Susan. *On Photography.* New York: Anchor/Doubleday, 1977.

———. *Regarding the Pain of Others.* New York: Farrar, Straus and Giroux, 2003.

SoRelle, James M. "The 'Waco Horror': The Lynching of Jesse Washington." *Southwestern Historical Quarterly* 86 (Apr. 1983): 517–36.

Sosna, Morton. *In Search of the Silent South: Southern Liberals and the Race Issue.* New York: Columbia University Press, 1977.

Sparks, Randy J. *Religion in Mississippi.* Jackson: University of Mississippi Press, 2001.

Spierenburg, Peter. *The Spectacle of Suffering: Executions and the Evolution of Repression.* Cambridge: Cambridge University Press, 1984.

Staiger, Janet. "*The Birth of a Nation*: Reconsidering Its Reception." In Lang, *Birth of a Nation,* 195–213.

———. *Interpreting Films: Studies in the Historical Reception of American Cinema.* Princeton, N.J.: Princeton University Press, 1992.

———. *Perverse Spectators: The Practices of Film Reception.* New York: New York University Press, 2000.

Stern, Seymour. "Griffith: *The Birth of a Nation.*" Pt. 1. Special issue, *Film Culture* 36 (Spring–Summer 1965).

Stewart, Jacqueline Najuma. *Migrating to the Movies: Cinema and Black Urban Modernity.* Berkeley: University of California Press, 2005.

Streible, Dan. "Race and the Reception of Jack Johnson Fight Films." In Bernardi, *Birth of Whiteness,* 170–200.

Sugrue, Thomas J. "Crabgrass-Roots Politics: Race, Rights, and the Reaction against Liberalism in the Urban North, 1940–1964." *Journal of American History* 82 (Sept. 1995): 551–78.

Taft, Robert. *Photography and the American Scene: A Social History, 1839–1889.* New York: Macmillan, 1942.

Tagg, John. *The Burden of Representation: Essays on Photographies and Histories.* Minneapolis: University of Minnesota Press, 1988.

Tambiah, S. J. "A Performative Approach to Ritual." *Proceedings of the British Academy* 65 (1979): 113–69.

Taylor, Clyde. "The Re-birth of the Aesthetic in Cinema." In Bernardi, *Birth of Whiteness*, 15–37.

Taylor, John. *Body Horror: Photojournalism, Catastrophe, and War.* New York: New York University Press, 1998.

Texas State Historical Association. *The New Handbook of Texas.* Austin: Texas State Historical Association, 1998.

Tolnay, Stewart E., and E. M. Beck. *A Festival of Violence: An Analysis of Southern Lynchings, 1882–1930.* Chicago: University of Illinois Press, 1995.

Trachtenberg, Alan. *Reading American Photographs: Images as History, Mathew Brady to Walker Evans.* New York: Noonday Press, 1989.

Turner, James. *Reckoning with the Beast: Animals, Pain, and Humanity in the Victorian Mind.* Baltimore: Johns Hopkins University Press, 1980.

Vandiver, Margaret. *Lethal Punishment: Lynchings and Legal Executions in the South.* New Brunswick, N.J.: Rutgers University Press, 2006.

Vasey, Ruth. "Beyond Sex and Violence: 'Industry Policy' and the Regulation of Hollywood Movies, 1922–1939." *Quarterly Review of Film and Video* 15, no. 4 (1995): 65–85.

———. *The World According to Hollywood, 1918–1939.* Madison: University of Wisconsin Press, 1997.

Vendryes, Margaret Rose. "Hanging on Their Walls: An Art Commentary on Lynching, the Forgotten 1935 Art Exhibition." In *Race Consciousness: African American Studies for the Next Century*, edited by Judith Jackson Fossett and Jeffrey A. Tucker, 153–76. New York: New York University Press, 1997.

Vinikas, Vincent. "Specters in the Past: The Saint-Charles, Arkansas, Lynching of 1904 and the Limits of Historical Inquiry." *Journal of Southern History* 65 (Aug. 1999): 535–64.

Wade, Wyn Craig. *The Fiery Cross: The Ku Klux Klan in America.* New York: Oxford University Press, 1987.

Waldrep, Christopher. *The Many Faces of Judge Lynch: Extralegal Violence and Punishment in America.* New York: Palgrave Macmillan, 2002.

———. *Roots of Disorder: Race and Criminal Justice in the American South, 1817–1880.* Chicago: University of Illinois Press, 1998.

Waller, Gregory A. *Main Street Amusements: Movies and Commercial Entertainment in a Southern City, 1896–1930.* Washington, D.C.: Smithsonian Institution Press, 1995.

Weiner, Jonathon M. "'The Black Beast Rapist': White Racial Attitudes in the Post War South." *Reviews in American History* 13 (June 1985): 222–26.

Wexler, Laura. *Tender Violence: Domestic Visions in an Age of U.S. Imperialism.* Chapel Hill: University of North Carolina Press, 2000.

Whites, LeeAnn. "Rebecca Latimer Felton and the Wife's Farm: The Class and Racial Politics of Gender Reform." *Georgia Historical Quarterly* 76 (1992): 354–72.

Whitfield, Stephen J. *A Death in the Delta: The Story of Emmett Till*. New York: Free Press, 1988.

Whitley, William Bland. "Precious Memories: Narratives of the Democracy in Mississippi." Ph.D. diss., University of Florida, 2004.

Wiegman, Robyn. "The Anatomy of a Lynching." In *American Sexual Politics: Sex, Gender, and Race since the Civil War*, edited by John C. Fout and Maura Shaw Tantillo, 223–45. Chicago: University of Chicago Press, 1990.

Williams, Kidada E. "Resolving the Paradox of Our Lynching Fixation: Reconsidering Racialized Violence in the American South after Slavery." *American Nineteenth Century History* 6 (Sept. 2005): 323–50.

Williams, Linda. *Playing the Race Card: Melodramas of Black and White from Uncle Tom to O. J. Simpson*. Princeton, N.J.: Princeton University Press, 2001.

Williams, Patricia. Diary of a Mad Law Professor. *Nation*, 14 Feb. 2000, 9.

Williams, Peter W. *Popular Religion in America: Symbolic Change and the Modernization Process in Historical Perspective*. Englewood Cliffs, N.J.: Prentice-Hall, 1980.

Williamson, Joel. *Crucible of Race: Black-White Relations in the American South since Emancipation*. New York: Oxford University Press, 1984.

———. *William Faulkner and Southern History*. New York: Oxford University Press, 1993.

Willis, Greg. *Democratic Religion: Freedom, Authority and Church Discipline in the Baptist South, 1865–1900*. New York: Oxford University Press, 1997.

Wilson, Charles Reagan. *Baptized in Blood: The Religion of the Lost Cause, 1865–1920*. Athens: University of Georgia Press, 1980.

———, ed. *Religion and the Solid South*. Jackson: University Press of Mississippi, 1985.

Woodward, C. Vann. *Origins of the New South, 1877–1914*. Baton Rouge: Louisiana State University Press, 1951.

———. *The Strange Career of Jim Crow*. New York: Oxford University Press, 1974.

Wright, George C. "By the Book: The Legal Execution of Kentucky Blacks." In Brundage, *Under Sentence of Death*, 250–70.

———. *Racial Violence in Kentucky, 1865–1940: Lynchings, Mob Rule, and "Legal Lynchings."* Baton Rouge: Louisiana State University Press, 1990.

Wyatt-Brown, Bertram. *Southern Honor: Ethics and Behavior in the Old South*. New York: Oxford University Press, 1982.

Wypijewski, JoAnn. "Executioner's Song." *Nation*, 27 Mar. 2000, 28–34.

Zangrando, Robert. *The NAACP Crusade against Lynching, 1915–1950*. Philadelphia: Temple University Press, 1980.

Zelizer, Barbie. *Remembering to Forget: Holocaust Memory through the Camera's Eye*. Chicago: University of Chicago Press, 1998.

INDEX